# *Above the Law*

## Police and the Excessive Use of Force

### JEROME H. SKOLNICK

### JAMES J. FYFE

**THE FREE PRESS**

New York  London  Toronto  Sydney  Tokyo  Singapore

The Free Press
A Division of Simon & Schuster Inc.
1230 Avenue of the Americas
New York, N. Y. 10020

First Free Press Paperback Edition 1994
Printed in the United States of America

printing number

   4  5  6  7  8  9  10


**Library of Congress Cataloging-in-Publication Data**

Skolnick, Jerome H.
   Above the law : police and the excessive use of force / Jerome H.
Skolnick, James J. Fyfe.
      p.      cm.
   Includes bibliographical references and index.
   ISBN 0-02-929153-4
   1. Police — United States — Complaints against.   2. Police —
Malpractice — United States.   I. Fyfe, James J.   II. Title.
HV8141.S56      1993
363.2'2 — dc20

                                                       92-38815
                                                          CIP

# Contents

# Acknowledgments

Each of us has been writing and thinking about police for more years than we care to remember. We wish to acknowledge scholars and practitioners who, through writings, conversations, and example, have been especially influential in shaping our ideas and visions of police and policing. These include David H. Bayley, Egon Bittner, Paul Chevigny, Herman Goldstein, Gary Hayes, Mark H. Haller, Roger Lane, Carl B. Klockars, Peter K. Manning, Joseph McNamara, William Ker Muir, Albert J. Reiss, Jr., James Richardson, Clifford D. Shearing, Lawrence Sherman, James K. Stewart, John Von Maanen, Samuel Walker, William Westley, and James Q. Wilson.

Most of all, we wish to acknowledge the contributions of Patrick V. Murphy, who has done more than any other cop in this century to improve the professional and human quality of American policing and to make the police officer's lot a happier one. We dedicate this book to him.

In addition, Skolnick wishes to acknowledge Elliot Currie for his insights into crime causation; also Joseph Brann, Lee P. Brown, Raymond Davis, Charles Gain, George Hart, Peter Sarna, Paul Walters, and Hubert Williams for showing him around the world of policing and police administration; Susan Martin for teaching him about women and policing; Robert Fogelson for introducing him to police history; Robert Reiner and Hans Klette for their colleagueship in England and Scandinavia; Abraham S. Goldstein, whose 1959–60 Yale Law School criminal procedure seminar made him recognize the importance of cops to the American system of criminal justice; and Richard D. Schwartz, who began as a teacher and continues as a colleague and friend.

At Berkeley, Skolnick discussed aspects of the project with colleagues

Meir Dan-Cohen, Malcolm Feeley, Philip Johnson, Sanford Kadish, Sheldon Messinger, Philip Selznick, Jeremy Waldron, and Franklin Zimring, all of whom have contributed to his writing and thinking more than they know. Robert Post, ever a constant friend, was especially encouraging at a time when the enterprise seemed immensely formidable.

Students in the Guggenheim Crime Seminar offered useful comments, and staff in the Jurisprudence and Social Policy program and the Center for the Study of Law and Society have been warmly supportive. Rod Watanabe has been, as always, indispensable as administrator and crony. Margo Rodriguez, resident computer whiz, was indispensable in solving software problems. Research assistants Richard Leo and Benjamin Douglas made valuable contributions at different stages of the project.

Skolnick has been the beneficiary of a grant to the Law and Society Center from the Daniel and Florence Guggenheim Foundation. He thanks the Foundation and Jameson Doig for generous support. Some of this book was written in Bellagio, Italy, at the Villa Serbelloni of the Rockefeller Foundation Study Center, in the summer of 1991. This was a magnificent setting with congenial scholars-in-residence, especially Albert Alschuler, Jack Greenberg, and Linda Kerber, who commented on parts of the manuscript. Skolnick's most kindred companion in Bellagio, as in Berkeley—in life itself—was Arlene Skolnick, who cultivates their "Embattled Paradise" to minimize combat and maximize pleasure.

Fyfe's thinking has been influenced in two phases: as a student and scholar and as a police officer. In the former, those who have been most important to him as friends, teachers, and colleagues have been Richard Bennett, Mark Blumberg, Thomas Brady, Fred Cohen, Brian Forst, Jack Greene, Robert Hardt, Michael Hindelang, David Klinger, Richard Myren, Donald Newman, Arthur Neiderhoffer, Carl Pope, Lloyd Sealy, Rita Simon, Jack Sulger, and Hans Toch. Fyfe's views on the police and their use of force have also been influenced by the work of Arnold Binder, Samuel Chapman, William Geller, and John Goldkamp.

However important these scholars and friends have been, Fyfe's consideration of police matters could not have developed without his years and associations during his first life in the New York City Police Department. Among those who showed him by example what it meant to be a *good cop*—or a *good boss*—there are Joe Barcia, Neil Behan, Joe Benson, Dick Condon, Walter Connery, Marty Delehanty, John Dovnar, Pete Edelberg, Pat Fitzsimons, Kenny Gooding, Larry Hanratty, Jerry Kerins, Eddie Lanzetta, Frank McGee, Bob McGuire, Bill McInerney, Tom McTernan, Vernon Musgrove, George Najarian, Bob O'Neill, Charley Reuther, Carl Sicignano, Dick Sullivan, Fred Thomas, and George Weinert. Although they were neither cops nor bosses, Betsy Gotbaum and Jean Michael were among the best of Fyfe's police partners.

One of the most pleasant discoveries during Fyfe's second life was the great number of good cops and good bosses to be found beyond New York City's limits. Among those who have been most inspiring and influential have been Samuel Baca, Eduardo Gonzalez, Daniel Guido, Sean Hayes, Bobbie Jones, Morton Solomon, Fred Taylor, Mack Vines, and John Wilson. Fyfe's colleagues and associates from the Commission on Accreditation for Law Enforcement Agencies, especially Sylvester Daughtry, John Duffy, Steve Harris, Dana Mitchell, Charles Plummer, and Charles Reynolds, have been excellent sounding boards.

Even more pleasant was the discovery that the civil rights bar across the nation, with whom Fyfe worked as an expert witness, included dozens of capable, ethical, even courageous attorneys who have made a genuine difference in policing and the law governing police.

Fyfe's final—and special—acknowledgment is to his wife, Candace McCoy, who has been his most inspiring and challenging colleague, critic, and good cop to his bad cop.

# Prologue
## *Whatever Happened to* Dragnet?

> The television program *Dragnet* was one of the great instruments to give the people of the United States a picture of the policeman as he really is. It was most authentic. We participated in the editing of the scripts and in their filming. If we had any objections on technical grounds our objections were met. This program showed the true portrait of the policeman as a hard-working, selfless man, willing to go out and brave all sorts of hazards and work long hours to protect the community.[1]
> —William H. Parker, Los Angeles Police Chief,
> interview by Donald McDonald, 1962

The videotaped beating of Rodney King destroyed the *Dragnet* vision of the Los Angeles police, and the Simi Valley verdict, followed by the Los Angeles riots, showed us how divided we are as a nation.

America is, culturally speaking, two countries. One is urban, cosmopolitan, and multicultural. It suffers disproportionately from crime, gang violence, poverty, and homelessness. The other is suburban, relatively safe, relatively prosperous, and—most important—unicultural. Like Simi Valley, and the King trial jury, it is predominantly white and middle-class.

The cops charged with assaulting Rodney King committed their crimes in the first America, but they were tried in the second. That they were was a failure of the local prosecutor, for reasons that remain obscure. The district attorney might have been overconfident or might have leaned over backward to be "fair" to the cops. After all, local district attorneys are normally on the side of the cops, which may explain other prosecutorial decisions in the King case, such as not bringing in outside police expert witnesses to interpret the videotape, or not putting King in the witness box. Yet the videotape was so compelling, had the assaulting cops been tried by a multiracial jury anywhere in urban America—in Los Angeles or San

Francisco, in Chicago or Detroit or Houston—they would, we believe, likely have been convicted.

When a jury in Simi Valley acquitted the officers who beat Rodney King, people everywhere were astonished, asking, how could the King trial jurors have reached such a decision? The answer, in part, is that *the jury* is not a narrowly rational fact-finding institution, and was never meant to be. Judges are perfectly capable of hearing evidence and deciding guilt or innocence. Historically, juries were conceived as a check on judges who were thought to be so close to the authorities that ordinary folks would be treated unfairly in the courtroom. The independence of juries is so valued that they are allowed to *nullify* the evidence and fail to convict, when it appears perfectly clear, as in the King trial, that the defendants were guilty. Without King's presence in the courtroom, he remained an abstraction, painted in sinister hues by the astute defenders of four young men who appeared in court every day.

Roger Parloff, a senior reporter for *The American Lawyer* magazine, wrote a powerfully argued, but ultimately unpersuasive, article in the June 1992 issue defending the decision of the Simi Valley jury to acquit. Parloff, who watched the trial on videotape, says that the television-viewing public missed the beginning of the action, when, he says, King did indeed seem to show superhuman strength. That missed part, Parloff asserts, clearly justified the first ten blows.

But what of the remaining forty-six blows? Parloff appreciates how much harder they are to defend, and writes:

> Whenever King moves his arm toward his waistband—remember, the officers have not been able to search King—they hit him. When King appears to get back into a push-up position or pulls his knees up under him—the positions from which he has twice before risen to his feet and advanced upon the officers—they hit him.

Parloff does not find this shocking. After all, these are "ordinary-size police officers trying to control a violent, resisting suspect who is the size of a professional football player" and who, Parloff reports, has not been searched for a gun. Parloff bought the defense. King was a speeder and an ex-con, King disobeyed the cops, King *threatened* the cops—those who beat him and those who watched. Like the Simi Valley jury, Parloff could perceive Rodney King as a massively strong and dangerous figure who could seriously harm a platoon of cops. We believe, however, that a jury composed of cops would not be so persuaded, nor were we.

Juries are supposed to be representative of, and the conscience of, the community—the *vicinage*—where the crime occurred. That is why the

Constitution requires not only an impartial jury, but also a jury "of the State and district wherein the crime shall have been committed." But tragically, when venue is shifted, that does not necessarily happen. In the King trial, the Simi Valley jurors were miles away from the deaths, fires, and property damage that followed their verdict.

It wasn't simply that the jurors were white and Rodney King (and the courtroom prosecutor) was black. Joseph Kelner, a former president of both the American and New York State Trial Lawyers' associations, and the author of an eight-volume work on litigation, analyzed the jury verdict for the *New York Law Journal* (May 26, 1992). Kelner first argues that, since the videotaped beating was played repeatedly on television and discussed widely on radio and in newspapers, a change in venue from Los Angeles was entirely unjustified on grounds that adverse pretrial publicity would jeopardize a fair trial. "The videotape," he writes, "was broadcast so frequently on national and local television that the change of venue served no purpose other than to provide a fertile field for acquittal before a totally white jury."

Nor was it solely the "whiteness" of the jury that made the difference. Most of the jurors were conservative people who resided in a conservative county. The prosecutor, Deputy District Attorney Terry L. White, did not use up all of his peremptory challenges during jury selection. The district attorney's office explained to the press that they had had no great hope of obtaining a more favorable panel than that selected, judging from the written statements of 264 potential jurors in the jury pool.

Virtually all the potential jurors expressed positive opinions of police. About 25 percent had relatives or friends who were police officers. Ventura County is home to many law enforcement officers. Only 6 potential jurors were black; only 2 percent of the Ventura County population is black. Four jurors were members of the National Rifle Association. Another was a registered Republican and a former shore patrolman.

The prosecutor's most promising jurors were Anna Whiting, a fifty-four-year-old printer from a working-class street near the Ventura oil fields, and Virginia Loya, a forty-year-old hospital housekeeper and the jury's only Hispanic. Mrs. Loya was interviewed by a number of reporters after the verdict, and said she felt that most of the jurors had already made up their minds when they entered the jury room. "It's like they saw what they wanted to see, like they already had their minds made up."

Among a public earlier nurtured on *Dragnet,* or even later on its raunchier and more realistic successors, like *Hill Street Blues,* viewers in every part of America had not come to expect anything like the beating of Rodney King. Shocked by what they saw, many asked themselves: Is this what cops are really like? In the first America, the brutality shown on the King videotape demonstrated the worst nightmare of African-Americans about police violence against blacks. The Simi Valley verdict confirmed black America's deepest suspicions of the criminal justice system. So, especially in the inner cities of the first America, the Rodney King videotape and the Simi Valley verdict shook the confidence of the public in the police and the system of criminal justice. In suburban America, residents and juries, who regard police brutality as "aberrant," are more likely to support the police reflexively.

We illustrate this difference with a true story. A friend, an editor, was called to serve on a New York City jury. Eight jurors were black or Hispanic, four were white. The defendant was a young African-American man accused of a mugging. He had assaulted a women near Columbus Avenue and 59th Street and had run away with her pocketbook. A white police officer witnessed the assault, bravely chased down and subdued the offender, and testified in Court. There was one other witness, an older woman, who also saw the mugging and recited her testimony with a Chinese accent.

The police officer was a straightforward and articulate witness. His testimony could not be shaken by the able defense attorney. By contrast, the Chinese woman stammered out what she had to say. The defense attorney asked her if she was excited when she witnessed the event. She answered affirmatively.

Was she nervous? "Yes," she answered.

Was she hysterical? "I was definitely hysterical," she replied in her broken English.

The day before, the jurors had seen on television news the videotaped beating of Rodney King. They suspected that the cops who administered the beating would lie about it, and that the officers who observed it would confirm the lie. Some of the jurors, especially the African-American jurors, had disbelieved cops before. Nothing they had seen about the videotaped beating generated much confidence in the validity of police testimony, whether in Manhattan or in Los Angeles. Consequently, they did not believe the New York cop.

Most of the first American jurors, however, credited the woman's testimony despite her acknowledgment that she had been hysterical, and voted to convict the mugger. Had the woman not seen the mugging, and had she not corroborated the policeman's testimony, the mugger would have walked out of the courtroom, free to find other victims. It's not that jurors in the first America are less susceptible to bias than those in the second—its just that they nullify different kinds of evidence. They tend not to believe cops, especially after they have seen cops brutally beating a black suspect lying on the ground, while others watched.

In the second America, viewers incorporate other biases, racial biases. They saw the videotaped beating of Rodney King and believed the police testimony that King's behavior controlled their response. They thought King got what he deserved. So they did not perceive police brutality in the videotaped beating. Overzealousness, perhaps, but not brutality. When some of the officers testified that King, who suffered multiple injuries and bone fractures after repeated blows, displayed "superhuman strength" and resisted arrest when he first got out of the car, the jurors believed the officers. After all, in the second America people are taught to believe that large black men enjoy superhuman strength. Sergeant Koon testified that King had not responded to a torrential number of blows, leading Koon to fear that he would have to shoot or choke King. Had King been compliant, one of the jurors said later, he would not have been beaten. Koon further explained to the jury that King was "buffed out," that is, muscular and, being black, showed characteristics that Koon read as sure signs that King was an ex-con. Koon decided to go with the option of serious injury and severe pain. The jury understood that the defendants were cops, not criminals, and that Rodney King, the ex-con, was a criminal. They voted accordingly.

The moral of these stories? America is a divided nation, and cops are perched perilously on the divide. The Los Angeles rioters, those who burned buildings, smashed windowpanes, and beat innocent motorists, were mostly angry young black men, the "Boyz 'n the Hood" portrayed in John Singleton's compelling movie about life in south central Los Angeles. None of the young men shown in that movie aspire to industrial jobs. William Julius Wilson explains how the black community in America has been transformed between the Martin Luther King crusade for social justice and the beating of Rodney King:

> The most fundamental change is that many poor black neighborhoods today are no longer organized around work. A majority of adults in inner-city ghettos are either unemployed or have dropped out of the labor force. Consequently, their everyday lives are divorced from the rhythm and reality of the American mainstream.[2]

Work is a positive and benevolent instrument of social control. Not only should work afford people a source of income, *a living wage;* work organizes lives by assigning responsibilities. Industrial workers do *not* hang out on streetcorners. They punch a time clock, raise families, take vacations.

Communities lacking in work rely more heavily on police to maintain public order. Policing such turf is unquestionably tough, hazardous, and frustrating. One response is to abuse the authority of law to control the "gorillas in the mist," as one of the Los Angeles cops called those whom he had recently encountered. A better alternative calls for professional training and reasonable restraint. Especially when black, Latino and Asian Americans are increasingly populating United States cities, it is ever more important that the police enjoy the confidence and respect of citizens who populate these inner-city areas throughout the country. When cops use more force than is necessary to carry out their assignment, when they employ excessive force to make an arrest, they undermine confidence in all police and the subsequent capacity of the police to capture criminals and to convict them with police testimony. After all, who, especially in urban America, will believe a cop on the witness stand when cops have a reputation for beating people up, or ridiculing them, or taking bribes—and then covering up the misdeeds? The King videotape enhanced the plausibility of any allegation against police everywhere in urban America.

Generations of thoughtful police—including William H. Parker—have understood how important public esteem is to their work, and how necessary it is for controlling crime, which is what cops are supposed to do. The King videotape and the verdict will make it harder for cops everywhere to do their job, which is to be *officers of the law*. Cops are not supposed to be security guards on the public payroll who, like bouncers in a rough-and-tumble bar, are on hand to mete out punishment as they see fit. Rather, in a free society, especially in the United States, where police derive their authority from law and take an oath to support the Constitution, they are obliged to acknowledge the law's moral force and to be constrained by it. Any sensible and reflective police officer will understand that when a cop reaches above the law to use more force or coercion than is necessary to subdue a suspect, he or she undermines the very source of police authority.

The lawless exercise of force employed in excess is popularly called police brutality. Like hard-core pornography, we may not be able to define it, but we know it when we see it. And when most of us saw the beating of Rodney King on the widely disseminated videotape, we knew that we were witnessing a significant incident of police brutality. Even a clear majority of residents of Ventura County, where the Rodney G. King beating case was tried, said they not only disagreed with the verdict, but were angered by it, according to a *Los Angeles Times* poll (May 7, 1992) taken a week after the verdict. How these same suburbanites would have cast ballots as jurors remains unknown. History suggests, however, that they may also have voted to acquit.[3]

The King beating, the Simi Valley acquittal, the subsequent riots, and the federal trial will be defining events in the history of the United States.

Rodney King's identity will be more than a trivia question, and the issue of police brutality will be a major concern of a broad and interested public for years to come.

Since the King beating, and especially since the Simi Valley acquittal, both police violence and rioting have been endlessly discussed in magazine and newspaper articles, on television and radio news and talk shows, and in legislative hearings. Unfortunately, both the content and the results of this attention show a tendency to oversimplify, rather than to analyze with any depth or meaning.

We two have been doing or studying policing for more years than either of us care to remember—nearly 60 taken together. We each teach graduate and law school seminars on police. We have appeared on TV shows, been quoted in the newspapers, testified before, and worked with legislative and investigative commissions after the King beating and after the astonishing acquittal. Everybody seems to want quick and simply answers and explanations—sound bites. But our experience has taught us that questions about how often police beat people, or where, or why, like the question of why people riot, do not have simple answers. Although we believe that police must be accountable to elected authority, the absence of such lines of reporting does not explain police violence. Experience has shown that brutality and needless violence have occurred in police departments that are administered in line with democratic principles, as well as in those that answer to nobody.

We have heard it argued that police beatings should surprise nobody because the people drawn to police work suffer a compelling need to exert authority over other people. This may be true of some cops in some places, but we have known too many fine, responsible and sensible officers to write the causes of brutality off so easily.

We've heard it said that brutality is the white cops' way of keeping minorities in line. But if this were the only reason for brutality, the white protesters and reporters at the 1968 Chicago Convention would not have been beaten, nor would other white victims who have experienced police brutality in the intervening years. And, of course, both black and white victims have needlessly and painfully felt the ends of nightsticks wielded by African-American officers.

We believe that there are explanations and answers, but that these are complex, and deserve full discussion. Consequently, following our first chapter, where we try to put police brutality in perspective by addressing the issues raised by the Los Angeles Police beating of Rodney King, we have organized this book to address three basic questions about police brutality and other excessive use of force:

What are the occasions for police brutality? (Part I)
How can it be explained? (Part II)
How can it be remedied? (Part III)

In the first of three chapters in Part I, our chapter on "Vigilante Justice," examines and interprets circumstances where police exceed the limits of the law to control a group they feel the law is, or will be, inadequate to contain. The next chapter, "The Third-Degree," delves into the traditional, but no longer prevalent, practice of brutalizing suspects who are being interrogated. This is a success story—there is a marked decline in police brutality in this arena—and we try to understand why. "Public Order Policing," discusses another major occasion for police brutality, where police are faced with controlling instances of such disorder as protests and riots.

If Part I examines the occasions for police brutality, Part II addresses its causes. We find a causal connection in the traditional culture of policing, that is, in the sorts of values and understandings street cops learn as they assume the job in many police departments. This is not to suggest that all cops have the same ideas. But just as bankers develop a special outlook on the world they inhabit, so do cops. The cultural world of the police is explored in Chapter Five, while Chapters Six and Seven develop two aspects of that world especially vital to encouraging excessive force: the idea that cops are like soldiers in wars on crime and drugs (Chapter Six); and the insularity, authoritarianism, and narrow-mindedness of some police administrators and, consequently, the parochialism of some police departments (Chapter Seven).

What can be done? Are there remedies? This is the focus of Part III. In it, we discuss administrative reform of police from both historical and managerial perspectives, and with a substantial appreciation for the limits of managerial police reform (Chapter Eight).

We review and expound in Chapter Nine on how police have and *have not* been made accountable by the courts. In Chapter 10 we examine how accountability can be boosted by the press, civilian review boards and internal management. In Chapter Eleven, our final chapter, we consider new visions of policing such as community-oriented and problem-oriented policing, plus other mechanisms of renewal such as a police cadet corps and *para-police*. And we reflect once more on what we think may be the most important single question in the entire debate over policing in American society, namely, *what makes a good cop a good cop?*

# 1

# *The Beating of Rodney King*

In many, but not all, Southern communities, Negroes complain indignantly about police brutality. It is part of the policeman's philosophy that Negro criminals or suspects, or any Negro who shows signs of insubordination, should be punished bodily, and that this is a device for keeping the "Negro in his place" generally.

—Gunnar Myrdal,
*An American Dilemma,* 1941

I'm glad you asked that question [about allegations of police brutality toward minorities], but before I get into it, I might point out that in a study I once made of the factors that militate against public understanding of the police service I said that two of the factors were the criticism of the police by certain minority groups in order to distract attention from the high incidence of criminal activity within those groups and the practice of the press in magnifying police failures and in minimizing their successes or accomplishments.

—William H. Parker, Los Angeles Police Chief,
interviewed by Donald McDonald, 1962

It all started when George Holliday brought home a camcorder, a Sony CCD-F77, on Valentine's Day, 1991. The thirty-three-year-old, recently married former rugby player, general manager of a local office of Rescue Rooter, a national plumbing company, hadn't had time to load it until March 2, the day before one of his employees was scheduled to run in the Los Angeles marathon. After setting his alarm for 6 A.M. so as to arrive in time for the race, Holliday went to bed early and was awakened at 12:50 A.M. by a blast of siren noise and screeching rubber. The racket was coming from Foothill Boulevard, the main thoroughfare of a middle-class, ethnically mixed Los Angeles exurb with a population about 60 percent Latino,

10 percent black, and the rest Asian and white. When Holliday, who is white, pulled the window shade aside, he could scarcely believe what he saw. The powerful spotlight of a police helicopter was shining on a white Hyundai surrounded by a half-dozen police cars. His first thought was, "Hey, let's get the camera!"[1]

The videotape Holliday shot showed a large black man down on hands and knees, struggling on the ground, twice impaled with wires from an electronic TASER gun, rising and falling while being repeatedly beaten, blow after blow after blow—dozens of blows, fifty-six in all, about the head, neck, back, kidneys, ankles, legs, feet—by two police officers wielding their 2-foot black metal truncheons like baseball bats. Also visible was a third officer, who was stomping King, and about ten police officers watching the beating along with a number of Holliday's neighbors.

Actually, twenty-three LAPD officers responded to the scene (an interesting number in light of the later claim that the Department is severely understaffed to respond to emergencies). Four officers were directly involved in the use of force; two hovered overhead in a helicopter; ten were on the ground and witnessed some portion of the beating; seven others checked out the scene and left. Four uniformed officers from two other law enforcement agencies—the Highway Patrol and the Los Angeles Unified School District—were also there.

Both Holliday and Paul King, Rodney's brother, tried to report the police abuse. Neither succeeded. When, on Monday morning, Paul King went to the Foothill station to report that his brother had been beaten, the officer at the front desk told him to wait. After waiting and growing impatient, Paul King returned to the desk. Finally, a sergeant came out of the back of the station and proceeded to give Paul King a bureaucratic hard time. The sergeant then left the room for about thirty minutes while Paul King, who had asked about procedures for making a complaint and had told the sergeant about the possibility of a videotape, waited impatiently.

When the sergeant returned, instead of addressing Paul's complaint, he asked whether Paul had ever been in trouble. He told Paul that an investigation was ongoing, and that Rodney was in "big trouble," since he had been caught in a high-speed chase and had put someone's life in danger, possibly a police officer's. The sergeant told Paul King to try to find the video, but at no time did the sergeant fill out a personnel complaint form. Paul King testified to the Christopher Commission that when he left Foothill Station, "I knew I hadn't made a complaint."

Holliday was busy on Sunday, the day he videotaped the beating. As he had planned, he took his videocam to the LA marathon, then to a wedding. On Monday, March 4, he telephoned the Foothill station, intending to offer his videotape to the police. He told the desk officer that he had witnessed the beating of a motorist by LAPD officers and asked about the motorist's condition. The desk officer told him that "we [the LAPD] do not release information like that." He neither asked questions about what Holliday had seen nor recorded a personnel complaint form as a result of Holliday's call. The officer seemed so uninterested in Holliday's information that Holliday decided to try another tack and called Channel 5 (KTLA) in Los Angeles. The station made arrangements with Holliday to bring the tape in, and it was broadcast Monday evening. CNN gave it national and international exposure, playing it repeatedly until it was seen everywhere in the world, from Tokyo to London to Zaïre. The beating of Rodney King became the lead story for several days on the major networks as well, the most explicit and shocking news footage of police brutality ever to be seen on television.[2]

In the ninety-second tape, viewers saw with their own eyes how a group of Los Angeles police officers could act out their anger, frustration, fears, and prejudices on the body of a black man who had led them on a high-speed chase. Like films of the police dogs in Selma or the clubs and tear gas of the 1968 Chicago Democratic Convention, the dramatic videotape gave new credibility to allegations of a sort that many people—including police officers— formerly dismissed as unbelievable. The tape was instantly etched in the memory of every American police chief who watched it and who knew that he or she could scarcely disregard its implications.

Shortly after the King beating occurred, Los Angeles Police Chief Daryl Gates condemned it as an "aberration." Actually, the King incident was simply the most visible in a lengthy series of police atrocities involving a police agency that had itself become aberrational. Between 1987 and 1990, 4,400 misconduct complaints were filed against the LAPD. Of these, 41 percent were filed by blacks, who make up only 13 percent of the population. In 1989 Los Angeles paid out $9.1 million to settle lawsuits alleging police misconduct. In 1990 that figure had risen to $11.3 million for suits alleging excessive force, wrongful deaths, false arrests, negligence, misconduct, and civil rights violations. The Christopher Commission found that a significant number of LAPD officers "repetitively use excessive force against the public and persistently ignore the written guidelines of the Department regarding force" and that "the failure to control these officers is a management issue that is at the heart of the problem."[3] What made the King beating different from those earlier events was not the conduct of the police, but the presence of George Holliday's video camera.

Most of those who lived in the south central sections of Los Angeles, in places like Watts, Inglewood, and Compton, knew this. Although the damage and the looting following the verdict could scarcely be justified by horrified viewers, many of whom were black, the origins of the riots could be traced to the history of tension and trouble between the police and black and Hispanic residents. "For many," *New York Times* reporter Seth Mydans wrote, "the riot was a simple message to the authorities and larger society. Treat us right. We've been pushed too close to the edge." Ervin Mitchell, a design engineer interviewed by Mr. Mydans, explained: "Young blacks and Hispanics have been persecuted, beaten and pulled out of cars because of stereotypes. We're tired of being treated like garbage. We're tired of living in a society that denies us the right to be considered as a human being."[4]

No one felt this oppression more powerfully than Jessie Larez and his family. Their name may be unfamiliar to those who focused on the King verdict and its aftermath, but their experience perfectly illustrates why so many south central residents bore such hostility to the authorities.

In 1986 Los Angeles police obtained a warrant that authorized them to search the Larez home for a gun. The judge who issued the warrant had not included in it a "no-knock" authorization that would have allowed the police to make an unannounced forcible entry. Instead, the Larez warrant required the police to knock and announce their presence and, presumably, prohibited them from forcing their way in unless they were denied admission or waited fruitlessly at the door for a response of any kind. According to a unanimous panel of the United States Court of Appeals for the Ninth Circuit, however, officers from the LAPD's appropriately named "CRASH unit[5] conducted a 'crisis entry' which involved breaking the back windows of the house to create a diversion ostensibly aimed at making a front entry safer."[6] The police did this at 7:00 A.M. on June 13, 1986, while Larez, his wife, and their seven children and grandchildren slept, some in beds and cribs directly beneath those windows. Once inside, according to the Court of Appeals' September 27, 1991 opinion, CRASH officers

> . . . hurled Jessie across the room, grabbed him by the hair, forced him to lie down on the floor with his knee on Jessie's neck and handcuffed him. Police kicked him and smashed his face into the floor. The officers laughed and sneered: they told him they had him where they wanted him. At one point Officer Holcomb pointed his service revolver at Jessie's head and said to him, "I could blow your fucking head off right here and nobody can prove you did not try to do something." Officer Keller told Jessie, "we finally got you motherfucker." Jessie sustained a broken nose during the incident. His knees required arthroscopic surgery, and neck surgery was recommended to alleviate the headaches which have persisted since the incident.
> 
> Police yelled to [Larez's daughter] Diane to "get up here with that fuck-

ing baby." Upon approaching, she was seized by her waist-long hair and arm and thrown face first to the floor where she, too, was handcuffed. Upon lifting her head to instruct a family member to take her baby away, Officer Keller grabbed Diane's hair and banged her head to the floor, demanding that she "put [her] fucking face on the floor."

[Larez's son] Katsumi, who was sleeping in his room attached to the garage at the time of the search, was awoken [sic] when his door was kicked in by police. An officer pointed his gun at Katsumi and shouted, "I'll blow your fucking head off." He was taken to the living room where he and his brother Frank, like Jessie and Diane, were also proned out on the floor and handcuffed. Katsumi was kicked in the head and side by Officer Holcomb.

The police left the Larez home "turned upside down." Pots, pans, and dishes had been taken from their cabinets and thrown to the floor, and various objects kept on the bar, as well as the VCR, had been thrown on the TV room floor. Katsumi's room looked as if a "hurricane [had] whipped through it." [Son] Albertdee saw beds turned over, clothing in heaps on the floor, broken crockery in the kitchen, and broken windows. His bedroom posters had been ripped from the walls, his punching bag had been cut open, and his plants had been dislodged from their pots. Jessie's prized Japanese albums, obtained while he was stationed in Japan [more than thirty years before], were broken by the [police]. Other broken items included a pitcher, a crockpot, a figurine, a dish, a vase, a music box, a lamp, a rice cooker, a coffee pot, wall paneling, a clock, a sliding glass door, picture frames, and a camera lens.

Despite the rigor of their search, the CRASH officers found no gun in the Larez home. No member of the family was charged with any offense related to the gun CRASH allegedly believed was in the house. Still, the police did not leave empty-handed: Jessie was arrested for battery on a police officer, a charge that was dismissed after trial. The police arrest report notes that Jessie, a fifty-five-year-old disabled veteran, was wearing "no shs, blu pajamas," and that he "received M.T. [medical treatment] at Jail Division for a small cut on the bridge of his nose and on the corner of his rt eyebrow, no stitches required."[7] The report includes no mention of other injuries or damage. Jessie's son Eddie also was arrested on unspecified grounds for violating the terms of his parole. According to the Ninth Circuit:

Jessie lodged a complaint with the LAPD. The department's Internal Affairs division assigned a CRASH detective not involved in the Larez search to investigate the complaint. In a letter signed by Chief Gates, Jessie ultimately was notified that none of the many allegations in his complaint could be sustained.

Outraged, Larez then filed suit against the six CRASH officers, the LAPD, and Chief Gates. When his case came to trial in 1988, one of us gave expert testimony on Larez's behalf. The LAPD investigation of Jessie Larez's complaint, Fyfe testified, was riddled with "a lot of holes," as were two years' worth of citizens' complaint investigations reviewed in connection with an earlier civil rights suit against LAPD. In these LAPD cases, Fyfe said on the witness stand, whitewashes were so frequent that, regardless of the seriousness or nature of complainants' injuries, "something has to be done on film for the department to buy the citizen's story."

The King incident was, of course, electronically memorialized by the amateur cameraman George Holliday and precipitated a national investigation by the Department of Justice and by the U.S. Congress of complaints against police. Within the city of Los Angeles, at least three major investigations were initiated—an internal investigation by the Los Angeles Police Department, another by the Police Commission, and a third by an independent commission formed by the merger of two groups appointed by the mayor and the police chiefs. This last, headed by a Los Angeles attorney and former State Department official, Warren Christopher, wrote of the difference made by the taping of the King incident:

> Our Commission owes its existence to the George Holliday videotape of the Rodney King incident. Whether there even would have been a Los Angeles Police Department investigation without the video is doubtful, since the efforts of King's brother, Paul, to file a complaint were frustrated, and the report of the involved officers was falsified. Even if there had been an investigation, our case-by-case review of the handling of 700 complaints indicates that without the Holliday videotape the complaint might have been adjudged to be "not sustained," because the officers' version conflicted with the account by King and his two passengers, who typically would have been viewed as not "independent."[8]

As information accumulated about the Rodney King episode, testimony about what happened became wildly contradictory. Both the Christopher Report and portions of a 314-page LAPD Internal Affairs report show wide differences of opinion about how King acted during the pursuit and after he stepped out of his car. The California Highway Patrol officers who first attempted to stop King for a traffic violation reported that King fled from them at "110 to 115 m.p.h." The Christopher Commission and others have suggested, however that such speeds are about 20 miles per hour faster than can be squeezed out of a Hyundai like King's.[9]

Some of the officers said that King, who suffered multiple injuries and bone fractures after repeated blows, displayed "superhuman strength" and resisted arrest when he first got out of the car. Sergeant Koon said that King had not responded to a torrential number of blows, leading Koon to fear that he would have to shoot or choke King. That was when he instructed his officers: "Hit his joints, hit his wrists, hit his elbows, hit his knees, hit his ankles," and, Koon told investigators, "that's what they did do, they did exactly as I told them to do and exactly as they're trained." Several of the officers reported that they had undergone baton training that night before going out on patrol. One of them, rookie officer Timothy Wind, according to Officer Rick Distefano, "demonstrated excellent technique and made contact in all the right places on the practice board."

Yet at least two of the bystanding officers saw no need for the vicious beating. Officer Melanie Singer of the California Highway Patrol, for instance, said she believed King was trying to comply with the officer's commands when he was beaten. "King did not aggressively kick or punch the officers," she said. "He was merely trying to get away from the officers."[10] Similarly, Officer Ingrid Larson, who had been out of the Police Academy only five days, said that "King did not appear to be combative, but merely used his arms to block the baton strikes." Paramedics who arrived on the scene also testified that King appeared to be coherent and was not acting violently.

On May 12, 1991, a guest editorial in the *Los Angeles Times* called for the resignation of Chief Daryl Gates. Published more than two months after the incident, this was not the first op-ed piece to call on Gates to resign. What was surprising was the identity of its author, the same Sergeant Stacey C. Koon who had been in charge at the Rodney King beating. Indicted and suspended without pay, Koon said he wrote the commentary to protest Chief Daryl Gates's handling of the incident, in particular his firing of rookie officer Timothy Wind, one of the indicted four. The editorial suggests that the Chief let the officers down, that he felt "justified to abuse the foundations of the organization to save the organization." Koon's essay became national news. Patrick Thistle, an attorney for one of the indicted officers, was asked by *CBS Evening News* (May 12, 1991) to comment on Koon's call for Gates's dismissal. "The LAPD has always stressed that they are a loving, caring family," said Thistle. "I think these officers believe that the family has treated them like they are not a member of the group."

The cops on the scene were responding to a code they believed in and considered to be moral. The code decrees that cops protect other cops, no matter what, and that cops of higher rank back up working street cops—no matter what. From the perspective of the indicted cops, Daryl Gates betrayed the code. Sergeant Koon was, in effect, alleging that Chief Gates was changing the unwritten rules, and consequently undermining the tradition of the organization.

Police department traditions and the norms police live by are sustained by street incidents. When cops brutally beat prisoners and others who challenge their authority, they must have learned from their fellow officers that such conduct is acceptable and will be protected from the top down; when they do so in public, they must understand that their immunity is virtually ironclad.

Mike Rothmiller, a former LAPD detective, recently told the story of his life in the department to writer Ivan G. Goldman. He describes a department where racism and spying were accepted and often even encouraged. So was lying on police reports:

> Again and again Rothmiller watched cops decide for themselves who was guilty, and then weave a spell over the arrest report to make it match their perceptions. Most of the arrest reports he encountered were doctored in some way—facts deleted or invented. It wasn't exactly the frontier justice of a lynch mob, but it wasn't justice either. It was just the way things worked.[11]

Police chiefs know about these unwritten messages. Brutality is an occupational risk of a profession that rides with danger and is trained and authorized to use force, even deadly force. Chiefs know this, and they know they cannot absolutely control their officers' behavior. Yet the best chiefs avoid any signal that excessive force is excusable or that any group of people is a legitimate target.

When brutality is alleged, good chiefs investigate thoroughly and objectively. When brutality is found, examples are made of those who committed it, those who failed to stop it, and those who covered it up. When brutality remains undiscovered in a well-run police department, it is because a few officers have managed to keep the incident a deep, dark secret. But there is no secretiveness in the Rodney G. King videotape. Officers and citizens alike could and did watch the beating. Officers—including a supervisor and, apparently, a watch commander—could joke about it in computer conversations they knew were being recorded. For these officers, the threat of review and censure by higher authority was nonexistent: after all, their comments memorialized their actions only on their department's electronic records, rather than on a citizen's videotape. In Los Angeles, the indictments and suspensions came as a shock to the involved officers. They expected the Chief to back them up, as he doubtless had done in the past. But the tape made that impossible, and they were grievously disappointed.

The four Los Angeles cops who beat King were indicted by a grand jury on serious felony charges, and appeared to face a bleak future of imprison-

*acquitted*

ment until they were acquitted by a Simi Valley jury. Yet a total of twenty-seven law enforcement officers were at the scene that night, including twenty-three Los Angeles Police Department officers. Although all or most were disciplined by their departments, those who watched and did nothing to interfere with the beating were not charged by Los Angeles District Attorney Ira Reiner. "However morally wrong their failure to intercede, in California law there is no criminal statute under which these officers can be indicted," Reiner said at a press conference on May 10, 1991. "No matter how reprehensible their action, or their inaction, no person can be charged with a crime unless they have violated a statute." But the officers were not entirely free of criminal liability. Reiner went on to say that he has referred the case to the U.S. Attorney's office to look into possible violations of federal civil rights statutes. The federal action was not activated until the Simi Valley acquittal, when the President himself expressed astonishment at the verdict and ordered the Justice Department to "proceed apace."

Many activists had demanded that the onlookers be charged and were dissatisfied when they weren't. They expressed reactions ranging from concern to outrage. Ramona Ripston, director of the Southern California chapter of the American Civil Liberties Union, argued that Reiner's announcement was a message to Los Angeles area law enforcement personnel that it is acceptable for police simply to stand by when they see other cops abusing people. "If citizens stand by and see a crime being committed, they are expected to report it," she said. "How can we expect less of our police officers?" John Mack, president of the Los Angeles Urban League, said he was deeply disappointed with Reiner's announced conclusion and commented, "It's a sad day in the history of Los Angeles that some seventeen police officers are going to be able to get away with being accessories to a crime."[12]

Daryl Gates and his Los Angeles Police Department had few defenders after the beating of Rodney King. One notable exception was Paul Walters, who succeeded Raymond Davis, a major innovator of community-oriented policing, as Chief of the nearby Santa Ana Police Department. In a March 11 guest editorial for the *Los Angeles Times,* Walters, who had been a protégé of Davis, wrote in an editorial that surprised Davis and others who had followed Walters's previous career:

> The task of leading the Los Angeles Police Department is formidable, but Chief Daryl Gates has been outstanding in the performance of his duties. The department, under Gates, has set for itself a high standard of excellence and is one of the few large police departments not tainted by major corruption. The chief has repeatedly sought to conduct his operations according to the letter of the law.[13]

## POLICE AND FORCE

Long before the riot probes and trials and the political conflicts within the city of Los Angeles are ended, police chiefs all over the country, however complacent they may have been about such abuses in the past, will have warned their rank and file that such conduct will not be tolerated. After the King beating, New York's Police Commissioner Lee P. Brown, then also President of the International Association of Chiefs of Police, in concert with a dozen other police chiefs, called on the federal government to develop a system for gathering information on the use of excessive police force. "The problem of excessive force in American policing is real," Commissioner Brown said. "It is, in part, related to the nature of the difficult challenges faced by the police in our urban centers. Regardless of its cause, it cannot be condoned and must be actively countered by concerned professionals."[14]

Clearly, more and deeper questions need to be raised about the nature of police violence, its centrality to the role of the police, and its prevalence. Obviously, it is nothing new. Part of the paradox of policing is that police are supposed to use necessary force. As anybody who has ever called a cop knows, police intervention is grounded in a round-the-clock capacity to take decisive action in handling all kinds of emergencies and to employ force where it is needed.

One leading police scholar, Egon Bittner, has even proposed that it makes sense to think of the police "as a mechanism for the distribution of non-negotiably coercive force employed in accordance with the dictates of an intuitive grasp of situational exigencies."[15] The question remains, however, as to how much force is justified and in what situations. Certainly, force is sometimes appropriate—that's why cops carry batons and guns. Police should not be labeled "brutal" simply because they employ forceful measures. Taken alone, a charge of brutality should not be regarded as evidence of guilt. After the Los Angeles riots, such a false charge was made by an ex-convict in Berkeley. The officer who was charged could prove that he was issuing a traffic violation ticket in another part of the city at the time the purported "victim" claimed to have been beaten. Yet the charge set off a protest march by indignant citizens who believed the allegations without hearing all the evidence.

Still, well-founded allegations of brutality following police vehicle pursuits are all too familiar. Florida's terrible Liberty City riot in 1980 had its roots in a fatal police beating at the end of a police chase and subsequent cover-up attempt. Indeed, long before the King incident, one veteran Los Angeles officer told Fyfe that he had never seen a police chase that did not end with at least a black eye delivered to the subject of the chase. What is it about these events that seem to generate such police rage?

Both authors have had long experience with police. During our years in police cars, we have been at the cop's end of more than thirty high-speed chases. Younger cops, hotshot cops, aggressive cops, relish the exhilaration of these pursuits. People who haven't ridden in patrol cars for a full shift cannot appreciate how tedious policing can be even in the world's most crime-ridden cities. Patrol policing, like military combat and the lives of cowboys, consists mostly of periods of boredom, broken up by interludes of excitement and even of terror. For police, a chase is among the most exciting of all work experiences: the sudden start of a chase is a jolt not unlike that experienced by the dozing fisherman who finds suddenly that he has a big and dangerous fish on the other end of his line.

More than representing excitement, the high-speed chase dramatizes two crucial elements of the policing enterprise: capturing daring criminals and meeting challenges to police authority. Anyone who speeds on a highway or, even worse, on city streets imperils other drivers and pedestrians. Those who speed with the intention of eluding police are, by definition, audacious and dangerous. The escaping driver is often believed to be a felon and—on rare occasions—may turn out to be a person who either has a cache of drugs in his car or has committed a serious crime. When the driver has passengers, as Rodney King had, he is thought to be even more dangerous. Such a driver, when captured, is rarely treated with consideration. He may be pushed, shoved, verbally assaulted, and tightly cuffed.

By now, however, police have learned from both experience and scholarly studies that most motorists who flee from them are not, in fact, threatening offenders. Instead, like King, fleeing motorists typically are troubled young men with bad driving records whose ability to reason has been altered by drugs or alcohol. But regardless of how relatively minor the violations that lead to their flight, fleeing motorists commit a cardinal sin against the police: instead of submitting immediately, they challenge the police and attempt to escape their pursuer's authority. In so doing, in the eyes of police officers accustomed to motorists and other citizens who not only submit immediately to police authority but even check their speedometers in the mere presence of police cars, fleeing motorists become prime candidates for painful lessons at the ends of police nightsticks.

Still, taking all that into account, everyone who watched the LA cops beat and kick Rodney King knew (intuitively, one might say) that the force used was not justified even as a reflexive striking out, that it went far beyond this. As the classical sociologist Emile Durkheim taught, we live in a society of shared moral norms, and we are presumed to know their boundaries. Two officers are seen beating a downed suspect with their nightsticks, even though he has already been hit with an electronic stun gun, has been subdued, and is no longer dangerous. Another officer joins in to kick the fallen man.

Los Angeles Mayor Tom Bradley, a former police officer, said he found the beating "shocking and outrageous." Chief Daryl Gates reviewed the videotape and said that he was "sickened" when he saw it. So did the President of the United States.

After the Simi Valley verdict of acquittal, in a prime-time speech to the nation on May 2, 1992, President Bush said, "What you saw and I saw on the TV video [of the King beating] was revolting. I felt anger. I felt pain. I thought, 'How can I explain this to my grandchildren?'"

"Viewed from the outside," he continued, "it is hard to understand how the verdict could possibly square with the video." In a *USA Today* poll, 86 percent of white Americans and 100 percent of black Americans answered that the King verdict was "wrong." Decidedly few voices were raised praising the conduct of the LA police in the King incident—in contrast to some of the responses to the flagrantly violent Chicago police conduct during the 1968 Democratic Convention, where the police conduct was said by some to have been provoked.

### "THE LAPD MENTALITY"

But if the brutality of Rodney King's beating was self-evident to everyone who watched it, why weren't the cops who beat and kicked him sickened? Were they as individuals beyond the pale of the moral understandings expressed by the Mayor, by the President, eventually by Chief Gates himself, and by virtually everyone else who saw the incident? Had they gone berserk? How about the cops who watched? Did they have defective personalities? Hardly. Two or three cops can go berserk. Maybe the cops who administered the beating were especially aggressive and insensitive. But when twenty-three others are watching and not interfering, the incident cannot be considered "aberrant," as Chief Gates initially suggested.

The incident and its cover-up must be seen in light of the overall philosophy of aggressive policing that began to dominate the LAPD when William Parker became its chief more than forty years earlier. In testimony before the Christopher Commission, Assistant Chief David Dotson said that LAPD clung to a 1950s version of tough policing:

> We reward our people—our field people, the people that got us here to this [Commission] meeting—we reward them for what we call hardnosed, proactive police work. We want them to go out and identify criminal activity

and stop it, either before it occurs, or certainly, after it occurs, we want to go out and determine who the criminals were who perpetrated this particular act and get them into jail.

. . . We expect people to go out and aggressively identify people, and investigate them, and that puts these police officers in the middle between what we evaluate them on and what they are able to do legally.[16]

The dominance of this philosophy—in Chief Gates's terms, "the LAPD mentality"[17]—suggests that King's beating could scarcely have been an isolated incident. More than twenty LAPD officers witnessed King's beating, which continued for nearly two minutes. Those who administered it assumed that their fellow officers would not report the misconduct and were prepared to lie on their behalf. In this respect, police brutality is like police corruption—there may be some rotten apples, but usually the barrel itself is rotten. Two cops can go berserk, but twenty cops embody a subculture of policing.

The written rule is clear: cops are to use no more force than is necessary to subdue a suspect. Where a departmental subculture condoning brutality prevails, the unwritten rule is: "Teach them a lesson." Santa Ana's former police chief, Raymond Davis, who, unlike his successor Paul Walters, was appalled by the King beating, told us that he had once visited the Ramparts Station of the Los Angeles Police Department and saw a sign on the wall that read: "Burglars Beware! Make Sure Your I.D. is Valid So We Will Know Where to Notify Your Next of Kin." Such expressions of cop humor, he said, send a transparent message about a police department's values, especially to rookie cops.

The King videotape confirms how these values play out on the street. More important than the beating was the passive witnessing by the other cops and the semi-jocular conversations on the police computer network. Sergeant Stacey C. Koon, who was the supervising officer on the scene of the King beating, reported by computer to the commander of his watch that "U (patrol unit) just had a big time use of force . . . tased and beat the suspect of CHP pursuit, Big Time." The response from the police station was, "Oh well . . . I'm sure the lizard didn't deserve it . . . HAHA I'll let them know OK."[18] All the officers involved—those who beat, those who watched, and those who talked afterward—had to be confident that their colleagues would remain silent or lie about what really happened and, further, that the Department would believe the officers and reject any citizen's description.

Four days after the incident, Daryl Gates held a press conference in a stuffy, overheated conference room jammed with seventeen television cameras and more than seventy members of the news media. It was here that he began his defense of his department and his record as chief by announcing that four officers would face criminal charges, and that the others who watched and did nothing could face administrative punishment.

"I preach—I mean I really preach—to every single person who graduates from the Police Academy about the law and their need for a reverence for the law," Gates said. "What they should have done, if they really loved their brother officers [was to] have stepped in and grabbed them and hauled them back and said, 'Knock it off!' That's what the sergeant should have done [and] that's what every officer there should have done."[19]

The news conference was contentious. Many of those present indicated by their questions that they did not believe Gates. Over the years he had made a number of highly publicized remarks, famous among Los Angeles reporters, suggestive of racial insensitivity, if not bias. A few months after Gates became police chief in 1978, he had offended Latinos by saying that some Latino officers were not promoted because they were "lazy." About two years later he drew complaints from women after he described a local television anchor woman as an "Aryan broad." Many Jews were angered when, in 1982, the press obtained an in-house report suggesting that the Soviets were sending criminals disguised as Jewish immigrants to disrupt the 1984 Olympics. Gates again angered Latinos by referring to the killer of a policewoman as a "drunken Salvadoran."[20] Nine years earlier, in his most widely publicized intemperate remark, he had said that "some blacks" may be more susceptible than "normal people" to police officers' use of a potentially fatal chokehold (which has since been banned). For this remark, the Police Commission publicly reprimanded Gates, and *Esquire* magazine honored him with one of its "Annual Dubious Achievement" Awards. In 1991 he won a second Dubious Achievement Award for appointing a panel to study reinstituting the chokehold in the wake of criticism about the use of batons and the TASER in the King incident. After the King beating, Gates declared that, "in spite of the fact that he's on parole and a convicted robber, I'd be glad to apologize."[21]

Given this background, besides raising questions about the King beating, reporters challenged the Chief about a number of incidents involving officers and blacks over the years—even about the 1979 shooting of Eulia Love, a black woman who was killed by officers after she was said to have been ready to throw a knife at them. Officers had gone to the Love home after she was reported to have struck a gas company employee who was shutting off her service because of an unpaid $22.09 gas bill.

More recent incidents were also raised. One involved Hall of Fame baseball player Joe Morgan; another, former Lakers basketball star Jamaal

Wilkes. Morgan collected $540,000 in damages after he complained in federal court that he was roughed up by a police officer who mistook Morgan for a drug courier. Wilkes was pulled over on his way home from work, ordered out of his car, and handcuffed by officers who gave conflicting reasons for having stopped him.

## MISTRUST OF THE LOS ANGELES POLICE

The questions at the press conference reflected a broad mistrust of the Los Angeles Police Department and other Southern California law enforcement agencies on the part of minority citizens and their representatives. Gregory J. Boyle, a Jesuit priest and Pastor of Dolores Mission Church in Boyle Heights, wrote in the *Los Angeles Times* that while most citizens were "stunned and uncomprehending" after viewing the tape of Rodney King being beaten by police officers, the members of his parish, a mostly black and Hispanic working-poor community east of downtown Los Angeles, experienced "grim memories of common and unchecked police brutality." Father Boyle criticized Chief Gates and others who interpreted the incident as an isolated event. "Most people of color," he wrote, "can recall such an incident happening to them or to a family member or neighbor."[22] That kind of recollection helped precipitate the riots after the Simi Valley acquittal.

But by the time of the trial, everybody who read newspapers and watched television should have known about the racism of the LAPD. The Christopher Commission's investigation affirmed Father Boyle's criticism, and was widely reported. Even within the LAPD, a survey of 960 officers found that about one-quarter of the 650 responding officers agreed that "racial bias (prejudice) on the part of officers toward minority citizens currently exists and contributes to a negative interaction between police and community."[23] Shortly before Officers Laurence M. Powell and Wind beat Rodney King, they had, it was reported, responded to a domestic disturbance call involving an African-American family. Using their in-car computer terminal, the officers subsequently informed their radio dispatcher that the call was "right out of *Gorillas in the Mist*." The message was returned with a remark that mimicked African-American dialect: "hahaha . . . let me guess who be the parties."

A *Los Angeles Times* poll of March 10, 1991, found that most Los Angeles residents maintained confidence in the department's crime control capacities but distrusted the police. Eighty-six percent said they had seen the oft-televised videotape showing King being beaten and clubbed by uniformed officers. King said that when he pulled his car over, he cooperated with police instructions, but the cops said he acted menacingly. A majority of those polled believed King. Among black respondents, 78 percent declared belief in King's version, while only 2 percent said they believed the police. Still, and regardless of whether they believed King, 92 percent of all respondents thought the arresting officers had used too much force against King.

Of more interest is the public perception of whether the beating of King was an isolated incident. Sixty-three percent of those surveyed said that brutality was common; 28 percent answered "very common" and 35 percent "fairly common." When broken down by ethnicity, however, the responses did vary considerably. Among Anglos, only 19 percent said it was very common and 39 percent fairly common. Among Latinos, 33 percent said it was very common, while 27 percent regarded it as fairly common. Among blacks, the breakdown was 44 and 36 percent, confirming Father Boyle's report of the perceptions held within the African-American community.

Those perceptions were likely shaped as much by the Los Angeles Sheriff's Department as by the LAPD. In December 1991, the Board of Supervisors of Los Angeles County appointed sixty-seven-year-old, retired Superior Court judge James G. Kolts, a Reagan appointee with a reputation as a law-and-order judge, to review "the policies, practices and procedures of the Sheriff's Department [especially] as they relate to allegations of excessive force, the community sensitivity of deputies and the Department's citizen complaint procedure." The Kolts Report to the Supervisors was released in July 1992, and its findings shone a harsh new light on law enforcement throughout Los Angeles County. "My staff and I," Kolts wrote in the introduction, "found deeply disturbing evidence of excessive force and lax discipline. The LASD has not been able to solve its own problems of excessive force in the past and has not reformed itself with adequate thoroughness and speed." Samuel Pillsbury, a professor at Loyola Law School, suggested in a *Los Angeles Times* Op-Ed column (July 22, 1992) that maybe the "loudest and wildest critics of criminal justice in Los Angeles have been right—or at least more right than we ever imagined."

The practices and communications employed in the so-called war on drugs have reinforced such mistrust. The drug war in Los Angeles focuses on paramilitary operations—sweeps, roundups, and battering rams. As Anthony Bouza, the former Minneapolis Police Chief, noted in a speech following the beating of Rodney King, such measures are "sure to lead to abuses and repression."[24] Mistrust and hostility predictably follow upon abuse and repression.

## THE BRUTALITY BAR

The aggressive policies of Los Angeles's law enforcement agencies have been accompanied by a rise in complaints. Karol Heppe, executive director of the Los Angeles Police Misconduct Lawyers Referral Service, reported that of the 2,624 complaints she received in 1990, 616 were against Los Angeles police officers, eight of whom were assigned to the Foothill Division, where those who beat King were stationed. In the first two months of 1991, the Lawyers Referral Service received 531 complaints, of which, according to Heppe, 127 were against Los Angeles police officers, seven of whom were assigned to the Foothill Division.[25] The nearly $21 million in settlements and court awards in excessive force cases filed against the Los Angeles Police Department from 1986 through 1990 does not include interest and attorneys' fees, which can be "staggering," according to Gail Diane Cox, who interviewed members of the "brutality bar" for *Los Angeles Magazine*.[26]

Unlike personal injury cases, where lawyers receive 30 to 40 percent of any award, most brutality cases are filed under the federal Civil Rights Act, which provides that reasonable attorney's fees be awarded to victorious lawyers, regardless of the size of the award to the client. Given this incentive, lawyers have annually filed some 200 to 300 lawsuits against the LAPD since 1986. In 1990, fifty-eight of these went to trial (many were settled out of court), and the city attorney reports winning all but seventeen. Brutality litigation is costly both to the city and to the involved lawyers. When the lawyers lose, they and their firms must absorb the cost. But when they win, they win big, or at least big enough to sustain a practicing "brutality bar."

The Rodney King videotape encouraged brutality bar lawyers to think big. Indeed, Stephen Yagman, the Larez family attorney, welcomed the Ninth Circuit's reversal of the $175,000 verdict he won against Chief Gates in that case. Noting that the judgment had been reversed on a technicality, Yagman said that he relished the chance to retry the case in this post-King era: "Gates got what he wanted," Yagman said, "He won a reversal because the trial judge let into evidence a damaging newspaper article without allowing the city's lawyer to examine the reporters on what Gates said. Now we get to retry the case with exactly the same evidence—plus the reporters' testimony. Gates got 'The Monkey's Paw.' He won his appeal and made this a million dollar case."[27]

John Burton, another member of the Los Angeles brutality bar, gained prominence in 1988. As the lead counsel of a team of ten Referral Service lawyers, Burton sued over an incident in which dozens of LAPD officers ran wild and trashed four apartments in a drug raid. So totally were the apartments damaged, and so extensive the injuries, that the Red Cross had to send aid. In February 1990 Burton and his team won a $3.4 million judgment, giving his fifty-five clients awards that averaged $60,000 each. In 1992 Yagman won a settlement in the $600,000 range for the landlord. Burton is involved in the King case, representing Bryant Allen, one of the two passengers in King's car. Like Yagman and other brutality bar lawyers, Burton has recently been thinking very big about legal fees. According to him, those who run police departments are going to have to make some major changes, "or else we are going to get very rich."

## IS BRUTALITY ON THE RISE?

Despite the current publicity given to police brutality, we believe that it has diminished in the past fifty years, even in the past twenty. We need to recall how much worse, how routine, police brutality used to be. Most Americans, even those of middle age, have grown up in an era in which Warren Supreme Court decisions, such as *Miranda* v. *Arizona,* are taken for granted. But *Miranda* was decided in 1966, not so very long ago.

A number of the cases decided by the U.S. Supreme Court have involved actual or threatened physical brutality or deprivation at the hands of the police. Suspects have been whipped, slapped, threatened, and deprived of food or water. Others have been subjected to extended periods of police interrogation. Psychological coercion used to be common. In one case a police psychiatrist posed as a general practitioner brought in to relieve an acutely painful sinus condition. In another, a policeman who was a close friend of the defendant told him that unless he confessed the policeman would be in deep trouble—would be fired—and that his wife and family would suffer.

Robert Fogelson, a leading historian of American police, observes that the Los Angeles police in the 1930s joined forces with the American Legion to prevent various left-wing and liberal groups, from the John Reed Club to the ACLU, from holding meetings in and around Los Angeles. Similarly, a few years later, when a large and orderly crowd gathered in Harlem to demonstrate against the trial of the Scottsboro Boys, New York City detectives tossed several tear gas canisters to break up the crowd. Still later in the 1930s, a vast but peaceful crowd tried to organize a picket line around a Republic Steel factory. Chicago cops, armed with revolvers, clubs, and tear gas, killed ten and wounded nearly a hundred of the picketers. "Although far from conclusive," Fogelson writes, "the evidence seems to indicate that the big-city police were probably less repressive in the mid-1960s than in the late 1920s and early 1930s."[28]

Nevertheless, the commissions investigating the riots and civil disorders of the 1960s found that police routinely used excessive force, especially against blacks. "Negroes firmly believe," the National Advisory Commission on Civil Disorders wrote in March 1968, "that police brutality and harassment occur repeatedly in Negro neighborhoods. This belief is unquestionably one of the major reasons for intense Negro resentment against the police.[29]"

Yet significant change has occurred in a number of police forces in the past twenty years. Those who work in organizations—whether IBM, McDonald's, or the FBI—reflect the values of their organization's leadership. This is especially true of police departments, because of their paramilitary character. Indeed, Gerald Uelman, a legal scholar, found that rates of police shootings in Los Angeles area police departments had more to do with individual police chiefs' personal philosophies and policies than with rates of crime and violence.[30] The chief who is interested in reducing use of force to a minimum must therefore make it absolutely clear that excessive use of force is not acceptable. Beating a prisoner should be a firing offense, and the best police chiefs make sure it is.

One impediment to police progress in controlling use of force is that even the police and some of their most sophisticated critics frequently fail to distinguish between brutality and unnecessary force.[31] Brutality is a conscious and venal act committed by officers who usually take great pains to conceal their misconduct. Usually, as in the case of the King beating, it is directed against persons of marginal status and credibility. And in an era notable for its high fear of crime, juries, who understand that cops routinely undertake risky and protective work, are reluctant to convict police without compelling evidence. Consequently, in the absence of videotapes or other objective recording of gratuitous violence, brutality rarely causes public controversy and is extremely difficult to prove.

Except for the immediate family and some friends and associates, nobody was much concerned about the Larez incident, for example, until the jury hit Chief Gates in his pocketbook. Even then, Los Angeles Mayor Tom Bradley and the City Council expressed no distress about what had happened in the Larez house, uttered no apology to the family, and took no action to discipline the officers involved. Instead, Bradley complained that the verdict against Gates would have a chilling effect on law enforcement and asked the Council to indemnify Gates for his liability. The Council agreed to pay it.[32]

When brutality is the isolated act of individual officers or small groups of officers, it must be rooted out harshly. When, as apparently occurred in Los Angeles, it is committed with impunity in the presence of an audience of police officers, it reveals a deviant organizational culture that must be changed.

Unnecessary force, by contrast, is usually a training problem, the result of ineptitude or insensitivity, as, for instance, when well-meaning officers unwisely charge into situations from which they can then extricate themselves only by using force. Hasty cops who force confrontations with emotionally disturbed persons and who consequently must shoot them to escape uninjured have used unnecessary force. Because such officers typically neither plan nor intend to hurt anybody, their acts usually are quite public and sometimes are quite controversial. But however tragic the outcomes of their misconduct, their actions and motivations—and the cures for them—differ from those that apply to the beating of Rodney King. Unnecessary force may be a good-faith police mistake. Good faith plays no part in brutality.

## POLICE AND THE PUBLIC

Perhaps the most significant explanation of the probable decline in police brutality is the increasing political power of minorities in many of the cities that experienced riots in the 1960s. This power has helped to elect a new cast of politicians and has led to the appointment of police chiefs who project a set of values more sensitive to the needs and wishes of inner-city communities. Such chiefs send a clear message that brutality will not be tolerated. San Jose, California, had a reputation for police brutality until Joseph McNamara was brought in from Kansas City as police chief and restored the community's confidence in the department. Santa Ana had a "kick ass and take names" policing stance until Raymond Davis became chief and cemented relations with the growing Spanish-speaking community. Houston had a notorious reputation as a gunslinger police force until Lee P. Brown, later to be appointed New York's police commissioner, was recruited by a woman mayor to be police chief. Brown turned the Houston department into one of the nation's most professional and innovative, and the Houston cops began to respect themselves. Despite Brown's competence and best efforts, however, even he could not eliminate brutality. One of his last official acts as he left office in Houston was to fire four officers who had shot and killed two citizens in separate events that began as minor traffic incidents.[33]

Until June 3, 1992, Los Angeles was politically unique as the only major police department in the United States to retain civil service protection for its chief. The voters, who had overwhelmingly lost confidence in Daryl Gates and his police department, supported a charter amendment to make the chief and other civil servants accountable to the Mayor. Charter Amendment F, which passed by a two-to-one margin, gives City Hall more power to remove the chief of police and limits the chief's tenure to two five-year terms. Even more important, the department's complex officer accountability system will change profoundly under Charter Amendment F. Officers will be subject to demotion as a possible punishment; the time period during which misconduct complaints can be made and investigated will be extended; and disciplinary boards will be allowed to consider patterns of old complaints against officers, even if the complaints could not individually be substantiated. While this last provision may appear draconian, it is not. In the absence of an objective recording—such as the King tape—the evidence in most citizens' complaints against officers consists only of the contradictory statements of the parties involved, so that the complaints cannot be resolved. In the LAPD, as in most other large agencies, a small number of officers account for a disproportionately large number of such "Yes, you did! No, I didn't!" swearing contests. Until the referendum, those patterns of past alleged misconduct could not be taken into account in determining what to do with officers found in more recent investigations to have engaged in abusive conduct. In short, the LAPD will now be authorized to use smoke in its search for the fire of excessive police force.

Even more significant than this new authority will be the addition of a civilian to the department panels, called "Boards of Rights." Hearings before them are usually reserved for more serious cases that could result in penalties harsher than twenty-two-day unpaid suspensions. In 1990—the last full year for which figures were available—only eight-five cases of the 1,699 investigated by the Internal Affairs Division went before a Board of Rights.[34] In police departments generally, however, any suspension without pay, even for a few days, is considered a serious penalty, since it can influence future career opportunities. Warren Christopher, the lawyer and former diplomat who led the special investigation of the LAPD after the beating of Rodney G. King, was also an architect of the complex Charter amendment. After the measure passed, Christopher described the disciplinary changes as "a critical aspect" of the measure, but they received little attention during the campaign because they are complicated and difficult to explain to voters, who mainly responded to the Chief's accountability and tenure provisions.[35]

Civil Service protection for the police chief may have been a good idea in 1936, when the Los Angeles Police Department was entangled in the corruption of the city's mayor and political establishment. But fifty years later it seemed an anachronistic and insulating requirement, one that permitted the philosophy of policing in Los Angeles to remain essentially unchanged and inappropriate. Under the system that produced the Rodney King beating, LAPD officers were accountable only to their Chief, except when they engaged in documented criminal misconduct. The Chief was accountable to nobody, except when increasingly frequent lawsuits were heard by the courts.[36]

In this arrangement, even the Mayor of Los Angeles—whose colleagues in other cities are powerful commanders-in-chief of their police—had virtually no influence on LAPD policy and practice. Indeed, when Mayor Tom Bradley was asked by an attorney in a civil case whether he was the Commander-in-Chief of the Los Angeles Police Department, Bradley chuckled at the question. After a pause, he answered, smiling, "I've never heard myself described in that fashion."[37] Civil service protection for police chiefs clearly is an impediment to reform.

Ironically, even though the LAPD took great pride in its officers' military mien and discipline, that system also violated the democratic tradition of military accountability to elected civilian authority. Just as an army led by generals who do not have to report to the President has no place in a democracy, this insular system—with its lack of accountability to a mayor or any other elected official—has no place in any American city. As a result of the sweeping Charter amendment victory in Los Angeles, it joins the ash heap of solutions to short-term problems but have long outlived their usefulness.

# PART ONE

# *Occasions*

# 2

## *Vigilante Justice*

In 1837, the young Abraham Lincoln delivered an address on "The Perpetuation of Our Political Institutions" and found that the chief threat came from "the increasing disregard for law which pervades the country—the growing disposition to substitute the wild and furious passions in lieu of the sober judgment of courts, and the worse than savage mobs for the executive ministers of justice."

—Richard Maxwell Brown,
*The American Vigilante Tradition,* 1969

[T]he beating of arrested Negroes—frequently in the wagon on the way to jail or later when they are already safely locked up— often serves as vengeance for the fears and perils the policemen are subjected to while pursuing their duties in the Negro community.

—Gunnar Myrdal,
*An American Dilemma,* 1941

One of us was interviewed at length about the beating of Rodney King by a thoughtful magazine reporter. She was shocked by the incident and, like so many others who saw it, was searching for a vivid metaphor to capture its essence. The near deadly rape and assault of a Central Park jogger in Manhattan had come to her mind, an act described by the youngsters who had participated in it as a "wilding." Was the beating of Rodney King another wilding? she asked. "No," was the reply, "These were not kids out of control. This was a symbolic lynching and came perilously close to being the real thing." That's also what it felt like to Rodney King's passenger, Pooh Allen, when the LAPD pulled them over: "Damn!" he said. "They gonna lynch us!"[1]

While most of us have come to regard lynching as a baleful relic of a distant past, the sort of brutality we witnessed on the Rodney King video-tape may not be so uncommon. Like lynching, such brutality is employed to control a population thought to be undesirable, undeserving, and un-derpunished by established law. Such beatings do not merely violate the law. They go beyond and above the law to achieve a fantasized social order. They are the most frequent, albeit usually most hidden, occasions for police brutality.

Although the term "lynching" may conjure up visions of mob violence, police often were implicated in Southern lynchings, frequently as partici-pants, more often as approving observers. Arthur Raper, who studied lynchings in the 1930s, estimated that at least one-half of the lynchings were carried out with police officers participating, and in nine-tenths of the others the officers either condoned or winked at the mob action. As Gunnar Myrdal observed in his monumental and authoritative study of the Negro in pre–World War II American society, Southern police officers routinely beat black captives to relieve the fears and avenge the perils they experi-enced in black communities.[2]

Evidence from historical sources, observational studies of police— our own and others—and legal materials shows that contemporary police bru-tality is both historically and sociologically related to lynching and related vigilante activities. The parallel is evident in several respects: both rely on legal authority to exonerate their extralegal use of force; both respond to perceived threats and fears aroused by outgroups, especially—but not ex-clusively— racial minorities. Both regard the legal order as too slow, too ponderous, too indolent, too unaware, or too constrained to deal with "the problem," however it may be defined. Most of all, police who conduct themselves as did those we saw beating Rodney King are, like lynchers, teaching a lesson of retribution outside the bounds of the penal code. In Los Angeles, this tradition came to mean that police were entitled to go to vir-tually any extreme in rendering curbside justice to people who, like Rod-ney King, were defined as deserving wrongdoers. The Los Angeles police were doubtless not conscious of it, but they were part of the American vig-ilante tradition.

## THE VIGILANTE PAST

American society has a long and dishonorable tradition of private violence to achieve domination and social control, coupled with a history of racism and nativism.[3] The historical record indicates an appalling and recurrent pattern of disorder and violence on the part of groups whose aim has been the preservation of an existing or remembered order of social arrangements, and in whose ideology the concept of "law and order" has played a major role.

No common term adequately describes the diverse groups who have fought to preserve their neighborhood, their community, or their country from forces considered alien or threatening. The Ku Klux Klan, the Minutemen, or related antiblack, anti-Hispanic, anti-Asian, anti-Semitic, or anti-Catholic groups have different origins, different goals, and different compositions, but they have one feature in common: they are willing to break the law to achieve what they see as a necessary and desirable social goal. Yet far from being "criminals," in their own eyes they are brave and moral actors, willing to pursue the punitive activities that more timid and hesitant others are disinclined to undertake.

Every social order is at some level maintained by the threat of punishment. A criminal code is, at its base, nothing more than a system of evaluating misconduct and of imposing measured penalties. But somewhere deep in the American experience is the idea that the legal order and its system of punishment are inadequate to cope with *the problem,* whether defined as crime, as immigrants, or as minority groups.

Usually we think of private associations—such as the Ku Klux Klan— as the instrument for administering or threatening such sanctions. These nativist groups see the formal enforcement of law and administration of justice as weak, inadequate, or inefficient. Such deficiencies justify "taking the law into their own hands." In practice, this means that ordinary law, the law of established authority, is rejected to achieve a self-defined conception of order and control of perceived dangers.

In the broader sweep of American history, the frontier produced the conditions that led to the rationale for the extralegal enforcement of the law. Indeed, organized law enforcement was often absent on the frontier. The deeply rooted American tradition of self-help seemed a practical response where settlement preceded the establishment of legal machinery of social control. There was an immediate problem of danger and insecurity in areas where the formal agencies of law had barely penetrated. To those sparsely settled areas, vigilante justice brought a crude yet necessary kind of policing. This was the context for the vigilantes of the Western frontier and the popular tribunals of the mining camps, as well as the South Carolina Regulators of colonial times. The goals of most of those early ventures at social control were simple. Since formal law enforcement institutions were absent or inadequate to accomplish the preservation of order, voluntary associations sprang up to fill the need. But however understandable the self-help tradition might have been in light of frontier conditions, it generated a series of questionable—even dangerous—premises and precedents. It meant that even where legal rules, procedures, and institutions were ade-quate, people could avoid these to achieve "law and order."

The common phrase "law and order" is often used mistakenly, as a mis-leading cliché, with emphasis on the "order" part of the phrase, with slight regard for "law." Under a regime of law, a developed legal system imposes restraints on the quest for order. By contrast, a self-help system bypasses such restraints and leans toward the extralegal enforcement of order. His-torically, private violence, sometimes in conjunction with constituted au-thority and sometimes not, came to be used as an instrument for enforcing a system of social, political, economic, and—perhaps most significantly—cultural arrangements against the claims of those whose actions, and whose very existence, were seen as threatening.

American Indians were unquestionably the first "alien" group to feel the combined assault of private and officially sanctioned violence. Regarded as threatening and exterminable, the native population of what was to be-come the United States was subjected to massive and sustained violence by private groups and government soldiers. Regarding the Indian, whose lands were being appropriated by white settlers along the frontier, "Many Americans cherished a conviction that they were waging what came to be called a 'war of extermination,' and they waged it with determination and hardly disguised enjoyment."[4]

The San Francisco Vigilance Committee of 1851 and others like it were, on the whole, composed of leading citizens who tried to control the justice system and employed private armies to achieve their aims. They were un-interested in legislative change or reform of existing institutions. Instead, they concentrated on the capture and punishment of "undesirables" and "criminals" whom they believed the courts had allowed to escape justice. Like those contemporary police who administer street discipline, they in-serted themselves and their punishments as a substitute for a judicial pro-cess they perceived as weak and inefficient. Those vigilance committees had counterparts in all states west of the Mississippi, but they were perhaps most pronounced in California. Rarely were blacks the focus of such com-mittees, because the major black migration to California did not occur until World War II, when African-Americans were invited to migrate—indeed, were subsidized to do so—to work in the shipyards and defense industries that flourished during wartime.

During the nineteenth century, the rough justice of the California vigi-lance committees actually worked hardest against Mexicans and Chinese. The hatred of these nativist vigilante groups was fueled in the fiercely com-petitive environment of the gold-rush mining camps and was institutional-ized in state law. In the context of official denial of Chinese rights, the preservation of "order" meant that outbreaks of criminal lawlessness might be overlooked or even encouraged by constituted authority. For instance, in Los Angeles, after a white person was killed during a tong war, mobs invaded the Chinese quarter, looting and "killing twenty-one persons—of whom fifteen, including women and children, were hanged on the spot from lamp-posts and awnings."[5] The pursuit of "law and order" in the West prompted—as it sometimes does today—a special effort against minority groups considered dangerous to constituted arrangements, moral values, and racial dominance. We get some flavor of contemporary "vigilance" by police in the following comments of the Christopher Commission:

> Witnesses repeatedly told of LAPD officers verbally harassing minorities; detaining African-American and Latino men who fit certain generalized descriptions; employing the so-called "prone-out" tactic . . . in minority neighborhoods, even for routine traffic stops; and using excessive force, particularly in African- American and Latino communities. While the Commission does not purport to adjudicate the validity of these complaints, the intensity and frequency of them reveal a serious problem.[6]

Vigilante justice was not confined to the West, however. It happened in the North as well, usually in connection with race riots. In fact, the bloodiest and most vicious lynchings in American history occurred not in Los Angeles or Atlanta but in New York City as an aftermath of the draft riots of July 1863. The city's Irish unskilled workers—Democrats all—did not want to fight a Republican President's war to free Negro slaves. Even apart from the dangers they would face as soldiers—a risk wealthier whites could avoid with a $300 payment—the Irish feared labor competition from freed Negroes who, they believed, if slavery were abolished, would cross the Mason-Dixon line and underbid them for jobs. African-Americans were killed with unbelievable ferocity during the riots. So many were murdered that it was impossible to count the many black bodies that bloodied the streets of Manhattan Island. When caught by the rioters, blacks were "hung up to lampposts, or beaten, jumped on, kicked and struck with iron bars and heavy wooden clubs." Homes were sacked and residents driven into the streets. Women and children, as well as men, felt the hands of the rioters. One of the city's newspapers reported:

> A perfect reign of terror exists in the quarters of this helpless people, and if the troubles which now agitate our city continue during the week it is believed that not a single negro will remain within the metropolitan limits.[7]

Those Negroes fled the city as best they could, escaping to Hoboken and Long Island and into the woods along the Harlem River. By the third day of the riots, one observer commented, "the Negroes have entirely disappeared from the docks. Many of them, it is said, have been killed and thrown into the river."[8]

The post–Civil War South faced the enormous problem of absorbing a population of former slaves while maintaining the dominance of the white caste. The solution, such as it was, led to enormous distortions in theories of natural racial superiority and the implementation of often brutal retaliations to keep the subordinate caste in its appointed place. The historian Allen W. Trelease comments:

> The physical and psychological necessities of keeping Negroes in subordination led to the wildest inconsistencies of attitude and expression. On the one hand, the black man was best fitted by nature and temperament for a life of servility and happiest in his carefree dependence on white protectors. On the other hand, he was only a degree removed from the wild beasts of the jungle, and the most constant surveillance was needed to keep him from bursting the bonds of discipline and turning upon his friends and protectors in a bloody insurrection.[9]

The Ku Klux Klan offered one part of the solution to the white Southerner's problem. It arose in the aftermath of the Civil War, when emancipation, the Fourteenth Amendment, and the ravages of the war itself had disrupted the traditional caste order and had weakened, to some extent, the effectiveness of class subordination. Originally begun as an amusement for a half-dozen former Confederate soldiers faced with postwar boredom, the Klan soon escalated as a powerful extralegal organization to assuage white Southerner's fears—"a state of mind bordering on hysteria"[10]—that followed the collapse of slavery. But unofficial violence was joined by legislation aimed at suspending the limited gains of the Southern blacks. The provisional legislatures established by President Andrew Johnson in 1865 adopted the notorious Black Codes, intended to establish systems of peonage or apprenticeship resembling slavery.[11]

After the Black Codes were struck down, Klan activity escalated to drive the freedmen out of politics and to restore power and control to the dominant white leadership. The night-riding assaults on blacks, Northerners, and their Southern sympathizers were justified as "the necessary effort to prevent crime and uphold law and order."[12] The Klan's first Imperial Wizard, General Nathan B. Forrest, justified the existence of the Klan in these words:

> Many Northern men were coming down there, forming Leagues all over the country. The Negroes were holding night meetings; were going about; were becoming very insolent; and the Southern people . . . were very much

alarmed. . . . Ladies were ravished by some of these Negroes. . . . There was a great deal of insecurity.[13]

Lynching was the typical weapon of the Reconstruction Klan and subsequent white terrorists. Lynching was a horrendous business. The victim was publicly tortured, mutilated, and hanged for all to see and remember— *Strange Fruit,* the novelist Lillian Smith called the human symbol of caste domination. The Tuskegee Institute has kept a record of lynchings in the United States since 1882. The record offers a shocking reminder that the white militant has been perhaps the single most violent force—outside of war—in the history of the nation. For the period from 1882 through 1959, Tuskegee has recorded a total of 4,735 lynchings, of which 73 percent were of African-Americans, and 85 percent took place in the Southern and Border states.[14]

In part, the rise of the later Klan was influenced by D. W. Griffith's racist film epic, *Birth of a Nation,* which portrayed the early Klan as a romantic defender of Southern white womanhood against the ravages of the freed blacks. Even Woodrow Wilson, a legendary symbol of patrician politics and scholarship, a President of Princeton University as well as of the United States, was impressed by the picture. " 'It is like writing history with lightning,' he said, 'and my only regret is that it is all so terribly true.' "[15]

The revived Ku Klux Klan of the 1920s mixed anti-Negro, anti-Semitic, and anti-Catholic agitation and spread throughout the country, rising to a membership of several million. It was deeply entwined with local and state governments, especially in the Midwest and the Western United States. The historian Richard K. Tucker describes a time in Indiana history in the 1920s when the Klan had so much control over state politics that its leader, David Curtis Stephenson, aspired to the United States Senate, and after that to the White House.[16] David Chalmers, a noted student of vigilante movements, writes that "Klan violence in California was as brutal as anywhere in the South, and in the town of Taft, in Kern County, the police and the best citizens turned out to watch an evening of torture in the local ball park."[17] Chalmers reports similar incidents in Oregon and Colorado, where the Klan exerted strong political influence in the Governor's mansion and in the state legislature.

## OFFICIAL JUSTICE

In the South, the line between vigilante justice and official justice was scarcely discernable at all—at least not until the beginnings of the Civil Rights movement of the 1960s and the subsequent demise of the segregation laws, and that was only thirty or so years ago. Until that time those laws remained the public as well as the private position of the South. In 1928 the historian Ulrich B. Phillips described the South as "a people with a common resolve indomitably maintained—that it shall be and remain a white man's country." That attitude remained steadfast into the 1950s. Phillips further observed that the conviction of white supremacy, "whether expressed with the frenzy of a demagogue or maintained with a patrician's quietude, is the cardinal test of a Southerner and the central theme of Southern history."[18]

However that theme might have been verbalized, it was plainly inscribed in the segregation laws and customs, which extended to schools, churches, housing, jobs, restaurants, public transportation, sports, recreation, hospitals, asylums, and even morgues and cemeteries. The historian Leon F. Litwack recalls that a black storyteller talked about the law in Richland County, South Carolina, in the 1920s: "Dere ain' no use. De courts er dis land is not for niggers. It seems to me when it come to trouble, de law an' a nigger is de white man's sport, an' justice is a stranger in them precints, an' mercy is unknown." Since the Bible instructed people to pray for their enemy, he offered up this prayer: "Drap on you' knee, brothers, an' pray to God for all de crackers an' de judges an' de courts an' soliciters, sheriffs an' police in de land."[19]

From the vantage point of America in the 1990s, it is hard to recall the pain and degradation of a segregated South. The concept of "separate but equal" was a deceptive and cruel myth. There was neither equality nor separation. The reality, especially in the deep South, in cotton farming states like Georgia and Mississippi, was "white supremacy" and subordination. Sociologists who studied the South described it as a "caste" society, where a break in the caste rules against any white person was seen as a challenge to all whites.[20] Even the most minor transgressions of caste etiquette did not go unnoticed and were punished, often by police. And the police were backed up by the courts, which accepted the police officer's word against that of any black person. Practically all public officials in the pre–civil rights south were white, but police were the public officials whose power most affected blacks. "The Negro's most important public contact is with the policemen. He is the personification of white authority in the Negro community," Gunnar Myrdal wrote.

Although the police generally were available to punish blacks for their transgressions, when private white persons took the law into their own hands, they were indulged. A social pattern of subduing blacks by physical force inhered in the system of slavery and continued through the Jim Crow period. As with slavery, white persons exercised a sort of delegated police power. Local police and courts, as with slavery, were expected to assist in upholding caste etiquette. Other functionaries were also assumed to have such powers. White operators of streetcars, buses, and trains were expected to enforce caste customs and segregation laws. But apart from laws, or even in violation of law, whites experienced little fear of legal reprisal. They could act above the law and get away with it. In such circumstances the descendants of slaves tried to avoid situations where violence might occur. Moreover, since white violence against blacks was rarely, if ever, punished, blacks could usually be controlled by mere commands or threats, without the use of actual violence. When violence occurred it was often severe.

Nicholas Lemann writes that Mississippi blacks passed around stories, which became legends, about sex, bloodshed, and the meaninglessness of the official legal order. From a social-psychology perspective, such stories suggest the internalization of social controls by the dominated group. An oral tradition may be more effective even than a written one in establishing the norms of transgression and punishment.

In one such story, a black boy who is working in a white family's yard is called inside by a partially undressed white woman. The boy understands his dilemma. If he refuses her advances, she will cry out and say he attempted to rape her, and he will be lynched. But if he accepts and is found out, he will also be lynched. In the story, the husband returns, the woman screams and claims she had been assaulted. The boy goes on trial for rape, but the husband, who had by then figured out what really happened, stands up for the boy in court, and he is freed. A gang of white boys lie in wait, waylay the black boy, tie his feet to the back of a car, and drive it to the next town "with the black boy's crushed, bloody head bouncing from the roadbed."[21]

Death is the most extreme outcome of violence. One way to kill is by lynching, often accompanied by torture and mutilation. Another is by capital punishment imposed by courts. On first thought, these seem like quite different events. The execution occurs after a trial by jury within the formality of the courtroom. If convicted, the defendant may exercise a right to appeal. When the execution is consummated, those who administer the death sentence are performing their sworn duty, at a designated time and place. It is a bureaucratic event, with standardized procedures, rules, and a measure of solemnity. "An execution," Charles David Phillips writes, "is an awesome exhibition of the law's true power: its ability to take the most precious of commodities—life."[22] By contrast, the lynching is an expressive, passionate event, usually occurring in a small town, at night, with frightening overtones of blood vengeance.

But Phillips argues that execution and lynching were often substitutes for responding to individual acts of deviance; people were either legally executed or lynched informally. An even more recent study by Beck, Massey, and Tolnay replicated Phillips's work using the data of a Deep South state and a longer time frame. They mainly confirm Phillips's substitution thesis but refine it, finding that execution was associated with murder, and lynching with rape. "Of all blacks executed in Georgia between 1882 and 1930, 88 percent were punished for murder and 12 percent for rape. Of those lynched, 34 percent allegedly committed murder, while 41 percent were lynched for rape or some other similar sexual offense." The record in North Carolina is similar."[23]

Those statistics, however, may be inflated. Gunnar Myrdal, who on our rereading appears still to be the most sensitive and perceptive writer on pre–civil rights Southern race relations, observed that when a mob made an accusation of rape, it was secure against any further investigation. But unsubstantiated accusations of rape that resulted in lynchings may have found their way into databases. Besides, rape was broadly defined as any sex relations between black men and white women. The very fears Southern white women were taught to have of black men tended to push rape statistics upward. The black boy in the story above was merely found in a room with a partially undressed white woman. The South had a double standard for interracial sex: between white men and black women, sex was common and understandable; sex between white women and black men was rare and damnable. Although both were illegal, the latter was considered an unthinkable, horrendous offense for which a lynching was justified, whether or not it actually occurred. When it actually happened, it was defined as rape. Even an interest shown by a black man in a white woman might be considered an occasion for which lynching was justified:

> When a white man in the South casts a roving eye upon a likely colored girl, the culture permits him to indulge in any type of affair that stops short of marriage, discreet consummation, or concubinage. For the Negro man who might be foolhardy enough to display a similar interest for women-folk across the color line there is a standing prescription—the noose.[24]

The informal and the formal norms were intertwined. Again, from the vantage point of the 1990s it is hard to recall the rigidity with which racist philosophies were engraved into law, particularly, but not only, in the South. Out of forty-eight states, thirty-nine had passed laws banning intermarriages, and thirty remained on the books into the 1960s, until the Warren Court in 1968, in its last major civil rights decision, struck down these "anti-miscegenation" statutes.[25] If Justice Clarence Thomas and his wife had tried to marry in Virginia prior to 1968, their marriage would have been void *ab initio,* that is, without any decree or legal process. They would also have been guilty of a felony. Mississippi even had a law categorizing as a misdemeanor the "urging or presenting for public acceptance or general information, arguments or suggestions in favor of social equality or intermarriage between white and Negro."[26]

Lynching was not, however, confined to sexual transgressions. Carried out primarily by lower-class and rural Southern whites, lynchings were employed to brighten and widen the fine social line between the lower-class white and the Negro. Myrdal reports a common saying—which a visitor to the South might have heard in the 1930s—that an occasional lynching is expedient or even necessary to keep "Negroes in their place." After World War I many lynchings of returning Negro soldiers—sometimes in uniform—were motivated by the fear that these soldiers had been unduly influenced by their foreign, particularly French, experiences during the war, and no longer accepted their subordinate status in Southern society.[27]

Police were deeply implicated in all of this. Police were not necessarily antagonistic to black persons so long as they did not violate caste understandings. When blacks behaved in their caste-appointed roles, they were treated pleasantly enough. Davis, Gardner, and Gardner found, however, that individual police were strongly antagonistic toward troublesome or "uppity" Negroes who showed less than proper respect for police authority. "They are," they write, "firmly convinced of the Negro's inherent inferiority, of his lack of control, of his proneness to lie and steal; and they regard any Negro who resists a policeman as a 'bad nigger,' one who must be 'taken care of' unofficially."[28] It is doubtful that contemporary Los Angeles police would use such language to a modern interviewer. Yet the beating of Rodney King, unless unrealistically considered an isolated, "aberrant" incident, suggests inescapable affinities between the motivations of Southern police of the first half of the twentieth century and the Los Angeles police of the second half.

## MODERN POLICE AND VIGILANTE JUSTICE

Public lynchings no longer occur anywhere in the United States, yet reports of police brutality, conducted under the cover of law, surface time and again. Sometimes a case arises that sounds almost like a lynching, except that the lynchers are cops, and the killing is done in police custody. One such case, unpublicized outside of Louisiana, arose on March 22, 1990, in the City of New Orleans. A white policeman, Earl Hauck, was trying to arrest a black male suspect, one Adolph Archie, when Archie shot Hauck, and, as it later turned out, the shots were fatal. Immediately after shooting Hauck, Archie turned around and ran. He was chased by eight New Orleans officers, who properly shot at Archie to apprehend him. One of the shots hit Archie in the arm and knocked him off his feet. Two of the officers, Steven Larroque and Chris Evans, plus three others who were not identified, hit and kicked Archie. By now Archie was bleeding and nearly unconscious and needed medical attention.

Archie was turned over to the custody of Officer Joseph Maumus, who was a close friend of the dying cop. The officers knew that Archie required medical attention and drove him to the nearest hospital. Yet when they arrived at the emergency ramp, they sat there with him. They refused to take Archie inside or to allow any medical personnel to treat him.

It was a tense time. Nobody knew whether Officer Hauck would survive. Officers and ranking members of the New Orleans Police Department were in the immediate vicinity of the ramp and the emergency room, waiting to hear whether or not Hauck would pull through. Some of the nearby officers began to threaten Archie, who was seen sitting up in the back of the police car. No ranking officers stepped in to intervene or to cool off the angry officers. No one tried to bring Adolph Archie into the hospital for medical treatment.

When the cops learned that Officer Hauck had died, they took Archie—by now identified legally as a suspect in the homicide of Officer Hauck, but informally as a cop-killer—instead to the 1st District Station. This was a violation of established procedure. Homicide suspects in New Orleans are normally booked in the main police building next to the Central Lockup. Forty-five minutes later, four cops brought Archie back to the hospital from the first District Station. This time he had two skull fractures, a broken larynx, and fractures of the cheekbones. He had bleeding testicles, and his teeth had been kicked in. The injuries to Archie's face varied in size and were, according to Dr. William G. Eckert, who examined the body, "characteristic of those made with a shod foot." His entire body, from his legs to his upper back and neck, had been, in the words of the examining doctor, "exposed to blunt trauma." Archie died twelve hours later.

This example of vigilante justice happened in 1990, not 1930. It was no longer possible for officers, even in the South, even in the town known as "The Big Easy," to take the law into their own hands. There had to be a cover-up. Officer Maumus, Hauk's good friend, was also a good friend to Dr. Frank Minyard, Coroner for New Orleans Parish. Maumus had worked in the Coroner's Office for years, was a neighbor and confidant, and was driving a Coroner's Office vehicle while transporting Archie to and from the hospital and to the 1st District Station.

Maumus and other officers persuaded the coroner to cover up the cause of death of Archie to make it appear that his injuries were consistent with a scuffle or a fall. Not until independent pathologists were called in, after complaints that Archie was seen sitting erect and apparently healthy while in police custody, was the true nature of Archie's injuries revealed. There was a public outcry, and several pathologists in the Coroner's Office resigned. Only then did the Coroner classify Adolph Archie's death as "homicide–police intervention."

That Archie deserved punishment seems to be beyond question, although given the subsequent behavior of the police, he may legitimately have been defending himself. Nor can there be much doubt that, had Archie been properly arrested, tried, and convicted, he would have been a prime candidate for execution under the laws of the State of Louisiana. Instead, Adolph Archie was beaten to death extrajudicially, as an act of police brutality and vigilante justice. Unless Adolph Archie acted in self-defense or was insane, there can be no justification for his having killed Officer Hauck. But police are law enforcement officers, sworn to uphold the Constitution, trained and paid by the public to maintain a civilized process of law. The anger of the police who did the brutal beating is understandable, but when cops act as extralegal avengers they obviously betray their own authority and forfeit any semblance of acceptable professionalism.

The American Civil Liberties Union and its affiliate offices around the nation receive two or three complaints of police misconduct each week. A number of these rival the King beating in the severity of the reported abuse and in the conspiracy of the officers to keep the abuse hidden from the public.

A recent ACLU pamphlet, published in the wake of the King incident, reports eight of these between 1988 and 1991. Although the list is not exhaustive, the ACLU claims that "they are emblematic of the wide variety of incidents nationwide that have raised public concern about the procedures of local police." Yet instances of vigilante justice can be handled differently in different police departments. Eight Palm Beach, Florida, undercover officers arrested a suspected drug dealer in the fall of 1990 for "trespassing." They searched him and found no drugs. They then proceeded to teach him a lesson. They handcuffed him, tied him to a truck bed, drove him to an abandoned dockyard, and roughed him up. Later they were found to have falsified their reports, but no discipline was imposed.

By contrast, when Police Chief Steven Bishop of Kansas City, Missouri, learned in the fall of 1990 that some of his officers had used a "slapper"—a small weighted club designed to inflict severe blows—to beat a high-speed chase suspect following his capture, Bishop fired the officers and permanently banned the use of slappers.

Most excessive force cases that reach the courts show that the questionable conduct either has happened because superiors are so indifferent to the misconduct as to be grossly negligent in the performance of their duties or occurs in fulfillment of administrative policy. A recent case in Mason County, Washington, depicts the first, while the Los Angeles chokehold cases illustrate the second.

On March 12, 1991, ten days after Rodney King was beaten, the Court of Appeals for the Ninth Circuit found Mason County, Washington, its sheriff, and several deputies to have violated the civil rights of five persons who were arrested without probable cause, beaten, and subjected to false criminal charges by Mason County Deputies. All the incidents, which took place in rural Washington, are suggestive of the traditional rural lynching and the way social control is exercised by lawless police authorities.

The Mason County cases (based on events in 1985 and 1986) seem like a replay of a B-movie about redneck cops. Unlike Adolph Archie, who allegedly had shot a cop, none of the complainants had committed serious crimes, if they had committed crimes at all. All of the cases arose out of traffic stops that resulted in "teach 'em a lesson" arrests, beatings, and false charges that were later dropped. The Ninth Circuit opinion describes several of these incidents, which resemble, but without a videotaped record, the beating of Rodney King:

> Early on the morning of June 29, 1985, as Doug Durbin returned home from a local tavern, Deputy Ray Sowers followed him and waited outside of Durbin's home. Deputy Tom Furrer later arrived as backup. Sowers, flicking an electric stun gun on and off, ordered Durbin out of his house. Durbin, who complied, was arrested for drunk driving. After taking one step toward his house, the two deputies tackled Durbin and threw him to the ground. Though Durbin never attempted to resist, Sowers began to beat him on the back of his head with his fist. In the patrol car on the way to the jail Sowers slammed on the brakes, causing Durbin, who was handcuffed and thus defenseless, to smash into the screen with his face.

In another case, John Davis and his fifteen-year-old nephew, Wayne Broughton, were driving a loaded hay wagon drawn by a team of four horses in the afternoon of July 28, 1985. Because some cars were slowed behind the wagon, Deputy Jack Gardner came alongside the wagon in his patrol vehicle and, using his loudspeaker, pulled in front of the wagon, took out his gun, pointed it at Davis and Broughton, and threatened to shoot if they did not stop. As Davis got down from the wagon to attend to his horses, Gardner beat him on the legs with his nightstick and struck him on the head. He then knocked him down to the ground and continued to beat him. After Deputies Pete Cribben and Garry Ohlde arrived at the scene, all three hit Davis, kicked him, and shocked him with an electric stun gun. According to one witness, Davis "looked like he had been dipped in a bucket of blood" after the officers finished beating him.[29]

## HOW MUCH FORCE IS NECESSARY?

As long as some members of society do not comply with law and resist the police, force will remain an inevitable part of policing. Cops, especially, understand that. Indeed, anybody who fails to understand the centrality of force to police work has no business in a police uniform. Jonathan Rubinstein spent a year watching Philadelphia police at work and noted that, for the officer,

> . . . a gun and a nightstick are not simply weapons that terrify some and intrigue others but extensions of himself whose use (and non-use) is linked to his notions about how he uses his body to do his work. But unlike anyone else whose body is the tool of his trade, the policeman uses his to control other people.[30]

So anybody who expects police to wear uniforms and patrol American streets should not be surprised or offended that police occasionally must use force in the course of their work. And force rarely, if ever, photographs well. Still, not all instances of excessive force should be labeled "police brutality" or "vigilante justice." Only in a small fraction of the cases where police exert force is it used in a way that could fairly be considered "excessive." To be sure, cops sometimes *threaten* force implicitly or explicitly to control suspects whom they want to put into custody. But most suspects are "reasonable" and know that it doesn't make sense to pick a fight or persist in one with cops. However, especially since the movement to deinstitutionalize unstable people began in the 1960s, cops often run into suspects who, emboldened by drugs, alcohol, mental illness, or all three, fight back. Unless these officers are sophisticated enough to identify such people quickly and to deal with them appropriately— on the whole, non-confrontationally—they may find themselves backed into corners and compelled to use more force than they intended, perhaps killing or seriously injuring a suspect who might have been talked into custody.[31] Regardless of how insensitive or incompetent they may be, officers who engage in force of this type cannot fairly be accused of conscious brutality like that inflicted on Rodney King or Adolph Archie.[32]

Instead, the conduct of these officers raises other issues. The most critical is the question of escalating force: How much and with what instrumentality is force appropriate in the myriad situations officers confront on the street? State criminal laws distinguishing criminal conduct from acceptable use of force attempt to operationalize the distinction with admonitions to the effect that officers should use no more force than is *necessary or reasonable,* or that force should be used only as a *last resort.* Such provisions, however, are too vague to serve as meaningful guidelines for cops in street situations. Hence, where officers are adequately trained (and not all are), the parameters of the police license to use force generally are conceptualized in training and policy as a scale from which officers should pick the least severe degree of force likely to accomplish the job at hand.[33]

Police use force to affect civilians' conduct. On a day-to-day basis, they do so most often by employing the least degree of force available to them, their *mere presence.* Cops wear uniforms and drive distinctly marked cars so that, without saying a word, they may have an effect on citizens' behavior. Indeed, the police tradition of *preventive patrol*—the single most expensive U.S. police activity—is based on the premise that the presence of uniformed cops and marked police cars will send would-be criminals elsewhere, will keep jaywalkers on the sidewalk, and will cause motorists to check their speedometers.

When officers' mere presence fails to produce desired conduct, police resort to *verbalization,* the second step on their ladder. For miscreant drivers, police verbalization typically begins with a red light or siren signal to pull to the side of the road. Then, when officers actually do speak, they are instructed to do so *persuasively* and in tones that are resolute but not commanding: "Good morning, Sir. I'm afraid that you were traveling at 66 miles per hour. The speed limit here is 45. May I see your license, registration, and proof of insurance, please?" If this type of *adult–adult* interaction fails to get the desired results or, in officers' reasonable assessments, would be inappropriate, they may proceed to, or begin, their interactions with more forcible options. The scale describes increasingly severe degrees of force but is not a suggestion that officers must start at the bottom and work their way higher until they find out what works. No cop is expected to say, "Pardon me, Sir. I'm afraid that we have a law against armed robbery in this state. May I have that sawed-off shotgun, please?" Instead, officers begin confrontations in such situations well up the scale of force.

One step up the scale from persuasion is another type of verbalization that the police call *command* voice. Motorists who reply with snappy comments to officers' requests for their drivers' licenses ("Why aren't you out catching a crook instead of harassing taxpayers?") are likely to hear command voices: "Sir, I asked you for your vehicle papers once. Now I'm *telling* you that you had better give them to me *now!*"

The first force option beyond verbalization is what police call *firm grips*. These consist of grips on parts of the body that let their subject know that an officer is present and that he or she wants the subject to remain still or to move in a certain direction, but that do not cause pain. An officer's grip on the elbow or shoulder of the drunk driving suspect he is trying to coax into a police station is a good example. So, too, are most of the means by which, without causing pain, officers cart off protestors at sit-in demonstrations.

The next level of forcible officer-to-citizen contact is *pain compliance*. This consists of grips designed to gain subjects' submission by inflicting pain without causing lasting physical injury. Cops are trained in a variety of *come-along* holds—hammerlocks, wristlocks, finger grips, and the like—which are very useful in breaking up bar fights and domestic battles and in arresting demonstrators whose protests have gone beyond mere passive resistance.

Next, officers put into action *impact techniques,* which, whether involving actual physical contact (kicks or batons, for example) or the use of chemical sprays or stunning electronic weapons, are designed to overcome resistance that is forcible, but less than imminently life-threatening. It is at this point that serious public misunderstanding arises regarding what may be legally and professionally—and reasonably—expected of police officers.

Most cops are not martial arts experts. Nor, unlike Secret Service Agents, are they expected by their employers to sacrifice their own lives unhesitatingly to save someone else's—*anybody* else's. In a jargon police trainers know well, cops simply are not paid enough to put their own lives on the line in order to avoid hurting somebody else—especially when that other person is attacking the cops. Thus, while cops should never force confrontations that might be avoided (as, unfortunately, they sometimes do with the growing population of mentally disturbed street people), they are under no obligation to counter force directed against them with a lesser degree of force.

Cops are trained not to try to use nightsticks to defend themselves against attacking knife-wielders, no matter how little the knife or how drunk its wielder. Instead, officers are taught to try to keep a safe distance between themselves and knife-wielders and to shoot when there is no other way to keep the distance from shrinking to unsafe ranges. Officers learn that trying to *play hero* by attempting to overcome force with lesser force allows no room for mistakes. The primary police obligation—to protect life—dictates that they not put themselves in harm's way to avoid using an appropriate degree of force.

In recent years traditional police impact methods—"intermediate force," in the language of the LAPD—have been supplemented by nonlethal devices. Perhaps the oldest of these are chemical sprays such as Mace, which has been available since the 1960s. More recently, police have been issued hand-held electronic "stun guns" that inflict a shock, and the Taser,[34] a gunlike device that allows officers to shock subjects through wires hooked to two electronic darts it is capable of shooting at close ranges. Careful viewers of the Rodney King tape were able to see Taser wires running from King's torso to the Taser with which Sergeant Stacey Koon had shot him.

The theory behind introducing these weapons was that they would provide officers with degrees of force midway between nightsticks and guns. Consequently, it was anticipated, police could use them to resolve confrontations that would otherwise end in shooting. In well-administered police departments, this theory has been borne out, and decreases in use of officers' firearms over the last two decades probably owe something to the new weapons. A constant temptation, however, is for officers to employ such devices as easier ways out of situations that, with only slightly more effort and no more danger, they could handle with lesser degrees of force. Thus, these devices have been a mixed blessing for police. If officers are to adhere to the principle of using no more force than necessary, their use of the newer technology must be monitored carefully.[35]

The most extreme use of force is *deadly force,* which, in policing, most often involves the discharge of firearms. Deadly force is defined in law as force capable of killing or likely to kill, a description that certainly applies when officers fire their guns at other people. This definition also applies, however, to other varieties of force. In 1985 the Philadelphia Police Department dropped an incendiary bomb on a house occupied by a militant cult, an act that proved deadly when it resulted in eleven deaths, including those of four children.[36]

Police in some departments also are trained in two neck holds that have proved capable of taking life. The first is the *carotid control hold,* the purpose of which is to induce unconsciousness by cutting off the flow of blood to the brain through the carotid artery, which runs up the side of the neck. In the emotions of street confrontations, this *sleeper* hold has resulted in fatalities. The second neck hold is the *bar arm control hold,* an extremely dangerous grip in which the forearm is forcibly squeezed in a viselike manner against the front of the neck in order to cut off air flow.

Police use of deadly force is governed by the criminal laws of individual states, which authorize officers to resort to this level of coercion in the imminent defense of their own lives or the lives of others. Until a 1985 challenge to the constitutionality of the fatal police shooting of an unarmed fifteen-year-old who was fleeing from a $10 burglary, police in about half the states also were authorized to use deadly force to apprehend all "fleeing felony" suspects. The Supreme Court's decision in *Tennessee* v. *Garner,* however, ruled that shootings in these situations violated the Fourth Amendment's protections against unreasonable seizure.[37] Since then, the prevailing rules on police deadly force have permitted officers to shoot in order to apprehend only those fleeing suspects who are demonstrably dangerous (e.g., armed with a weapon; fleeing from a violent crime). Again, because of the vagueness of criminal laws defining justifiable use of deadly force by officers—and because proceedings against cops who have shot people in apparent violation of law are such political hot potatoes for prosecutors[38]—well-run police departments generally have supplemented them with clearer and more easily enforceable administrative guidelines and policies.

The issue of when cops should *draw* guns is less clearly understood than the question of when they should *fire* them. We have run into unsophisticated police chiefs who argue that if a cop is able to return a drawn gun to its holster without having fired it, the gun should never have been drawn in the first place. Thankfully, we have found this twisted logic—a permutation of the principle that cops should never draw their guns unless they are prepared to fire them—only among police in small, quiet police departments where it is likely that guns are unholstered only for target practice.

In reality, the difference between drawing a gun and firing it is as big as the difference between showing the fleet and using it to launch an invasion. Police officers in well-run departments are trained to draw their guns only when circumstances present a reasonable expectation that they will encounter life-threatening violence. In busy police jurisdictions, this means that police officers draw their guns far more often than they are fired. Guns sometimes are discreetly drawn when officers respond to reports of violent crimes in progress. When, as is usually the case, it is discovered that reports were false or that criminals are long gone, the guns are just as discreetly put away. When officers make arrests for serious crime, guns sometimes are displayed more prominently as a means of inducing quick compliance by suspects. When the subjects of police concern are mentally disturbed or otherwise irrational, however, the display of guns may stimulate violence rather than defuse it. Similarly, officers generally are discouraged from approaching suspected dangerous people too closely while carrying unholstered weapons. Each year, about a quarter of U.S. police officers shot in the line of duty are wounded or killed by people who have disarmed them and turned their own weapons against them.[39] The fear of disarming also is the reason that corrections officers in even the most dangerous prisons do not carry guns while they are on duty among inmate populations.

## A POLICY ENCOURAGING BRUTALITY

Clearly, questions of how much and when force is justified presents some complex policy and training issues. Often these are matters of judgment rather than simple dichotomies split by what lawyers call a *bright line* distinguishing the permissible from the impermissible. Still, in lawyers' terms, some instances of use of force are so unambiguously excessive that they shock the consciences of all reasonable people. Like the King incident, most of the brutality cases that have drawn wide public attention and have led to expensive litigation have been characterized by truly outrageous police conduct rather than by borderline misbehavior. Further, some of the most sensational of such cases have involved officers who were following obnoxious policies rather than individual cops who acted out on their own.

The use of chokeholds in Los Angeles offers a prime and disastrous example of a misguided policy that tacitly encouraged vigilante justice and fostered public hostility toward the police. Virtually alone among large American police departments, the LAPD instructed officers that carotid control holds were pain compliance techniques rather than a form of deadly force. Hence, according to the LAPD, such holds could permissibly be used to gain the compliance of such offenders as loudmouth traffic violators or unruly black teenagers. These grips—referred to as "departmentally approved upper body control holds"—are mentioned in hundreds of LAPD reports dismissing complaints that they had been used unnecessarily.[40] The LAPD reclassified them as a form of deadly force only when Adolph Lyons, a traffic offender who had been choked unconscious by an LAPD officer, brought a legal challenge that went as far as the U.S. Supreme Court. Lyons proved in court that, during the five years preceding his encounter with Los Angeles police, sixteen people had died after LAPD officers applied this hold to them, twice as many chokehold-related deaths as the combined total of the other twenty largest U.S. police departments. The fact that fourteen blacks were included among the victims stimulated Chief Gates's speculation about the relative vulnerability of blacks' circulatory systems.[41] The consequences of such policies and the philosophies and beliefs underlying them as an aspect of so-called "professional" policing, has raised deep concerns among thoughtful police as well as civilians, over how far we have actually progressed from our vigilante past.

# 3

# *The Third Degree*

The third degree brutalizes the police, hardens the prisoner against society, and lowers the esteem in which the administration of justice is held by the public.
—*National Commission on Law Observance and Enforcement,*
George Wickersham, Chairman, 1931

The "third degree," like lynching, has proved another major occasion for police brutality. Nobody actually knows the origins of the expression. It is one of those obscure legal mysteries, like why criminal trial juries are composed of twelve persons. One theory traces it to the highest order, the "Third Degree" of Freemasonry. "Its use to refer to relentless grilling of a suspect by police officers is thought to come from the rigorous tests that, formerly at least, the candidate for the Master Mason rank had to pass."[1]

Another, proposed in 1910 by Richard Sylvester, President of the International Association of Chiefs of Police in 1901–15, finds its origins in the system of criminal justice. The "first degree" is presumably the arrest, the "second degree" the transport to a place of confinement, and the "third degree," the interrogation. Whatever its origin, the term third degree signifies a prime occasion for police brutality. Sylvester also describes the "sweat box," which was introduced after the Civil War to combat the "marauder, the bank robber and highwayman, thieves and criminals of every kind, [who] took advantage of the exciting times to engage in their nefarious undertakings." The "sweat box" he describes as

> . . . a cell adjoining which in close proximity was a high iron stove of drum formation. The subject indisposed to disclose information which might be securely locked within his bosom, without ceremony or formality . . . would be confined within the cell. A scorching fire would be encouraged in the monster stove adjoining, into which vegetable matter, old bones, pieces of

rubber shoes and kindred trophies would be thrown, all to make a terrible
heat, offensive as it was hot, to at last become so torturous and terrible as to
cause the sickened and perspiring object of punishment to reveal the inner-
most secrets he possessed as the compensation for release from the "sweat
box."[2]

Captain Cornelius Willemse of the New York police, in a book titled
*Behind the Green Lights* (of the police station), contrasted the public and
the police idea of the third degree. "To the public," he wrote, ". . . the 'third
degree' suggests only one thing—a terrifying picture of secret merciless
beating of helpless men in dark cells of the stations." The detective,
Willemse said, saw it differently. To him, it was strategic, *purposeful* pressure, not the imposition of punishment for the sake of retribution. "To him
it means any trick, idea and stunt, risk or action he may use to get the truth
from a prisoner." Although Willemse acknowledged a repertoire of coercive and deceptive police tactics, he took care to point out that these were
not necessarily violent. Detectives might roll up their sleeves and carry a
rubber hose but would not actually beat the suspect. They might arrange
for shrieks or groans accompanied by slapping sounds to come from an
adjoining room; they might construct lies about the evidence in their possession; they might insert police officers in cells to masquerade as prisoners; they might play on the suspect's jealousy or keep drugs from addicts.
    But Willemse acknowledges that there were no limits on how far police
might go to break down a suspect: "The 'third degree,' too, means rough
stuff when required . . . against a hardened criminal," he boasted. "I never
hesitated. I've forced confessions—with fist, blackjack and hose—from
men who would have continued to rob and kill if I had not made them
talk."[3]
    The tactics used by police, then, were ultimately grounded in the moral
character and perceived toughness of the interviewee, as well, of course, as
that of the interviewer. A New York police reporter, Emanuel H. Lavine,
described a specimen of the third degree he had witnessed: A Polish immigrant was thought to have mortally wounded the man who had succeeded
him in the affections of his betrothed. The man was about twenty-five
years old "and almost as broad as he was tall," with a powerful neck and
seeming immunity to pain. The detectives beat him repeatedly with a rubber hose, but it was no use. The man wore out their arms and their patience,
but he would not talk.
    The cops were friendly with a dentist who solved their problem. The
police took the prisoner to the dentist's office, where the dentist proceeded
to grind into the man's molars with a rough burr until a "voluntary" confes-

sion was elicited. Then the dentist filled the holes and assured the detectives that it was impossible to determine the age of a filling since, after several hours, "the acids of the mouth quickly discolor the area."[4] They were assured that they could lie confidently about how the confession was obtained.

The prevalence of the "third degree" was scarcely a secret. The American Bar Association's Committee on the Lawless Enforcement of the Law reported in 1930: "We can only say that the 'third degree' in the sense of rigid and severe examination of men under arrest by police officers or prosecuting attorneys or both, is in use almost everywhere if not everywhere in the United States."[5]

The most influential report on the third degree was made by the National Commission of Law Enforcement and Observance, appointed by President Herbert Hoover and headed by George W. Wickersham, a law partner of William Howard Taft. Hoover had promised to appoint such a commission when he was nominated by the Republican Party in 1928. To the dismay of the Democrats and Wets, he extended its mandate from an examination of how well Prohibition was working to a "searching investigation of the whole structure of our federal system of jurisprudence."[6]

The Wickersham Commission, like the Bar Association, concluded in 1931 that the third degree, which it defined as "the inflicting of pain, physical or mental, to extract confessions or statements" was widespread throughout the United States.[7] So appalled were the Commission's investigators by the police interrogation tactics they discovered that they described the harsher forms as "torture."

Third-degree questioning did not usually begin, however, with torture. Protracted questioning was the method most commonly employed. Relays of examiners would badger the suspect until his energies were depleted and his resistance overcome. Prisoners who held out too long would eventually experience physical torture.

The police showed considerable ingenuity and sadism in devising these routines. In addition to fists, blackjacks, and rubber hoses, preferred because they left no marks, the interrogation might include hot lights, confinement in fetid and airless rooms, beating the suspect over the head with a telephone book, or hanging him from a window on a high floor.

In addition to the physical brutality they found, the Commission also was concerned about illegal detention and a refusal to allow suspects to see counsel. What the law required about producing prisoners promptly simply did not matter. The police commonly ignored the law and delayed bringing their prisoner before a magistrate. "The practice of holding the accused *incommunicado,* unable to get in touch with their family or friends or counsel," the report concluded, "is so frequent that in places there are cells called 'incommunicado' cells."

It would be mistaken to attribute these measures of detention and torture to the aberrant inventions of sadistic individuals. Those who kept suspects incommunicado and wielded their fists, blackjacks, and hoses in the interest of eliciting confessions were part of a larger *system*. Emanuel Lavine's publisher, James Henle, was careful to emphasize this point in his foreword to Lavine's book. He said that it would be manifestly unfair to punish individual police for what is reported in the book, since the third degree, "is not an exhibition of blood lust on the part of a single policeman: it is an integral and regular part of police routine and in the police station itself excites no more comment than the arrest of a riotous drunkard."

However commonplace the third degree, the Wickersham Commission found that corruption was equally, if not more, pronounced. Payoffs and the favors tied to them were an everyday feature of policing. Cops played in and robbed floating crap games, hijacked trucks, and took bribes for every conceivable regulatory violation. According to Grover A. Whelan, a former New York City Police Commissioner, more than thirty-two thousand speakeasies operated in greater New York during the Prohibition era. It was understood that the cops would be paid a dollar for every half-barrel of beer.

Gangsters who bribed the police or who had "connections" with the political machines were rarely subjected to the third degree. Although organized criminals and gangsters were occasionally beaten by police, most of the time they escaped such suffering, even the most vicious of them. "Under the present system," Lavine wrote, "the 'third-degree' is applied, for the most part, to the poor, the ignorant, and the friendless."

It is self-evident that the third degree could not have flourished without the complicity of higher political authority and of the lower courts. In 1931 American law enforcement in most big cities was manipulated by politicians. The legendary James J. (Jimmy) Walker, famous for his man-about-town life-style and easy virtue, was Major of New York City and accountable to Tammany Hall. When the Wickersham Commission investigators asked informed sources about lawless law enforcement, instead of hearing about the third degree they were first told about "shakedown arrests," how cases were "squared" or "thrown," and how charges were "fixed" with crooked district attorneys and crooked judges who had been appointed through machine politics. What Ernest Jerome Hopkins called "the paralyzing touch of Tammany Hall on the processes of justice" was commonplace.[8]

It was evident that cops who were willing to accept bribes and to beat confessions out of suspects would also be unhesitant, indeed find it necessary, to perjure themselves during testimony at trial. Since third-degree practices were well known, and since lower court judges were also beholden to the political machines, most judges would accept the false testimony of police. Under the applicable law, even in those pre–Warren Court days, the rule against self-incrimination was embodied in the U.S. Constitution; more important at that time, it was written into the constitutions of all the states except Iowa and New Jersey, where it was invoked by judicial decision.

For the system to have worked, when cops lied about how they had treated a prisoner, judges must have accepted the lie. Coercive cops were usually careful not to leave bruises or other marks that could easily be seen by judges or juries. Even when bruises were visible, however, they could be explained away. The defendant had resisted arrest, the police might testify, or the defendant had fallen down the stairs. Abused suspects routinely signed their confessions, and the presence of a signed confession would be considered proof of its "voluntariness."

## WICKERSHAM'S IMPACT

The 1931 Wickersham Commission report documented corruption and brutality in the criminal justice system, expressed shock at what it found, and deplored its existence in high-minded rhetoric. The Commission's members and other police reformers of the 1920s and 1930s were part of a social elite that sought to contain the rough-edged corruption and brutality of police who were mainly Irish, Catholic, urban, and connected to the political machines of the time. People like George Wickersham; August Vollmer, the Berkeley, California, Police Chief; Raymond Fosdick, a police reformer who was later to head the Rockefeller Foundation; and Arthur Woods, a New York City Police Commissioner from 1914 to 1919, who was later invited by Yale University to deliver the Storrs Lectures, were products of the thinking of the staunch and upright reformers—usually Republicans—of the Progressive era. The Progressive goal was clear: to instill middle-class virtue into all Americans and American institutions. "Everyone," the historian David Rothman observes, "was to become hardworking, to abandon Old World vices, to respect and accumulate private property."[9]

However slight the influence of the reformers might have been with rank-and-file cops, they did influence each other, that is, police reformers who aspired to "professional" policing and elite lawyers and law professors who began to write reformist articles in law reviews. More importantly, appellate courts began to pay attention to and exclude confessions that had been admitted into evidence at trial but had been elicited by the third degree. Through the 1950s, when California's Supreme Court succeeded it, New York's was the most important state supreme court. Called the "Court of Appeals," it had boasted Benjamin Cardozo as its Chief Justice, and its opinions persuaded judges across the country. In 1932 it reversed a conviction where the defendant was questioned for twenty-four hours without food and agreed to confess if food was given to him. He also claimed that the officers beat him, but they denied it. The opinion, however, revealed a deep suspicion of the police: "The growing number of instances in which officers of the police force stand accused at our bar of threats and brutality in the extortion of confessions is a cause of deep concern to all the judges of the court."[10]

Not until 1936 did the U.S. Supreme Court exclude a confession coerced by local, not federal, police. The case, *Brown* v. *Mississippi,* disclosed extraordinary police brutality and judicial complicity, exposing the Southern caste system at its ugliest. The defendants were three Negroes suspected of murder, although no evidence, aside from their confessions, was presented at the trial. When one of the men denied the charges to the Mississippi sheriffs, they hanged him with a rope from the limb of a tree, and let him down. When he again denied the charges, they hanged him again. Again he denied the charges. Then they whipped him severely. Still, he did not confess. A day or two later, a sheriff told him that he would whip him until he confessed. The prisoner finally complied. The two other men were whipped and pummeled until they confessed.

The confessions were admitted by the trial court, and the Supreme Court of Mississippi affirmed. The justices of the U.S. Supreme Court, in 1936 known as "the nine old men" and scarcely a collection of liberals, were shocked not only by the conduct of the Mississippi police but that the highest Court of Mississippi could admit into evidence confessions that had been elicited by these open admissions of brutality. "It would be difficult to conceive of methods more revolting to the sense of justice than those taken to procure the confessions of these petitioners," Chief Justice Charles Evans Hughes wrote, "and the use of the confessions thus obtained as the bases for conviction and sentence was a clear denial of due process."[11]

*Brown* v. *Mississippi* was a landmark case, and yet an easy one. One need not be a legal expert to understand that a confession gained through physical torture can scarcely qualify as "voluntary," and furthermore might be false. The Mississippi authorities were responding to an unwritten racial code, not to be found in the statute books or in the Constitution. Although law professors have cited the New York and the Mississippi cases as examples of the third degree,[12] there was a notable difference between them. In New York, the cops understood that they needed to lie about their methods, and they compounded their offense by regularly perjuring themselves. Ironically, the Mississippi sheriffs were truthful, because they did not need to lie. That such beatings occurred was understood and accepted by all-white juries and court officials, including the highest judges in the state. The deputy who had presided over the beatings acknowledged in open court that one of the defendants had been whipped, but, he testified, "not too much for a Negro; not as much as I would have done if it were left to me."[13]

Once the Supreme Court established that confessions must be "voluntary" and not "coerced," the question became what this meant in practice. Clearly, cops could not beat people with whips or rubber hoses and then claim the confession was uncoerced. One persistent problem was, however, that defendants repeatedly claimed under oath that the cops had beaten them, while the cops would, under oath, resolutely deny that they had. The problem of the "swearing contest" has never been, and by its nature cannot be, resolved. As we shall see, it is one of the reasons the *Miranda* warnings were formulated.

But even when cops and defendants agreed on what had happened, courts were repeatedly faced with novel examples of police practices. The Supreme Court had, for example, ruled that a confession produced after thirty-six hours of questioning was unconstitutional. But would thirty-five hours be permitted, or would five? The next year the court defined as "coerced" a confession obtained after a defendant, subjected to the third degree, was humiliated by being stripped naked and made to stand for three hours before being questioned for an additional ten.

*Spano* v. *New York* was heard and decided in 1959, after the Supreme Court had been reviewing confession cases for more than two decades. The case is not, like *Miranda* v. *Arizona,* a watershed in the annals of criminal procedural jurisprudence, being only one of many that eventually led to *Miranda.* Nevertheless, it arose at a critical time, as third-degree practices were being transformed from physical to psychological coercion.

Vincent Joseph Spano was born in Messina, Italy, but by the time he was twenty-five he had settled in the Bronx, in New York City. Vincent didn't have much of an education—he had graduated from junior high school—but he worked regularly and stayed away from trouble. After work he enjoyed going to a neighborhood bar to drink with his friends.

On January 22, 1957, Vincent ordered a drink and left his change on the bar. One of the neighborhood toughs, a man named Palermo, a burly 200-

pounder who had fought as a professional boxer in Madison Square Garden, reached over, picked up Vincent's money, and casually walked out of the bar. Vincent, smaller than Palermo and no match as a fighter, nevertheless followed the bigger man out of the bar and demanded his money.

The ensuing fight was no contest. The ex-pugilist knocked Vincent to the ground and kicked him repeatedly in the head. Vincent vomited from the force of the blows. Vincent's friends brought him inside, where a sympathetic bartender applied ice to Vincent's head. Vincent recovered enough to navigate his way home to his apartment, where he picked up a gun.

He searched the neighborhood for his tormenter and found him in a candy store, a hangout for local hoodlums. Also present were three of Palermo's friends, two of whom were ex-convicts. There was another witness, a boy who was supervising the store. Vincent drew his gun and unhesitatingly fired five shots into Palermo's body. Later the boy was the only witness who acknowledged he had seen the shooting. The friends, true to the neighborhood code, said they had seen nothing. Vincent left the store and disappeared.

The Bronx County Grand Jury indicted Vincent Spano for first-degree murder on February 1, a week after the shooting. Two days later, Spano called a close boyhood friend, Gaspar Bruno, who had recently joined the police department and was not yet out of the academy. According to Bruno's testimony, Spano told him that he had taken a terrific beating, that he hurt "real bad," that he was "dazed" and didn't know what he was doing, and "went and shot at him." Vincent told Gaspar that he intended to get a lawyer and turn himself in. The next day, accompanied by a lawyer, who had cautioned Vincent not to answer any questions from the police, Spano turned himself in to custody at the Bronx County Courthouse.

Spano was immediately taken to the office of the Assistant District Attorney for questioning, which was "both persistent and continuous." He refused to talk, on grounds that his attorney had advised him not to. Teams of prosecutors and detectives took turns badgering Vincent, but he wouldn't crack. "It was back and forth," Detective Farrell was later to testify. "People just came in, spoke a few words to the defendant or they listened a few minutes and they left."

By 12:40 A.M., the questioners were stymied. They decided to insert Gaspar Bruno, Vincent's close boyhood friend, into the questioning. Gaspar was told to tell Vincent that his telephone call had gotten him "in a lot of trouble" and that unless Vincent agreed to talk, he, Gaspar, would be fired, and his pregnant wife and three children would suffer. At first, Vincent resisted. Later on, for whatever reason, perhaps fatigue, the continuing pressure of the interrogators, or perhaps sympathy for his friend, Vincent's resolve not to confess broke down. At 3:25 A.M. he admitted to shooting his tormenter. He completed his statement at 4:05 A.M.

Vincent thought he would be allowed some rest. Instead, three detectives bundled him into an automobile and took him on a tour of Manhattan's bridges to help him recall from which one he had thrown the murder weapon. During the ride Vincent told the detectives that the man he had killed was "always on his back," "always pushing" and that he was "not sorry" that he had killed him.

Despite objections, the confession was introduced in evidence at trial. The jury returned a guilty verdict, and Vincent Spano was sentenced to death. New York's highest court affirmed the conviction over three dissents, and the case was appealed to the U.S. Supreme Court.

Spano had, in fact, been treated with what might be called the new third degree, epitomized by a movement from physical to psychological coercion. He had not been a victim of police brutality. He had been questioned hard, but for five rather than thirty-six hours. Under the tenets of the old third degree, the police might have introduced rubber hoses after five unproductive hours. Instead, the police decided to trick a confession out of Spano by bringing in Gaspar Bruno to play the part of a worried father, harried by his superiors. Bruno's entreaties ultimately persuaded Spano to confess and inspired Justice Warren, in his opinion, to quote John Gay's couplet:

*An open foe may prove a curse,*
*But a pretended friend is worse.*

We can only speculate as to what the cops were thinking when they brought Spano in. Yet their actions were consistent with what police were being taught about effective ruses by police reformers following the publication of the Wickersham Commission report. The reform movement's leaders were a Northwestern University law professor, Fred E. Inbau, and John E. Reid, the man usually credited with developing the polygraph into a "lie detector." Like the false story told to Vincent Spano, the lie detector exemplified the new psychologically, but not physically, coercive interrogatory style. The theory underlying lie detection had four connected premises, each of which was flawed: the act of lying leads to conscious conflict (but untruthful people may believe what they say); conflict between truth and lying statements induces fear or anxiety (some people are very anxious, and others, such as sociopaths, are hardly at all); anxiety results in measurable physiological change (bodily responses do not vary regularly, either with each other or with emotional states; if they did, only a unigraph, not a polygraph, would be required); such measured changes permit a trained examiner to determine whether a person is lying. None of the premises is true, but the myth of the lie detector's accuracy encouraged persons accused of crime to confess for fear they would be found out and would be punished even more severely.

As with Gaspar Bruno's false story told to Spano, detectives were encouraged to employ a variety of ruses to elicit incriminating admissions from suspects. They were told to interview suspects in their own offices, where the suspect would be "deprived of every psychological advantage." Detectives were told to insinuate themselves into the suspect's confidence by suggesting legally incriminating rationalizations for their actions. Thus, a rapist might be told that his victim probably "asked for it" by the way she walked, dressed, or otherwise comported herself. Or the detective might suggest that the suspect was a victim of poverty or a bad family life. In blaming the victim or society, detectives would, falsely, minimize the moral seriousness of the offense and encourage admissions.

For police manual writers like Inbau and Reid, psychological coercion and trickery seemed a reformist achievement. The new third degree disposed of the most horrifying forms of police brutality. It was, in effect, proposed as a synthesis, resolving the contradiction between the violence of the old third degree and constitutionally mandated due process. Their benchmark test was: "Although both 'fair' and 'unfair' interrogation practices are permissible, nothing shall be done or said to the subject that will make an innocent person confess." The detectives in the Spano case had perfectly exemplified the Inbau and Reid benchmark.

But Earl Warren was unwilling to settle for that standard. Beyond the "inherent untrustworthiness" of involuntary confessions, the former prosecutor deeply believed in due process values "that the police must obey the law while enforcing the law; that in the end life and liberty can be as much endangered from illegal methods used to convict those thought to be criminals as from the actual criminals themselves." Nevertheless, as inspirational as such pronouncements might be, aside from fist, blackjack, and hose, it was unclear what methods "the law" considered to be "illegal." Because Vincent Spano's case did not clearly suggest police brutality, it posed a delicate balancing problem for the Supreme Court.

Of all the justices, Earl Warren was the most experienced with law enforcement and most appreciated its needs. He was acutely aware of the problems posed for court oversight of police by the movement from physical coercion to trickery and psychological persuasion. "As law enforcement officers become more responsible, and the methods used to extract confessions more sophisticated," he wrote, "our duty to enforce federal constitutional standards does not cease. It only becomes more difficult because of the more delicate judgments to be made."

Warren voted to overturn Spano's conviction basing his conclusion on an assessment of "all the facts." The problem is, of course, that an examination of "all the facts," a concept eventually enshrined in constitutional jurisprudence as the "totality of the circumstances," is behaviorally standardless. It simply does not answer the "illegal methods" question. Even with the best of intentions, how could police possibly interpret such a standard? Suppose Spano had been grilled for two, rather than five, hours before Bruno had been inserted? Would the conviction have withstood constitutional scrutiny? The "facts" of every interrogation are unique. How long, how isolated, how deceptive may an interrogation be?, police could reasonably ask after Spano had been decided. And what about the suspect—whose age, education, race, and mental stability will also vary from case to case? In sum, how would other courts, and other cops who conduct interrogations, know what bundling of "all the facts" would pass constitutional muster? Yale Kamisar, a prominent critic of the "voluntariness" standard, once characterized the concept as a "fiction" used to vilify or beautify varying techniques of interrogation.[14]

The "voluntariness" yardstick's vagueness generated administrative problems for trial courts, which had to decide whether a confession was "voluntary," and for appellate courts, which were required to review whether the trial courts had made the proper judgment. Students of the law believed that this burden contributed toward the development of the more objective "rules" later to be developed in *Miranda* v. *Arizona*.

Spano, for example, had repeatedly asked to see his lawyer, but that request had been denied. The denial had been considered merely a contributory factor in Justice Warren's cluster of "all the facts," but some of the other justices thought the denial of counsel was critical. Justices Douglas, Black, and Brennan insisted that Spano's conviction should be overturned because a man formally charged with a capital crime needed, and was entitled, to see his lawyer.

Justice Stewart spelled out the problem: Spano had been indicted, that is, formally charged and, instead of being brought before a magistrate and "arraigned" in a court of law, was subjected to "an all-night inquisition in a prosecutor's office, a police station, and an automobile." From Justice Stewart's perspective, Spano had been subjected to an inquisition rather than a trial. Several years later, the law professor Yale Kamisar would highlight the distinction between the "gatehouse" of American criminal procedure, "a police station with bare back room and locked doors," and its "mansion," the courtroom, "a splendid place where defense attorneys bellow and strut and prosecuting attorneys are hemmed in at many turns."[15] Spano had been tried in the gatehouse.

## FORCE VERSUS FRAUD

By 1963, the Court was to decide several cases suggesting that a person, having been formally accused by indictment, was entitled to a lawyer's counsel, and that after he had it, the police could not talk to him without his lawyer being present. In 1964 that principle was adopted in a case where there was not a hint of police brutality, nor even of direct questioning by police. Two men, Massiah and Colson, were indicted for federal narcotics violations. Massiah retained a lawyer, was arraigned before a federal magistrate, pleaded not guilty, and was released on bail. In the meantime, Colson was offered a deal by federal agents, who had recruited him as an informer. He talked with Massiah in an automobile that had been wired by the federal agents and was able, in the course of discussing the pending case, to persuade Massiah to make damaging admissions.

So here was a case far removed from the 1930s third degree fist, club, and hose interrogations, and even very different from Spano's. There was no isolation, no police station, no grilling, no fatigue. As the dissenters complained, there was no "inherent danger of police coercion justifying the prophylactic effect of another exclusionary rule." Nor, in the view of the dissenters, was there any interference with Massiah's right to counsel; he was not prevented from consulting with his lawyer, nor did the government spy on his consultations with his lawyer.

The majority recognized the difference between Massiah's treatment and Spano's and then introduced a novel standard for its decision. Massiah, it held, was "more seriously imposed upon" than Spano, "because he did not know that he was under interrogation by a federal agent," suggesting that police deception, even as in the case of Spano, would violate the constitutional rights of someone under indictment. Massiah had, in effect, been defrauded into making his incriminating admissions, and a fraudulently obtained admission cannot, said the majority, have been "voluntary." (Yet only two years later, the Court allowed as evidence incriminating statements by Jimmy Hoffa, the corrupt head of the Teamsters Union and its Central States Pension Fund, made in somewhat similar circumstances. Hoffa, a high-priority target of the Justice Department, was on trial for jury tampering. A false "friend," secretly working for the government, was planted in Hoffa's entourage. Hoffa, the Court said, had not been "compelled" by the friend to talk, and if he chose to make incriminating remarks, that was his choice.)

The Massiah case was followed in only five weeks by another landmark case, or at least so it seemed at the time. Danny Escobedo was a small-time hoodlum who had been taken into custody and questioned about a fatal shooting. Danny's attorney had succeeded in having him released, but he was again arrested when the cops were told by his friend, a man named DiGerlando, that Danny was the killer. Escobedo was rearrested and repeatedly asked to see his attorney, a request that was denied. The police brought Escobedo face to face with DiGerlando, at which point Danny incriminated himself in the killing. Based on his statements, the assistant prosecutor was able to elicit a more elaborate written confession. Danny's confession was introduced at the trial, and he was convicted of murder.

Once again the court was faced with a case of custodial interrogation, and once again there was no issue of police brutality. Unlike Massiah and Spano, Escobedo had not been indicted, but he was clearly thought to be the murderer, and thus he was the "focus" of the investigation. He had an attorney, with whom he wanted to consult and who wanted to see him.

The police had not deceived Danny, but they had pressured him by making him face his accuser. They had done what Justice Stewart had found so objectionable in the Spano case. They had, in effect, pretried the case in the "gatehouse" according to their own set of procedures. Escobedo was removed from his attorney, friends, and family, and was required to face his accuser without the right to cross-examine and without a disinterested judge to oversee the proceedings and to tell him that he had a right to remain silent—which of course he did not really have in the confines of the police interrogation room. Once Escobedo's confession had been elicited and introduced into evidence, the public trial was a predictable formality. The jury was virtually required to convict.

The facts of the Escobedo case were disconcerting. The majority of the Court expressed deep skepticism about "a system of criminal law enforcement which comes to depend on the 'confession'." Such a system, they added, "will, in the long run, be less reliable and more subject to abuses than a system which depends on extrinsic evidence independently secured through skillful investigation." The Court said further that "no meaningful distinction can be drawn between interrogation of an accused before and after formal indictment," and that an interrogation before indictment was a "critical stage" in the process, akin to the trial. Lawyers who read the opinion thought the Court was about to announce that suspects had a right to counsel in the station house, but that was not to be. Instead, the Court issued a confusing and limited holding, from which it was difficult to derive larger principles.

The big and underlying issue was whether police should be permitted to engage in gatehouse justice, that is, "custodial interrogation" of suspects who, they have reason to believe, have committed a crime, and whom they have arrested; and to introduce into evidence the resulting confessions. The Court need not have pronounced a "No Confessions Allowed" rule. Confessions would have been outlawed by indirection. All that was needed were two clear guidelines that would have been entirely consistent with the direction the Court had been heading. First rule: Suspects have a right to an attorney immediately after they have been advised of their Constitutional rights following an arrest. There can be no waiver of rights, unless advised by an attorney. Second rule: Once a suspect invokes the right to remain silent, there can be no further questioning. If there is, anything learned directly or indirectly cannot be used in evidence. Had such rules been in effect, attorneys would typically have advised their clients, as had Spano's, Massiah's, and Escobedo's, to exercise their right to remain silent and to refuse to talk to the police.

Criminal justice professionals—judges, lawyers, and cops alike—understand that the criminal justice system can be perilous to those who represent themselves, even those who work in it and understand it. When cops or attorneys are accused of a crime, they call a lawyer. So do others, especially criminals, as had Spano, Massiah, and Escobedo. But many persons accused of crimes do not and cannot comprehend why a lawyer is so important, especially if they are poor and uneducated. In 1963, in the landmark case *Gideon* v. *Wainwright*,[16] the Court had ruled that everyone charged with a felony has a right to be represented by an attorney in a courtroom. But it did not grant persons the right to consult with a lawyer when arrested.

Four of the justices—Douglas, Warren, Black, and Brennan—had signaled their support for such a position as dissenters in a 1958 case where they said, "The right to have counsel at the pre-trial stage is often necessary to give meaning and protection to the right to be heard at the trial itself."[17] The key issue facing the Court after Escobedo was whether to follow the logic of its previous decisions and recognize that, just as a defendant cannot have a fair trial without an attorney, so too does a suspect need an attorney to advise in making such critical decisions as the waiver of the Constitutional right to remain silent. Practically speaking, such a requirement would have virtually eliminated custodial interrogation and confessions.

If not these *bright line* rules, the Court needed to devise some other benchmark. It responded with the rules announced in the renowned case *Miranda* v. *Arizona,* where a rapist and kidnapper was tricked into confessing by being told he had "flunked" the lineup and had been identified. Although sometimes celebrated (and often denounced) as the pinnacle of the

Warren Court's liberal rulings, in retrospect the *Miranda* ruling seems an awkward compromise between those who would effectively have barred station house confessions by granting everyone an attorney when they were arrested and those who preferred to test whether a confession met standards of due process and voluntariness by reviewing "all the facts."

The five-to-four majority began by examining police manuals and texts, which they considered to be a "valuable source of information about present police practices." *Miranda* was thus the first case to recognize and discuss the new third degree, that is, the assertion by professional police that custodial interrogation was an indispensable tool of law enforcement and that it passed Constitutional muster, provided the tactics employed were not so coercive as to induce an innocent person to confess.

The majority expressed considerable dismay with the tactics recommended by the police manuals and discussed them at considerable length. Although such tactics might have been acceptable under the traditional test of voluntariness, the Court reasoned that "the potentiality for compulsion is forcefully apparent." No one tactic was singled out, but the majority seemed especially distressed by the Mutt-and-Jeff technique. There, one investigator, Mutt, plays the tough guy role, that of the canine enforcer. Mutt threatens the suspect, is impatient, and won't stand for prevarication. He is dogged. He wants a confession, and he wants it *now*. Jeff plays the kind-hearted family man, whose brother was involved in a similar scrape. He doesn't like his partner, he doesn't approve of his tactics, he'll try to have him transferred, but he's not sure how long he can hold him off. When Mutt leaves the room, Jeff pleads for cooperation.

The Mutt-and-Jeff technique is, of course, simply a sophisticated variation of the old third degree, where detectives slapped their palms with rubber hoses and arranged for screams and groans to emanate from the next room. No rubber hoses are shown by Mutt, but they are implied by Jeff. Someone who confessed after experiencing a Mutt-and-Jeff interrogation, or even some less blatantly coercive tactic, could scarcely have given statements that could be considered genuinely "voluntary." Thus the Court concluded that "unless adequate protective devices are employed to dispel the compulsion inherent in custodial surroundings, no statement obtained from the defendant can truly be the product of his free choice."

Instead of mandating that a suspect must consult with an attorney before consenting to be interrogated, the Court developed the heralded *Miranda* rules. When police decide to interrogate someone who is in custody, everyone, regardless of how much they might have been aware of their rights, must be told that they have a right to remain silent. They must also be told that anything they say can and will be used against them in court; that they have a right to consult with a lawyer and to have a lawyer present during interrogation; and that if they are indigent a lawyer will be appointed to represent them. They must also be told that the interrogation must stop if they say they want to cease talking, and that if they want an attorney, the police must stop interrogating until the attorney is present.

It is not clear whether the majority thought that, with the *Miranda* warnings in place, custodial interrogation would be a thing of the past. The dissenters seemed to think so. They disparaged the warnings as a "constitutional code of rules for confessions." The police, outraged, believed that the *Miranda* requirements would "handcuff" them in solving important crimes. But surveys and empirical research on police found that the *Miranda* warnings did not influence custodial interrogation nearly as much as liberals had hoped or conservatives had feared. No one, probably, could have anticipated how little effect the warnings would have. Without an attorney's on-the-spot advice, most defendants were, and are, unable to understand the consequences of talking with police. They usually waive their right to remain silent and to consult with an attorney.

Besides, police soon learned how to give the warnings so as to diminish their significance. Police have learned how to "soften up" the suspect by avoiding the subject of the crime, talking instead about the suspect's life, his hobbies, Michael Jordan's moves on the basketball court, and so forth. Police use their understanding of underlying norms of interaction to invite the suspect's trust. When the warnings are then given in the soft and compassionate tones of "Jeff," suspects feel encouraged to cooperate. Many believe that if they can explain themselves to this agreeable and sympathetic figure of authority, they will be released. Suspects rarely understand what kind of language is or is not incriminating— that by agreeing with the detective, for example, that the victim provoked the attack, they might be making a critical admission.

More importantly, police have learned that they need to "interrogate" far less than they formerly thought they did. Usually, when they have focused in on a suspect, they have extrinsic eyewitness and physical evidence to make the case without a confession. In cases involving drug possession, rarely is there a need to interrogate. The incriminating evidence is the possession of the drug itself, not the suspect's statement. Knowledgeable narcotics detectives who arrest street drug dealers often don't bother with *Miranda* warnings, since they do not plan to elicit an admission of guilt from the dealer.

Police who are seeking admissions have learned how to *interview* rather than *interrogate*. The distinction is critical. *Miranda* warnings apply only when the subject is under arrest, that is, in custody and not free to leave.

"Interviews" do not require Miranda warnings, because the subject of an "interview" consents to the discussion and is free to leave. When police are investigating a homicide, for example, they will usually try to interview the victim's spouse, friends, neighbors, relatives, or lovers. One of those might, of course, be the murderer. When police invite truly *innocent* friends to be interviewed, either in the police station or at home, these actually innocent persons usually cooperate willingly, even enthusiastically. Innocent persons who are contacted by police investigating the murder of a friend, spouse, or lover ordinarily elect to help police find and convict the murderer. The actual murderer above all wants to appear to be innocent. The guilty understand, as we all do, that innocent people cooperate with police. They therefore mimic the innocent so as to suggest that they, too, are unoffending.

Finally, there is the matter of the waiver. Is it possible for someone accused of a serious crime to waive his or her Constitutional right to silence and the right to consult an attorney "voluntarily, knowingly, and intelligently" as Miranda requires? Except in the case of an experienced criminal, who has developed a prior relationship with the police; or an innocent person who can clear up the matter immediately; or a truly remorseful person who wants to confess, it seems unlikely that anyone could "intelligently" waive his or her Constitutional rights, unless by "intelligent" we mean merely a literal rather than informed understanding of the implications of waiving one's rights. Indeed, before *Miranda* was decided, the then Los Angeles Police Chief, William Parker, wrote an article in the *Los Angeles Bar Bulletin* making exactly that point. He feared that if the police were required to apprise the defendant of his Constitutional guarantees of silence and legal counsel, "and that he intelligently waived these guarantees," a "whole Pandora's box" would be opened "as to what circumstances . . . can a defendant intelligently waive these rights."[18]

Knowledgeable criminal defense attorneys rarely, if ever, permit their clients to be interrogated by police. When they do, they make sure they are present at the interview. The *Miranda* rules seem internally contradictory, virtually an oxymoron. In practice, a waiver cannot be genuinely "intelligent" unless it has been counseled by a lawyer; but "knowing and intelligent" lawyers usually counsel their clients to remain silent. As Justice Jackson recognized in his 1949 dissent in *Watts* v. *Indiana,* "any lawyer worth his salt will tell the suspect in no uncertain terms to make no statement to police under any circumstances."[19]

The Supreme Court has been especially sensitive to the Sixth Amendment and the right to a lawyer that it guarantees. Recall the *Massiah* case, where the Court overturned a conviction because the government had tricked Massiah, who had been indicted and had engaged an attorney, into making admissions to a confederate who was working for the government and was secretly recording the conversation. After the *Miranda* decision, legal scholars were puzzled by what it implied for the rule handed down in *Massiah,* which seemed to be this: Once a suspect has been indicted and has engaged an attorney, police can no longer question him.

Then, in 1977, the Court reviewed an odd and much discussed case, *Brewer* v. *Williams.*[20] By 1972 it had been decided that suspects enjoyed the right to counsel "at or after the time that judicial proceedings have been initiated."[21] Legal authorities were not certain of what the initiation of "judicial proceedings" meant. But in Williams's case, where a warrant had been issued for his arrest, he had been arrested, and he had been arraigned before a judge and sent to jail, "judicial proceedings" were found to have been initiated. And Williams had retained a lawyer, who told him not to talk to the police and made certain the police understood that they were not to "interrogate" Williams.

Williams was an eccentric character, a religious zealot who had been charged with the murder of a young girl in Des Moines, Iowa. He had been captured in Davenport, Iowa, and needed to be transported to the Des Moines authorities. In an almost classic illustration of the new third degree, a police captain *persuaded* Williams to reveal the location of the dead girl's body. He used no fist, no rubber hose, no threats of violence. Instead, he appealed to Williams's conscience by noting that it was almost Christmas, that it was snowing, that the weather was worsening, and that it would be necessary to find the body as soon as possible to ensure that the murdered girl would have a Christian burial. Moved by the plea, Williams led police to the body and provided the evidence leading to his conviction.

The Supreme Court overturned the conviction, ruling that the captain had violated his promise to Williams's lawyer and "deliberately and designedly set out to elicit information from Williams just as surely as—and perhaps more effectively than—if he had formally interrogated him." But had Williams initially waived his right to remain silent and to an attorney, it would have been perfectly acceptable for a detective to have urged Williams to clear his conscience and show the police where he had buried the body. Had there been such a waiver, in what sense could it have been "knowing and intelligent," even if voluntary? Ironically, when a waiver occurs, the familiar "totality of the circumstances" formula becomes the benchmark for testing the validity of any confession that might afterward be elicited. Consequently, in an instance of magnificent irony, once a subject waives the right to remain silent, many of the psychologically coercive and deceptive tactics that the *Miranda* majority deplored in the police manuals may come into play. The question once again becomes, as it was prior to *Miranda,* was the confession "voluntary" under the "totality of the circumstances"?

## THE PRESENT AND THE FUTURE

Although it is unlikely that we shall ever again experience the sort of routine third-degree brutality in police stations that was commonplace in the 1920s and 1930s, deceptive techniques, even more advanced than those decried by the *Miranda* majority, have become the hallmark of the police interrogation trade.[22]

Among the most effective and commonly used is the "fabrication of evidence" ploy. This takes a number of forms. One is to tell the suspect falsely that he has been identified by an accomplice. Another is to present the suspect with faked physical evidence, such as fingerprints, bloodstains, or hair samples, to confirm that suspect's guilt. In yet another ruse, police tell the suspect he has been identified by an eyewitness. The police may even stage a line-up where a pretend eyewitness identifies the suspect. Even more commonly, the suspect is persuaded to take a lie-detector test and then told that the test proves he is guilty. In a recent Florida case, police officers fabricated two scientific laboratory reports, one from the Florida Department of Corrections, the other from a private testing organization, purporting to show the suspect, a man named Cayward, that semen stains on the victim's underwear were his.[23] Cayward subsequently confessed. The social psychologist Richard Ofshe remarks that deceptive practices are not a problem when the defendant is actually guilty, but they may confuse an innocent person into disbelieving his own recollection of the events.[24] After all, if the police say they have physical evidence proving your guilt, you may question the validity of your own recollection.

What should we think of these practices? Part of the problem is that trickery by police is permitted by law and has become so common as to be an entrenched institution.[25] Detectives are trained to turn criminals into informers, especially in narcotics investigations. Moreover, every narcotics enforcement agency in America trains undercover detectives to pose as drug dealers. But if police deception is worrisome, why is the evidence based on deceptive techniques accepted?

One important reason is that the Constitutional protection of the rights of defendants isn't the only value held by judges, even by the most liberal. Controlling crime is a powerful competing consideration in which the government is seen to have a strong legitimate interest. When, as in narcotics enforcement, deception seems necessary, it is also considered lawful.

These sentiments were expressed by Justice Potter Stewart when he wrote that "the government's use of undercover activity, strategy, or deception is not necessarily unlawful. Indeed, many crimes, especially so-called victimless crimes, could not otherwise be detected." Thus, when cops investigate narcotics offenses, the good ends of catching and convicting criminals come to outweigh the bad means of deception.

Should the good end of convicting criminals also justify deception during interrogation? One's answer is likely to depend on the balance of one's attachment to due process as against crime-control values. The injunction "Thou shalt not lie" doesn't seem to apply to trickery in interrogation. Conservatives who lean toward crime-control values do not countenance lying as a general matter. But they approve of police deception as a necessity, measuring the cost of police deceit against the benefits of trickery for victims of crime and the safety of the general public.

As in the investigation of narcotics dealing, the good end is said to justify the bad means. Custodial interrogation and accompanying confessions are likewise considered a practical necessity for convicting the most serious sorts of criminals—murderers, rapists, and child molesters.

Yet in the *Cayward* case, where the cops falsified evidence, the Florida court saw that as an offense to "our traditional notions of due process of law." The court was evidently alarmed by the *unfairness* of a system that allows police to "knowingly fabricate tangible documentation or physical evidence against an individual." In addition to its "spontaneous distaste" for the conduct of the police, the court added a longer-range utilitarian consideration. Documents manufactured for such purposes, the court feared, may, because of their "potential of indefinite life and the facial appearance of authenticity," contaminate the entire criminal justice system. "A report falsified for interrogation purposes might well be retained and filed in police paperwork. Such reports have the potential of finding their way into the courtroom." The court also worried that if allowed in evidence, police might be tempted to falsify all sorts of official documents "including warrants, orders, and judgments," thereby undermining public respect for the authority and integrity of the judicial system.

Yet the slippery slope argument surely applies to lying as well as to falsification of documents. When police are permitted to lie in the interrogation context, why should they refrain from lying to judges when applying for warrants, violating internal police organization rules against lying, or lying in the courtroom? An *Oakland Tribune* columnist, Alix Christie, recently received a letter from a University of California science professor who had served on an Alameda County (Oakland) murder jury. He was dismayed that a defendant, whom he believed to be guilty, had been acquitted because most of the jurors did not believe the police, even about how long it takes to drive from west to east Oakland. "The problem," Christie writes, "predates Rodney King. It's one familiar to prosecutors fishing for jurors who don't fit the profile of people who distrust cops." She locates the problem in "the ugly fact that there are two Americas." In the first America, the one she was raised in, the police are the "good guys." In the other, police are viewed skeptically. As we suggested earlier, the police who beat Rodney King were tried in one America for acts they had committed in the other.

Police misconduct—and lying is ordinarily considered a form of misconduct—undermines public confidence and social cooperation anywhere, but especially in urban America. People living in these areas often have had negative experiences with police, ranging from an aloof and legalistic policing "style," to corruption, even to the sort of overt brutality that was captured on the videotape of the Rodney King beating in Los Angeles. "Community-oriented policing" is being implemented in a number of American police departments to improve trust and citizen cooperation by changing the attitudes of both police and public.

Police deception may thus engender a paradoxical outcome. Although affirmed in the interest of crime-control values by its advocates, like Fred Inbau, who has had a strong influence on generations of police interrogators, it may generate quite unanticipated consequences. Rarely, if ever, have advocates of greater latitude for police to interrogate—which, as interrogation is currently taught, is synonymous with lying and trickery—considered the effects of systematic lying on law enforcement's reputation for veracity.

Police lying might not have mattered so much to police work in different times and places in American history. But today, when urban juries are increasingly disposed to be distrustful of police, deception by police during interrogation offers yet another reason for disbelieving law enforcement witnesses when they take the stand, thus reducing police effectiveness as controllers of crime.

There is an additional reason for opposing deceitful interrogation practices. It does happen that innocent people are convicted of crimes—not as often as guilty people are set free, but it does happen. In a 1986 study of wrongful conviction in felony cases, C. Ronald Huff and his colleagues conservatively estimated that nearly six thousand false convictions occur every year in the United States.[26] Hugo Bedau and Michael Radelet, who subsequently studied 350 known miscarriages of justice in recent American history, identified false confessions as one of the leading sources of erroneous conviction of innocent individuals.[27] When an innocent person is convicted, the price of the error to society is doubled. Not only is an innocent person treated unjustly, but a guilty, and possibly dangerous, person goes free.

## THE REHNQUIST COURT

The Supreme Court has moved in a more conservative, crime-control, direction in recent years. It has softened the *Miranda* rules in important and complex ways, especially since the appointment of William Rehnquist as chief justice. If the public safety requires it, a five-to-four majority held in 1984, a suspect may be questioned without advising him of his rights. The "facts" justifying a "public safety" exception were these: The police chased a rape suspect into a supermarket. They thought he was armed and when they cornered and arrested him, they frisked him and discovered an empty shoulder holster. One officer asked him, without giving *Miranda* warnings, "Where is the gun?" He replied, "The gun is over there" and gestured to a stack of soap cartons.[28]

The Court said that "so long as the gun was concealed somewhere in the supermarket, with its whereabouts unknown, it obviously posed more than one danger to the public safety; an accomplice might make use of it, a customer or employee might later come upon it." But as the criminal law authorities Wayne LaFave and Jerrold Israel note, the danger was slight. The suspect, Quarles, was handcuffed and in the custody of four armed officers. There was no way Quarles could reach the gun. Nor did he have an accomplice. And the likelihood that some other person could have found the gun was slight. The events happened after midnight, the store was apparently deserted, and the police knew that the gun had been discarded in the immediate vicinity.[29]

Deference to the fact that a lawyer has been involved has also declined, as has the court's concern for deception by police. In *Moran* v. *Burbine* (1986)[30] the Supreme Court let stand a murder conviction even though the police denied a lawyer to the man being questioned. Brian K. Burbine, a twenty-year-old man, was arrested in Cranston, Rhode Island, on a charge of breaking and entering. Although he was read his *Miranda* rights, he did not ask for a lawyer. While he was in custody, the police linked him to the murder of a woman who had been severely beaten with a metal pipe.

In the meantime, Burbine's sister had called a public defender to represent her brother on the breaking-and- entering charge. The lawyer, who knew nothing of the murder charge in the making, called the police station at 8:15 P.M. A detective told him that Burbine would not be questioned that night about the burglary. Questioning began a few minutes later. Burbine, who was never told that a lawyer had called, confessed to the murder and was subsequently convicted.

The Supreme Court, in a decision by Justice Sandra Day O'Connor, upheld the conviction. The justices were not pleased by the "misleading" police actions, but, since Burbine had been told of his rights and had voluntarily waived them, the conviction stood. The dissenters, led by Justice Stevens, decried the "incommunicado questioning" and denounced the majority for having embraced "deception of the shabbiest kind."

Finally, the notoriety of the Rodney King beating overshadowed the significance of the Supreme Court's recent portentous self-incrimination decision. In *Arizona* v. *Fulminante* (1991)[31] a confession was obtained when a prison inmate, an ex-cop who was also an FBI informer, offered to protect Fulminante from prison violence, but only if he confessed to the murder of his daughter. In a sharply contested five-to-four opinion, the Court reversed its previously held doctrine that a coerced confession could never constitute merely a "harmless error." Previously, when a confession was found to have been coerced, the resulting conviction was automatically invalidated. *Fulminante* ended this rule. Whether the ruling will be as important in *encouraging* police coercion of confessions as the King videotape will be in discouraging future street brutality remains to be seen. Will the police now rely more readily on the fruits of tainted confessions, rather than the products of skillful investigation? Will more innocent suspects falsely confess to crimes they did not commit and be wrongfully convicted? Not only does the *Fulminante* decision perhaps foreshadow these outcomes, but, in concert with other recent U.S. Supreme Court decisions cutting back on the rights of defendants, it may also send a message that police can use violence as well as threaten it.

If courts allow police to deceive suspects for the good end of convicting criminals, can we really expect the police to be truthful when offering testimony? If we interpret coercion as "harmless error" for the good end of crime control, should we be surprised when cops employ violence for the good end of maintaining their authority in the street? There are no easy answers to these dilemmas, no easy lines to suggest when the need to keep our police moral and honest brushes up against the imperatives of controlling crime. Nevertheless, police deception must be considered a heavy cost in a free society that believes in a fair system of criminal justice.

That *Miranda* will be overturned by the Rehnquist Court is unlikely, but constitutional limitations on police interrogation will unquestionably be further relaxed. The fist, the blackjack, and the hose probably will not return to interrogation rooms, except to administer justice outside the law, primarily to punish, not to convict. Still, fraud and psychological coercion such as "Mutt-and-Jeff" questioning and other forms of deception will almost certainly rise as a result of the message—that the courts will not look askance at questionable police conduct—being sent to police by the Rehnquist Court. Most important of all, we should understand that our rules for police procedures are not merely obscure legal technicalities. These rules impart to police meanings whose significance is conveyed in the locker rooms and acted out in the streets.

# 4

# *Public Order Policing*

The Whole City, My Lord, is alarm'd and uneasy; Wickedness has got such a Head, and the Robbers and Insolence of the Night are such, that the Citizens are no longer secure within their own Walls, or safe even in passing their Streets, but are robbed, insulted and abused, even at their own Doors.

—Daniel Defoe, London, 1730

## THE POLICE AS CONTROLLERS OF RIOT

Although most of us think of police as crime controllers, they were, from the beginning, at least as prominent as controllers of public disorder. Yet London was not, for nearly a century after Daniel Defoe's complaint, to establish a police force for either purpose, although both riots and crime were threatening the growing city, especially its propertied classes. Looking back at that time, the social historian Allen Silver wrote: "Crime and violence evoked complaints which have a quite contemporary theme." Those who owned property felt increasingly threatened by the rapidly multiplying poor of cities whose size had no precedent in Western history.[1]

England was in what the historian John J. Tobias described as "violent transition." As England moved from a feudal and agricultural economy to an urban and industrial one (just as today we are moving from an industrial to a postindustrial high-technology and service economy), the towns, especially London, developed enclaves of criminality among the poor who had migrated there. Jobs were scarce, and new arrivals had to fend for themselves. "Receiving no assistance from their families or their employers (if they had families or employers) or from the municipal authorities," Tobias writes, "they found solutions by adopting the techniques, the habits and the attitudes of the criminals."[2] As crime flourished, so, of course, did the issue of protecting persons and property.

But crime was only part of the problem. The last half of the eighteenth century was also a revolutionary period, when workers began to think of themselves as a class apart. Workers did not own property and could not vote their interests. Public protest and riot were fairly common means of communicating grievances and demands.

Historians generally mark the years 1780 to 1850 as the main period of public disorder in England, beginning with the anti-Catholic Gordon riots of 1780 and highlighted by the so-called Peterloo massacre of 1819. Hundreds of people were injured and eleven killed in St. Peters fields outside of London, when the army and the smaller landholders, the yoemanry, panicked during a peaceful protest against high wheat tariffs, food prices, and other parliamentary abuses.[3] (Opponents of the Tory government predicted it would be the government's "Waterloo," hence the term "Peterloo.")

The most severe period of economic depression and social unrest followed the Napoleanic wars. The English social historian Asa Briggs found that in 1816 and 1817 nearly one-fifth of the population was on relief in Birmingham; in the iron-producing areas of the Black Country there was "the silence of unmingled desolation" inside many of the ironworks, and bitter cries of angry men outside. In Lancashire, the weavers were complaining that "now, when the waste of war is over, our sufferings are become more general and deeper than ever." The colliers at Newcastle were also resentful and expressed that resentment by rioting, as did the farm laborers at Ely and the townspeople of Bridport.[4] All over the country, as Samuel Bamford, a social activist of the time, put it, "Whilst the laurels were yet cool on the brows of our victorious soldiers, the elements of convulsion were at work amongst the masses of our labouring population."[5] Working-class unrest and agitation were met with a sharp backlash by the "silent majority" of the middle class and anyone who owned property. This was a revolutionary era, and memories of the American and French revolutions were keen, recent, and ominous. The response was a reign of terror by the nobility and the middle class "more formidable, though more silent, than the noisy demonstrations" conducted by radicals and reformers.[6]

Parliament's response to the Peterloo massacre was unyielding and retributive. Parliament augmented the army with 10,000 men and sharply curtailed civil liberties. The notorious "gag acts" limited public meetings, taxed periodicals, authorized the seizure of publications that could be called seditious libel, and allowed magistrates to search houses for arms. Although Parliament succeeded in suppressing all forms of political expression, it failed to solidify the government's authority. On the contrary, Charles Reith, a leading historian of the British police, wrote, "They greatly increased the prevailing indignation against the government." The younger generation, especially those at the universities, began to question the principles of old-fashioned Toryism.[7]

Repression prevailed as the principal instrument of social control. The death penalty was prescribed for more than 160 offenses. Melville Lee, a turn-of-the-century captain in the London Metropolitan Police and a historian, concluded: "Such indiscriminate infliction of the extreme penalty of the law could serve no useful purpose, on the contrary it undoubtedly aggravated the very offenses it was intended to check."[8] Witnesses refused to give evidence that might condemn a defendant to the gallows, and juries sometimes failed to convict even when the evidence given was perfectly clear. Why successive English governments continued to retain, and even expand, the range of capital statutes at a time when fewer and fewer capital punishments were actually carried out has puzzled several English historians. The most intriguing and controversial explanation has been offered by Douglas Hay, who argued that the unreformed criminal law served as an ideological expression of social values and enhanced the status of constituted authorities when they granted mercy to those accused of capital crimes. As Hay puts it, "the criminal law was critically important in maintaining bonds of obedience and deference, in legitimizing the status quo, in constantly recreating the structure of authority which arose from property and in turn protected those interests."[9]

Strenuous efforts were made by Jeremy Bentham and Samuel Romilly to persuade the government to reduce the number of offenses punishable by death, but even those influential figures had little success. Robert Peel, a leading Tory and former chief of the Irish Constabulary, at first opposed such reforms, but when he began to think that an organized police was necessary to control both riots and crime, he realized that a "reformed police could not function effectively until the criminal and other laws which they were to enforce had been made capable of being respected by the public, and administered with simplicity and clarity." Although he had boldly announced plans for police, he postponed them and concentrated his energies on reforming the law.[10] As Prime Minister, Peel abolished the death penalty for more than one hundred offenses and erased numerous criminal penalties entirely.

Peel understood that he was not the first to propose an organized police. Despite rising crime and riots, Parliamentary commissions had considered and rejected instituting a police force in 1770, 1793, 1812, 1818, 1822, and 1828. A surprising consensus opposed the establishment of a formal police organization, because everyone, property holders and workers alike, feared the force of an organized police. Chateaubriand's tracts against the French police system were read and quoted in England, and it was widely believed that any police system would soon resemble the French. "Tories feared the over-ruling of parochial and chartered rights, and of the powers of the local J.P.'s," E. P. Thompson explains. "Whigs feared an increase in the powers of Crown or of Government; Radicals like Burdett and Cartwright preferred the notion of voluntary associations of citizens or rotas of householders; the radical populace until Chartist times saw in any police an engine of oppression."[11]

Consequently, it was difficult to persuade Parliament to approve a police organization. Peel was, however, an extraordinarily shrewd and flexible politician. Besides reforming the criminal law, he compromised on his police plans and excluded the City of London from their jurisdiction. Moreover, the crime problem was worsening, as was the threat of riot. Some formal, organized means of social control began to seem essential. Perhaps most compelling of all, Peel developed a philosophy of policing intended to assuage public anxiety about possible despotism.

Although the police organizational chart reflected a military structure, it was clear from the beginning that, philosophically, the police were to be altogether distinguishable from the army. Soldiers, who had formerly been responsible for public order, were often hated by the masses of people who might publicly demonstrate or even riot. Peel comprehended the political significance of symbols. Since the Army wore red coats, the police were issued blue coats. If the Army carried rifles and muskets, patrolling police were to carry a baton and no firearm. Yet police needed to be respected for their capacity to employ force, so they were issued tall and distinctive hats, which made them seem to tower over the populace.

Police were taught that the only way they could be successful was to rely on the good will of most of the citizens, but not of course, the criminals. "The basis upon which our theory of the police ultimately rests," Melville Lee wrote, "is the assumption that every lawful act performed by a police officer in the execution of his duty has the sanction and approval of the great majority of his fellow citizens." The very first set of instructions to constables, published in 1829, reminded the new police:

> There is no qualification more indispensable to a Police Officer than a perfect command of temper, never suffering himself to be moved in the slightest degree, by any language or threats that may be used; if he does his duty in a quiet and determined manner, such conduct will probably induce well-disposed by-standers to assist him should he require it.[12]

By the mid-1830s what had formerly been unthinkable was slowly becoming acceptable. Parliament, in an 1834 committee report, pronounced the attainment of an "efficient and systematic establishment of Police."

The committee was especially pleased that "on no occasion since the establishment of the Metropolitan Police has the military authority been called upon to assist the civil power in repressing any disturbance." Twelve years earlier a Parliamentary committee had found that the principles of liberty and police were irreconcilable. The 1834 committee, by contrast, found the new police to be "one of the most valuable of modern institutions."[13] By insisting that the police be unarmed; by designing distinctive uniforms and tall hats; and by demanding exemplary public conduct of officers even when provoked, the police under Peel were able to convey a sense of benign and sensible authority that was especially helpful in dealing with crowds and other forms of protest. Melville Lee chronicles the success of the English policeman's exemplary command of temper in dealing with crowds in its first forty years by citing an extraordinary and compelling statistic. "Personal injuries sustained by the aggressors were invariably less severe than those suffered by the constables," he writes, "though the latter were all men of exceptionally fine physique, and were armed with truncheons."[14]

## RIOTS AND THE AMERICAN POLICE

No American police department was so carefully organized and philosophically grounded as the London Metropolitan Police. "The employment of police in municipal administration was governed not by theory but by convenience," Roger Lane observes in his classic history of the Boston police.[15] Public order and rioting posed a more serious problem than crime in early-nineteenth-century Boston, when the city established its first full-time police department in 1837. The precipitating event was akin to a race riot—roving bands of Protestants destroyed nearly every Irish home on Broad Street.[16]

The police also performed services that are no longer assigned to police, including the enforcement of laws governing refuse and sewerage. When sewer, health, street, and building departments were launched, the role of the police contracted toward the end of the century to what it is today, that is, to enforce the criminal law and to maintain public order.

Boston was by no means the only city to have experienced riots in the early history of America. Like their London contemporaries in the eighteenth century, New Yorkers thought themselves engulfed in what the historian James Richardson called "a rising tide of crime and disorder." Foreigners and Negroes were held responsible, although native-born Americans were accountable for more crime than the foreign-born. Negro slaves made up one-fifth of the population and were, according to Richardson, "an unstable and unruly element often treated with great brutality."[17]

The New York Police, organized in 1845, faced their greatest public disorder challenge during New York City's Civil War draft riots, which occurred on July 12 and 13, 1863. This was the most violent and famous of several anti-Negro riots to take place in the North during the Civil War. New York City had a large Irish population and a powerful Democratic machine, which dominated the city and opposed, or was at the very least unenthusiastic about, fighting the Civil War.

The New York Irish lived in extremely trying conditions. They were crowded into dreary and noisome tenements in a city with the worst disease mortality and highest crime rates in the Western world, a city that was already being compared unfavorably to London as a refuge for criminals. The Irish, who worked in low-skill jobs for marginal wages, were caught between the competition from free black workers and the disdain and exploitation of the Protestant middle and upper classes who employed them. "The Irish," James McPherson concludes, "were ripe for revolt against this war waged by Yankee Protestants for black freedom."[18] The police, who were untrained, could not handle the situation and had to yield to the National Guard and to troops brought in from Gettysburg. With New York's Civil War riot in mind, Charles Loring Brace considered the city possibly the most hazardous venue in the Western world, worse even than London. In New York, he said, rioters seemed inclined "to sack an entire city," whereas in London "rioters merely battered policemen or smashed lamps."[19]

The themes of riot, hostility and brutality against blacks, and black antagonism toward police, fueled even further by ethnic and class conflict, were to arise time and again in the Northern states. Riots were more commonplace than exceptional, with the police, who by the mid-nineteenth century were predominantly Irish and Catholic, siding with the Irish against the blacks.

James Richardson describes a New York City riot in 1900 that grew out of persistent competition between Irish and blacks for jobs in New York City. He recounts a "classical precipitating incident between a black civilian and a white policeman," the sort of episode that was to foreshadow many of the later race riots during the twentieth century. He describes rampaging crowds moving in to beat blacks and police swarming over the area, "cracking the heads of Negroes and doing nothing to restrain the Irish mob." A city commission was appointed to investigate the incident, but lawyers for the Negroes were not allowed to cross-examine witnesses who favored the police. Police witnesses were said to have testified in an impartial manner, while Negro witnesses were said to have displayed strong and bitter feelings while testifying. "That the Negroes were bitter is hardly surprising," Richardson observes, "seeing that the police did not only not protect them against a white mob, did not arrest any of the whites involved, but also indulged in gratuitous clubbing. The police did not stop the white rioters, they joined them."[20]

Lynchings were primarily a Southern phenomenon, while race riots occurred in the North. As Southern Negroes migrated to the Northern municipalities, race riots became common. Although the greatest impact of Negro migration occurred after World War II, the urbanization and migration of Negroes had important consequences after the turn of the century and World War I. Northerners, some of whom were even Abolitionists, began to accept the Southern view of racial domination. In addition to the anti-Negro riots in New York in 1900, there were riots in the Midwest: Springfield, Ohio, 1904; Greensburg, Indiana, 1906; Springfield, Illinois, 1908.

World War I spurred black migration to border and Northern cities and fomented conflict between white and black workers. We have earlier described the flourishing of the Ku Klux Klan in the North after World War I. That was a period when labor unions excluded black workers, and so the migration of Negroes to the North generated great hostility as black workers were hired as a source of cheap labor. When white workers struck, black workers were recruited to replace them, in effect relegating black workers to the hated role of strikebreaker.

Such was the case in a major incident in East St. Louis, Illinois, in 1917, when the labor force of an aluminum plant struck and the company hired black workers as "scabs." The white workers demanded that further migration of blacks to East St. Louis be stopped by the city authorities. There were rumors that a black man had shot a white man in a holdup, that a white woman had been insulted, and that two white girls had been shot. Thousands of whites roamed the streets beating Negroes. The National Guard restored order for a time, until white pickets clashed with Negro workers. Once again whites rioted, and bitter fighting ensued. Negroes were pulled off streetcars, clubbed, and kicked. "Mob leaders," according to the Civil Disorder Commission, "calmly shot and killed Negroes who were lying in blood in the street. As the victims were placed in an ambulance, the crowds cheered and applauded."[21] Eventually, rioters set fire to the entire Negro section of town and left forty-eight dead, hundreds injured, and more than three hundred buildings destroyed.[22]

The famous Chicago riot of 1919 has likewise been attributed to tensions resulting from the black population increase. The number of blacks in Chicago had more than doubled in ten years as a result of the influx of thousands of African-Americans from the South, then referred to politely as "Negroes" or "colored," who were attracted to the city by what seemed to be high wages in the steel mills and slaughterhouses.[23] The meatpacking industry was able to defer unionization by playing on the racial antagonisms of white and black workers, discord which spilled over into the city, especially as housing became scarce. The 1919 riot broke out after a young black man, who was swimming at a beach reserved for blacks, drifted into water reserved for whites and drowned. Blacks, believing he had been struck with a stone, demanded the arrest of a white man. Instead, the police arrested a black and touched off a riot that went on for nearly a week.

Similar riots occurred during World War II. The most famous was perhaps the Detroit race riot of 1943, which began in Belle Isle Park, a large recreational area, especially popular among African-Americans. It is difficult to pinpoint exactly why the riot began, but all observers agreed that racial tensions were high and that fights broke out between white and black youths. The brawl escalated into a couple of days of rioting and looting that lasted until federal troops arrived. The Governor's Committee to Investigate the Riot did not acknowledge the riot's underlying political and economic conditions, laying blame partly on the youthfulness of the rioters, both black and white, and on their "irresponsible" character. The committee also singled out "the positive exhortation by many so-called responsible Negro leaders to be 'militant' in the struggle for racial equality."[24] The committee singled out for special rebuke a statement by A. Philip Randolph, head of the Pullman Porter's Union and a legendary figure in the civil rights movement, appearing in the January 2, 1943, issue of the *Detroit Tribune*. Randolph wrote, in language prefiguring the spirit of the civil rights movement:

> Justice is never granted, it is exacted. It is written in the stars that the darker races will never be free until they make themselves free. This is the task of the coming year.

The committee's conclusions that the police behaved lawfully and competently and that such supposed "Negro militants" as A. Philip Randolph were responsible for the riot were challenged by other presumably militant Negroes, such as Thurgood Marshall, then a young civil rights attorney. Writing in *Crisis* in 1943, Marshall complained that the police "enforced the law with an unequal hand." The police, he maintained, "persuaded" the white rioters, while against Negroes "they used the ultimate in force: nightsticks, revolvers, riot guns, submachine guns, and deer guns." He pointed out that twenty-five of the thirty-four persons killed in the riot were Negroes, seventeen of whom were killed by the police. "This record by the Detroit police," Marshall concluded bitterly, "demonstrates once more what all Negroes know only too well: that nearly all police departments limit their conception of checking racial disorders to surrounding, arresting, maltreating, and shooting Negroes. Little attention is made to check the activities of whites."[25]

The armed forces were segregated during World War II, and blacks in Detroit mistrusted both the service personnel who were stationed in Detroit, some of whom joined in the rioting, and the police. Every observer of the riot, including spokesmen for the police, agreed with Detroit Police Commissioner John H. Witherspoon, who wrote in his "white paper" reviewing the riot: "For many years the Negroes in this and other communities have had an antagonistic attitude toward the police officer." But the National Association for the Advancement of Colored People developed a more specific criticism of the police, accusing them of both ineptitude and racism: "So inefficient is the police force," the Detroit Chapter wrote, "and so many of its members are from the deep South, with their anti-Negro prejudices and Klan sympathies, that the trouble may break out again as soon as the troops leave."[26]

## GHETTO RIOTS IN THE 1960s

Race riots broke out again, and especially hard, in the 1960s, first in the South, then in Los Angeles, Cincinnati, Cleveland, Newark, Detroit, and elsewhere, and the police were, once again, deeply implicated. The U.S. Civil Disorder Commission found that, in the first nine months of 1967 alone, there were 164 disorders of varying intensity. Of these, 41 outbreaks in 39 cities were considered to be major.[27] "Triggering" incidents immediately preceded the riots, but they were usually trivial and could scarcely be identified as the "cause" of the riot. Usually a number of such similar episodes preceded the disorder in what is described as "an increasingly disturbed social atmosphere." Yet of the dozen grievances listed in the more than 1,200 interviews conducted by the commission, "police practices" were ranked number one, followed by "unemployment and underemployment" and "inadequate housing." The least serious issue was "inadequate welfare programs."[28]

As early as 1963, serious disorders broke out in Birmingham; Savannah; Cambridge, Maryland; Chicago, and Philadelphia. Whites and blacks battled each other. More frequently they fought the police. The most violent encounters occurred in Birmingham, Alabama, where police used dogs, firehoses, and cattle prods against civil rights marchers, many of whom were children. Negro victims of white racists and their burned-out residences were shown on television and aroused the sympathy of the nation.

In the spring of 1965 the nation's attention shifted to Selma, Alabama, where a peaceful civil rights march, led by the Reverend Martin Luther King, was forcibly interrupted by police and state troopers.

The Los Angeles riots of August 1965 devastated the Pacific Coast's largest black community, centered in the Watts area of south central Los Angeles. The Los Angeles riot was the nation's most damaging racial disorder since the St. Louis massacre of 1919, and it took a grim toll—not as bad as the riot of 1992 was to exact, but bad enough. Thirty-four persons died, 1,032 were injured, 3,952 were arrested, hundreds of buildings were damaged, and tens of millions of dollars of property damage could be counted.

To the commission headed by John McCone, a businessman and former CIA chief who investigated the facts and causes of the 1965 riot, the "rioters seemed to have been caught up in an insensate rage of destruction."[29] Scholars who studied the riot came to a different conclusion. For example, the social historian Robert Fogelson argued that traditional race riots "were interracial, violent, reactionary, and unsuccessful attempts to change the status quo at a time of rapid social change." By contrast, the riots of the 1960s, he maintained, were not race riots at all but were—"ignoring profound differences in grievances and responses"—articulate protests comparable to the preindustrial riots that led to the formation of the British police, protests against the social conditions of the inner city and the racism of the wider society, especially of the police. The rioters were young, but not "riffraff, that is, the unemployed, ill-educated, and criminal." Rather, Fogelson contended, basing his interpretation on statistical studies of the participants, the rioters were fairly representative young Negro adults who were widely supported within the community and were expressing its grievances.[30] (The perpetrators of the 1992 violence were also not confined to any single age, racial, or ethnic classification.)

The McCone Commission also examined grievances complaining of lack of employment, racial discrimination, and inadequate transportation and educational opportunity. It did not dismiss them. Yet the main expressed grievance of Negro witnesses was with attitudes and behavior of the Los Angeles Police Department. "The bitter schism we have heard evidences a deep and long-standing schism between a substantial portion of the Negro community and the Police Department. 'Police brutality' has been the recurring charge," the commission wrote.[31] That the department's chief, William H. Parker, was singled out as a "focal point" for criticism, mistrusted by Negro witnesses who asserted that he evidenced "a deep hatred for the Negro community," puzzled Commissioner McCone. Chief Parker's statements and previous actions, McCone judged, should not have aroused such intense animosity.

The inconsistency between the hostility expressed toward Parker and the McCone Commission's appreciation of him is understandable. Chief Parker was one of the most respected figures in American law enforcement, an articulate and intelligent man who shaped a department that, throughout the 1950s and the early 1960s, was considered a model for others. To be sure, Parker had stamped out corruption in the LAPD, but he had done so by developing an efficient and semimilitary organization. Journalist Paul Jacobs, writing after the riot, described "The Glass House," now known as the Parker Center, as having the atmosphere of a *General Headquarters,* the directing center of a war. Parker himself wore four stars on the shoulders of his dress uniform and called his deputy chiefs, who wore two stars, *the general staff.* "The department," Jacobs wrote in a brief passage that captured its animating vision, "stresses automatic efficiency and absence of compassion; its greatest concern is with 'fundamental' police work—crime detection and the capture of law-breakers." In retrospect, it is not hard to comprehend why such a department could be admired by a highly placed establishment figure, a former CIA director, and at the same time be berated by the population being policed.

If the Los Angles Police Department was disliked by the city's community of color because of its semimilitary policing philosophy, in other American police departments the rank-and-file cops were perhaps even more overtly racist—and corrupt as well. George Edwards, who served as Judge of the United States Court of Appeals for the Sixth Circuit in 1967, and as Commissioner of the Detroit Police Department from 1961 to 1963, told the Civil Disorder Commission investigators that there had been open warfare between Detroit Negroes and the Detroit Police Department during the 1943 riot and that Detroit was in the 1960s a city waiting for a race riot to happen. Edwards was all too prescient about the possibilities of riot in Detroit when he had written a polite but telling criticism in 1965 in the *Michigan Law Review:*

> Although local police forces generally regard themselves as public servants with the responsibility of maintaining law and order, they tend to minimize this attitude when they are patrolling areas that are heavily populated with Negro citizens. There, they tend to view each person on the streets as a potential criminal or enemy, and all too often that attitude is reciprocated. Indeed, hostility between the Negro communities in our large cities and the police departments, is the major problem of law enforcement in this decade. It has been a major cause of all recent race riots.[32]

Once again, the Detroit riot began with a relatively minor "precipitating incident" on Saturday, July 22, 1967, when the Detroit police raided five "blind pigs," private and illegal after-hours drinking and gambling places that persisted after Prohibition. Judge Edwards and his successor, Ray Girardin, had tried to restructure the police department, but with little success. The "blind pigs" were in an area of high vice and crime, and there were persistent rumors about both police corruption and brutality. John Hersey's book *The Algiers Motel Incident* laid bare the nightstick justice of the Detroit police, who killed three black men and brutally beat two women during the riots. An older officer was interviewed in Detroit about that period for a study of police reform. "Sure there was prejudice," he said as he looked back with mixed feelings "but there was respect too, and that's been lost."[33]

Every city in which a riot occurred could claim a unique style, history, and urban identity. If the Los Angeles Police Department seemed efficient and paramilitary, the Newark, New Jersey Police Department of the 1960s appeared to be its opposite, mired in a history of disorganization, lack of productivity, and overstaffing. Its precinct houses were minimally serviceable ruins, their holding cells Dickensian in their squalor. The department was also, during the early 1960s, corrupt throughout.[34]

Yet the cities experiencing the most massive inner urban riots, Los Angeles, Newark, and Detroit, shared a tragic similarity with respect to underlying social conditions. Across the board, the inner urban areas suffered from low employment, inadequate housing, drug problems, broken homes, and welfare dependency. Riots in such cities have prompted an almost predictable aftermath. A blue ribbon commission of leading citizens is appointed to assess causes and lay blame; the police are usually found to be at fault or are deeply implicated. Thus, the Harlem Riot Commission Report of 1935 reserved its most severe criticism for the police: "The insecurity of the individual in Harlem against police aggression is one of the most potent causes for the existing hostility to authority," it concluded.[35]

Nothing seemed to have changed when, in 1968, the Civil Disorder Commission singled out the police as the activating cause of the urban riots that shocked and mystified the American public. "Harlem, Watts, Newark and Detroit, all the major outbursts of recent years," the report declared, "were precipitated by arrests of Negroes by white police for minor offenses."[36] Twenty years later, Detroit and Newark had taken active steps to introduce community-oriented policing (which we discuss in Chapter 10), but the philosophy of policing in Los Angeles seemed to reflect and to be stuck in the 1960s, the era of William H. Parker. The departure of Daryl Gates and the appointment of Willie Williams as Chief to replace him should move the Los Angeles Police Department into the 1990s era of community-oriented policing.

For many African-Americans in the 1960s, however destructive the riots, they seemed to offer an outlet for expressing deep frustration with the persistent consequences of racism in American society. One major riot, however, was not touched off by police action. Of all the disturbing manifestations of American racism, the assassination of Martin Luther King, Jr., on April 4, 1968, one month after the release of the Civil Disorder Commission report, was undoubtedly the most painful and shocking. Riots broke out throughout the country in its aftermath, following an already rising incidence of disorder in the first three months of the year. Indeed, in April 1968 alone there were nearly as many disorders as there were in the entire disorderly year of 1967; more cities and states were involved than in the previous year; more arrests and injuries occurred in April 1968 alone than in all of 1967, and nearly as much property damage.

Yet, until the Los Angeles riot of 1992, 1968 seemed to be the peak of ghetto rioting in America. Why that should be so is not entirely clear. Certainly the riots were enormously destructive to the communities in which they occurred. Businesses that once served the communities left in their wake, in fear of future riots. Perhaps rioting declined because 1968 also represented a pinnacle in the official response to racial outbreaks. In April alone, more National Guard troops (34,900) were called in than in all of 1967 (27,700), and so were more federal troops (23,700 to 4,800).

As civil disorder declined, the crime rate rose precipitously. During the early 1960s prisons in America had empty beds. Prison populations were to double in the 1970s and triple in the 1980s, even as increasingly punitive sentencing laws were supposed to raise the price of crime. Was there a connection between the decline in civil disorder and the rise in crime? The Civil Disorder Report observed that a large proportion of riot participants were between fifteen and twenty-four years old. This is the age group in the African-American community that has experienced extraordinarily high unemployment rates, often around 50 percent. This age group also has a disproportionately high crime and imprisonment rate and feeds the gangs in Los Angeles and Detroit and New York City.

The commissions that studied the civil disorders and protests of the 1960s—the National Advisory Commission on Civil Disorders and the National Commission on the Causes and Prevention of Violence, and the McCone Commission on the Los Angeles riot—were largely composed of moderate and Establishment figures. Otto Kerner was Governor of Illinois and a product of its politics. The Violence Commission Chair, Milton Eisenhower, was a distinguished educator and brother of the former Republican President and war hero. John McCone had replaced Allen Dulles as head of the CIA. The executive directors were all leading corporate attorneys. Yet every commission recognized that behind the riots were genuine and significant social and economic underpinnings ranging from institutional racism through underemployment to sheer poverty. There have been some attempts in the intervening years to remedy these "causes," but in many respects the social and economic position of African-American youth in south central Los Angeles, Detroit, Newark, Harlem, the South Bronx, and other ghetto communities has worsened. During the 1970s and beyond, it could plausibly be argued, crime, not protest, was the result.

## POLITICAL PROTEST AND PUBLIC DISORDER

The year 1968 was, moreover, extremely turbulent on the political front, as the war in Vietnam became the nation's principal domestic preoccupation. Rodney King's beating is by no means the first instance of police brutality to be captured on film, nor has police brutality during riots been confined to African-Americans. The response of the Chicago police during the 1968 Democratic convention was extensively and dramatically covered by television networks and excoriated by the media with a unanimity comparable to the condemnation of the Los Angeles police who brutalized Rodney King. Yet those who felt the end of the police batons were nearly all white.

Daniel Walker, then a prominent Chicago attorney and civic leader, President of the Chicago Crime Commission and vice president and counsel to Marcor, Inc. (the result of a merger between Montgomery Ward and the Container Corporation of America), was recruited by the National Commission on the Causes and Prevention of Violence to investigate the fierce confrontation between demonstrators and police. Walker, a tall, handsome and consummately self-possessed attorney, the embodiment of the legal establishment, in theory reported to Jerome Skolnick and his Task Force on Violent Protest and Confrontation. Actually, Walker (who was later to become Governor of Illinois) conducted his own investigation, with the assistance of a staff of more than two hundred highly trained interviewers and lawyers, free from any reporting constraints from anyone, including the commissioners. Chicago's Mayor Richard Daley lambasted Walker's report and its interpretations, while the press applauded it, since it confirmed their version of the events.

Walker's report, *Rights in Conflict,* offered a vivid, comprehensive, and politically explosive account of the violence that occurred in Chicago during the Democratic National Convention, August 25–29, 1968. Walker observed that when demonstrators compared the Chicago police to the Soviet troops who were then occupying Prague, news commentators thought the comparison justified and relayed it to the world. "Not since Birmingham and Selma had there been so heated a mood of public outrage," Walker wrote in his report to the Violence Commission.[37]

The police were surely provoked. Obscene epithets, rocks, sticks, bathroom tiles, even human feces were hurled at them. Yet the police, like an urban army run wild, responded with vicious obscenities of their own, plus gas, mace, and club attacks directed partly at bands of provocateurs but also at innocent bystanders, peaceful demonstrators, and large numbers of residents who lived in the convention vicinity or were walking through the parks and streets. Because these persons had "broken no law, disobeyed no order, made no threat," the violence against them was all the more shocking. Reporters and photographers were singled out for assault, and their equipment was deliberately damaged. The response, Walker concluded, "was unrestrained and indiscriminate police violence, on many occasions, especially at night . . . in what can only be called a police riot."[38]

Mayor Daley and other Chicago politicians aside, there was never a question that Walker's damning characterization of the police as having "rioted" was accurate, just as there was never a question that the beating of Rodney King epitomized police brutality. Televised images offer a compelling and unassailable verification of an event. Yet, as Walker's report documented, the violence captured by the television cameras was actually less fierce than the brutality witnessed by bystanders when the cameras were not turned on.

There was an immediate counterresponse to the disorder in Chicago. Many observers thought that, because of the provocation, the demonstrators got what they deserved. Similarly, in Los Angeles, there were the beginnings of a defense of the Los Angeles Police Department and of its philosophy and history of policing. Nobody supported the police brutality shown in the Rodney King videotape, but many supported the system that produced it.

Significantly, the Chicago police riot was not unique, except in these respects: It was extensively covered by every form of media, already primed to report on the great quadrennial event of American politics, the nomination of a presidential candidate; the best journalists from every media form were therefore present, so the quality of the reporting was high; and it was investigated by a national commission with the resources to undertake a thorough inquiry. In fact, similar outbreaks of police violence had occurred earlier in many places, including Los Angeles, San Francisco, New York, and Chicago itself.

The 1960s was one of the most disorderly and confrontational periods in the history of the United States. The civil rights movement, the black militancy movement, the antiwar movement, and student protest all combined to catapult social protest into a familiar and sometimes painful aspect of the domestic American experience. Televised images of urban riots, middle-class peace marches, and campus demonstrations became as familiar to the television watching public as the scenes of battle in Vietnam. Nevertheless, organized protests and demonstrations were, for the most, peaceable, and the police often handled these professionally, even with equanimity.

Much depended on who was protesting and the political context of the protest. White middle-class adults, blacks, or counterculture groups such as the "Yippies," the self-styled Youth International Party of Abbie Hoffman and Jerry Rubin, could expect different treatment. A raucous counterculture group, the predominantly white Yippies specialized in pot-smoking, dancing, and outrageous humor, such as dressing in red, white, and blue to mock the American flag. They staged a rally in Grand Central Station in 1968 and were exactly the sort of protesters the police despised. Naturally enough, they were never given the opportunity to disperse peacefully. The police suddenly appeared and enthusiastically clubbed the Yippie demonstrators, whom they doubtless regarded as wayward, deficient, even treasonous, children.

What happened to the Yippies, however amiss, was understandable, since provocation was the Yippies stock-in-trade. Yet college students fared scarcely better. Cops, who were mainly working-class and patriotic, regarded college student protesters as privileged, ungrateful, and un-American. They could also be provocative, some of them rivaling or even outdoing the Yippies. At Columbia University, a student protester jumped out of a window and landed on a policeman's back. The officer never fully recovered and remained a paraplegic.[39] The more the radical students challenged the authority of the police, the more the cops hated them. The language used by police to describe such student protestors bears no repetition and slight imagination.

Ironically, the animus of police, and their actions, often drove moderate students into the ranks of the radical. Daniel Bell, in 1968 a sociology professor at Columbia University and an editor of the neoconservative journal *The Public Interest,* was appalled by the arbitrary punishment bestowed by the New York Police on the Columbia University campus. It was not so much the violence itself that was so "horrible" to Bell. Ever careful to offer a balanced description, Bell observed that although students bled, not one required hospitalization.

More than anything, however, Bell was shocked by the "capriciousness" of the police. "The police simply ran wild," he wrote, after seeing the cops arrive on campus to tame the student protesters. "Those who tried to say they were innocent bystanders or faculty were given the same flailing treatment as the students." As on many college campuses, the encounter with the police was a first for most of the Columbia College students, who had been raised in affluent suburbs or educated in fashionable private schools. "In a few hours," Bell concluded, "thanks to the New York City Police Department, a large part of the Columbia campus had become radicalized."[40]

The Los Angeles police were similarly violent in dealing with demonstrators in an antiwar protest in 1967, involving a march of thousands, men, women, and children, who were parading to Century City. The protesters were not a threatening crowd, and the decision to disperse them was questionable at best. The paraders had a permit and did not violate its terms. A report prepared by the Southern California American Civil liberties Union concluded that "the order to disperse was arbitrary and served no useful purpose."[41]

Three key and similar words punctuate the descriptions of the above events: "indiscriminate," "capricious," and "arbitrary." The police, it is said, ran wild. What circumstances allow that to happen? One theory might be that it is really not possible to control police in such fast-breaking and tumultuous situations. There is something to be said for that theory, but it does not explain the following report of the discipline and restraint shown by the London Metropolitan Police during a Vietnam War protest:

> The police never drew their truncheons and never showed anger. They held their line in front of the embassy until, as they attackers tired, they could begin to push the crowd down South Audley Street and away from the square. Americans who saw the Grosvenor Square events could not help drawing the contrast with the violence that erupted between the Chicago police and demonstrators at the Democratic Convention in August.[42]

Part of the explanation may lie in the absence of strong personal feelings about the war. In contrast to American police, who had brothers and cousins on the front lines, the London police could consider crowd control a professional matter and a challenge. In the United States, Vietnam War protest was often a conflict between two social classes, especially when the police were pitted against college student protesters, as at Columbia University. Each side felt itself to be morally and politically justified. The students believed they might be drafted to fight in an unwinnable and unjustifiably destructive war, while to cops who had brothers and cousins actually fighting in that war the student protesters were considered unforgivable traitors who were offering aid and comfort to the enemy.

Another part may be ascribed to the tradition of British crowd control. The British police deliberately chose public support rather than overwhelming force as a means of crowd control up to and beyond the Vietnam War period. The traditional British crowd control strategy was grounded in their mistrust of Continental European police, the *gendarmerie,* who symbolized oppressive force maintained to control the populace. By contrast, the British police were considered to be of the people, deriving their authority from a population *consenting* to be policed. London's Police Commissioner Sir Robert Mark is said to have articulated the London Metropolitan Police philosophy of crowd control as follows: "The real art of policing a free society or a democracy is to win by appearing to lose." Mark claimed that the police had during the 1970s even trained a handsome horse to collapse when crowds became unruly, to win the support of the animal-loving British public.[43]

Nevertheless, partly because police had to face protests, marches, strikes, and even terrorism during the 1960s and 1970s; partly because of conflicts with the rising racially diverse population of London; and partly because of the Thatcher government's "law and order" ideology, the London Metropolitan Police and other British forces have largely abandoned their traditional response to crowd control and have militarized their capacity to deal with public order problems. "Without much public debate *de facto* 'third forces' developed," Robert Reiner writes, "specifically trained and readily mobilizable to cope with riots."

In a recent book, the British criminologist Tony Jefferson contrasts the consent response to the 1968 anti–Vietnam War demonstrations with contemporary public order policing in England. In the former, the predominant picture is of "dense cordons of police" in "eyeball-to-eyeball" contact with the demonstrators and, during lulls in the protest, exchanging humorous comments with the protesters. There are, to be sure, aggressive arrests, drawn truncheons, and mounted police in pursuit of demonstrators. But overall, conventionally uniformed officers are joined together to form a "relatively static and defensive human shield."[44]

The 1980s brought about an important shift, as the bitterly contested miners' strike of 1984–85, coupled with inner-city race riots, dictated a change in strategy by the Thatcher government. Instead of a line of bobbies pushing and shoving to hold back protesters, the London police organized Special Patrol Groups and Police Support Units, military-style teams of fourteen to sixteen officers that traveled in vans to the scene of disturbances. Of these tactics, Jefferson is sharply critical, arguing that the training and values of such paramilitary units can scarcely be controlled by legal or democratic structures.[45]

How police should respond to public disorder in a democratic society is sometimes unclear and often controversial. America has experienced numerous protests since the 1960s, especially, in the 1990s, over such issues as homelessness and gay and abortion rights. Often the police have behaved in a manner that police observers themselves have described and would describe as "professional." That term normally is followed by such adjectives as "restrained," "controlled," and "well-planned." Its opposite, "unprofessional" tends to elicit such modifiers as "brutal," "arbitrary," and "run wild."

Some years ago, in an analysis of police riots, the sociologist Rodney Stark argued that such riots were unusual only in their relative infrequency. His analysis is shaped by the concept that whatever ideas and practices cops bring to everyday police work, that is, the culture of policing, is simply exacerbated during riots. Excessive violence against persons who "anger, offend, or frighten" police is commonplace. "What is abnormal about police riots," Stark concludes, "is the number of policemen and civilians involved in a single incident during a relatively condensed timespan."[46]

Although there is no precisely paradigmatic example of police misconduct, an investigation by New York's Chief Robert J. Johnston, Jr., of police wrongdoing in Tompkins Square Park on the evening of August 6, 1988, will serve.[47] The review was prompted by what the chief called "the appalling behavior of some members of the department," which had been captured on film and video taken by the media and private citizens following a demonstration to oppose a curfew in the park. Although not as widely publicized nationally as the beating of Rodney King, the pictures showed, in the words of the chief, "police officers striking demonstrators with night sticks and kicking other apparently defenseless people while they were lying on the ground." Several cops, he added, tried to conceal their identity by covering or removing their shields. There is no question that, ultimately, a number of cops were out of the control of any authority. "The seriousness of individual police officers taking independent unlawful action cannot be overstated," the chief wrote. What happened was that the cultural predispositions of rank-and-file cops took over through a series of administrative blunders, including that of the commanding officer, who left the scene at a critical moment.

Sometimes the "mistakes" made at crowd-control events can result from a combination of cultural predisposition and dysfunctional policy. For example, until recently it was the policy of the San Francisco Police Department to permit officers to ride horses into groups of demonstrators to disperse them. Of course, from time to time a demonstrator would be kicked by a horse and seriously injured, as a demonstrator was at the 1984 Democratic National Convention.

A lawsuit was filed on June 7, 1990, against the San Francisco Police Department accusing officers of beating and insulting demonstrators, and trapping passers-by inside homes during an "ACT-UP" AIDS demonstration on October 6, 1989, on Castro Street, the heart of San Francisco's gay community. The plaintiffs also claimed that the police behavior was part of a pattern of police brutality toward demonstrators, especially as evidenced by the baton thrust of a police officer who broke the spleen of Dolores Huerta, Vice President of the United Farm Workers, during a demonstration. In that case, the Office of Citizen Complaints found the technique of baton thrusting might have been appropriate, but "unnecessary force" was nevertheless used because of the "amount, degree and severity of the force applied." Then Chief (and later Mayor) Frank Jordan disagreed, but nevertheless issued a set of recommendations that would limit the use of baton thrusting only to after "an overt or hostile act on the part of hostile or violent demonstrators." Jordan further recommended "twelve major steps to improve the existing policies," including new written policy statements; reorganization of the Special Operations Bureau; annual review of tactical unit personnel records to weed out the most aggressive police officers; stress evaluation exams for officers; and increased training in crowd control.

Police do not always overreact to crowds. Sometimes they underreact. The most powerful illustration of this was demonstrated in the aftermath of the Simi Valley verdict, when the Los Angeles cops underreacted to flagrant rioting, looting, arson, and assault in Los Angeles, which far exceeded in intensity and damage even the Watts riots of 1965. As of May 2, 1992, police reports placed the number of deaths at thirty-eight, with at least ten killed by law enforcement officers. At least 1,400 injuries were reported, including around two hundred critically injured, while property damage exceeded $500 million. Although not the worst rioting in American history—that occurred in Detroit in July, 1967, leaving forty-three dead, more than 2,000 injured, and $200 million in property damage—the 1992 Los Angeles riots gave new and vivid meaning to the term "domestic problems" during a presidential election year.

Why the police underreacted was not entirely clear, but the evidence suggested that top police officials failed to plan for the possibility of rioting and failed to follow standard procedures once the rioting occurred. Even Los Angeles Sheriff Sherman Block lambasted the Los Angeles Police Department before the County Board of Supervisors, saying that the LAPD's initial response to the riots "didn't make any sense" and that its failure to react lent "an aura of legitimacy" to the looting.[48] The most scathing, even sarcastic, criticism came from an unusual source, California Supreme Court Justice Armand Arabian, a politically conservative member of the court who had been appointed by Republican Governor George Deukmajian. "Where was the protection and the service?" Justice Arabian asked. "Any slower response and we would have seen photos of policemen pasted on milk containers and listed as missing."[49] The Commander of South Los Angeles, Deputy Chief Matthew W. Hunt, said that he and his men did their best, but that the department was simply ill prepared. He said that he had pressed Chief Daryl F. Gates prior to the verdicts to offer greater resources but that he was rebuffed. Consequently, officers in the field were not properly prepared or equipped and were overwhelmed by the exploding violence.[50] A day later, at a press conference, Chief Gates denied that the department was ill prepared and blamed the outbreak of violence on a lieutenant who, Gates alleged, failed to regroup his officers and rout rioters from a South Los Angeles intersection where officers had been pelted by debris. "He had a responsibility to regroup and form up in squads and obtain additional people and go back to that location and clean it up," Gates said. "Unfortunately, he did not do that. That was a mistake. We admit that mistake."[51] In a radio interview, Chief Gates also blamed the police response on politicians and the news media for their unrelenting criticism, which, he said, had turned the department into taking a softer stance to policing. "I'm retiring," said the Chief. "But for those who have their careers to think about, they're looking at what has been said we ought to do, and that's the soft approach to policing."[52] Less than a week later, Stanley Sheinbaum, President of the Police Commission, who had long been at odds with Gates, appointed former FBI Director William Webster and, as his assistant, Police Foundation President Hubert Williams to direct an investigation into the police response.

In sum, it appears that the way police conduct themselves when controlling crowds is not always predictable. Most of the time, police are prepared for crowds and act properly. But protests, especially riots, often confront police with novel problems, and any breakdown in command or preparation augurs trouble. Finally, these events are also political in a larger sense. Whether the issue is the assassination of Martin Luther King, the invasion of Cambodia in 1969, or the Los Angeles riots of 1965 or 1992, the police response is rarely entirely impartial. Partly, it is governed by how politically inspired events are defined for the police by higher authorities within the police department and city government; partly on how the police are trained to deal with crowds and demonstrators—especially those who may be hostile to the police—and partly on the personal political views of police occupying positions on the line. All of these factors are combined with the world view of cops into a sometimes explosive mixture. That world view, the culture of the police, is the subject of the next chapter.

# PART TWO

## *Explanations*

# 5

# *The Culture of the Police*

The police value orthodoxy, loyalty, obedience and silence. . . . The entering recruit's expectations of service and good deeds founders on the cold shoals of the secretive internal culture, the cynicism and the unspoken assignments pushed by the overclass.

—Chief Anthony V. Bouza, Ret.
*The Police Mystique,* 1990

Peter Marsala was a hero cop. During his ten-year career as a New York City Transit Police officer, Marsala was cited for bravery twelve times. On almost twenty occasions he had pulled fallen passengers from between subway cars. Once, when he had ventured above ground to patrol bus routes in a police car, a woman waved him to the side of the road. She pointed at a nearby building that was afire; Marsala ran into it and led twelve women and children out of it to safety.

Marsala's police career came to an end when he was convicted of assaulting a man he had originally arrested for violating the subway's antismoking regulations. According to Marsala, the smoker was handcuffed after he threatened to kill Marsala's partner. "Then," Marsala told the *New York Times,* "he said he was sorry, that he just lost his job, his father was dying of cancer, that his brother was a police officer. I told him that instead of arresting him I was going to give him a summons, and I removed the handcuffs. He turns around and throws a punch. I became so incensed that I pushed him against the wall and punched him three times. In the trial, it came out that as a result he had permanent brain damage." In the trial, Marsala was convicted and subsequently spent twenty-eight months behind bars.[1]

How can police, who can be exemplary heroes, beat people and then even be prepared to lie about it? We shall explain this paradox with the proposition that two principal features of the police role—danger and authority—combine to produce in them a distinctive world view that affects the values and understanding of cops on and off the job, sometimes leading to admirable valor, sometimes to brutality and excessive force, and sometimes to a banding together, a cover-up, a conspiracy of silence. And as Chief Bouza suggests, when police go astray they are often fulfilling the unwritten assignments of those of us who have real and personal property to protect.

## THE WORK OF POLICE

Like a tribe or an ethnic group, every occupational group develops recognizable and distinctive rules, customs, perceptions, and interpretations of what they see, along with consequent moral judgments. Although some recognitions and prescriptions are shared with everyone else—we all live in the same society—others are mandates peculiar to and appreciated only by members of the craft or profession. In this sense, a specific world of work is rather like a game: One has to know the rules in order to play properly. Even those who play games develop such informal rules. "Baseball has evolved a set of unwritten and rarely even spoken norms, mores, habits, and customs," George Will writes. "The code governs such matters as when it is appropriate to pitch at, or very close to, a batter; when and how to retaliate for that; which displays of emotion are acceptable and which constitute 'showing up' an umpire or opposing player; what sort of physical contact, in what sorts of game situations (breaking up a double play at second, trying to score when the catcher is blocking the plate), is acceptable."[2]

Police also live by a profusion of such unwritten rules. Some have been adopted by police all over the Western world, such as customary ways of dealing with people who challenge police authority. Others are the unwritten norms prevailing in a specific department. Every police department has such written and unwritten guidelines, including the proprieties of accepting gratuities, discounts, bribes, or favors.

Even in those American police departments enjoying a reputation for "legalistic" and therefore incorruptible policing, such as the Los Angeles Police Department, police may enjoy certain favors but not others. Basing his observations on years of service as a Los Angeles police officer and detective, Joseph Wambaugh, in his novel *The Choirboys,* observes that one of his characters, an ordinary LA policeman, "had accepted a thousand packs of cigarettes and as many free meals in his time. And though he had bought enough clothing at wholesale prices to dress a dozen movie stars, he had never even considered taking a five dollar bill nor was one ever offered except once when he stopped a Chicago grocer in Los Angeles on vacation."

Like most of us, and unlike economists, police do not make their choices by a rational calculation of comparative economic values. Choices are made instead on moral grounds, developed within the subculture of a police department. Thus, Wambaugh interprets his character's conduct as being in conformity with a distinction the police department and its members made "between gratuities and cash offerings, which were considered money bribes no matter how slight and would result in a merciless dismissal as well as citizen prosecution."[3] Robert Daley describes a similar, but more sinister, dichotomy in *Prince of the City,* his account of a New York City narcotics detective's decline into corruption. Among this work group, the elite Special Investigations Unit, it was permissible to steal drug dealers' money and to reward snitches with some of the drugs seized in raids made possible by their information. Money earned from selling drugs, however, was *dirty.*[4] By the same logic, according to the Knapp Commission's report on police corruption, other officers considered bribes from bookmakers and illegal numbers operators to be *clean money* and would have nothing whatever to do with drug dealers.[5]

We have read and heard boundless and unresolvable arguments over whether, like doctoring, lawyering, or ministering, policing qualifies as a "profession." However that argument might be resolved, there is no question that policing is a defining identity. "The day the new recruit walks through the doors of the police academy," the late New Haven Police Chief James Ahern wrote, "he leaves society behind to enter a profession that does more than give him a job, it defines who he is." "For all the years he remains," Ahern added, "he will always be a cop."[6]

Doctors and lawyers are often at odds, because doctors understand why other doctors behave the way they do, while lawyers are largely unappreciative of the dilemmas of doctors—though they do empathize with other lawyers. So police are not alone in retaining a distinctive outlook on the world and a set of understandings peculiar to the craft of policing, when dealing with *their* occupational environment. As the sociologist Emile Durkheim observed, although a common political community is preeminent in forming our conceptions of morality, our conceptions of right and wrong are mostly shaped by the smaller social groups to which we belong. "Morality is complete," Durkheim wrote, "only to the extent that we feel identified with those different groups in which we are involved—family, union, business, club, political party, country, humanity."[7]

Policing, particularly because it is a twenty-four-hour-a-day identity, generates powerfully distinctive ways of looking at the world, cognitive and behavioral responses which, when taken together, may be said to constitute "a working personality."[8] How working cops learn to see the world around them and their place in it has come to be acknowledged by scholars of police as an indispensable key to understanding their motives, fears, and aspirations, and the moral codes by which they judge themselves and affect the lives of others. "It is a commonplace of the now voluminous sociological literature on police operations and discretion," Robert Reiner observes, "that the rank-and-file officer is the primary determinant of policing where it really counts—on the street."[9]

Social scientists have studied police in every part of the United States, in Europe and in Asia. The fundamental culture of policing is everywhere similar, which is understandable since everywhere the same features of the police role—danger, authority, and the mandate to use coercive force—are everywhere present. This combination generates and supports norms of internal solidarity, or *brotherhood*. Most police feel comfortable, and socialize mainly, with other cops, a feature of police culture noted by observers of police from the 1960s to the 1990s. Every cop has a story about a social occasion where an inebriated guest would make a joking or half-joking remark that deprecated police or set them apart. Most cops prefer to attend parties with other police, where drinking and carousing can occur without fear of civilian affront or knowledge. Cops don't trust other people— which is practically everybody who is not a cop. "They know the public generally resents their authority," Mark Baker says, "and is fickle in its support of police policy and individual police officers. Older officers teach younger ones that it is best to avoid civilians."[10] Different philosophies and styles can be introduced into policing, a point we shall elaborate in our chapter on police administration. Yet cops on patrol in New York, Philadelphia, Los Angeles, London, and Stockholm—with whom we and others have ridden and observed—are remarkably comparable, with kindred occupational perspectives and working personalities.

However skeptically police may be viewed by outsiders, police often identify themselves as a moral force, protecting innocent and productive members of the public against those who would brutalize and victimize ordinary decent citizens. People who are attracted to policing do not see themselves as bullies, nor does the literature on policing suggest that those drawn to it are authoritarian personalities. On the contrary, they tend to be upright, virtuous, and civic-minded. The typical police recruit is white, physically fit and agile, of the lower-middle or working class, male, in his twenties, and with some college education. Following each of the nation's wars, veterans have gravitated toward the police world, where they are welcomed because of their ease with adapting to the uniform; their acceptance of the deference owed to, and the authority of, rank; and their familiarity with firearms. Students of police who have interviewed recruits, or who have themselves been recruits, report a combination of self-interest—it is a good, well-paid, and stimulating job—plus idealism as the motives for entering the occupation.[11]

Those who choose policing as an occupation or profession are not entirely idealistic. Few Americans (or Britons or Swedes, for that matter) appreciate how well paid are their contemporary police in many departments. In no big U.S. city are they better paid than in Los Angeles.[12] Nor do pay scales fully capture the compensation given to high-ranking officers. In a California city with sometimes desperate fiscal problems—not Los Angeles—a captain of our acquaintance disclosed during a luncheon conversation that his 1990 salary, *with overtime,* was $97,000. Additional fringe benefits included the use of a new four-door sedan, plus generous health insurance and pension plans. (So generous was the dental insurance plan that several officers, who were thirty-something, were wearing orthodontic braces.) Twenty Washington, D.C., police officers—most of whom were street cops rather than administrators or supervisors—earned enough in overtime to put their 1990 salaries into six figures.[13] Recruits, of course, do not earn nearly so much, but they do share in the health and benefit packages, and many can look forward to remunerative careers.

Nevertheless, when asked, police recruits point to opportunities afforded by policing to serve the community as their primary motivation.[14] Similarly, Robert Reiner, perhaps the leading contemporary British police scholar, has argued that a sense of mission is a central feature of the culture of police. "This is the feeling that policing is not just a job, but a way of life with a worthwhile purpose, at least in principle."[15] Oddly enough, it may be precisely this sense of mission, this sense of being a "thin blue line" pitted against forces of anarchy and disorder, against an unruly and dangerous underclass, that can account for the most shocking abuses of police power.

## THE POLICE ROLE

A by now sizable number of observers of police have made strikingly similar commentaries about the police role and how it shapes its occupants. Forty years ago Colin MacInnes, a British suspense novelist and student of police, portrayed police as neither the courteous, charming English "bobbies" so often portrayed in the British cinema nor as the equally distorted opposite fantasy, the devil-may-care-adventurer. Instead, MacInnes depicted the cop as an utterly conventional character, averse to risk, who above all prefers a predictable and orderly world. "The true copper's dominant characteristic, if the truth be known," he wrote, "is neither those daring nor vicious qualities that are sometimes attributed to him by friend or enemy, but an ingrained conservatism, an almost desperate love of the conventional. It is untidiness, disorder, the unusual, that a copper disapproves of most of all; more, even, than of crime which is merely a professional matter."[16]

These preferences are understandable, even inevitable. Consider that the world inhabited by cops is unkempt, unpredictable, and sometimes violent. Statistics suggest that the risk of physical injury is greater in many lines of industrial work than in policing,[17] but cops are the ones to whom society accords the right to use, or to threaten to use, force. This assignment and the capacity to carry it out are said to be *the* central feature of the role of police in society. "Whatever the substance of the task at hand," the sociologist Egon Bittner writes, "whether it involves protection against an undesired imposition, caring for those who cannot care for themselves, attempting to solve a crime, helping to save a life, abating a nuisance, or settling an explosive dispute, police intervention means above all making use of the capacity and authority to overpower resistance."[18] Bittner is well aware that police may not use force so very often. But he concludes: "There can be no doubt that this feature of police work is uppermost in the minds of people who solicit police aid or direct the attention of police to problems." It is also in the minds of police, and its potential hazards, however statistically remote, are never far away in the everyday life of the cop.

"You never know what's going to happen," one cop told Connie Fletcher, who interviewed more than a hundred. "The whole world can come to an end in your last few minutes of duty, right before you leave your watch. Or—right before you retire from the force. We've had cases of police officers working their last tour before going on pension. And they've run into a situation where they're killed."[19]

Every arrest, every handcuffing, involves an imposition of force on an essentially unwilling person, no matter how compliant. The volatility of even routine police field investigations—as well as the degree to which they dehumanize their subjects—is made plain by Jonathan Rubinstein:

> [The patrol officer] may not only circumscribe a person's liberty by stopping him on the street, he may also completely violate the suspect's privacy and autonomy by running his hands over the man's entire body. The policeman knows that a frisk is a humiliation people usually accept from him because he can sustain his authority by almost any action he feels necessary.

While he does not frisk people often just to humble them, he can do so; when he feels obliged to check someone for a concealed weapon, he is not usually in a position to request their permission, even if this were desirable.[20]

Understandably, police prefer to encounter citizens who appear stable, well-dressed, normal, and unthreatening enough not to warrant a field patdown. But precisely because they are society's designated force-appliers, police often encounter those who are unstable, ill-dressed, pugnacious, and threatening.

Students of police have frequently remarked upon the *machismo* qualities of the police culture. The typical police recruit is chronologically and temperamentally young, male, and athletic. Recruits often lift weights—like football players—so as to offer a more formidable appearance on the street. They are trained in self-defense. They are trained to handle a variety of offensive weapons, including deadly ones. They are taught how to disable and kill people with their bare hands. No matter how many warnings may be issued by superiors about limitations on the use of force, no matter how much talk about policing as a profession, police training continually reminds recruits that coercive power is a central feature of police life.

## THE PARADOXES OF COERCIVE POWER

The informal norms that cops develop on the street are, at least in part, a paradox noted by William Ker Muir: "The nastier one's reputation, the less nasty one has to be"; in other words, *the stronger one's reputation for being mean, tough, and aggressive, the less iron-handed one actually has to be.*[21] Cops and everyone else understand the reality of this paradox. And whether or not they actually articulate it, cops develop styles of policing in response to it. One style, as we have seen, was used by Southern police to keep the African-American population in a subordinate position. The cops made clear how nasty and brutal they could be. As a result, the Southern black population was, by and large, compliant to the rules of caste subordination.

Nevertheless, when police rely on coercive power to control a population, they may not be successful. The Southern police of the 1930s were agents of the power elite, and those who might have opposed them were virtually powerless. That is no longer true even in the South, and it is certainly not true in Northern cities. However much racist opinions may be expressed in private, the caste society of the Southern United States of the 1930s, a society of legal segregation of the races, is no longer acceptable to the wider society. Our laws will not tolerate explicit racism. Nor can police publicly resort to coercive power without eliciting criticism from portions of the citizenry and the public, and from higher police and public officials. They may also subject themselves to criminal and civil liability.

Furthermore, even when iron-handed law enforcement proves effective in general, it also invites retaliation by those who are *not* intimidated by it. Abusive police must then raise the force ante, employing ever more severe violence to continue to seem formidable. This, for Muir, generates a competing paradox: *Police who rely on coercive force to make the world a less threatening place make it more dangerous place for themselves and for other cops.* Those who are being policed do not distinguish among blue uniforms. All cops come to be defined as brutal, and thus appropriate targets for retaliation. Hated cops are not safer cops.

William Ker Muir was the first police scholar to call attention to the paradoxes of coercive power. He saw how police who are gifted with maturity, empathy, and interpersonal skills could escape from the trap of relying on the threat of force. As he had seen in his observations of police, some accomplished cops could intuit how to handle even the most difficult and potentially explosive situations. He believed that appropriate "training and enhanced language skills" could diminish police violence,[22] a possibility we shall explore in our chapter on police administration.

In connection with the need to use force, police and their culture are a complex and often contradictory combination of cautious values and risky undertakings. Mark Baker, who unscientifically, but convincingly, interviewed more than a hundred cops for his book on police and their lives, concludes that police lean to the right politically and morally. "They advocate the straight and narrow path to right living," he writes. "They believe in the inviolability of the marriage vows, the importance of the family, the necessity of capital punishment." In this, cops are in tune with the constituency that elected Ronald Reagan and George Bush to be President of the United States, that most politically conservative portion of the majority of Americans whom Anthony Bouza calls "the overclass."

The occupational vision of police and its culture is grounded in these beliefs. But cops do not necessarily abide by the apple-pie-and-motherhood values that they assert. As with most human beings, spoken values are often an aspiration, not necessarily something to embody. At least half the married male police officers whom Baker interviewed told him about their girlfriends and mistresses. After a few years on the job the cops interviewed developed a distinctive, but scarcely exemplary, hierarchy of wrongfulness: "dead wrong, wrong but not bad, wrong but everybody does it."[23] Skepticism, cynicism, mistrust—all are words observers of police apply to them and that they apply to themselves, especially after years on the job.

Suspicion and skepticism are especially congruent with the capacity to use force and enforce the laws. We all make distinctions between the normal and the abnormal, the safe and the unsafe, the appropriate and the inappropriate. Police are, however, specially trained and required to make these interpretations. The distinction between what is "normal" and what is threatening or "abnormal" usually depends upon the context in which it appears. Is a man with a gun in a bank "abnormal?" That depends. The possession of a deadly weapon is appropriate for a bank security guard, but not for an armed robber. Similarly, we expect to see an electric light switched on to illuminate a room at night. But if the room is in a warehouse, and it is two in the morning, the policeman must understand whether the lighted room signifies that someone is, as usual, working late, or whether the warehouse is being burglarized. We want police to draw such distinctions and to act upon them.

Complaints about police conduct do not usually arise because police are apprehending burglars in the middle of the night, or robbers who are holding up a bank. Trouble arises out of social interactions, especially when cops encounter people who may not be engaging in criminal activity, but whose conduct suggests that they might be, or might be the sort of people who would if they could. A police manual cautions police to attend to the unusual, listing among the persons and conditions for which to be especially watchful and cautious: "suspicious persons known to the officer from previous arrests, field interrogations, and observations"; "persons who loiter about places where children play"; "known trouble-makers near large gatherings"; and "cars with mismatched hub caps, or dirty car with clean license plates (or vice versa)." Years ago, in our studies of police, one of us observed that because police work requires cops continuously to be alert, they become much attuned to deviations from the normal, especially those suggestive of potential violence. As a necessity and a consequence of maintaining this high state of readiness, police develop a perceptual shorthand to identify certain kinds of people as "symbolic assailants," that is, as persons whose gestures, language, or attire the police have come to identify as being potentially threatening or dangerous. This sort of apprehension and sensitivity sets police apart and tends to isolate them from those whom they are policing. Such isolation may be especially pronounced when police are patrolling in vehicles, rather than on foot, since the vehicle segregates the police from the people who are being policed. Well before community and problem-oriented policing became as acceptable as it has become in some police circles, the 1967 Civil Disorder Commission advised patrolmen to get out of their cars, into the neighborhoods, and on the same beat or assignment long enough to know the people and the neighborhood's prevailing conditions.

But even when police know the people with whom they are dealing, they still must distinguish the known from the unknown or unfamiliar. How much latitude police enjoy in making such distinctions and acting upon them has been a continuing issue in the constitutional law of search and seizure. When police do not have grounds for an arrest, do they have the right to stop and question suspects without their consent?

## SUSPICIOUS PERSONS

The Supreme Court addressed that issue for the first time in the landmark case of *Terry* v. *Ohio*.[24] There, a police officer saw three men who were apparently "casing" a store for a stickup. The officer approached the men, asked them who they were, and when they mumbled an answer, patted them down and found weapons on two of them. Justice Earl Warren, often tagged a "liberal" but actually an experienced former prosecutor sensitive to the needs of the police, wrote an opinion that artfully evaded the "probable cause" requirements of the Fourth Amendment. The holding of the case is especially deferential to the need of the police to be suspicious in the interests of crime prevention, particularly where the crime may endanger the cop or members of the public. The opinion, rich with possibilities for interpretation, affirms the central features of the police role. It suggests that police are supposed to be suspicious of "unusual conduct" denoting "criminal activity" by possibly "armed and dangerous" criminals who threaten "safety."

But suppose a cop observes unusual conduct that seems to her or him to denote criminal activity merely because it violates a social preconception or prejudice? Such was the case of Edward Lawson, who perfectly fulfilled the stereotype of a burglar. Tall, angular, energetic, black, and athletic-looking, Edward Lawson could have been taken for a guard or small forward for a college basketball team, except for one thing. He had let his hair grow out naturally into long, coiled "dreadlocks."

Given his singular appearance, when Lawson took nocturnal walks in lily-white San Diego neighborhoods, he would often be stopped by cops, who would ask for his ID. Lawson invariably refused to identify himself on grounds that there was no reason to stop him since he was engaged in no criminal activity and was not planning to commit a crime. Nevertheless, he was arrested fifteen times by the San Diego police between March 1975 and January 1977. He was prosecuted only twice, was once convicted; the second charge was dismissed.

From what we know of police culture we can only speculate on how the cops involved might have viewed Lawson. John Van Maanen, who studied police in a place he called "Union City," a large metropolitan force employing more than 1,500 uninformed officers, developed a tripartite typology to categorize how police viewed the citizens with whom they came into contact.[25] Like other social scientists who had studied the police, Van Maanen came to understand that such "typifications," and the reasons behind them, are an important guide to understanding police behavior.

Suspicious persons, the first category of Van Maanen's typology, are those who, like Lawson, seem incongruous in their surroundings. Van Maanen says that when the police stopped such persons they were usually treated in a brisk, professional manner, as Lawson, in fact, was. (Once Lawson began to speak, it must have been plain to the San Diego police who arrested him that Lawson was well-spoken and articulate, however eccentric his appearance might have seemed.)

Lawson, who was in fact not a burglar but a disk jockey and promoter of rock music concerts, understood perfectly well what the police reaction would be to someone of his appearance.[26] Lawson sued to have the California statute requiring that persons provide "credible and reliable" identification to police declared unconstitutional. To the surprise of many legal experts, Lawson, who himself undertook and completed much of the legal research, won his case and later collected substantial civil damages from the City of San Diego. Justice O'Connor found that the statute Lawson had challenged was overbroad and vested police with "virtually complete discretion . . . to determine whether the suspect has satisfied the statute." In effect, Lawson had capitalized on his understanding of the police assignment to protect property, plus his realistic assumptions about how San Diego police would respond to a black man with dreadlocks walking about in a white neighborhood in the middle of the night.

In reality, of course, the environment police inhabit is extraordinarily complex, and legal rules stemming from cases like *Lawson* have an effect on only a small part of the normative climate of policing. Even after the *Lawson* case, police were not forbidden to ask a strolling citizen for identification, but if he refused, they could not arrest him for refusing.

Police have developed all sorts of strategies for legally extracting information from citizens. Cops can usually find some pretext to stop an automobile, particularly in inner-city neighborhoods where automobiles often have visibly defective equipment. Once a stop is made, the officer can ask to search the car. At that point the driver, usually confused as to "rights," perhaps frightened, often intimidated, rarely refuses.

In carrying out the war on drugs, police have taken to stopping individuals in airports, train stations, and bus depots when their demeanor suggests in some vague way, that they are carrying illegal drugs. Police will ask entirely innocent persons for their identification and will even ask to search their belongings without any probable cause to believe they have committed a crime, or even without a reasonable suspicion that they are engaged in criminal activity. So long as the stopped person feels that he or she is free to leave, the provisions of the Fourth Amendment forbidding "unreasonable searches and seizures" have not been violated. Fourth Amendment jurisprudence has it that a person who feels free to leave has not been "seized;" and cannot therefore have been *unlawfully* seized.

In Broward County (Fort Lauderdale), Florida, Sheriff's Department officers developed a program of boarding buses at scheduled stops and asking passengers for permission to search their luggage. Whatever pressure passengers feel in a terminal or depot must be heightened on a bus. Here is how the Florida Supreme Court described what happened in the case of Terrence Bostick:

> Two officers, complete with badges, insignia and one of them holding a recognizable zipper pouch, containing a pistol, boarded a bus bound from Miami to Atlanta during a stopover in Fort Lauderdale. Eyeing the passengers, the officers admittedly without articulable suspicion, picked out the defendant passenger and asked to inspect his ticket and identification and both were returned to him as unremarkable. However, the two police officers persisted and explained their presence as narcotics agents on the lookout for illegal drugs. In pursuit of that aim, they then requested the defendant's consent to search his luggage.[27]

Bostick denied that he "consented" to the search, while the police maintained that he did. The Florida Supreme Court said that any encounter on a bus is a "seizure" *per se,* because people who ride buses scarcely are free to leave. If they do, they are stranded. Consequently, the Florida court ruled that cops cannot search luggage on a bus unless they can articulate why they thought the person they searched was holding drugs or some other contraband.

But the United States Supreme Court overruled the Florida Court. Justice O'Connor said that people on buses are not necessarily intimidated when cops in raid jackets and guns ask questions of them. She recognized that people on buses are restrained but rejected the "not free to leave" analysis on which Bostick relied to win his case in the Florida Supreme Court.

Justice O'Connor held that "in such a situation, the appropriate inquiry is whether a reasonable person would feel free to decline the officers' requests or otherwise terminate the encounter," and sent the case back to the trial court to make that determination.

Did Bostick consent? Would a trial court be able to tell? That depends on what we mean by consent. Fourth Amendment jurisprudence and social reality are scarcely commensurate. Those who have studied police have observed that rarely will people who are stopped by police officers refuse to show their ID, and rarely even understand when they are not required by law to show it, such is the authority that police ordinarily command. Cops know this, and also learn how to manipulate such encounters so as to appear forceful in the encounter, using a *command* voice, while later testifying that the person "volunteered" to be searched when it was clearly in their self interest not to be.

Paradoxically, people in the "overclass" may be especially likely to respond politely to a police officer's request for information about themselves or others. They fit the description of what Van Maanen calls "knownothings," ordinary citizens who are not police and who know nothing of the world police inhabit, that peculiar spot on the bridge between the *first America* and the *second America*. These are the good citizens for whose benefit police will present a courteous and efficient performance.

Besides, those who comply with police requests for identification are probably discerning to do so, regardless of Constitutional prerogatives. For those who are carrying drugs, it would, of course, be more prudent to decline a police officer's request to search their bags. But being questioned by police is often intimidating. This is especially so in bus sweeps since, as the dissenters argued in Bostick, such sweeps are inherently "inconvenient, intrusive, and intimidating."

Imagine standing up to armed police in that situation. Most of us learn early to respect the authority of a police officer, and that it is impolitic for a citizen to challenge that authority. When he or she does, especially when he does, he may find himself occupying Van Maanen's third and most evocative category, that of "the asshole," that is, a person who denies, resists, or questions the authority of the police. The following story, offered by Van Maanen, exemplifies the category: A cop stops a motorist for speeding and politely asks for license and registration. "Why the hell are you picking on me," says the motorist, "and not somewhere else looking for real criminals?"

"Cause you're an asshole," replies the policeman. "But I didn't know that until you opened your mouth."

Paul Chevigny similarly explains the origins of much police brutality in

*Police Power,* his classic study of police abuses in New York City in the 1960s.[28] Following an extensive two-year study of complaints against police, Chevigny identified as "the one truly iron and inflexible rule" he could deduce from the cases he reviewed was this: "any person who defies the police risks the imposition of legal sanctions, commencing with a summons, on up to the use of firearms."[29]

Chevigny goes on to describe a three-step process leading to excessive force. Step One involves a perception by police of a challenge to authority. Those who take the police on high-speed chases are, of course, among the most extremely confrontational. But Chevigny reports instances of much lesser defiance, such as merely questioning an officer. Such a person, in the New York of the 1960s, was called a "wise guy," a term that seems in retrospect antiquated and mild but conveys the appropriate connotation. The speaker is thought by the police officer to be presenting himself as superior to the cop. In the parlance of the police studied by Van Maanen, he is said to be an "asshole, creep or bigmouth," or any number of other dismissive names used by cops to describe a person who resists police authority.[30]

In Step Two, when police have so defined the malefactor, as in, "So you're a wiseguy," an arrest, according to Chevigny's respondents, would almost invariably follow.

Whether it did or not depended on the offender's response (Step Three). If the citizen admitted that he was, in fact, a wiseguy, or turned polite and complied with the officer's request, he was usually released. If he persisted in defying police authority, an arrest would typically follow. If he further persisted, he would be taught a lesson of compliance by being beaten, and then charged with resisting arrest, in addition to the original charge.

Albert Reiss, Jr., who with Donald Black conducted a systematic observational study of police coercion for the President's Commission on Law Enforcement and Administration of Justice, reported that, of the incidents of excessive force recorded by observers, nearly half occurred when the victims verbally defied police authority. The authority that was defied was not "official" but the personal authority of the individual officer. Reiss was surprised to find that in 40 percent of the cases of what the police considered open defiance, the police never executed an arrest, nor did they file charges of resisting arrest to "cover" their improper use of force. Reiss inquired further into what police interpreted as defiance. "Often he seems threatened," Reiss observed, "by a simple refusal to acquiesce to his own authority. A policeman beat a handcuffed offender because, when told to sit, the offender did not sit down. One Negro woman was soundly slapped for her refusal to approach the police car and identify herself."[31]

Recently, one of us was riding alongside a patrol officer in a Midwestern city. The officer saw a young white woman seated behind the driver's seat of a car parked in the area of a predominantly black housing project noted for drug dealing. Since the cop suspected that the woman was picking up drugs, the officer waited until she left, determined to stop her for something, anything, such as running a red light, so he could search her car. He noted that one of the taillights on her car was slightly damaged and stopped her for that. He checked out the car on his computer and discovered that the owner, her boyfriend, had failed to pay three parking tickets.

The officer asked to search the car, and she reluctantly consented, clearly unaware of what rights she had, if any. He found no drugs, and she denied ever using or selling them. She did act annoyed, talked back to the officer, and complained that she was being harassed. In return for her seeming insolence, the officer committed no act of brutality but had the car towed, arrested her for a traffic violation, and booked her at the police precinct. In reality, she had committed two police cultural crimes: She was a white driver in a black neighborhood where drugs were sold, and she had challenged the authority of the officer, a serious transgression in the police cultural statute book, where it is an offense to talk back to a cop.

Chevigny was sensitive in his three-step paradigm to two other important considerations. First, an ordinary citizen begins to assume the status of a pariah only when actively defying the police, while an outcast group member may be presumed to be a potential offender. Consequently, when such a person is arrested, the arrest can be considered the ethical, if not the legal, equivalent of arresting a criminal. The arrest can be justified on grounds that even if the outcast has not committed a crime this time, he has been guilty many times in the past.

Second, Chevigny notes that it also may be more difficult for members of minority groups to show the submissive qualities middle-class people learn to use to when dealing with authorities. He further observes that the words "Sorry, Officer" often feel like galling words of submission to the downtrodden and are especially hard for African-Americans to say. "The combination of being an outcast (step one)," he writes, "and refusing to comply in step three is explosive; thereby hangs the tale of many police brutality cases."[32]

## THE UNDERCLASS

Chevigny's is a book of the 1960s and reflects the deep social divisions of those troubled and turbulent years. The economic and social conditions of America's inner-city ghettos have cruelly worsened in the intervening years. "The urban black poor of today," Wacquant and Wilson wrote in 1989, "differ both from their counterparts of earlier years and from the white poor in that they are becoming increasingly concentrated in dilapidated territorial enclaves that epitomize acute social and economic marginalization." This "hyperghettoization" has brought in its wake a tangle of unfathomed social miseries, including crime, drug use and sale, high rates of unemployment, high teenage pregnancy rates, the highest homicide rates in American history, and unprecedented homicides and interpersonal violence among young black males. For several years, black-on-black homicides have been the leading cause of death for young black males.[33]

No scholar on any part of the political spectrum denies this reality, although scholars differ considerably as to how to interpret its significance for social policy and whether the term "underclass" inappropriately mislabels and demeans all residents of inner-city areas. Astute scholars of poverty, such as Michael Katz, are supremely sensitive to the politics of its discussion. Most American political discourse, he observes, has transformed poverty into an issue of "family, race and culture rather than inequality, power and exploitation."[34]

Structural theorists and liberals (for whom William Julius Wilson has become the most prominent spokesman) detail how economy, society, and history have imposed severe limits on the life chances of inner-city African-Americans.[35] They highlight such *causal* factors as the loss of jobs in a postindustrial economy; the internationalization of manufacturing and the associated flight of capital and jobs to low-wage havens; the loss of housing and concomitant family stability; the lack of connection to employment or business opportunity; the impoverishment of educational facilities; and the legacy of racism.[36]

If liberals tend to stress the environmental and historical roots of poverty, conservatives (among whom Charles Murray is one of the most prominent spokesmen) stress the ethical and cultural inadequacies of "the underclass." Murray defines the "underclass" as the parasitical poor, a subclass of the impoverished "who chronically live off mainstream society (directly through welfare or indirectly through crime)." To Murray, the underclass are people who *choose* to be bad. Their malfunctioning is attributable primarily to moral failure: "They characteristically take jobs sporadically if at all, do not share the social burdens of the neighborhoods in which they live, shirk the responsibilities of fatherhood and are indifferent (or simply incompetent) mothers."

Although liberals locate the underlying *causes* of antisocial and criminal behavior in the inner city in structural unemployment, inadequate education and housing, and blocked opportunity linked to historical racism, such explanations, Robert Kuttner says, "lose much of their resonance against the reality of a junkie, a middle-class kid panhandling, or a crack-using teen mother, or other seemingly irresponsible forms of urban low-life."[37]

In fact, both visions of the underclass can be justified. The behavior of young men who assault strangers, neighbors, and friends, and who deal drugs on the street and in housing projects, are harmful and destructive of self and community. Former Washington, D.C., Police Chief Isaac Fulwood, himself a product of a poor black District of Columbia family, has seen the drug culture wreak havoc with that area's public safety and civic values. "1988 changed us," he observed. "We can never go back to being what we were. It's not just the volume of murders, it is the viciousness—the kinds of wounds that you see—where young people have had their kneecaps shot off, had their testicles shot off. We charge these cocky kids with taking another person's life and there's no remorse."[38]

What they are, however, is not adequately described by such terms as "culture of poverty" or "the underclass," which in any case should encompass the homeless and the deinstitutionalized mentally ill. Instead they express capitalism run amok, a robber baron behavior of the streets. The street world, especially the drug trade, is harsh and dangerous. For many young men, especially gang members who live in that assertive and lawless world, the appearance of vulnerability may invite aggression. Gang members, Martin Sanchez Jankowski reports, are defiant individualists and outlaw capitalists. They cannot call the police when they are robbed or sue for breach of contract when they are cheated. Like nations that stock an oversupply of nuclear weapons in the interest of deterrence, outlaw capitalists need to present an impenetrable exterior to those seen as threatening their status, honor, or economic advantage, especially when they are marketing drugs.[39] The drug business is vividly described by Terry Williams, a sociologist who spent more than 1,200 hours over a period of five years observing a primarily Dominican drug gang in Washington Heights, the upper Broadway locus of Manhattan's drug scene. While not denying that the "cocaine kids" are antisocial dealers responsible for violence and death, Williams also portrays them as "struggling young people trying to make a place for themselves in a world few care to understand and many wish would go away."[40]

Cops usually resonate to what they see happening in front of them, not to underlying causes or sociological explanations, although many cops are surprisingly sensitive to these. Yet, no matter how discerning, when doing their policing job cops do not interpret *why* someone is mugging, raping, or selling drugs on the street, just that they are doing it or are threatening to do it. If cultural beliefs shape the working personalities of police, as we have argued they do, the cop, like the majority of Americans, is unlikely to define the street drug dealer as a victim of inequality, structural unemployment, and exploitation. What the cop perceives is a bad and dangerous person who preys on the *deserving* poor and exacerbates the social conditions found in the inner cities. Such preconceptions profoundly influence police behavior, especially their use of force.

Still, problems of excessive force rarely arise when police address actual crime and criminals. A clean, straightforward apprehension of a robber or of a drug dealer who has been busted following an undercover police officer's "buy" is rarely an occasion for exercising excessive force. Abuses occur when police develop two visions of their work that are often a prelude to excessive force. One is described by the Christopher Commission as a "siege mentality."[41] The other is "the Dirty Harry" vision, which rationalizes vigilante justice.

## THE SIEGE MENTALITY

In the course of its investigation, the Christopher Commission, the 1991 blue-ribbon commission headed by Warren Christopher to investigate the LAPD following the Rodney King beating, found general agreement among all sources, from senior and rank-and-file police to the general public, that the LAPD reflected an organizational culture, based on its time-honored notion of "professionalism," that "emphasized crime control over crime prevention and isolated the police from the communities and the people they serve."[42] This organizational culture insisted on both the aggressive detection of such major crimes as murder, burglary, and auto theft and a rapid response to calls for service. Officers were rewarded for the number of calls they handled and arrests they made, as well as for being "hardnosed." As a result, the LAPD consistently outperformed other big-city police departments in the number of violent crime arrests per officer, but at the risk of creating what the Commission calls a "siege" (us–them) mentality that alienates the officer from the community. Obviously, not every police department encourages a siege mentality. But the Los Angeles Police Department's policing style for many years served nationally as an important model of police professionalism. Consequently, its vision of hardnosed and impersonal policing influenced the training of thousands of American cops—so much so that its vision and values became entrenched as an element of traditional police culture.

## THE DIRTY HARRY PROBLEM

The Dirty Harry dilemma was so named by the sociologist Carl B. Klockars, who drew its name from a 1971 Warner Brothers film. "Dirty Harry" Callahan, played by Clint Eastwood, is on the trail of a psychopathic killer who has kidnapped a fourteen-year-old girl and buried her with just enough oxygen to keep her alive for several hours. Harry meets the kidnapper with the ransom. The kidnapper reneges on his bargain, wounds Harry's partner, and escapes. Harry manages to track him down, illegally searches his apartment, finds guns and other evidence of his guilt, and captures the kidnapper on a football field. He shoots the kidnapper in the leg and tortures him, twisting the injured leg, into revealing where the girl has been hidden. Unfortunately, she is already dead, and the killer must be set free because none of the evidence—the gun, the confession—was legally obtained.

Released in 1971, *Dirty Harry* could properly be interpreted as a right-wing attack on "legal technicalities." But, as Klockars astutely saw, it also raises a fundamental problem constantly confronting police, namely, "When and to what extent does the morally good end warrant or justify an ethically, politically, or legally dangerous means for its achievement?"

The Dirty Harry dilemma faces every cop in the course of his or her career, and its ultimate resolution is always problematic and subject to hindsight criticism. Extralegal resolution of the Dirty Harry dilemma is difficult enough when the "bad guy" is an identifiable and factually guilty individual. It is most problematic when the criminal is not an individual but a loosely defined gang or criminal organization, where the consequences of a mistake can be tragic for innocent individuals or bystanders, and where a gut-level racism can be imputed to the officers involved.

This was the case in the LAPD's Gang Task Force raid in South Los Angeles on August 1, 1988, which by mid-June 1991 had cost Los Angeles taxpayers $3.4 million. Police believed that four apartments at 39th Street and Dalton Avenue were gang-controlled "crack" cocaine houses. Police Captain Thomas Elfmont, who was in charge of the raid, was accused of having urged his officers to render the apartments "uninhabitable" and was later charged in a criminal court of "aiding and abetting vandalism," a misdemeanor.

According to testimony, police believed that the Rolling 30s, a gang associated with the Crips, were selling drugs and terrorizing a family that lived between two apartment buildings where the drugs were being sold. They also believed that the drug dealers were heavily armed and had threatened a family that had put up security lights. The police decided to raid the apartments and destroy the young drug-dealing gangsters. Three days before the raid, the captain in charge held a roll call and told the assembled officers to "hit hard." He used such words as "leveled" and "uninhabitable" to describe how the apartments should appear after the raid.

Thus advised, police raided the apartments with guns and axes. Nobody was killed, but the police methodically destroyed beyond recognition the four apartments where the "search" occurred. They broke all the toilets, tore them from the floor, and left water running everywhere. They smashed in plaster walls with sledge hammers, breaking everything in sight, including TV sets, VCRs, and typewriters. Bedroom and living room sets were smashed, couches and chairs were cut, bottles of wine and jars of baby food were emptied on clothes and bedding. Phone wires were cut, light fixtures were destroyed, and "LAPD Rules" graffiti were spray-painted on the walls. According to eyewitnesses, the thirty-three people who were brought to the Southwest Division police station "were forced to whistle the theme from the old Andy Griffith television show, and to run a gauntlet of police officers who allegedly struck them with fists and flashlights."[43]

But no gang members lived in the Dalton Avenue apartments, where scarcely any drugs were found—just a small amount of cocaine and marijuana—and no guns. Captain Elfmont and two other police officials were charged with crimes but were ultimately acquitted of "aiding and abetting" vandalism, because, the prosecutor said, the LAPD's "code of silence" prevented police who were eyewitnesses from testifying in court about what had actually happened.

## THE CODE OF SILENCE

We have both heard comments that, in near mystical terms, describe or speculate about a highly conspiratorial police code of silence. Those who propound this theory assert that, like gangsters who understand that death is the penalty for violations of *omerta*—the Mafia rule of absolute secrecy—police officers risk their lives when they violate their brotherhood's unwritten regulations.

Frequently used in support of this theory is the movie version of Frank Serpico's efforts to get action on his allegations of police corruption. The film begins with an incident where Serpico is shot in circumstances that make it appear that he was set up by his colleagues to be killed. The evidence does not support this interpretation.[44]

Frank Serpico was shot while on a drug raid in what New York cops knew as "Brooklyn North," one of two umbrella commands into which the NYPD had divided the city's most populous borough. He got there when

Brooklyn North narcotics officers—whose jurisdiction included ten police precincts and a resident population of more than 840,000—learned late one night that the services of a Spanish-speaking undercover officer might help them make a drug buy and arrest. They called the NYPD's Narcotics Bureau's central headquarters in Manhattan and asked whether any Spanish-speaking narcotics officers were on duty in the city at that late hour. Headquarters then called Serpico, who left his assignment in "Brooklyn South," which included the sixteen precincts and nearly 2 million residents of the borough's other end, to help in the Brooklyn narcotics bust.

When Serpico arrived, he met officers who knew him only by reputation. They had never previously worked with him, had not been implicated by him in any misconduct, and never were. They worked in a unit—Brooklyn North Narcotics—that had nothing to do with the corruption that Serpico had exposed in his anti-gambling squad across the city in the Bronx. Indeed, he had been assigned to Brooklyn South Narcotics because it was as far removed as possible from his old assignment.

The officers planned a "buy-and-bust" in which Serpico would go to an apartment door, use code words in Spanish that had been provided by the Brooklyn officers' informant, and buy a small amount of heroin while his colleagues remained out of sight a few feet away, ready to assist. This would all be done while Serpico stood at the threshold of the apartment's front door, which, in the tradition of small-time urban heroin dealing, would be opened only far enough to accommodate a short chain of the familiar type that serves as a failsafe lock by connecting the door to its frame. Once Serpico had completed the buy, he was to put his shoulder to the door, identify himself as a cop, signal his colleagues, and, with their help, force the door open and *bust* the drug dealer.

At the time, buy-and-bust operations were the routine procedure of the NYPD's narcotics units. They were also very dangerous. In the first four months of 1971, the year in which Serpico was shot, two detectives on two similar operations were beaten unconscious and robbed. Another was shot and wounded. One killed a suspect in a gun duel. Another detective shot a man who had tried to rob him with a weapon that turned out to be a starter's pistol. Another officer shot and wounded one of three suspects who attacked him with lengths of two-by-four planks. Another, shot at twice by a suspect, grabbed the suspect and engaged in a struggle; the suspect's gun discharged between the two men, and the suspect was shot in the leg.[45]

Things went wrong in Serpico's buy and bust as well. After making his buy, Serpico yelled that he was the police and tried to force his way into the apartment. The dealer slammed the door, trapping Serpico's head, arm, and shoulder between it and its frame. Serpico managed to unholster his gun, but the dealer shot him in the face and fled out a window. Several hours later the dealer was found at another location, pulled his gun on the cops who had come to get him, and was shot, wounded, and arrested.

These facts do not support the conclusion that the cops who were with Serpico put him into harm's way and intentionally left him there to be shot. Those officers didn't even know Serpico. While they may have wished that headquarters had sent them someone other than this *troublemaker* whose name was then vaguely floating around their department, their professional involvement with him would have ended with this single case. We agree with Patrick V. Murphy, New York's Police Commissioner at the time Serpico was shot. Murphy writes: "I do not believe Serpico was set up, and, even more, I do not believe that Detective Serpico believes it either."[46]

Further, although it probably has occurred at some point in American police history, we know of no other cases in which police have punished those who betrayed the code of silence with anything as extreme as a shooting. Instead, the code—and there is a code—typically is enforced by the threat of shunning, by fear that *informing* will lead to exposure of one's own derelictions, and by fear that colleagues' assistance may be withheld in emergencies.

In our experience, this last incentive to silence—denial of help in street emergencies—is more often imagined than real. Officers who by their own admission "do not see eye-to-eye" with their work groups frequently complain that colleagues intentionally fail to respond promptly to their calls for urgent assistance. On close examination, however, these complaints usually reflect a variety of paranoia that itself accounts for these officers' unpopularity among their peers. In other words, some officers perceive situations as more threatening than they are (or, through bungling, make them worse than they began), call urgently for help, and draw the rapid response of colleagues who arrive and can't figure out what all the fuss was. After a few such incidents, such officers' credibility is damaged, and their colleagues come to regard their calls for help like that of the boy who cried wolf too often.

The first two disincentives to violating the code of silence—shunning and exposure of one's own derelictions—are real and are discussed further in Chapter 6. For now, having claimed that the police code of silence is not a mafia-style life-or-death pact with the devil, we shall confine ourselves to some observations about what the police code of silence is.

Most important, a code of silence is not unique to the police. In every identifiable group, there exists an unspoken understanding that one reports on members' misconduct only at some risk. The sociologist and police scholar Albert J. Reiss, Jr., has suggested that even his Yale University students share such a set of understandings.[47] In the pressure cooker of elite academic institutions, Reiss points out, students sometimes are tempted to cheat to maintain the grades necessary for a big job or a slot at a prestigious professional or graduate school. On occasion, other students become aware of such cheating but, despite academic codes of honor, rarely will call their peers' misconduct to official attention.

In our own university discussions of the code of silence, we regularly ask for students who have become aware of classmates' cheating at some point in their educational careers to raise their hands. Invariably, almost every hand in the class is raised. When we ask for only those who have called such cheating to teachers' attention and have been willing to be publicly identified as accusers, virtually every raised hand is lowered.

The point, of course, is that it is not easy in any group to be identified as the *rat*, the *squealer*, the *busybody*, the one person who cannot be trusted absolutely. Doctors rarely expose the incompetence of their colleagues, even though, as the great frequency and size of medical malpractice verdicts suggests, it certainly must come to their attention. College athletes don't usually talk about alumni boosters' under-the-table payments to superstars, and office workers do not inform on co-workers who take supplies home. Similarly, real estate agents and banks remain mum about *de facto* discrimination and redlining in apartment rentals and mortgage lending. Regardless of where, any member of any group who considers becoming a *whistle-blower* must know that, however laudable one's motives, doing so will forever change one's own life and status in the group.

In the closed society of police departments, especially in departments or units that see themselves and the public in terms of "us and them" and adopt the siege view of the world, the pressure to remain loyal is enormous. In such societies, there is no need for violent means of enforcing the code, because, having subsumed their individual identities into the whole, cops know that betraying the group betrays themselves and destroys their identities.

Consider Robert Leuci, the *Prince of the City* whose testimony eventually put his whole squad and about seventy other New York city narcotics detectives behind bars. According to Robert Daley, before blowing his whistle, Leuci had a conversation with his wife, telling her of his intentions:

"I'm not going to implicate any one close to us."
"Do you think they will allow you to do whatever you choose to do? Do you think they will say: Okay, Bob, whoever you want to tell us about. You decide. I don't think they will allow you to do that."

After a moment she added, "I know you feel guilty. Other people are responsible, not you. They are guiltier than you are."

In a low voice, he replied, "I want to end this life I have been living."

"Then quit the Police Department."

But he loved the Police Department. "And do what? Sell insurance? Work in a bank?"

Gina said, "I know you. It's going to kill you. They will force you to hurt friends, people who have done no harm to you, only good. When you were sick, they all came. They called me every day. I know what kind of man you are. I know what you can live with and what you can't live with. This will kill you. You tell me the feelings you have for informants, and now you are going to be an informant. How are you going to live with that? How am I going to live with you, as you live with that?"[48]

There is no mention in this conversation of Leuci's safety, because Leuci anticipated—correctly—that none of the people he "hurt" would try forcibly to silence him or to avenge his turnaround. In the end, he suffered great stigmatization and the reality that, having broken the code, he could never be what he once was: the "Prince of the City," the hotshot member of the most envied and prestigious detective unit in the biggest police department in the country.

A conversation one of us had with a former Special Investigations Unit detective who had been imprisoned on Leuci's testimony shows how strong was that group's cohesiveness. "Whatever happened to Leuci?" this detective was asked, "Has anybody heard from him?" "Nah. And that's too bad," the detective replied. "We run an SIU reunion every year, and we always send him an invitation. We never hear from him, though. He probably thinks the guys are pissed at him, but it's water under the bridge. He did what he had to do, and we know that."

The code of silence, then, is not one that is enforced by assassins lurking in dark alleys or arranging for drug dealers to terminate cops who inform. The police code of silence is an extreme version of a phenomenon that exists in all human groups. It is exaggerated in some police departments and some police units because cops so closely identify with their departments, their units, and their colleagues that they cannot even conceive of doing anything else. Like Bob Leuci, they live in a world of desperately conflicting imperatives, where norms of loyalty wash up against standards of law and order. So mostly, like the cops who witnessed the beating of Rodney King, they see, hear, and speak no evil. As we shall discuss later, special efforts can and must be made to overcome these powerful prescriptions of silence and loyalty in the culture of policing.

# 6

# *Cops as Soldiers*

The difference between the quasi-military and the civil policeman is that the civil policeman should have no enemies. People may be criminals, they may be violent, but they are not enemies to be destroyed. Once that kind of language gets into the police vocabulary, it begins to change attitudes.

—John Alderson, *The Listener,* 1985

Identifying the enemy makes us very uncomfortable because the enemy happens to be a great many of us.

—Daryl F. Gates, Address to Attorney General's Crime Summit, March 4, 1991

Military jargon shows up in virtually any discussion of the police. Police departments are "paramilitary," complete with "chains of command," "divisions," "platoons," "squads," and "details." In many places, patrol officers are "privates" or "troopers." In virtually all places, officers report not to supervisors, middle managers, or executives, but to sergeants, lieutenants, captains, majors, and colonels. In police training academies, much attention is devoted to close order drill and military courtesy.

The military metaphor also colors the public's expectations of the police. Our police have been engaged in a nonstop "war on crime" for the last sixty years. Most recently the battle has focused on ridding the country of the scourge of drugs and the profiteering "drug kingpins." Just a few days before Rodney King's beating, then Attorney General Richard Thornburgh opened a national "crime summit," at which Chief Gates spoke of the enemy among us. In his keynote address, Thornburgh asked law enforcement officials to attack street crime and "violent drug traffickers" with the same vigor and valor shown by our troops in the Persian Gulf:

> [L]et me turn once again to the example of Desert Storm and the great might that was brought to bear upon a threatening and violent enemy. Under brilliantly coordinated "command and control," the Gulf coalition forces made the best use of firepower guided by great ingenuity and relentless certainty. We had the weapons to do the job: "smart" weapons that worked with deadly effect against an enemy finally reduced to desperate encounter, ineffectual response, and abject retreat.
>
> Here at home in the fight against violent crime we should employ, to be sure, the same command and control, the same ingenuity and certainty. Only here we battle not with the weapons of the military, but with the far stronger weapon of our laws. We need to make certain that our laws are just as smart—just as efficient and effective against criminals—as those weapons that turned back the ruthless and violent intrusion by Saddam Hussein's forces.[1]

However stirring this call, it relies upon an inexact analogy and is far more likely to produce unnecessary violence and antagonism than to result in effective policing. The lines between friend and foe were clear in the Arabian desert, but police officers on American streets too often rely on ambiguous cues and stereotypes in trying to identify the enemies in their war. When officers act upon such signals and roust people who turn out to be guilty of no more than being in what officers view as the wrong place at the wrong time—young black men on inner-city streets late at night, for example—the police may create enemies where none previously existed.

In addition, this faulty analogy has had the effect of putting the police on the front lines of crime wars they cannot win. There, like soldiers who know they are fighting for a lost cause, some police officers become frustrated and demoralized. In effect, they surrender. Working in environments far harsher than the executive offices in which ill-conceived wars usually are planned, such officers turn cynical, taking few risks and doing as little as possible. None of these officers wants to become a casualty of a no-win war plotted in an isolated ivory tower, so they waste their working lives simply marking the days until they are eligible for pensions. Other officers, perhaps more naïve and certainly more zealous, heed their leaders' calls to battle. They also hear frequent claims that they are losing the war only because *others*—typically, liberals and the courts—have handcuffed them. They hear fundamental Constitutional principles and due process rights—the rights to appeal, *habeas corpus,* and the Fourth Amendment's protections against unreasonable search and seizure—described as technicalities and unreasonable limits on their ability to fight the enemy among us. Then, angered and seeing themselves as the beleaguered *Blue Knights* and *New Centurions* of the former Los Angeles cop Joseph Wambaugh's novels, they commit atrocities against people like Rodney King.

American policing is not a monolith, however, and police leaders do not present a united front in this war on crime. The recent trend toward community-oriented policing is promising evidence of a police sentiment that the confrontational style encouraged by some has not worked. Darrel Stephens, the former Police Chief of Newport News, Virginia, and now director of the Police Executive Research Forum, a Washington-based research and policy organization, said recently: "To cast the modern American police force in a military way, as in the war on drugs, is wrong. . . . It's not a proper characterization."[2] Another prominent, and longer-term, dissenter is Patrick V. Murphy, who served as chief police executive in Syracuse, Washington D.C., Detroit, and New York, and as president of the Police Foundation. In 1977 he concluded his autobiography with this protest against wars on crime directed by police chiefs and other high-ranking officials:

> What the police chief—behind his big oak desk in his private office, insulated from the outside world by hordes of officious aides and layers of bureaucracy—must do, by all means, is to focus the entire institutional effort around one job: that of the police officer closest to the communities. Everything else should be secondary. It's a bosses' job only if we permit the bosses to make it one, if we permit both the institutions of the police and the officers themselves to become alienated, literally and figuratively, from their primary role in society, which is to keep the peace and maintain order in a sophisticated, humane, and Constitutional way. Policing should not be a bosses' job but rather a cop's job, because it is my view that perhaps the American police officer in this last quarter of the twentieth century has the most important job around.[3]

Murphy's observation captures much of the thesis of this chapter: The view of police officers as soldiers engaged in a war on crime not only diverts attention from more effective strategies for crime control but also is a major cause of police violence and the violation of citizens' rights. Those who hold and urge this view wrongly presume—or worse, *pretend*—that grand strategies devised by police chiefs, no-nonsense prosecutors, drug czars, law-and-order politicians, and other would-be generals can banish crime, disorder, and the scourge of drugs. They have urged a *war model* of policing that aggrandizes these top cops, hardnosed prosecutors, and other assorted tough guys in suits, most of whom have never made a drug buy, never made an arrest, never faced physical danger, and never come face to face with a criminal on a dark street. Less obviously, it reduces the role of the cop on the street to that of unquestioning grunt in the trenches. This wrongheaded emphasis has led us to evaluate the performance of the police and the criminal justice system by counting bodies—bodies arrested, convicted, confined, and executed—rather than by trying to determine whether our war efforts have made our streets safer and more civil. The current war on drugs has made cynics of much of the population, adding them to the great numbers of street-level police officers. On the streets, too many cops long ago stopped believing that their lives were on the line for anything that could be regarded as a viable grand strategy. Instead, most cops see drug and crime wars for what they are: *politics,* in all the pejorative senses of that word.

Most directly to the point of this book, however, the *war model* of policing encourages police violence of the type that victimized Rodney King. When any soldiers go to war, they must have enemies. When cops go to war against crime, their enemies are found in inner cities and among our minority populations. There, in a country as foreign to most officers as Vietnam was to GIs, cops have trouble distinguishing the good guys from the bad. In this environment, the more cynical officers give up and do nothing or, worse, occasionally become corrupt and share in the profits of the illegal underground markets that flourish around them. There, some of the more passionate officers, who are not so easily discouraged from fighting the battles to which they have been assigned, and who typically are incorruptible, become frustrated and angry. Soon, *everybody* becomes suspect in their eyes. The community and the police become alienated and distrustful of each other, and incidents like the King beating occur more frequently than we would like to think. A bright, highly motivated, and well-educated young officer assigned to a crime-ridden inner-city district recently told us:

> The people in headquarters think we're doing fine because we're giving them lots of arrests and nobody's complaining about us. Bullshit. Drugs are all over the place, kids shoot each other as soon as the patrol car drives around the corner, and nobody complains because they know the department doesn't want to hear it and won't do anything about it. If people complained about us every time we kicked somebody's ass, I'd be in big trouble. I can't think of a single day when I didn't put my hands on somebody.

## ORIGINS OF THE VIEW OF COPS AS SOLDIERS

How did the view of police as soldiers in a war against crime develop? Its origins lie in the establishment of the police themselves. The police as we know them—with uniforms and nightsticks, out patrolling the street—are, we noted earlier, a relatively new invention. After a brief test in Dublin, the first modern police were created in Great Britain in 1829 at the urging of Sir Robert Peel, who sought to replace London's antiquated night-watchman service and to develop a humane force to suppress London's increasingly frequent food riots. With appropriate adjustments for American decentralization and home rule—in the United States, the federal government has less power over local policing than is true of virtually any other country— Peel's concept of a *New Police* soon spread across the Atlantic.

Peel well knew the traditional British mistrust of official authority and took great pains to make certain that his brainchild would not be perceived merely as some form of domestic army, put in place to protect the Crown at the cost of individual liberties. Even though Britons bridled at the thought of the nation's soldiers being used against its own citizens, the military was a widely admired British institution. The British military did its job very well and with tremendous efficiency. True, it had lost the American Colonies, but it had also expanded the small island nation so much that "the sun never set on its empire." Despite his great efforts to distinguish *individual* police constables from soldiers, therefore, Peel borrowed heavily from the military *organizational* model in order to convince critics that his New Police would do its job as flawlessly and as incorruptibly as the military did its. He also appointed two experienced and admired military commanders to head his police.

Thus, modeling the police on this organization helped to ease Peel's difficult task of convincing the skeptical British public that a new form of official authority was needed to deal with disorder and crime. Besides, Peel and those who worked with him to assemble the London Metropolitan Police had few options. Like the police, large organizations themselves are a fairly recent innovation: Until the Industrial Revolution, few large organizations existed, other than the military, and most other organizations that evolved—large businesses, government bureaucracies—generally were designed in the same hierarchical fashion as the military. In some ways, then, the organization of police along military lines was a historical accident. Had other efficient models been available, our police might well be differently organized.

## THE MILITARY MODEL AND FRONT-LINE DISCRETION

Indeed, since Peel's time, new models have emerged and, critics such as scholar and former police chief John E. Angell have noted, may be more appropriate than the military model to the realities of American policing.[4] The pyramidal shape of the military model originally was designed to accommodate a distribution of official discretion that gave those at the top the greatest and broadest decision-making authority and closely limited discretion at the lowest organizational levels. In the military, after all, the generals and their commander-in-chief make all the great decisions—Should we go to war? How extensive should our commitment be? Will it be an air war, or shall we also commit ground troops? When will we consider ourselves victors or losers? Meanwhile, soldiers are limited to doing and dying, rather than wondering why.

Angell reasoned that a more "democratic" organizational structure akin to that characteristic of hospitals, universities, and law firms would be more appropriate for the police. In such places, Angell argued, administration is by and large a ministerial function—making sure that enough personnel are available at any time, that they have the support they need to do their jobs, and that there is enough money on hand to keep the enterprise afloat. As in police departments, however, the big decisions related to direct delivery of services in these organizations are made by those on the line. Doctors, not administrators, decide whether to operate or to medicate; professors, not deans, decide whether students' work is passing or failing; trial lawyers, not managing partners, decide whether to advise clients to settle or to go before juries; police officers, not chiefs, decide whether and when to shoot.

The great commonality between police departments and other organizations in which discretion is greatest at the line level ends here. Both within their organizations and among the public, doctors, professors, and lawyers—rather than administrators who have spent most or all of their careers far from the line—enjoy the lion's share of their professions' prestige. Not so in police departments, where the cop on a patrol beat is regarded both inside and outside his or her department as someone who hasn't yet figured out how to advance professionally. Doctors, professors, and lawyers are well paid and need not leave the line for management positions in order to advance either economically or in terms of status. Not so the cop, who typically must enter supervisory ranks and be lost to the line in order to "get ahead." Appropriately, doctors, professors, and lawyers also are presumed to be their professions' main reservoirs of expertise. Consequently, they play great roles in governance, discipline, and assessment of their organizations, as well as their professions and their colleagues. Not so the cop, who sits at the bottom of a long chain of command that separates him or her from the organization's policy-makers.

The military model probably is appropriate to most large organizations where those at the top make the great decisions while those on the line—be it the front line or the assembly line—exercise little discretion. Despite allowances for greater employee participation suggested by the increasing sophistication of the workforce and the successes of Japanese corporations, the top brass assembled by Lee Iacocca still decide what new Chryslers will look like, while auto assembly line workers exercise little discretion and work under close supervision. In government organizations other than police, line workers engage in closely supervised work directed at a common goal. In most government agencies responsible for dealing with emergencies, precise coordination and direct and immediate central control over a large group of skilled people who unhesitatingly and expertly do their jobs is absolutely critical. Without such control and precision, military operations would fail and firefighters could not function effectively.

Even though the *raisons d'être* of both the military and the police involve the use or threat of force, these justifications for military-style organization are only rarely applicable to the police. The military model probably is the best way we know to coordinate the efforts of large numbers of people who work collectively to solve the same great problem or to achieve the same grand goal. But, except for large public gatherings, demonstrations, and disorders, police officers generally do not work in such conditions.[5] As James Auten has pointed out, a cop typically works alone or with one other officer and deals with large numbers of small, isolated, unconnected problems.[6] Every day, out of their supervisors' sight, police officers at the lowest levels of their departments make what law scholar Joseph Goldstein called "low visibility decisions" that have great effects on the lives and liberties of individual members of the public.[7] At any moment, for example, police officers throughout the United States are deciding whether to ticket or merely to warn this motorist; whether or not to destroy the marijuana cigarette that kid was found holding and send him on his way without marking his life history with a record of arrest; whether or not to arrest this abusive husband; whether to back off a bit or stand firm and shoot the oncoming emotionally disturbed person wielding the knife.

These are momentous decisions that can be reviewed only after the fact and, often, only after their consequences have been realized. Before there is any opportunity to determine whether the officer has acted appropriately, the ticket has been issued, the arrest or release has occurred, the shot has struck flesh. Further, absent videotaping or other reasonably objective recording, reviews usually must rely solely upon the accounts of the officers and citizens involved. When citizens benefit from officers' exercise of discretion, as when they are given what police call *scares* rather than tickets, any opportunity officially to review the appropriateness of officers' decisions disappears with them as they leave the scenes of their encounters with police. When the wisdom or reasonableness of officers' actions is challenged, review frequently consists of trying to *eff the ineffable*—attempting to resolve irresolvable swearing contests between citizens and police officers. Conversely, whenever police chiefs make decisions, their discretion is recorded and subject to comment by myriad critics, both before and after the fact. As an old saw has it, police chiefs' decisions are put on paper in the form of orders and policy statements and are there for everybody to see; but cops' decisions quickly disappear into the ozone, where there is nobody to criticize the cops' version of what occurred. It is hard to think of any hierarchical organization in which the lowest-level employees routinely exercise such great discretion with such little opportunity for objective review.

This is no meaningless anomaly. Trying to shoehorn street-level officers' great discretion into the lowest level of a military organizational style has resulted in the creation of elaborate police rulebooks that pretend to be definitive but provide little meaningful guidance for police officers. Hard and fast rules are viable in mechanical work situations, but they are of little assistance in dealing with the fluid discretionary situations that are the core of police work.[8] No rigid directive can tell officers to arrest every time they witness a violation of law; to do so would severely damage the ends of justice and drain the resources of the police and the rest of the criminal justice system. No directive can tell police never to arrest; no directive can precisely define the circumstances distinguishing cases in which arrest is appropriate from those in which it is not. Yet, especially in police agencies that aspire most directly to the ideal of military spit-and-polish philosophy, top administrators persist in perpetuating the myth that officers adhere to the ideal of full enforcement. In such "legalistic" departments, James Q. Wilson suggests, this façade serves

> ... to disassociate the department from the law-making process, which is essentially a political process, thereby making it clear that so long as the department "does its job" the responsibility is on others to decide what it shall do and thus no one can accuse the department of being "political" by making its own decision as to what laws to enforce. It is harder to keep the department out of politics if it appears to be making political judgments, and it may appear in just that light if it does less than enforce all the laws all the time.[9]

In fact, officers in even the most legalistic departments do not enforce all the laws all the time. Instead, they routinely violate the letter of their departments' rule books by issuing warnings rather than tickets and by releasing minor offenders, sometimes in exchange for information about more serious criminals. Nor do they closely follow the detailed rules that their administrators promulgate and use as a way of fixing blame at the lowest levels for things gone wrong. Indeed, if officers were to follow the rules of the most bureaucratized departments, their work would grind to a halt, as it occasionally does when police protest labor conditions by conducting rulebook slowdowns: Only when rules are irrelevant can adhering to them hinder progress toward organizational goals.[10]

Irrelevant or overly rigid police regulations also create the less readily visible tension of making it impossible for officers to do their jobs without routinely violating rules. Peter Manning spoke with a British police constable who explained his department's rule book:

> 140 years of fuckups. Every time something goes wrong, they make a rule about it. All the directions in the force flow from someone's mistake. You can't go eight hours on the job without breaking the disciplinary code.... But, no one cares until something goes wrong. The job goes wild on trivialities.[11]

Consequently, offices are inclined to devalue rules and find shortcuts around *all* of them, regardless of the justifications for their existence. Early in James Fyfe's NYPD career, officers' common rationalization for violating rules of any degree of merit was that "the job is not on the level." This perception, in turn, creates among line police officers a sense that they are on their own and that the brass is unrealistic and more interested in protecting itself than in seeing that police goals are accomplished.

This sense of isolation is exacerbated by the difficulty of communicating up and down the rigid *chains of command* that characterize the military-style hierarchy. In the NYPD, the biggest of all U.S. police departments, for example, police officers who wish to communicate with the department's chief executive generally must do so on paper and "through channels." While en route to the Police Commissioner through these channels, officers' original letters are amended by the addition of positive or negative "endorsements," or recommendations, by a sergeant, an administrative lieutenant, the captain or deputy inspector in command of the officer's precinct, the inspector in command of the "area" in which the precinct is located, the assistant chief in command of the borough in which the area is located, the Chief of Patrol, the Chief of Department, and the commander of any specialized unit that might be affected by any action suggested in the correspondence.

Since virtually every police officer's attempt to communicate with the Police Commissioner involves at least implicit criticism of existing practice or an appeal from a decision made at lower levels in the chain of command, such communications generally are subject to more distortion than one might expect even if they threatened to gore nobody's ox. Communications down the chain run a similar gauntlet of interpretations and often reach the front lines altered in both intent and substance.[12]

The sense of isolation that develops from this organizational arrangement—cops against bosses, as well as against a hostile clientele—helps to account for a rare degree of camaraderie and group loyalty among police officers. *Esprit* among police is desirable and necessary, but when coupled with the necessity of routine violations of the rules in order to get the job done, it delegitimatizes everything the brass does. It also effectively neutralizes officers who might otherwise speak out about *serious* misbehavior by their colleagues. As David Simon suggests, there is no privacy in police working groups—everybody who is an active member of every police squad knows everything about everybody else in the group.[13] When rulebreaking is part of the routine in such groups, everybody also *has something* on everybody else. Group members cannot easily inform on or otherwise assist in the downfall of colleagues who commit misconduct without risking public airing of their own many small sins. Even when wrongdoing is serious, this code of silence applies.

This trap also affects officers who move up and out of line squads into supervisory and management positions. As products of such systems, they are vulnerable to subtle blackmail by former colleagues who know of their old sins. Often, they cannot be strong leaders because their own histories are so well known that they can invoke disciplinary action only at the risk of exposure or, more likely, of being rejected as hypocrites by the very society of which they were so recently a part. We spoke with a police official who believed that much-needed reform in his department would be possible only if his mayor appointed an "outsider" as chief. This official told us of his disappointment when a widely known veteran was given the reins to the department:

> He's a nice guy, but he'll never straighten out the department. He's been around it too long. The people he needs to push out of the way know about every free cup of coffee he took when he was a cop, every time he stole a half-hour from work, every time somebody went to bat for him when he was caught off base. If he does anything to hurt anybody in the department, he'll wind up being humiliated. Sure, he knows all the actors in the department, but his big problem is that they know him too.

Supervision in rule-laden military-style police departments is hurt in other ways as well. A prominent complaint of most police chief executives is what they see as the failure of first-line supervisors to exercise effective control over their personnel. At a national law enforcement conference within a week or two of the King incident, the videotaped beating was the main topic of conversation. Most of the chiefs and administrators in attendance analyzed it as an illustration of first-line supervisory failure. Had the sergeant on the scene done what he was supposed to do, they argued, the beating would not have occurred.

This interpretation is no doubt correct, but is far from a complete explanation of the King beating in particular or of the absence of strong first-line supervision in policing generally. Virtually every act of collective police misconduct not authorized at the highest organizational levels[14] can be dismissed as a result of supervisory failure. The demonstrators at the Chicago Convention and Tompkins Square Park would not have been beaten had sergeants done their jobs, but knowing that this is so does not provide us with any information about *why* first-line supervision frequently seems to fail in critical times.

In good measure, the answer is that police organizational structure and the pretense that hard and fast rules govern police conduct make it very difficult for sergeants to supervise according to the book on a day-to-day basis. Consequently, it should not be surprising that the weak link of first-line supervision is most dramatically exposed in crises. Consider the job of police sergeants assigned to supervise patrol officers in the tough neighborhoods where police violence is most likely. Because of civil service procedures and safeguards, such sergeants have little authority to reward or punish their officers formally. Hiring and firing are not within the sergeants' province. Lesser disciplinary measures also are meaningless or difficult to employ. Even though disciplinary transfers are regarded disapprovingly in the literature of police administration, for example, sergeants usually can recommend such actions. Officers assigned to patrol tough areas, however, already are doing their departments' most dangerous, sensitive, onerous, ill-paid, and least prestigious work. Hence they typically regard the possibility of transfers with favor rather than dread. A former colleague once told Fyfe:

> There's one nice thing about working in the South Bronx. The bosses can't do anything to me. What can they do? They couldn't possibly send me anyplace worse, and they're not about to send me anyplace better because that would be doing me a favor. They can take me out of the radio car and put me on a foot post, but that's no punishment because riding a car here is no bargain. They can't give me worse hours, because I'm already working the worst they've got. They can't harass me because I can just stop working. All in all, I like it here because I'm my own boss. I can do what I think is right, and I don't have to worry about their chickenshit.

Small wonder that, when the researcher Larry Tifft studied the Chicago police, he found that variations in the supervisory and motivational styles of sergeants made a big difference in the work of detectives, but that sergeants' personality, style, and example mattered hardly at all in patrol units.[15] Detectives do the prestigious and rewarding work of catching crooks; they know that crossing their sergeants can lead to loss of their plum assignments. Patrol officers have little or nothing to lose by ignoring their sergeants.

Sergeants repeatedly are told that they are part of their departments' *management teams,* but in fact they almost invariably identify and develop much closer relationships with the troops than with the brass. Sergeants are responsible for getting their people to produce, and to do so they must routinely overlook rules violations. Since sergeants themselves must violate rules to do their own work and to get officers to do theirs, they become vulnerable to betrayal by their officers. In such circumstances, according to Elizabeth Reuss-Ianni, the relationship between sergeant and officer becomes a *reciprocal* understanding between near equals rather than the clear superior–subordinate relationship presented in police organizational charts.[16]

Indeed, the costs of disruptions in this relationship may be greater for sergeants than for officers. Sergeants typically are bright and upwardly mobile young careerists much concerned that the promotion boards in their futures see only clear records of achievement and managerial success through inspiration rather than intimidation. Consequently, sergeants run a risk when they resort to formal disciplinary action often enough to lead their officers to retaliate or to cause their superiors to believe that they cannot get officers to produce without flogging them. In short, the sergeant typically is compromised. Jonathan Rubinstein notes of the Philadelphia Police Department:

> Since every supervisor violates regulations to produce the conditions and circumstances which enable him to get the required work from his men, each must bear in mind the possibility of betrayal. No matter how rare its occurrence, it is both a barrier against petty tyranny and a brake on the capacity of the supervisors to enforce stringent control on their men. They are as much colleagues as they are executives.[17]

Thus, the highly centralized military organizational model often works to weaken police supervision and leadership in the places where it is most needed: on the front lines of inner-city patrol units. One way to address this problem might be adoption of the Continental European police tradition of a separate *officer class,* whose members are recruited at advanced ranks out of colleges and professional schools. In our view, however, reliance on such a model would serve mainly to exaggerate the pathologies of the existing military model and to enlarge the existing differences between street cops and management cops.[18]

## THE POLICE NUMBERS GAME

The police, like most bureaucracies, tend to measure their performance in purely quantitative terms and to ignore the more fundamental question of how well they are doing the tasks with which they have been charged. Instead of learning whether or not officers solved the problems to which they were summoned, for example, readers of police annual reports learn how many calls were received by 911 and, on average, how many minutes and seconds it took officers to respond to them. Instead of telling us whether police activities have increased safety and decreased congestion on our roads, police reports present elaborate tables telling us how many tickets the police issued. To use Herman Goldstein's term, the police are locked in a *means/ends syndrome,* in which they tell us how often they employ the tools they have been provided to achieve their goals rather than whether the goals themselves have been achieved.[19] It is as though doctors measured their performance by counting operations without bothering to determine whether patients were cured; as though lawyers counted their cases without regard to whether they won or lost for their clients.

Like the military body counts of the Vietnam era, the police numbers game—how *many* rather than how *well*—can be severely misleading. Perhaps its most extreme example appears in a New York State Commission of Investigation report on New York City's narcotics enforcement efforts. In 1970, the commission reported, undercover NYPD narcotics officers made 7,266 purchases of suspected heroin. Operating under a policy of attempting to strengthen prosecution cases by making two buys of suspected heroin before arresting dealers, the narcotics unit made 4,007 drug sale arrests as a result of these activities.

These are impressive numbers, but the amount of controlled substances taken out of the drug traffic by all these buys and arrests was incredibly small. The commission's report indicates that the total weight of controlled substances seized in these activities was *4.97 pounds.*[20] Since street-level heroin in New York City at that time ranged between 4 and 12 percent "pure" (the other 88 to 96 percent consisting of milk sugar, quinine, or other additives), the net effects of this very dangerous undercover work[21] were the removal from the drug market of something less than a half-pound of pure heroin and the arrests of many minor dealers. Such arrests, the commission noted, were not likely to affect the availability of drugs, because the low-level dealers involved—typically addicts who sold drugs to sustain their own habits—were remote from the "higher echelons of heroin being trafficked in New York city."[22]

Certainly, overreliance on quantitative measures of police performance might exist even if police organizations were not structured along military lines. We doubt, however, that it would be nearly as marked as it has been in the United States during our lifetimes. Peter K. Manning writes that Robert Peel's original mandate required the police

> ... to prevent crime without resort to repressive legal sanctioning ... ; to manage public order nonviolently, with the application of violence viewed as an ultimate means of coercing compliance; to minimize and indeed reduce, if at all possible, the schism between police and public; and to demonstrate efficiency by the absence of crime and disorder, not police action in dealing with them.[23]

In twentieth-century America, Manning suggests, this set of responsibilities has proved an impossible mandate. Because the police know that they cannot achieve these states, he argues, they have embraced a highly bureaucratized and impersonal version of professionalism and have engaged in a variety of strategies designed to make it look as though they are doing well when they are not. These strategies rely heavily upon quantitative measures of performance, which appear to be far more characteristic of highly centralized, rigidly structured bureaucracies than of more decentralized large organizations or of small organizations.

The reasons for the bureaucratic preference for numbers are clear. When organizational policy-makers and those with the power to reward and punish workers are remote from the line, it is very difficult for them to measure the quality of performance and to present it to their consumers in ways that make sense. Consequently, they develop standardized, objective performance measures that are presumed to be equally applicable to everybody in the organization, but may not tell us what we really want to know. As our auto makers have recently discovered, knowing how many cars come off the assembly line how quickly tells us little about how well they are put together or whether they meet consumers' needs. But when authority resides close to the line—as when supervisors can reward or punish—or when those on the line themselves have some input into identifying and rewarding good and bad performance, questions about the quality of work may be addressed on a face-to-face basis. In such circumstances, purely quantitative measures of performance have less meaning.

In big, centralized police departments, however, those near the line have little authority. Consequently, as Jonathan Rubinstein wrote, "activity" becomes the standard measure of performance:

> "Activity" is the internal product of police work. It is the statistical measure which the sergeant uses to judge the productivity of his men, the lieutenant to assure himself that the sergeant is properly directing his men, the captain

to assure his superiors that he is capably administering his district, and the department administrators to assure the public that their taxes are not squandered.[24]

Nobody who spends day after day in the tight and closed societies that are police work groups needs to measure "activity" to know who the *good cops* are. In our experience, the best way to identify the good cops is to ask their colleagues who they are.[25] When this is done, the assessments obtained often have little or nothing to do with numbers and, in that and other ways, are similar to what one hears when asking doctors, professors, and lawyers to comment on their colleagues. Good cops, according to street officers, are level-headed and never get their colleagues into "trouble."

Good cops always seem able to identify the causes of problems and to come up with the least troublesome ways of solving them. Good cops think ahead and always leave a way out of any tough situation. Good cops rarely have to resort to the law to solve minor order maintenance problems like drunks or noisy kids on the street. Good cops spend their time finding out about the people and places on their beats instead of lurking at speed traps or near badly marked stop signs. Good cops know the people on their beats well enough to put an end to problems like double parking merely by telling store owners to warn customers against illegal parking. Local criminals know the good cops and stay away from their beats when they are working. Detectives know that good cops are tapped into the neighborhoods they patrol and frequently turn to them for information about serious crimes.

As a consequence, the officers known to their colleagues as good cops may be virtually invisible beyond their immediate work groups. The numbers on their activity reports rarely are boosted by what street officers in many places call "piss collars" for contempt of cop charges such as disorderly conduct, obstructing justice, or resisting arrest. They are not among those who issue large numbers of parking tickets or traffic citations. They rarely become heroes by making the kinds of spectacular arrests that lesser officers occasionally stumble into. Their information and sources may solve many serious crimes, but the arrests in these cases are recorded over detectives' names, rather than over their own. A veteran officer told us that good cops do their jobs so well that it may appear to the distant connoisseur of statistics that they are not even needed:

> You know what they figure in headquarters? "Hey, nothing ever happens on this guy's beat. There's no crime, no traffic problem, no noisy kids. We put him out there and he shows us nothing. Never makes any arrests, no tickets. Nothing. Zip. What are we paying him for? Let's take him out of there and put him where he's needed. Let him help the guy on the next post. There's

lots of crime there and no matter how many arrests and tickets we give out, the people still complain that they don't get enough protection. Isn't it funny how two streets so close to each other can be so different?" Hah! If the bosses ever came out to look, they'd see that the streets are the same, but that the difference is the cops. The bosses can tell you what kind of numbers look good in a report, but they wouldn't know a good cop on a bet.

The message is clear: prevent things from happening and go unrecognized; take strong and formal action after the fact—give a ticket, make an arrest—and be viewed as a valuable contributor to the unit's statistical reports of "activity."

## THE DEVELOPMENT OF WARS ON CRIME

Thus, in retrospect, it might be wished for a variety of reasons that Sir Robert Peel had had alternatives to military organization when he sired the first police departments in Dublin and London. Still, the American variant of Peel's vision has experienced more violence and controversy than have police in England. Apparently—and although the English police recently have experienced plenty of violence themselves—some combination of American social and historical forces has blended with the military model to produce a volatile mix.

Some of these forces are obvious and external to the police. Over the years, American police have had no reasonable way to avoid much of the violence in which they have become involved. Instead, they have had to use force more than the British police simply because they have worked in a society more violent than Britain's. Our police first patrolled the streets unarmed but—after great debate both inside and outside their ranks—began wearing guns in the middle of the nineteenth century only when it became unavoidably clear that it was not safe to do otherwise.[26] Just recently, as British heterogeneity and rates of crime and violence have increased, the country has began to debate seriously the paramilitary nature of police organization and the question of whether police should be armed.[27] Thus, the weaknesses of the military model may have been apparent here longer than in England because they have been exposed by the great social pressures to which our police have been subjected.

In addition, high-level official venality also has encouraged a considerable amount of American police violence. On occasion, politicians have used their police forces as armies to crush those protesting labor conditions and racial inequities, as well as those holding unpopular or opposing political views.[28] But these events are infrequent enough to make them aberrational. Something else is at work when, without conscious and specific encouragement from the highest levels, police use violence or excessive force in the course of day-to-day business.

## J. EDGAR HOOVER'S FBI

The view of the American police as soldiers locked in combat gained substantial impetus from J. Edgar Hoover's successes in rounding up the celebrated criminals of the 1930s. The overwhelming fact of American life at that time was, of course, the Great Depression, which made police and law enforcement work attractive to large numbers of well-educated young men who, in better times, would have spurned it. At the same time, American policing was beginning to recover from the country's great adventure with Prohibition, during which, it is fair to say, virtually every large American police department had become riddled with corruption and politicization. The Chicago Police Department, probably the worst of the lot, was so far off the chart that a blue-ribbon citizen's commission suggested seriously in 1931 that the only way to clean it up was to fire all 4,000 officers and to "concentrate upon a fresh start, unimpaired by even a trace of the old tradition."[29]

The entire nation was ready to flush away the old tradition, and Hoover, taking advantage of the high-quality labor pool, furnished a model. As a twenty-nine-year-old Justice Department lawyer, he had been named to head—and to reform—the corrupt and hack-ridden two-hundred-person "Bureau of Investigation" in 1924.[30] He set about turning the Bureau into a model bureaucracy. He altered its identity by renaming it the *Division* of Investigation. He staffed it with fine and well-educated young men, trained them carefully, and isolated them from the community and its corrupting influences. For as long as Hoover lived, the Division and its successor, the FBI, took no part in corruption-prone activities like narcotics or alcohol enforcement, and he long refused to acknowledge even the existence of organized crime.

Hoover summarily fired many agents who had been hired before his tenure and encouraged others to leave by frequent transfers. He developed a merit personnel system independent of and better compensated than the federal civil service system. He instituted rigid inspections of field offices. He built a national constituency of local law enforcement officials by establishing and making available to them the nation's largest repository of fingerprint, criminal, and fraudulent check records, *modus operandi* files, and a sophisticated crime laboratory. He also took over the International Association of Chiefs of Police Uniform Crime Reporting (UCR) program and turned it into the nation's principal provider of official crime statistics.

Hoover's assumption of responsibility for the UCR was no small event. More than any other single action, it introduced and legitimized *numbers* as measures of police effectiveness. This was particularly significant because, at nearly the precise time that Hoover began systematically publishing crime figures, the United States entered a three-decade-long period of extreme domestic tranquility that lasted through the early 1960's. Consequently, for an entire generation, police were able to claim that low crime rates reflected the success of their efforts to emulate the FBI's high degree of professionalism. Although we now recognize that police activities probably had little or no impact on the actual incidence of crimes included in the UCR,[31] this was not clear at the time. Thus, most chiefs no doubt believed their own claims about the credit due them for low rates of crime.

During the earliest years of Hoover's administration, the Bureau was limited by statute to investigation rather than enforcement. Its agents were unarmed, and their direct anticrime activities were generally confined to two federal offenses: interstate transportation of prostitutes and interstate transportation of stolen motor vehicles. By the early 1930s, however, Hoover's Bureau was a smooth-running machine, and he was anxious to expand its role. President Franklin D. Roosevelt, a longtime advocate of stronger federal law enforcement and centralized power, gave Hoover all the support he needed to accomplish this. By 1934, with Roosevelt's support, Congress had made escape across state lines, interstate transportation of stolen property, extortion by telephone, and bank robbery federal crimes and had allowed the FBI to intervene in cases in which kidnap victims were not recovered within a week. Congress also gave FBI agents the powers to arrest and to carry guns.

Thus equipped, Hoover's Bureau went to war against "Public Enemy Number One" and the other bad guys included in his new "Ten Most Wanted" program. The Bureau quickly won this war: One by one, they captured or killed "Machine Gun" Kelly, "Pretty Boy" Floyd, "Baby Face" Nelson, Ma Barker, Bonnie Parker and Clyde Barrow, and—most dramatically—the bank robber, murderer, and master prison breaker John Dillinger. Hoover then turned his agents' attention to threats from abroad. Throughout the late 1930s and the World War II years, they achieved great successes in counterespionage and antisabotage.

Thus, within less than a decade, Hoover made law enforcement respectable. He showed that a war on crime could be won and the streets could be made safe for democracy by an elite corps of steely-eyed professionals who mastered technology and scientific crime detection methods, who reported only to a charismatic and virtually autonomous chief executive, and who could demonstrate with numbers how well they were doing. This, especially after the recent disgraces of the Prohibition years, was an extension of Peel's military model that was very appealing to police throughout the country. Many adopted it and, so long as crime rates remained low, remained satisfied that their new style of *professional* policing was the answer to crime and disorder.

## THE FBI AND COPS: ANOTHER BAD ANALOGY

Over time, however, the analogy between local police and the FBI has proved no more apt than that between the military and the police. Hoover was successful because the enemy in his war was not so much crime as a few sensational public enemies—the John Dillingers and Baby Face Nelsons—who were relatively easy to catch. This, we began to discover during the mid-1960s, is not the crime problem facing our local police.

Today the police work in inner cities, where poverty, unemployment, teenage pregnancy, and drug use have achieved nearly institutional status and where young men are steered by their peers to commit crimes before they have reached puberty. In such circumstances, cops' wars on crime are unwinnable. Police detectives—or FBI agents—can track down a few *individual criminals*. They do so with some success, considerable prestige, and the resulting sense of a job well done. But in the grand picture, all police administrators know that their investigators' best efforts and most spectacular arrests will never solve the *problem* of inner-city violence.

Instead, these administrators ask their patrol officers to keep a lid on the crime factories that have replaced industrial work in our inner cities. Over the past decade, news reports and movies have made a broad public increasingly familiar with urban gang colors, hand signals, and rap refrains. To most Americans, and to the police, these have emerged as symbols of a fearsome and depressed urban America and of American economic and moral decline. As America has moved from an industrial economy that promised jobs to a broad range of workers to a postindustrial world that increasingly offers rich rewards to skilled professionals but low-paying service jobs to the least educated, we see an increase in economic inequality as well as poverty, accompanied by a rise in crime and violence. Studies of the causes of crime invariably stress blocked opportunity as an important factor in gang and associated activities, such as drug selling.

Of these studies, John Hagedorn's analysis of gangs in Milwaukee, Wisconsin, is the most emphatic and systematic in linking gang development and behavior to the decline of the traditional American industrial base.[32] However bad the economy might have been for the African-American community in Milwaukee during the 1960s and 1970s, the 1980s were devastating. Thirty-five thousand jobs were lost to the Milwaukee area between 1980 and 1985. The unemployment rate for black workers in 1985 was 27.9 percent, the second highest in the nation. Tragically, the Milwaukee story is scarcely isolated. Between 1973 and 1986, real earnings of black males in the work force continued to decline. Nearly one-fifth of black men in America have spent time in jail or prison, and minorities populate our correctional institutions far in excess of their percentages in the population. Male bonding groups and delinquency exist in all communities, but street gangs are a correlate of impoverishment, checked economic opportunity, and a tearing of the social fabric. The data from an early 1980s National Bureau of Economic Research survey of young black men aged 16–24 identify the problems—which have worsened during the Reagan and Bush administrations—of black youth in the most poverty-stricken areas of U.S. inner cities:

> [Black youths living in the poorest areas of inner cities were] much more likely to be unemployed and less likely to be employed than white youths or all black youths. They tend to have slightly lower wages than other youths and they work fewer weeks per year. In addition, those youths have far worse family backgrounds than others. One-third of them live in public housing; almost one-half of them have a family member on welfare. Only 28 percent of them have an adult man in their household.[33]

These are the kids who populate gangs and contribute to the ranks of street drug dealing. Day after day, patrol officers—trained and socialized to think of themselves as soldiers—see around them the evidence that their enforcement efforts are in vain. One of us (Skolnick) was riding with an NYPD cop in Washington Heights, the main marketplace of New York City's drug scene. Youthful drug sellers were standing in threes and fours on virtually every corner.

Our police companion, an experienced narcotics officer, was asked, "How effective are the police in controlling the drug trade?"

"We are," he answered, "like a gnat biting on a horse's ass."

New York's Commissioner Lee P. Brown made a similar observation in a more dignified tone in a newspaper interview: "I look at the message coming out of Washington that we're winning the war on drugs and I don't know what city they're talking about," he said. "It's certainly not New York City."[34]

Frustration grows, and it should surprise no one that some patrol officers, those who operate directly in the streets, rather than detectives working out of offices and assigned the unambiguous task of investigating specific crimes, apparently account for most of police brutality against citizens.

## REDEFINING THE STREET COP'S JOB

In fact, police patrol officers are not automatons or grunts and should not be treated as low man—or low woman—on their departments' totem poles. Street cops exercise greater discretion than any police officials. They are society's first responders to an incredible array of human problems, some of which simply are beyond resolution. Good street cops should not be encouraged to leave their patrol assignments for more rewarding specialties. They should be encouraged to stay on the street and to develop their talents. The good ones—and most, but not all, are good ones—should be appropriately rewarded for their extraordinary work, both financially and in terms of prestige and influence within their occupation, agency, and community. Most important, street cops should not be encouraged to see themselves as soldiers locked in a war.

In fact, police brutality is inevitable when, as has happened in some places, officers describe themselves as *ghetto gunslingers* or as troopers assigned to isolated outposts of civilization. Police must be recognized, and must recognize themselves, as valuable members of the communities they serve. Before this can happen, street cops must be recognized as the most prized members of their departments, rather than as simple low-level grunts laboring in trenches far removed from the sterile offices in which foolhardy wars are plotted.

# 7

# *Beyond Accountability*

You can take community policing and stick it in your ear. . . . When I was chief, we were relating to the good people and we were relating to the other people too—we were throwing those people in the can. . . . I always said, "The good people of Milwaukee, they bought what the Department was selling."

—Harold Breier, former Milwaukee Police Chief, 1991[1]

The citizens get as good a police service as they want.

—Leonard Fuld, 1909[2]

## INTRODUCTION

Even though Robert Peel took great pains to see that his New Police would be a police of the people, modern police departments are far more insular than the military organizations on which they are modeled. Soldiers and sailors enter the services at varying levels, both as enlisted personnel and as officers, but virtually all cops enter their departments at the same level: the lowest. The ranks and ambience of the military constantly are refreshed by the comings and goings of those who leave after serving only single enlistments, by the activation of reservists, and by career paths designed to enrich military leaders' experiences and perspectives. Except for a few top administrators who move from department to department, however, the great majority of police officers spend their entire careers within only one agency. Rarely are they exposed to the practices and policies of other departments or to the reasoning of other disciplines.

Insulation from the public, from the rest of officialdom, and from other police agencies may enhance group loyalty and *esprit de corps,* both of which are desirable. But insularity also may breed abuse, violence, and secrecy. When insularity exists in an agency headed by a charismatic chief executive who has managed to move beyond accountability, police mistreatment, excessive force, and secrecy have proved virtually inevitable.

At the federal level, this progression was evidenced by J. Edgar

Hoover's FBI, in which abuse and secrecy generally were more subtle than the street-level bloodshed and transparent whitewashes that have been caused by local police departments out of meaningful control. At the local level, abuses, violence, and collusion have arisen when police chiefs have been permanently tenured in their positions. In addition, in at least one notable case—Frank Rizzo's Philadelphia—a police chief temporarily won total autonomy through democratic processes.

During the years when former Police Commissioner Frank Rizzo reigned as Mayor in the City of Brotherly Love (1972–79), the Philadelphia Police Department (PPD) answered to nobody but a Mayor who encouraged officers to brutality and who backed up this invitation by insulating abusive officers from accountability. In the end, however, Rizzo himself had to answer to the voters. After losing a referendum that would have allowed him to serve a third term, some semblance of democratic policing returned to Philadelphia.

But, while Rizzo could be voted out of office in Philadelphia, two other American big cities have operated under systems that granted civil service tenure to police chief executives. There, as secure in their jobs as federal judges, police chiefs have been able to formulate life-or-death policies and practices entirely on the bases of their own ideologies and biases. The LAPD is the best-known such department, but, until Chief Breier's retirement, the Milwaukee Police Department (MPD) also operated under a *chief for life*. Although MPD chiefs since Breier have been named only to five-year terms, Breier's legacy has lingered after his departure, and the department remains a prime example of police parochialism and inbreeding.

The record tells why this is so. Breier entered the MPD as a police officer in 1940 and went on to serve as Police Chief from 1964 to 1984. According to the report of a blue-ribbon commission that recently investigated the Milwaukee Police Department:

> Approximately three-fourths of the Department, including all those in the ranks of Captain and above, joined the Department while Harold Breier was Chief. After Chief Breier's retirement in 1984, former Inspector Robert Ziarnik came back from retirement to serve as Chief.... After Chief Ziarnik's retirement in 1989, the Fire and Police Commission instituted a national search which resulted in the hiring of Chief Philip Arreola, a former Commander of the Detroit Police Department, and Police Chief of Port Huron, Michigan. Chief Arreola was the first person ever hired by the MPD above the entry-level rank of police officer.[3]

Incoming chiefs may find that such great insularity causes reactions like former Chief Breier's evaluation of Arreola's plan to adopt a community-oriented style of policing. Indeed, former Philadelphia Police Commissioner Willie Williams received similar greetings when it was announced that he would succeed Daryl F. Gates as the LAPD's chief. Gates, who referred to his successor as "Willie from Philly," noted that Williams had made improvements in the Philadelphia Police Department but added that anything one did would be considered an improvement in Philadelphia. "When you've got 8,000 police officers" inside the department, Gates said, "you would believe that within that 8,000, there ought to be somebody that is acceptable, and should be selected as police chief. That has always been my opinion."[4] In departments full of civil service–tenured Breier and Gates loyalists, such comments deliver another message that goes far beyond simple condemnation of a newfangled way of using police officers: *This, too, shall pass. This outsider is trying to change the way you and I always did things. I don't approve of this, and I don't think you should either. The best way to make this pass quickly is to make his life miserable. Slow things up. Appear to cooperate, but don't really. He can't hurt you for that, and eventually he'll get the message. He'll go back to where he was, one of you will get the job that should have gone in-house in the first place, and things will go back to the way they've always been.*

## PRODUCING CONSISTENT POLICE BEHAVIOR

No outsider truly understands *the way things have always been* inside any police department. Although the general reputations of particular agencies may draw different types of candidates, new officers really do not know what their departments or their work will be like until they are on the inside. Regardless of what they may have seen on television or heard from recruiters or from family or friends already in policing, new officers enter their departments essentially as blank slates. Until they become cops, they are, in John Van Maanen's term, "know-nothings": just ordinary citizens who, unlike police officers, cannot possibly understand what the world is really about.[5]

Once they are inside, new officers' behavior, perceptions, and values are influenced enormously by their administrators, and there develops within police departments a shared view of the world and the role of the police in it.[6] To be sure, the routine of policing is governed in large measure by peer pressures and by the desire for peer approval, but, whether through act or omission, the chief is the main architect of police officers' street behavior. This is so because the strength and direction of street-level police peer pressures ultimately are determined by administrative definitions of *good* and *bad* policing and by the general tone that comes from the top.

When administrations are weak or too far out of touch with the reality of the streets—as when police chiefs pretend that hard and fast rules govern officers' behavior—they are rejected by officers. Then, unrestrained by any sense that their administrators' authority is legitimate, cops become free agents. They develop their own *sub rosa* codes of behavior, their own loyalties, their own systems for defining and dealing with good police work and bad police work, their own methods of telling headquarters what it wants to hear. The vice and narcotics corruption scandals that came to light in New York City during the early 1970s were caused by weak administrations that kept their heads in the sand while field units kept them supplied with superficially impressive arrest statistics.

When things are as they should be, the tone set by administrators creates a shared view and commonly held values that provide a happy compromise between unworkable hard and fast rules and the risk that officers' individual idiosyncrasies may lead to arbitrary treatment of citizens. Good administrators want their departments' organizational culture and rhythm to reflect varying community values, but they also want their officers to behave predictably and in accordance with their training. Good administrators strive for a diverse department, but they try also to ensure that it does not matter whether the cop who shows up in response to a citizen's call for help is black or white, male or female, fundamentalist or atheist. Good administrators seek diversity at the broadest level, but they want consistency at the one-to-one level of the cop on the street. Good administrators get these results by enforcing vigorously a bit of cant that all new officers hear over and over again from their instructors and supervisors: *I know you have prejudices. We all have prejudices, and there's not much the department can do about them. But if you let your prejudices affect your work, I'll do everything I can to put you out of this job.* Good administrators expect that this same rule will be applied to themselves by those to whom they are accountable; administrators who are accountable to nobody can do as they please.

Reducing the chance that prejudices will be acted out is one of the main reasons for trying to increase the representativeness of police agencies. It is more difficult to treat women and ethnic minorities badly when one is sharing a patrol car with a female or minority officer. A second reason for increasing police representativeness is to introduce views and values to police ranks that may vary from those characteristic of the white males who have long dominated policing. Here, the hope is that the presumably kinder and gentler policing styles of women and nonwhite officers will rub off on the entire organization, producing a less aggressive police agency. Yet, despite the LAPD's success in recruiting women and minorities,[7] the evidence suggests that things have not followed this pattern in that city. According to the Christopher Commission, no female officers are among the LAPD's 132 "top . . . officers ranked by the combined use of force reports, personnel complaints, and officer-involved shootings," and many "officers, both male and female, believe female officers are less personally challenged by defiant suspects and feel less need to deal with defiance with immediate force or confrontational language."[8] Although there is no way to tell what the records of those 132 officers would look like without the presumably restraining influences of female colleagues, the LAPD apparently has not produced consistency among its officers where response to provocation and use of force are concerned. However strong the LAPD's administration, it apparently has not succeeded in rendering officers' characteristics irrelevant: the gender of the officers who show up in response to Los Angeles citizens' calls for police probably does help determine how calls are handled.

Further, the consistency that flows from the LAPD's administrative philosophy and departmental culture may be very negative. In a recently completed study, George Felkenes of the Claremont Graduate School reported that regardless of race and gender, virtually all Los Angeles police officers see themselves as detached from the public, at war with the press, and underappreciated and disliked by an ungrateful public.[9] As Felkenes suggests, the organization apparently has hardened the newcomers' views far more than they have mellowed the department:

> [T]he officers do appear to take on an attitude that can be described as "cloning," in which a diverse group is so indoctrinated into the police culture that they become all but indistinguishable.[10]

## SIGNALS FROM THE TOP

The sentiments discovered by Felkenes do not develop in a vacuum. Instead, they filter down from the top and are part and parcel of what Chief Gates referred to as "the LAPD mentality." Although many scholars have suggested that it is rare for police officers to act out such negative sentiments violently,[11] these sentiments are important, because the shared view they reflect ultimately determines whether—and how—officers distinguish among citizens as *good* or *bad,* deserving or undeserving, and whether to arrest, ticket, help, or ignore the people with whom they come in contact.

These negative views also help officers to choose sides in what they see as the war between police and community. When citizens are defined as undeserving and ungrateful, or even hostile, the actions of the most violent officers are seen as expressions of justifiable overzealousness and are tolerated. Most of the officers present at the Rodney King beating, for example, never laid a finger on him—but neither did they do anything to stop the beating or to see that the conduct of the officers who did it was brought to official attention. Instead, although most LAPD officers (let us assume) would not engage in violence like the King beating, it was treated as an understandable response to provocative conduct on the part of an *asshole* badly in need of reeducation. This view is strengthened each time a police administrator signals that some groups are unworthy or that street justice against them is a tolerable prerogative of the street officer.

## FRANK RIZZO'S PHILADELPHIA

At the extreme, police administrators may even determine who will be killed. When the late Frank Rizzo was Philadelphia's hard-line Police Commissioner and Mayor, he also made headlines with provocative statements. "I'm gonna make Attila the Hun look like a faggot after this election's over," he told one reporter. "The way to treat criminals is *spacco il capa*"—to bust their heads—he told another. During his term as Mayor, Rizzo informed a national television audience, he had armed his officers so well that "we could invade Cuba and win."[12] Of Rizzo's relationship with the PPD and Joseph O'Neill, the man he appointed to head it, an internal U.S. Justice Department report noted in 1979:

> There is no firm evidence as to how or whether Rizzo remains directly active in PPD decision-making, only conflicting rumors. Whatever informal decision-making balance there may be vis-à-vis O'Neill and Rizzo, O'Neill formally makes all decisions on hiring officers and disciplining them. He is a strict moralist who uses the PPD disciplinary processes to investigate and punish officers for such matters as extramarital affairs and failure to pay debts. O'Neill knows the extent of the PPD police abuse problem. . . . However, he has resisted not only pressure from outside the PPD, but proposals from his own head of Internal Affairs, Chief Scafidi, for more discipline of officers using excessive force. O'Neill told us that disciplining officers for use of excessive force on duty would seriously impair police willingness to take aggressive action and impair morale. Commissioner O'Neill believes very strongly in protecting "his men" and expects compliance with his views on morality in return. Publicly he discounts the police abuse problem as "minuscule" and blames the popular view of the PPD as abusive on unfair press, fee-chasing lawyers, and persons who would undermine respect for authority.[13]

Whatever the formalities of this relationship, in 1973 O'Neill suspended the department's restrictions on officers' use of deadly force. Contrary to

practice in most large police departments, O'Neill also assigned investigations of police shootings to the department's Homicide Bureau rather than
to Internal Affairs or to some other high-level unit established just for this
purpose.[14] According to the Justice Department:

> The proffered explanation of why Homicide should investigate police
> shootings is that Homicide Division personnel have the expertise, derived
> from their other work, to investigate shooting matters. Chief [Joseph]
> Golden's Detective Bureau, not Internal Affairs, also investigated allega-
> tions of PPD brutality which come from detained prisoners, apparently be-
> cause detectives are working up "the case" against such prisoners anyway.
>
> [Chief Golden] dismisses all suggestions of on-duty abuse as the product
> of perjured or fabricated testimony and media distortions. Golden's atti-
> tudes are crucial in the PPD. He meets at least twice daily with Commis-
> sioner O'Neill as part of the Detective Bureau meetings to discuss major
> crimes and crime statistics.
>
> At one point in his career [Golden] was a working partner or "car-buddy"
> of Frank Rizzo, and is viewed by some in PPD and the community as retain-
> ing great power because of the Rizzo connection.
>
> Golden refuses to discipline or even admonish officers for "bad" on-duty
> shootings. The investigations into shootings are inadequate.[15]

O'Neill told the U.S. Civil Rights Commission very much the same
thing about disciplining police officers for "bad" shootings. In testimony at
a 1979 hearing, O'Neill said that if an officer "did shoot, if [the officer] felt
that he was doing that which is right, I'd most certainly defend him."[16]

The results of these attitudes and practices were dramatic. During
Rizzo's eight years as Philadelphia's mayor, fatal shootings by PPD officers increased by about 20 percent annually.[17] In a study conducted for the
U.S. Justice Department, one of us reported that, while individual Philadelphia cops were no more likely than New York cops to make arrests or to
come face to face with armed people, they were *thirty-seven times* as likely
as New York cops to shoot unarmed people who had threatened nobody
and who were fleeing from suspected nonviolent crimes. The Justice Department summarized forty-seven of the more controversial Philadelphia
"Police Shooting File" cases. Among them are the following:

75–86: 17-year-old black male who stole 3 bath mats and one toilet seat
cover from a store was shot in the back and killed as he tried to run
away.

75–119: 22-year-old black male involved in consensual homosexual
act in an alley was shot in the back of the leg as he ran from the police
who were responding to a burglary call.

76–2: 20-year-old white male prowler who ran from the officer with his hands up was shot in the ankle. The officer said it was a warning shot.

76–58: 18-year-old black male who had robbed a drunk of two packages of cup cakes was shot in the buttock as he ran [the suspect had knocked down the drunk and taken the cupcakes].

77–50: 16-year-old white male was shot while running from the theft of sneakers and albums.

78–13: 19-year-old white male was killed while running away from a traffic violation.

78–62: 19-year-old black male was killed while running from police headquarters while handcuffed with hands behind him [at the time he died, this individual was in custody for traffic violations and for leading police on a high-speed vehicle pursuit. After his death, it was discovered that he was the subject of an outstanding robbery arrest warrant].[18]

The Pennsylvania criminal law, which authorized police to use deadly force only in defense of life or to apprehend persons suspected of "forcible felonies,"[19] apparently was violated in most of these shootings (as in most of the forty others described by the Justice Department), but none of the officers involved was arrested or charged. Further, as O'Neill's comments regarding discipline might lead one to anticipate, officers who shot people invariably were found to have acted within whatever *ad hoc* departmental rules O'Neill applied after he had abandoned the former written policy on shooting. During the four years 1975–78, Fyfe could find only one Philadelphia police officer who was disciplined for an on-duty shooting: he killed his wife when she came to his police station on pay day to argue with him about the disposition of his paycheck.[20]

Perhaps the best evidence that the lawlessness of the Philadelphia Police Department was attributable to Rizzo and O'Neill was what happened when they left. During Rizzo's first year out of office, 1980, reform Mayor William Green's new Police Commissioner, Morton Solomon, reinstated and vigorously enforced the former shooting policy. Fatal shootings immediately declined by 67 percent, and officer injuries and deaths declined as well.[21] Thus, outrageous police practices in Philadelphia changed because the man who put them into place—Frank Rizzo—ultimately was rejected by the electorate.[22]

Evidence of administrative influence on police decisions to kill has been found beyond Frank Rizzo's Philadelphia. When Gerald Uelman studied the fifty police departments in Los Angeles County in the 1970s, he found that the best predictor of the rate at which officers killed people was not the level of violence they faced but the personal philosophies and policies of their chiefs.[23] It is critical, therefore, that police chiefs' philosophies and policies be consistent with the primary police responsibility to protect life, and that chiefs be held accountable for meeting this standard.

## POLICE AUTONOMY: LOS ANGELES AND MILWAUKEE

Ironically, especially in police departments that purport to adhere most closely to the military model, a key concept of the military metaphor—accountability to elected officials—frequently is missing. The LAPD has long clung to the military model and, until a June 1992 referendum overturned it, had a tradition of autonomous chiefs that dated back to August Vollmer's recommendation that police chiefs needed independence from the dirty politics of most city halls. In 1931 Vollmer wrote in the report of the prestigious Wickersham Commission that there was some merit to fears that autonomous police chiefs might eventually possess too much power, but that

> ... the people have gone too far in attempts to limit the control of police executives ... [T]heir attempt to protect themselves from a powerful autocratic chief of police has served to place them and the government in the hands of unscrupulous cutthroats, murderers, and bootleggers.[24]

Vollmer's conclusion was informed by his one year, Prohibition-era (1923–34) stint as Los Angeles's Chief of Police. Of that experience he wrote nine years later:

> [I]t is my opinion that under the present system and laws the police department of Los Angeles can never be separated from politics, nor be free from some of the vicious and frequently unfounded attacks made upon the department by some of the newspapers and preachers of Los Angeles.... And from what I know of the people of Los Angeles, it is unlikely that they will make any radical change.[25]

Vollmer's prediction held until the early postwar years, by which time Los Angeles had become a booming good-government city with a rapidly growing population much different from the days when he had been chief there. In 1950, when William Parker became the LAPD's chief, he put into place most of a blueprint for reform that had lain dormant since Vollmer had written it in 1924. With Parker's appointment, Los Angeles honored for the first time a 1936 city regulation granting the LAPD chief a civil service–tenured appointment from which he could be removed only *for cause,* which generally has meant that chiefs are guaranteed continued employment as long as they do not commit crimes. With this change, Los Angeles joined Milwaukee as one of the only two major American cities to have, in effect, a police chief for life.

These were not the only similarities between the LAPD and the MPD. Both departments were subjects of blue-ribbon mayoral commission reports stemming from controversial police incidents in 1991.[26] Both departments served populations that have changed color dramatically during the last generation. In 1950, for example, Los Angeles was 89 percent white; by 1990, the city was only 37 percent white and had become a highly segregated collection of white enclaves amid large black, brown, and yellow communities.[27] While Milwaukee's population is shrinking in numbers, it has experienced ethnic shifts much like those of Los Angeles:

> [T]he [1960] population of Milwaukee was 741,324, and was 90% White. . . .
> The 1990 United States Census reported a population of 628,088 . . . 63.3% were White, 30.5% African-American, 1.9% Asian-Pacific Islander, .9% Native American, and 3.4% other races. . . .
> Milwaukee is a racially segregated city. The 1990 Census showed that the population of two inner-city Aldermanic Districts was more than 90% African-American, while three of the 16 Aldermanic Districts, all on the far South Side, had less than 1% African-American population.[28]

Both the LAPD and MPD have long histories of depending exclusively on insiders for leadership. All four LAPD chiefs who served between the time Parker took the helm in 1950 and the appointment of former Philadelphia Police Commissioner Willie Williams as LAPD's chief in July 1992 had worked their way up through the department's ranks. Between them, Parker and Gates alone held office for more than thirty years.[29] While Milwaukee's Breier may regard Chief Arreola as an unwelcome outsider, Gates's accession to the LAPD's chief's job would certainly have met with Parker's approval. A Los Angeles police officer since 1949, Gates spent seven years on Parker's personal staff and was head of LAPD operations for Edward Davis, who served as chief from 1968 to 1978. Gates's style, according to critic Frank S. Donner, has

> . . . confirmed that he was cast in the same mold as the three Big Men who preceded him: James Davis [chief in 1926–29 and 1933–38] and Gates's two revered mentors, William H. Parker and Ed Davis—arrogant, moralizing, intolerant of critics, and hostile to dissent generally. Like his predecessors, Gates personified the California countersubversive tradition and inherited the legacy of extremism that has long flourished in Los Angeles's political culture.[30]

Like Parker and Davis, Gates was succeeded by a person selected in a civil service process that made it nearly impossible for any candidate from outside the department to get the job:[31] In a development we and many others found even more surprising than the King verdict, however, Wil-

liams the outsider did win the job. A similar line of succession also has
long existed in Milwaukee. In Milwaukee, Vollmer's Wickersham Commission reported admiringly in 1931, there had been only two police chiefs
in forty-six years.[32] When Chief Arreola was appointed in 1989, he became
the MPD's third chief in twenty-five years.

According to the commissions that investigated them in 1991, both departments apparently have tolerated nasty racial and ethnic humor and gay-
bashing by officers. Both departments have defined their primary work as
warring on crime, and both derogate the other services urban police are
called upon to provide. In both cities, beatings following police vehicle
chases have created great public scandals. Ten years before the Rodney
King incident, three MPD officers were fired and criminally charged for a
beating and cover-up involving a lewd behavior suspect who had fled on a
motorcycle.[33]

Both departments also have suffered spectacular losses in civil rights
suits.[34] In 1984 the Seventh Circuit U.S. Court of Appeals affirmed a $1.6
million award to the family of Daniel Bell, a twenty-three-year-old black
man who had been unjustifiably shot and killed by a Milwaukee police
officer.[35] More important, the Circuit Court agreed with a verdict that this
shooting, which occurred in 1958, had been the subject of a cover-up that
had lasted for *twenty years* and that had involved Chief Breier's predeces-
sor. During that time the dead man's family brought two suits against the
MPD. One was dismissed by a judge whom the police had deceived; unable to prove what they suspected had really happened to their son and
brother, the family had agreed to a small settlement in the other. Only in
1978, when the truth finally was told by a police officer who had seen the
shooting and found that he could no longer live with his conscience, did
this whitewash end. The Circuit Court agreed with the trial judge, who had
written of the earlier settlement and dismissal:

> [T]he [police] fraud in this case is sufficient to nullify an otherwise valid
> settlement and dismissal. This is not a case in which the defendant simply
> lied and thereby made the plaintiff's proof of his case difficult. Rather, this
> is a case of massive conspiracy by high ranking Milwaukee officials to pre-
> vent the disclosure of the true facts of the shooting of Daniel Bell. Given the
> monopoly on force held by the government, this conspiracy prevented the
> proper functioning of the judicial system.[36]

There were also significant differences between the LAPD and the
MPD. The LAPD closely adhered to the military ideal of an omnipotent
command structure, while Milwaukee's officers were organized into a
powerful labor union that had much to say about work rules; MPD person-

nel assignments are based on seniority rather than supervisors' estimates of officers' merit. Still, the differences between these departments are minor in light of the fact that, until Breier and Gates retired, both were led by chief executives who, in effect, had no bosses. Consequently, both departments long were able to fashion important policies in virtual autonomy.

## CONCLUSIONS ABOUT INSULARITY

One effect of such a long leash is suggested by Chief Breier's comments about the "good people of Milwaukee": police policy may be formulated in response to majority demands for strong law enforcement. Such responsiveness, however, may create a tyranny of the majority or, at least, a tyranny of those who have the chief's ear. A veteran police commander told us:

> You can't decide what the police should do exclusively on the basis of what the public wants. Most of the people who take the time to talk to the police do it because they want quiet neighborhoods and high real estate values. If it were up to them, the cops would be kicking ass and making people disappear to keep their streets quiet. Even the nicest people are like this. They just want whatever's troubling them to go away, and they don't care how it happens. I've had sweet little old ladies tell me that the cops have forgotten what their nightsticks are for, and that we need a "goon squad" to make examples out of kids who hang out on streetcorners.[37]

Lifetime tenure and the consequent absence of accountability for police chiefs also create the danger that important policy decisions may be made without consideration of any views but the chief's, or that structurally isolated chiefs may misperceive who the "good people" are or what they want. A highly critical 1972 Wisconsin State report on his department suggests that former Chief Breier may have been mistaken in assuming that he was tapped into the wishes of the "good people":

> Almost all of the major deficiencies of the Milwaukee Police Department enumerated in this report are attributable to the isolated condition of the department in relation to the citizenry its serves. The responsibility for law enforcement policymaking and implementation is concentrated in an office whose incumbent is directly accountable to no one ... the erosion [of MPD's high national reputation] is due not so much to any personal inadequacy of the police chiefs who ruled during this time, but rather to the department's structure, which has insulated the entire organization from, and rendered it ill-equipped to cope with, significant changes in Milwaukee neighborhoods.[38]

## GOOD AND BAD PEOPLE

Administrative insularity breeds administrative arrogance, which generates independence from legal constraints or values. As we discussed in our chapter on vigilante justice, cops become a law unto themselves, based on their understanding of who are *good* and who are *bad* people, judgments that are not necessarily tied to race. It is easy to conclude that many critical LAPD decisions related to use of force have reflected idiosyncratic views of the distinctions between *good people* and *bad people*—and of what each *deserves*—rather than systematic application of sound police principles. As we discussed in Chapter 2, the LAPD's use of choke holds to subdue nonviolent citizens ended only after a traffic violator who had been choked unconscious brought a suit that went as far as the U.S. Supreme Court. By that time, Los Angeles had seen sixteen choke hold–related deaths in five years.

A lesser known, but even more lethal, LAPD innovation has been the Special Investigation Section (SIS). Formed in 1965, this elite unit's clientele is an outgroup—robbers and burglars—that has no defenders among the public. As a consequence, with strong support from the LAPD's chiefs, SIS has been free to make up its own rules for dealing with these worst of all *bad people*. The most controversial of the home-baked rules is the SIS practice of standing by and watching as its surveillance subjects victimize innocent citizens, and then confronting offenders as they leave the scenes of their crimes. The *Los Angeles Times* reporter David Freed asked SIS's commander, Captain Dennis Conte, about the dangers of this practice. According to Freed, SIS had ample grounds to arrest most of its surveillance subjects before they committed the violent crimes for which they eventually were confronted. Why, Freed wondered, did SIS not attempt to prevent bloodshed by arresting these subjects for lesser crimes, on authority of outstanding warrants or for attempting to commit the violent crimes witnessed by SIS? Conte explained, "Public safety is certainly a concern, but we have to look beyond that because if we arrest someone for attempt, the likelihood of a conviction is not as great."[39]

Many of SIS's subjects have not survived long enough to tell whether the unit's tactics make conviction more likely than would be true of more conventional police operations. According to Freed, the nineteen men in SIS killed twenty-three suspects, wounded twenty-three more, and shot at but missed at least twenty others during the unit's first twenty-three years.[40] By 1992, SIS's totals had increased to twenty-eight dead and twenty-seven wounded in forty-five separate shooting incidents.[41] During this time, one SIS detective has been shot and killed, but he died after being hit by another officer's shotgun blast.

All this blood and guts is not a result of an enormous volume of business on SIS's part. According to Freed, SIS—the only full-time surveillance unit Freed could find among more than twenty of the country's largest municipal police departments—accounted for only thirty-six arrests, or less than two per officer, during 1987. The 1992 testimony of SIS commanders and supervisors suggested that 1987 was an average year and that SIS officers had by then made slightly more than a thousand arrests over the unit's twenty-six-year history.[42] In other words, nearly one in twenty SIS arrest attempts—45 of about 1,000—has resulted in shooting.

## JOHN CRUMPTON AND JANE BERRY

Two cases illustrate both the violence of the SIS operating style and the unit's emphasis on the *big arrest* over the lives and safety of innocent citizens. For seventeen of forty-three days during the summer of 1982, SIS officers followed John Crumpton and Jane Berry, two ex-cons suspected of robbing banks. A police report states:

> The suspects' method of operation was believed to be a "bank-take-over" in which the suspects wore gloves and masks and were armed with handguns. The suspects would force the patrons and employees of a bank to lie on the floor at gunpoint. The male suspect would vault the teller's counter as the female stood guard over the persons in the bank.[43]

Crumpton and Berry first came to SIS attention in July 1982. According to a court document:

> [O]n Wednesday, July 14, 1982, the Security Pacific Bank, 2496 Glendale Boulevard, Los Angeles, was robbed by a lone suspect described as a male of unknown descent, wearing a flesh-colored Halloween mask, gloves and armed with a small-caliber automatic handgun. The witnesses observed the suspect leave the bank and enter a 1975 Ford Grenada [sic], California license 369 RDN, driven by a female Caucasian who then drove from the scene.[44]

The LAPD detectives who investigated this case visited the car's owner, an acquaintance of Crumpton. He told them that he had loaned his car to Crumpton and Berry on the day of the Security Pacific robbery and had had no idea that they had intended to use it in a crime. Reportedly unable to arrest Crumpton and Berry "due to disguises and gloves worn during the robbery," the robbery detectives requested that SIS begin a surveillance of the pair.[45]

The police decision merely to watch Crumpton and Berry perplexes the veteran police investigators to whom we have spoken; even before the surveillance began, the two were what most police would regard as *likely sus-*

*pects*. Both had long records and, indeed, had been sentenced to federal prisons in 1975 for robbing a bank together. Berry was paroled in 1980 and had been wanted since April 1982 for parole violations. Crumpton had been released from prison in November 1980 and was free on bail while awaiting trial for a grocery store stickup. As the surveillance went on, things got worse. In August a parole violation warrant also was issued against Crumpton. The SIS detectives who watched them reported that they "appear[ed] to randomly select and 'case' numerous banks."[46] On surveillance "off-days," hidden bank cameras took "photographs believed to be of Crumpton and Berry committing several bank robberies."[47]

SIS kept its distance from Crumpton and Berry until September 15, 1982, when a team of nine SIS detectives followed the couple as they cruised near a Burbank branch of the Security Pacific Bank. The police were

> . . . aware that [the bank] had been robbed approximately two weeks prior. The robbery had been committed by a male and a female using the suspected method of Crumpton and Berry; wearing masks and gloves, both armed with handguns. Based on the prior robbery and the suspects' actions, the detective believed that the Security Pacific Bank was the suspects' possible target.[48]

The police watched as Crumpton and Berry drove to an isolated parking lot to switch cars—and to give Berry an opportunity to don the "Bozo-style" red wig that had been part of the description of the female half of the robbery team the police were looking for. Instead of stopping the pair at that point, however, the police followed them as they drove in a stolen 1961 Corvair to an alley behind the bank. There, without having provided the bank's staff or customers with any warning that they anticipated a bank takeover, the police waited outside as Crumpton and Berry "alighted from the Corvair and approached the bank wearing [Halloween] masks and gloves," then entered. Once inside, according to the police, the two ordered the bank's personnel and customers (eleven in all) to the floor at gunpoint, executed their bank takeover, and left, dropping money as they fled.

Rather than confront the two as they emerged from the bank, police followed them back to the isolated lot where they had parked their first car. There, when the police challenged them, Berry allegedly pulled a pistol (which she did not fire), and Crumpton repeatedly reached toward his waistband where, it was subsequently discovered, there were only an empty holster and a screwdriver.

> The four detectives believed that Crumpton and Berry intended to shoot Detectives Sirk and Niles and fired 16 rounds from their shotguns, almost si-

multaneously, in rapid succession. The suspects fell to the ground; however, Crumpton continued in his attempt to remove the object [the empty holster] from his waistband. Detectives Sirk and Niles observed Crumpton's movement and believed that the suspect was still attempting to withdraw a handgun from his waistband. Detective Sirk fired one round from his service revolver at Crumpton as Detective Niles fired one additional shotgun round at the suspect.

The suspects were taken into custody without further incident. . . . Berry was treated for multiple gunshot wounds [and] was booked for murder.

Crumpton was treated for multiple gunshots wounds to the upper body, however, failed to respond to medical treatment and expired at 1226 hours.[49]

Crumpton's death led to a murder charge against Berry. Even though she had killed nobody, California law (like that of most other states) defines *felony murder* as engaging in a felony in which a death occurs. LAPD found that the officers had acted justifiably. From her prison cell, Jane Berry filed a civil rights suit against the officers, Chief Gates, Mayor Bradley, and the City of Los Angeles. Not surprisingly, Berry failed to convince a jury that an imprisoned bank robber deserved compensation for injuries she had sustained in the course of her crime. Still, her case produced intriguing information about the shooting and about the history of the officers involved in it.[50]

Each of the seventeen rounds of double-O buckshot discharged by the police in this incident contained nine .32 caliber pellets. Thus, counting the single police pistol shot, the police fired 154 projectiles at Crumpton and Berry. Crumpton was struck by forty-four of them, and Berry, who was two months pregnant, was hit thirteen times. Contrary to what one might expect from a reading of the police reports, however, none of these shots struck Crumpton in the front of his "upper body." Instead, four hit him in the left arm; six in the right arm; six in the right back; one in the left back; thirteen hit his right hip, buttock, and the rear and side of his right thigh; six hit his left buttock and thigh; three hit his right leg; one entered the sole of his right foot; three entered his left sole; and one hit his right hand.[51] Thus, his back and side and, eventually, the soles of his feet were facing the police as they shot him. According to the police report:

[E]xamination revealed a combination of 23 tears and holes on the back of [Crumpton's] shirt. . . . All of the holes were consistent with pellet entry holes. No holes were observed in the front of the shirt.

Crumpton's tank-top shirt was examined and found to contain seven entry-types holes on the back of the tank top with no corresponding exits in the front.

Crumpton's blue levis pants contained 32 entry-type holes in the back side. These holes corresponded to wounds on the body. Thirteen of these holes appeared to be a combination of entries from both an upright and supine position with the head faced away from the point of entry. The front side of the trousers had four holes on the lower pants leg consistent with exit holes.

Crumpton's undershorts contained 16 holes in the back side with no corresponding exit holes. There were two minor tears in the fly opening.

Crumpton's left shoe contained three holes. The trajectory of the pellets causing these holes appeared to be from bottom to top. The right shoe had two holes approximately 5 inches from the toe, with the trajectory apparently from top to bottom.

Crumpton's two white socks had a total of 10 holes in them . . .

One of the gloves worn by Crumpton was observed to have a hole which corresponded to the wound on Crumpton's right ring finger.[52]

When the police obtained Berry's clothing from the hospital, they found:

Berry's long-sleeved white blouse contained seven holes to the back of the garment which appeared to be entry bullet holes. The front of the shirt contained one hole which was possibly grazing entry/exit hole.

Berry apparently was wearing a red T-shirt under the long-sleeved blouse. The red T-shirt contained 10 holes in the back which were consistent with bullet entry holes. There were no corresponding exits to these holes.

The brown corduroy pants worn by Berry contained eight holes which appeared to be entry bullet holes. There were no apparent corresponding exits. Two of these holes were possibly ricochets.

Berry's bra contained a hole to the back which appeared to be an entry wound with no apparent exit. One of the socks worn by Berry contained 11 bullet holes, but entry or exit could not be determined.[53]

The police report also indicates:

The only information available regarding Berry's physical injuries was received from Dr. A. Renner, St. Joseph Medical Center. Dr. Renner treated Berry for multiple gunshot wounds to the front and back of the upper torso and the back of both legs. Due to the Right of Privacy Act, detectives were unable to obtain further medical information.[54]

In fact, the report of the ambulance personnel contained in the police files indicates that Berry sustained "'00' shotgun wound to back. No visible exit wound." The sketches in the police file on the case show that one of the eight holes in Berry's trousers appears on the outer seam of the left leg; there is no sketch to show the seven that entered through the rear. In all, Berry sustained thirteen shotgun wounds to the back of her torso and legs.

If one believes the police account of this event, therefore, Crumpton was hit forty-four times in the back and side and the bottoms of his feet while he allegedly reached again and again for a holster that held no gun. By the police version, Berry was hit thirteen times in the back of her torso, legs, and feet while she threatened the police with a gun she never fired. If one believes Jane Berry, she and Crumpton tried to surrender to the police immediately but were shot down as they tried to protect themselves by turning away from the police and dropping to the ground.

This shooting raises significant questions about LAPD policy. Why didn't the police attempt to take Crumpton and Berry down early in their robbery spree? There apparently was sufficient evidence for a warrant, and an early morning raid on the pair's apartment could have resulted in bloodless arrests. Indeed, why didn't the police see to it that Crumpton and Berry were summarily taken off the street for their parole violations?[55] Warrants had been issued for both of them. Why didn't the police attempt to confront them as they cased the bank on the day they robbed it? The pair had robbed this same bank a few weeks earlier; immediately prior to the holdup, an SIS detective who was posted "100 feet north of the bank . . . did observe them make 'several passes' by" the bank.[56] Why didn't the police confront them when they drove to the parking lot the first time? There, the police saw Berry put on a distinctive red wig that was part of the description from the couple's earlier robberies. Why didn't the police stop them as they drove to the bank? They were in a twenty-one-year-old Corvair, so there was virtually no possibility that they could outrun the police. Why didn't the police confront the pair as, wearing masks and gloves, they walked from their car to the bank? Instead, while a police radio transmission warned all the SIS personnel to don bulletproof vests before confronting Crumpton and Berry, the police let these two walk into and take over a bank full of unsuspecting employees and customers. Why didn't the police confront Crumpton and Berry as they left the bank? Instead, the police let them drive to an isolated spot where there would be no civilian witnesses to what happened next.

The records of the nine detectives involved in this surveillance strengthen the suspicion that they let Crumpton and Berry go on about their business until they could be cornered in a lethal trap from which there was no escape. During the thirteen years before the Crumpton–Berry shooting, these nine had been named as defendants in no fewer than twenty-eight civil rights and misconduct suits. Two of these officers—Detectives John Tortorici and Jerry Brooks—had accumulated truly spectacular records as defendants in civil litigation. For Tortorici, who reportedly did not fire any shots in this incident, the Crumpton–Berry suit was his second in 1982; before it, he had been sued twice in 1975; once in 1977; three times in

1978; three times in 1979; and once in 1981. When Berry's case came to
trial in 1990, Tortorici was present, still assigned to SIS.[57] The Crumpton–
Berry suit was the ninth in ten years for Brooks, who had fired four shotgun
rounds at the two robbers.

## THE McDONALD'S BANDITS

Both Tortorici and Brooks also were involved in the second SIS case we
examine, perhaps the most spectacular in the unit's bloody history.[58] In this
latter case, Brooks did much of the shooting, and Tortorici, by then assigned to LAPD's Robbery-Homicide Division and a member of its
Officer-Involved Shooting Team, did much of the investigating, *including
the official interview of his old SIS colleague and co-defendant, Jerry
Brooks.*

In late 1989, twenty-five-year-old Jesus (Jesse) Arango came to
LAPD's attention as a suspect in a series of armed robberies in which the
safes of Los Angeles area McDonald's restaurants were the usual targets.
Arango and his brother-in-law, thirty-seven-year-old Hector Burgos, had
previously been suspected of complicity in a series of robberies and thefts
from McDonald's franchises over the five years in which one or both had
worked for McDonald's.

By the time they ran into SIS, the evidence against Arango and Burgos
was fairly compelling. In late 1988, while working for a McDonald's franchise in Culver City, Arango made some lame excuses for bungling a Saturday transfer of store receipts to an armored car company. His "mistake"
made it necessary to safeguard heavy weekend receipts in the store's safe.
When the store manager opened for business on Monday morning, he
found that the safe had been broken into and robbed. The following day,
Arango "showed up at work driving a new 1987 Ford Thunderbird (gray)."

About 1:00 A.M., August 25, 1989, four young Hispanic men confronted
a cleanup employee as he opened the rear door of a Westwood area
McDonald's in order to remove trash. The men, masked and armed with
shotguns, pistols, and a knife, forced the manager to open the safe, took its
contents, and left in an employee's car. The car was found the following
day; in it was a "toy plastic rifle resembling a shotgun."

At 11:15 P.M., Sunday, September 4, according to Arango, by then—*in-
explicably*—the manager of a downtown McDonald's franchise,

> . . . as he was exiting via the rear door, two or three males, possibly Hispa-
> nic, forced their way in and made all the employees lay [sic] on the floor.
> Two of the victims had their hands, feet, and mouths taped with duct tape.
> Arango was taken to the office and made to open the safe. Arango was then

put on the floor and his hands, feet and mouth were taped. One of the suspects put a McDonalds shirt on so as not to draw attention from passersby. . . .

Detective B. Cureton, #24975, Central Detectives, was assigned as the original investigating officer as to this robbery. On 9-8-89, Detective Cureton interviewed Arango regarding the robbery. Arango told Cureton that after he had opened the safe, one of the suspects wrapped tape around his mouth and legs. Arango stated that his hands were also taped behind his back. Cureton noticed that where the tape supposedly was wrapped around Arango's wrists, there was *no hair missing* from either wrist. During the interview of the other victims that had their hands taped, Cureton noticed hair missing from the wrist areas.

When Detective Cureton interviewed the owner of the business . . . , he told Cureton that he suspected Arango may be involved in this robbery. [The owner] based his suspicions on a robbery that occurred in June 1989 while Arango was employed at the Central Avenue and Olympic Blvd. store. Arango had failed to count and withdraw excess money from the drive-up window position and had told two of the four employees working the window to leave. Shortly after Arango left the window, it was robbed by two male Hispanics in a white, 4-door, possibly Ford Granada.

On 9-15-89, Detective Cureton conducted a polygraph examination of Arango. Arango gave conflicting statement and failed the exam. Several days later, Arango quit his job with McDonalds. [Emphasis in original.]

Had the police checked, they would have discovered that Jesse's cousin Aramus Arango, later identified by one of the ring as a member, owned a white 1977 Ford Granada four-door sedan. Further, the file includes a memo in which McDonald's security personnel note that, after the maintenance men had been blindfolded, they "thought they heard a third party conversing with the robbers" in a "funny accent" about security precautions taken by the robbers. The memo also describes other irregularities:

*Incidents Not Normal*

1) Jessie [sic] normally left between 9:30 and 10: P.M., never later.
2) Robbers familiar with & knew *all* about our store.—Inside Job
   a) Basement
   b) Lobby
   c) Safe
   d) Building Security
3) Bun delivery arrived at 9:45. Manager never stays to sign for buns. This is always verified in morning. Jessie stayed to help bun driver leave early.
4) Jessie's car parked directly behind store. Never parked there before. Always parked on street.
5) Jessie was too calm. Never appeared shook-up by incident.

6) Robber very familiar with maintenance men's situation and threatened them about their families.

7) Jessie's watch had been stolen in robbery. 3–4 days later, he walked in wearing a very expensive gold watch.

8) Various other McDonald's incidents.

9) Police Department (LAPD) feels he is "dirty." Polygraph test proves it.

On Sunday, September 18, at 2:30 A.M., the night manager of another McDonald's arrived at his home after closing his store. Three armed Hispanic men were waiting for him. They blindfolded and bound him with duct tape and drove him back to his store. The men took his keys, but "asked him no questions regarding keys, door locks or alarms," because they "knew which keys unlocked doors and which turned off alarms" and "were familiar with the store layout." They did ask the manager for the combination to the safe, with which they opened its outer door. They then pried open the safe's inner door and looted it.

At 12:35 A.M., Sunday, October 9, another McDonald's night manager was abducted as he walked home from his shop. His assailants were two men driving a "gray colored vehicle, with an eagle design across the taillights (possibly Ford T-Bird)," a description that matched the car Arango had first driven to work the day after the 1988 McDonald's robbery in which he had been a suspect. The men, who "wore something over their heads," blindfolded the manager with duct tape and drove him to his store. They remained there for an hour while, wearing "McDonald's shirts so as not to draw attention," they opened the outer door to his safe with the combination he had provided at gunpoint, pried open its inner door, and looted it.

At 4:15 A.M., Sunday, October 23, two McDonald's employees were closing up shop when they were approached at gunpoint by three Hispanic males who bound their eyes and hands with duct tape, coerced from them the combination to the safe's outer door, forced its inner door, took the money, and ran. Six days later, on Saturday, October 29, again at 4:15 A.M., four Hispanic males wearing nylon stockings on their heads met four employees of a Carl's Jr. franchise as they arrived at work and repeated this drill.

On Monday morning, November 13, two McDonald's franchises were robbed in the same way. The first robbery, at 2:45 A.M., involved a team of four Hispanic men; the second, at 5:00 A.M., involved only two Hispanic men.

On Sunday, November 26, SIS began an intermittent surveillance of Arango and his brother-in-law but observed no untoward activity. The surveillance apparently had been stopped when, at 3:30 A.M. on Thursday, December 30, a McDonald's employee and her father—who had driven her home from work—were abducted from their home's carport by five Hispanic men wearing costume masks. They were then driven to the store and, with another employee, were blindfolded and bound with duct tape while the safe was robbed. Two days later, at 11:55 P.M., January 1, 1990, four Hispanic men wearing clear Halloween masks and carrying guns, used plastic ties and duct tape to bind and blindfold six McDonald's employees. There, while using "McDonald's terminology" related to store operations and security, they robbed the safe. In this case, apparently for the first time, two victims suffered some undisclosed minor injuries at the hands of the robbers. The surveillance was reinstated.

On February 4, 1990, SIS detectives followed Arango and Burgos as they drove to the home of nineteen-year-old Alfredo Olivas, picked him up, and drove off. Although this surveillance all took place after 11:30 P.M. on a Sunday night and the records include no indication that Arango and his associates knew that they were being followed by police, SIS's elite detectives reported that they soon lost the car in traffic. A short time later, a McDonald's employee was confronted by two armed and masked men as he was being dropped off at his residence after work. He was blindfolded and taken back to his store in a car occupied by his two assailants and driven by a third man. The employee told the robbers that he was not the store's manager and therefore did not have its keys or the combination to its safe. The robbers stopped their car, pushed him out of it, and went on their way.

On the following Sunday, February 11, SIS massed twenty-two detectives and a police helicopter to begin a surveillance at Arango's home. At 10 P.M., he, Olivas, and twenty-year-old Juan Bahena left the house and moved two bags from the trunk of Aramus Arango's white Ford Granada to the trunk of Arango's Thunderbird.[59] All three then returned to the house, only to leave a short time later with Burgos, driving off in the Thunderbird. The Thunderbird traveled to a McDonald's restaurant on LA's Foothill Boulevard, drove around the parking lot, and exited. The car stopped on a nearby side street, where three of its occupants went to its trunk to "put on additional clothing." At 11 P.M., the Thunderbird parked on the cross street adjoining the McDonald's parking lot and, with all four occupants obscured by heavily tinted windows, remained there for an hour and a half while police watched unnoticed.

At 12:30, the Thunderbird moved off, drove around the block, and parked on Foothill Boulevard, directly across the street from McDonald's. Burgos emerged from the car, which was parked immediately behind a large truck, walked up and down the street and around the McDonald's parking lot, and got back into the car. A few minutes later, Burgos and Olivas took a similar stroll before returning to the car. Inside, the restaurant had closed and employees had started on their way home, eventually leaving the manager, twenty-four-old Robin Cox, alone in the store. Ms. Cox was totally unaware of what was happening outside.

Shortly after 1:00 A.M., Burgos, Bahena, and Olivas got out of their car, reached into the trunk, and either retrieved or deposited something the surveillance officers reportedly could not see. The three then walked to the restaurant and slunk around it in the dark, at times moving near a side door that was out of police sight. Soon the three were joined by Arango. According to the reports, SIS had anticipated that the "suspects were most likely preparing to do one of two things: Case the location for a future robbery attempt, or await the departure of the manager after closing at which point they would follow the employee and kidnap her."

This reasoning would befuddle any experienced police officer. Given the history of weekend robberies and the ideal circumstances they apparently believed to exist, it would be highly unlikely that these four bandits would put off a robbery until a better time. The bandits had Ms. Cox alone and vulnerable. For them, there could have been no better time than this. Nor could there have been a better place than this. Kidnapping Cox would have required Arango and company to wait for her to leave the restaurant so that they could abduct her and transport her *back* to their starting point. In any event, because the suspects had parked their car directly across Foothill Boulevard from McDonald's, and because some unknown citizen reportedly made notes while standing near the car, the police also ruled out the kidnapping scenario, concluding instead that Arango and his companions were merely casing the restaurant.

Inside the restaurant, Ms. Cox ("C") had spotted the prowlers at her door. At 1:19, she called an LAPD 911 operator ("O"):

O: Operator 838.
C: I have an attempted robbery in progress.
O: Where are you calling from?
C: 7950 Sunland Boulevard—Foothill Boulevard.
O: Are the suspects still there?
C: Yeah, they're outside. I'm inside a McDonald's restaurant and they're there right now.
O: How did they try to rob you?
C: I don't know but they're trying to get inside.
O: Is it a closed business?

C: Yes, it's a McDonald's. They're trying to break through the door.

O: White, black, Mexican—how many?

C: Mexican. I just seen two.

O: Any clothing description on them?

C: I seen a black shirt.

O: On how many of them?

C: On one of them. I didn't see what the other one had on.

O: Do they have any weapons?

C: I don't know. I didn't look that well. They're coming in the back. ....
They're coming in the doorway in the back. I was taking a reading
'cause I was getting ready to leave and I saw them duck and hide and
I saw the other one run the other way.

O: They say anything to you?

C: No, they didn't. I don't know if I saw them or not. They're outside.
I'm inside. They're trying to get in.

C: I understand that, Ma'am. What is your name please?

C: My name is Robin.

O: Okay, Robin. We'll get the police over there immediately.

C: Please, 'cause I'm here by myself.

O: Okay, we'll get the police there immediately.

O: Is there anything else you want me to say?

C: Are you going to hang up?

O: Well, Ma'am. What else do you want me to do? I need to talk with
police officers to dispatch them. Either we can sit here on the telephone and you can waste my time and keep me from getting officers
over there or we can hang up.

C: Okay.

Neither the 911 operator nor local patrol officers had been advised of SIS's operation. At 1:23 A.M., a black-and-white unit was dispatched in response to Ms. Cox's call. The SIS officers, who were using a tactical frequency, did not hear this transmission, but the helicopter crew assigned to the stakeout did. They informed Brian Davis, the SIS detective in charge of the surveillance, that patrol cars were en route to the scene. At 1:24 A.M., Davis "caused the call to be canceled." There then somehow began a twenty-four-minute gap in the transcripts of SIS's radio transmissions.

According to Davis, he then decided to "immediately move in and arrest the suspects outside the restaurant when it could be established all the suspects were together." The detective closest to the restaurant, however, reportedly radioed that this would be unsafe because Burgos, Olivas, and Bahena had already succeeded in gaining entrance to the lobby.

Based on the unexpected action of the suspects, Detective Davis instructed the surveillance teams to hold their positions. The detectives were aware that during the commission of the prior crimes the suspects generally did not physically harm the employees and it was believed that to confront the suspects inside the location would severely jeopardize both the safety of Robin Cox and the detectives. A tactical plan was now formulated which would allow the suspects to exit the restaurant and return to their vehicle. Once the suspects were together contained in the vehicle, designated teams would employ a vehicle jamming maneuver and take the suspects into custody, before they could pull away from the curb.

Inside the restaurant, the robbers

> ... approached [Ms. Cox], produced a handgun and demanded money. The suspects taped her eyes and tied her hands behind her back. She was taken to the back of the restaurant and told to sit down. Ms. Cox ... thought [correctly] the suspects were inside the location for approximately 30 minutes beating on the safes. At one point during her ordeal, one of the suspects put a gun to her head and demanded the combination to the safe. She gave it to them several times and explained how the safe worked.

According to the police report sent to Chief Gates, Arango then left the restaurant, deposited a dark bag and a toolbox in the trunk of his car, started the car, and turned its lights on. Quickly, his three companions ran from the restaurant to join him in the Thunderbird.

> Detectives Brooks and Spelman ... stopped [their unmarked Buick] adjacent to the driver's door of the suspects' vehicle, which prevented the suspects from moving away from the curb. Simultaneously Detectives Helms and Zierenberg positioned their vehicle at the rear of the suspects' vehicle. Detectives Harrison and Weaver stopped their vehicle to the rear of Detective Brooks' vehicle as Detectives Strickland and Tippings stopped their vehicle to the rear of Detective Helms' vehicle. Detectives Eggar and Callian approached on foot.

In fact, Brooks drove up alongside Arango's car, slowed, and turned right, driving the right corner of his bumper into the Thunderbird's door. At the same time, Helms struck the rear of the Thunderbird so that, with a large truck directly in front of it, it was trapped on three sides. What happened next was a bloodbath. According to the police report:

> Immediately upon the stop of his vehicle against the driver's door of the suspect's vehicle, Detective Spelman, the passenger officer, observed Burgos, in the right front seat, pivot counterclockwise and point what appeared to be a blue steel semiautomatic pistol at him. Detective Spelman shouted, "Gun" to alert the other detectives and in defense of his own life

fired one shotgun round at Burgos. Detectives Brooks and Harrison shouted at the suspects, "Police, drop the gun." The suspects failed to comply and Detectives Brooks, Eggar and Harrison fired several rounds at the suspect. Detective Brooks then observed a suspect in the rear of the vehicle brandishing a handgun. Detective Brooks alerted the other detectives to the presence of a gun in the rear area of the vehicle, at which time Detective Helms began firing at the suspects inside the vehicle to prevent them from shooting at Detective Spelman who was in close proximity to the armed suspects. Burgos quickly exited the right front door of the vehicle and ran north into a vacant dirt lot. Burgos held a blue steel handgun in his right hand and as he ran he pivoted his torso and pointed the handgun in the direction of the detectives. In the belief Burgos was preparing to shoot at them, Detectives Spelman, Zierenberg, Tippings and Callian fired several rounds wounding Burgos who fell to the ground.

The detectives continued to observe a gun being brandished in the rear of the vehicle and they directed gunfire into the vehicle to prevent the suspects from firing at them. Upon termination of the gunfire, and when it appeared the suspects had lowered their weapons, they were ordered out of the vehicle. When the suspects failed to exit, Detectives Helms and Zierenberg announced that they were going to approach and secure the vehicle from the passenger side. . . .

When [Helms and Zierenberg] reached an area near the open passenger door, they observed a handgun on the right rear floorboard of the vehicle and movement towards the weapon from both Bahena and Olivas who were now both in the right rear seat area of the car. Additionally Arango, who was still in the driver seat area, quickly moved his upper torso and shoulders upward. In the belief the suspects were armed or attempting to arm themselves and preparing to shoot at them, Detectives Helms and Zierenberg fired several additional rounds each from their .45 caliber semiautomatic pistols at the suspects who now ceased their movement. Detective Zierenberg again ordered Olivas to raise his hands away from his weapon, Olivas now complied. Detectives Callian and Weaver approached and removed the suspects from the vehicle where they were handcuffed without further incident. (NOTE: The officers manning the air unit were unable to witness the shooting incident, due to the fact that at the time of the shooting their orbiting altitude was 7,000 feet).

In all, the police fired 24 shotgun rounds (each containing nine .32 caliber pellets) and eleven .45 caliber pistol rounds—a total of 227 projectiles—at the four suspects. Arango, Burgos, and Bahena died at the scene. Like Ms. Berry, Olivas survived, was charged with felony murder, eventually was convicted of robbery, and was sentenced to a long prison term.

The suspects fired no shots. Indeed, the weapons they had so successfully used during their string of holdups turned out to be empty $CO_2$ pellet pistols rather than real guns. The nature of these guns raised a question that could be debated—*would robbers, trapped and under shotgun fire, persist in brandishing realistic but harmless guns?* Regardless of which side one might choose in such an argument, much of the physical evidence and the original police reports leave no room for debate. They unambiguously contradict the account of this incident approved by Chief Gates.

The police accounts of this event claim that Burgos was fired upon as he pointed a gun at police from the right front passenger seat of the Thunderbird. Then, as he fled on foot, Burgos is alleged to have turned on the police with a gun in his right hand. He was shot, fell down, rose to a sitting position, and "raised the handgun with his right hand as he began to pivot his torso clockwise toward the police" when he was shot again. But none of the thirty-five shotgun and pistol entrance wounds Burgos suffered hit him in front of his body. Instead, he was hit nineteen times in the back of his torso; ten times by back-to-front wounds in the right side of his torso; once in the rear of his biceps; once in the inner elbow; three times in the back of his skull, and—*most tellingly*—once in the "palmar surface of the right hand, at the web of the ring and little finger" by a shotgun pellet that proceeded straight through, and exited the back of his hand. According to the police, Burgos was holding a gun in that hand at the time he sustained this wound. According to the testimony of the pathologist who found and classified the wound, that was impossible.

Arango reportedly was shot while he sat in the driver's seat of his car. But, according to the police account, the only gun in the front seat of the car was the one Burgos took with him when he fled. Arango suffered one shotgun blast that caused a "pattern of twelve (12) injuries to the left side of the back consisting of entries, exits and graze wounds . . . 15 1/2 to 19 inches below the top of the head"; a second that caused "twelve (12) entries or abrasions on the back, located 3 1/2 to 18 inches below the top of the head"; another shot that caused a "3 inch defect" in the center of his back; and a pistol shot in the left lower back.

Bahena was hit by a pistol shot to his upper back, a second to the back of his chest, and a 10-inch spread of about twenty-eight shotgun pellets "to the back of the head, neck and upper shoulders." In addition, his "entire midbrain [was] destroyed" by a back-to-front pistol shot to the top of his head. The preliminary report of Lieutenant William D. Hall, the LAPD's Officer Involved Shooting investigator, includes handwritten notes apparently drawn from a taped interview the morning of the shooting and describing the sequence in which Detective Helms fired this shot. After Helms had emptied his shotgun into the car during the initial explosion of gunfire, he drew his .45 and, according to the notes, took a

... slight pause to evaluate. Still movement within vehicle both sides. [An] officer on left (unknown which) shouted "There's still guns—he's still got a gun." [Helms] believed suspect still armed, fired (1) round at a suspect moving in left rear of veh [Olivas]. [Helms] then directed attention to rt. of veh. detected movement fired (1) round at susp moving in rt. rear [Bahena]. . . .

[Helms] with [Zierenberg] moves west up to rt. rear side of the side window. From this position [Helms] illuminates interior. Alerts [Zierenberg]. Appears to be more than one suspect in rt. rear seat area. [Helms] can see head & shoulders of one suspect [Bahena] draped over the other suspect's lap [Olivas], head facing north. Susp. was moving his shoulders as if reaching downward. Other susp. slumped down on seat. [Helms] continues stepping west to get better angle to view rt. rear. As [Helms] moves he instructs susp's to put their hands up. [Bahena, who has already been hit in back of head, neck, and shoulders by 28 shotgun pellets] cont's to move shoulders as if reaching downward. When [Helms] reached a point where he could see around door post, he obs. a gun lying on the rt. floorboard. [Bahena's] hand was inches above gun. [Bahena] cont. to reach downward. [Helms] fired (1) round into top of his head. Ceased his movement (leaned torso forward quick 1st round poss miss leaned back fired 2nd round through side window).

In the trial of the civil rights suit subsequently brought by Olivas and the survivors of his three companions,[60] Helms acknowledged the accuracy of this early account, which is more detailed than Hill's final report. This final, sanitized document says of Helms's shot into the top of Bahena's head:

When Detective Helms reached a position on the sidewalk which enabled him to look around the door post into the right rear seat area, he observed a handgun lying on the right rear floorboard between the feet of Olivas. Detective Helms shouted to his partner, "There's a gun on the rear floorboard." Bahena continued to move his shoulders and it appeared to Detective Helms that the suspect, whose hands were now several inches above the aforementioned handgun, was reaching for the weapon. Detective Helms shouted at Bahena to put his hands up. When Bahena failed to comply and continued to reach for the handgun, Detective Helms utilized a standing right "Harries" stance and quickly leaned his torso forward past the plane of the door post and fired one round (his 3rd) from his .45 caliber pistol at Bahena. Due to the somewhat awkward position from which he fired, Detective Helms believed his 3rd round had missed the suspect. In the belief Bahena still posed a deadly threat and to prevent him from obtaining the weapon and shooting at him and Detective Zierenberg, who were in a position without cover, Detective Helms quickly leaned his torso back out of the suspects' direct line of fire through the open passenger door and fired one round (his fourth) [actually his tenth, counting his six shotgun rounds] from a standing right "Harries" stance, through the rear side window. Bahena now ceased his movement.

According to medical testimony, however, Behana's movement stopped instantly with Helms's first shot, which disintegrated his brainstem and killed him instantly. After this, Helms fired another shot at Olivas, whose upper torso was under the sprawled body of Bahena. Olivas, the only robber to suffer front-to-back wounds (in the abdomen and hip), survived, he claims, precisely because he had burrowed under Bahena's body in order to avoid Helms's gun. According to Olivas, the instantly fatal shotgun blast to Arango's head and the pistol shot to the top of Bahena's head were gratuitous *coups de grace* inflicted after the initial smoke had cleared.

Olivas's statements raise other questions. He claims that no pellet guns were brandished during this shooting, because they had been put into the Thunderbird's trunk, along with the safecracking tools, masks, and $14,000 booty. This, he says, was the robbers' usual practice, and was followed on the reasoning that any police they might run into en route home from a robbery would be less likely to discover the incriminating evidence if it was stashed in their car's trunk than if it were more easily visible in the passenger compartment.

Certainly, Olivas's credibility is questionable. But, in addition to the issue of whether robbers persist in pointing toy guns at cops who have real guns, other evidence suggests that he is truthful. The police did see the robbers remove or deposit something in the Thunderbird's trunk at the beginning of this incident. They also saw Arango deposit a tool box and a bag in the trunk after he had emerged from McDonald's. The masks, money, tools, and a third pellet gun were found in a search of the car's trunk. The police claim to have clearly seen the guns through the Thunderbird's closed windows, but this was late at night, and the Thunderbird had heavily tinted windows of the type cops hate because they can't clearly see what's behind them. At fairly close range, the police fired 227 projectiles at people who reportedly were brandishing or reaching for guns. Yet, although it riddled the Thunderbird and three of its occupants, none of this flying lead hit any of the robbers' pellet guns. Some crime scene photos showed the two pellet guns alleged to have been inside the car lying, unstained and pristine, atop all the shattered glass and litter of the shooting; the guns were absent in other photos. At the first of the civil trials to follow this shooting, police suggested that the guns were missing from some photos because these pictures had been taken late in the investigation, after the guns had been removed for examination and safekeeping. The sequence of numbers on the negatives and photos, however, suggests that the reverse was true: the guns were absent in early photos, but prominent in pictures taken later in the investigation. In short—and except for the statements of the police them-selves—every bit of evidence in the case is consistent with the theory that the guns were planted on the bodies after the shooting had stopped.

Moreover, in this case, as in the Crumpton-Berry shooting, it is un-fathomable that the police would let things go as far as they did unless they specifically intended the bloody ending they achieved. In his charge to the jury who heard the robbers' subsequent civil rights suit, Judge J. Spencer Letts told the jury that, as a matter of law, the evidence available to the police before Arango and company entered the Foothills McDonald's was sufficient to justify the arrests of all four suspects. Further, as Fyfe testified in the case, even if the police on the scene were not aware of *all* the evi-dence that had been developed over the preceding months or otherwise had doubts about their authority to arrest the men in the Thunderbird, they cer-tainly had authority to stop, question, and frisk their suspects.

*Terry* v. *Ohio*,[61] the 1968 decision that we discuss in Chapter 5, and that is well known to the greenest police officers, gave police officers the U.S. Supreme Court's permission to exercise this "stop-and-frisk" authority in circumstances involving conduct that is suspicious but that, by itself, does not justify arrest. Although the details differ somewhat, the facts that led to the *Terry* decision are strikingly similar to what the SIS officers in the Arango case—and in the Crumpton–Berry case—claimed to have per-ceived.

Terry and two companions had aroused the suspicions of Martin Mc-Fadden, a Cleveland plainclothes officer, by nervously appearing to be "casing" a local store. After watching the three strangers for several min-utes, McFadden, who had worked the same area for thirty years, ap-proached and questioned them. They "mumbled something" and, fearing for his safety, McFadden turned Terry around, patted him down, and felt what turned out to be a revolver in Terry's coat pocket. In the same way, he found another gun on Chilton, one of Terry's companions. McFadden arrested them both and later testified in a trial in which both were convicted of unlawfully carrying concealed weapons.

Terry and Chilton appealed their convictions, arguing that they had been unlawfully searched. Their case reached the Supreme Court, which re-jected it, saying:

> We merely hold today that where a police officer observes unusual conduct which leads him reasonably to conclude in light of his experience that crim-inal activity may be afoot and that the persons with whom he is dealing may be armed and presently dangerous, where in the course of investigating this behavior he identifies himself as a policeman and makes reasonable inquir-

ies, and where nothing in the initial stages of the encounter serves to dispel his reasonable fear for his own or others' safety, he is entitled for the protection of himself and others in the area to conduct a carefully limited search of the outer clothing of such persons in an attempt to discover weapons which might be used to assault him. Such a search is a reasonable search under the Fourth Amendment, and any weapons seized may properly be introduced in evidence against the person from whom they were taken.[62]

Even without attempting to make immediate arrests, use of this "stop-and-frisk" authority would probably have led to arrests for carrying concealed weapons and subsequently to line-up identifications of Arango and company by their earlier victims. Even if, fortuitously, the suspects' realistic pellet guns were not found during police frisks, such an action certainly would have scared the suspects off. At minimum, therefore, police *tosses* of the suspects would have prevented Ms. Cox's agony, which, despite the reported absence of physical injury, was considerable: The robbers had held her at gunpoint, bound and blindfolded, for a half-hour. After the robbers left, Cox freed herself and, upon hearing the shooting in the street, hid in the restaurant's walk-in refrigerator, where police subsequently found her. Chief Gates did not see it this way. According to him:

> If we had taken them outside [the restaurant before they entered it], they would have been out on bail today, and probably robbing someone else. Now there won't be any more of these robberies at McDonald's. Perhaps we accomplished something.[63]

The jury that heard the robbers' civil suit did not agree. After a thirteen-week trial, they heard the attorney Stephen Yagman conclude his case by acknowledging that neither Olivas nor the deceased robbers deserved to be rewarded for their part in all this. Nonetheless, Yagman argued, he represented *robbers* while the police officers' attorney represented *assassins*. Yagman asked for a "nominal" award to send LA's City Hall a message that the jury deplored the police conduct in this situation. The jury complied with a $44,000 punitive damage judgment personally against Gates and the five officers who had fired shots in this incident. Yagman, who represents other survivors in a second suit stemming from the McDonald's shooting, expected a lengthy appeal of this verdict. Instead he was surprised when, in short order, he received a check for the amount of the verdict, not from Gates and the officers, but from the Los Angeles treasury. Again the City Council had intervened. In an unannounced executive session—held even as the trial of the officers who beat Rodney King proceeded—the Los Angeles City Council had voted to indemnify Gates and the SIS cops.

## OPERATION RESCUE

Despite this stunning verdict, police shootings of the likes of Berry, Crumpton, and the McDonald's bandits may not cause much sympathy or draw much critical scrutiny. As the judgment against Gates suggested, however, they seemed to reflect an official LAPD philosophy that the rules can be suspended when police deal with indefensible or unpopular conduct. One type of conduct that is extremely unpopular with most liberals is the anti-abortion activism of Operation Rescue, the group that has garnered national headlines for its sit-ins and demonstrations at abortion clinics. In 1988 the Los Angeles City Council learned that Rescue was preparing an offensive in Los Angeles. At the initiative of Michael Woo, one of the council's leading liberals and most vocal critics of the LAPD and Chief Gates, the Council passed a resolution urging the LAPD to engage in "vigorous enforcement" at Rescue demonstrations.[64] Woo subsequently testified that he and Zev Yaroslavsky, another of the Council's outspoken critics of Gates,

> ... had met with Gates before [Rescue's first] protest to discuss the Police Department's law enforcement policies at Operation Rescue demonstrations. And when asked by [Rescue attorney Cyrus] Zal if he had attended any other demonstrations this year, or authored motions requesting rigid law enforcement at protests by groups other than Operation Rescue, the councilman answered no.[65]

At Rescue's first Los Angeles demonstration, in March 1989, LAPD's elite Metro Squad removed demonstrators, in Rescue attorneys' language, by using

> ... pain compliance holds, such as wrist locks and twisting the demonstrators' arms behind their backs in an attempt to induce the demonstrators to violate their consciences and walk away from the abortuary, allowing killing of unborn babies to resume. Because the demonstrators were committed to their cause, the pain compliance holds resulted in many cases in personal injury, including broken bones, muscle strains, and bruises and contusions, although the injured demonstrators were not actively resisting arrest.[66]

Although Councilman Woo testified that he had seen no excessive force at the March demonstration,[67] these were harsher means than typically are used by police to remove sit-in participants. Most often, as was the case in demonstrations in other cities targeted in Rescue's 1989 Southern California offensive, police simply carry or cart off demonstrators. By the time Rescue returned to stage another Los Angeles demonstration in June 1989, the LAPD had decided to move the demonstrators by even more forceful means. At an April 1989 Rescue, for apparently the first time in American police history, the San Diego Police Department had used *nunchakus*[68] against nonviolent participants in a peaceful demonstration. In doing so, according to Rescue lawyers, the San Diego Police Department broke one demonstrator's arm and injured four or five others.[69] In June the LAPD went San Diego one better by using nunchakus against Rescuers vigorously enough to break bones and cause sprains and nerve, tendon, ligament, and soft tissue damage to several Rescue demonstrators.[70]

Nunchakus—in this case, two identical pieces of high-tensile plastic connected by a short rope—originated in the Orient, where they were used by farmers as scythes and, later, as a choking device to move oxen. More recently, they have developed into a martial arts weapon and staple of B-Movies of the Bruce Lee–Chuck Norris genre. In California, as in many other states, they are considered such a deadly single-purpose offensive device that their mere possession by a citizen is a felony.[71] Like switchblade and gravity knives, brass knuckles, sawed-off shotguns, and blackjacks, nunchakus are classified by the California legislature as a thug's weapon.

Nunchakus apparently found their way into American policing in Thornton, Colorado, during the early 1980s. There, Officer Kevin Orcutt, a First Degree *Jukado* Black Belt, developed and patented the Orcutt Police Control Nunchaku ("OPN"), the device subsequently used against Rescue's demonstrators. "In 1982," according to an LAPD training syllabus, the sixty-seven-member "Thornton Police Department initiated a comprehensive one year study implementing the OPN. With the successful completion of the Thornton study, the Thornton Police Department adopted the OPN as its primary and standard intermediate defensive and controlling instrument in 1984."[72] Nowhere, however, does any document indicate that Thornton's police have ever used nunchakus on peaceful demonstrators. Nor, despite selling the nunchakus to both the LAPD and San Diego and training a group of LAPD instructors in their use, did Kevin Orcutt appear in court to testify that using them against peaceful demonstrators was appropriate or reasonable.

Orcutt or any other expert on police practices would have been hard put to do this. Videotapes taken by both Rescue and LAPD very graphically and audibly show a demonstrator's arm being snapped. A slight young man is brought to his feet by officers who have his armed trapped at an awkward rear-facing angle. Suddenly, a *crack* is heard and the man winces as his arm suddenly jerks skyward. A female voice, apparently that of the photographer or an assistant close to the camera is then heard to shout,

"Oh, my God! They broke that guy's arm!" In addition, the LAPD's own tape of eighteen numbered uses of nunchakus against demonstrators was shot with the advantage of closer proximity to its subjects and shows that most demonstrators apparently resisted only by writhing and screaming in pain. In one incident, Stanley John, the lead plaintiff in Rescue's subsequent attempt to obtain a federal injunction against continuing use of the nunchakus, is heard to plead with officers who are using the device to apply pressure to his wrists that his passive resistance to them has ceased: "I'm not limp any more. . . . I'm not limp any more. . . . I can't move my arm."

Between sequences 11 and 12 of the LAPD tape, a formation of uniformed officers is shown marching on foot and on horseback. As they pass the camera, the following words scroll the screen:

*The Thought for the Day:*
*Some People Wait for Things to Happen . . .*
*Others Wonder What Happened . . .*
*Metro and Mounted Make It Happen!!!!*

In court papers filed in the litigation that followed the June demonstration, the LAPD offered several justifications for the decision to adopt the nunchaku.[73] Police officials testified in deposition that they believed Rescue had been schooled so extensively by sympathetic police officers that normal crowd control techniques had become useless against them. In videotapes of the June demonstration, however, demonstrators are seen to be doing nothing new; they merely sit on the ground and remain limp when lifted to their feet. One commander testified that he had heard that Rescuers at the March demonstration had greased themselves to make it more difficult to remove them, but there was no evidence that this rumor was accurate. LAPD officials also argued that it was speedier to use nunchakus than to cart or carry off demonstrators. The tapes, however, show teams of three to five officers awkwardly and haltingly walking, half-dragging, and carrying off writhing demonstrators one at a time in what is hardly an efficient assembly line process. The LAPD suggested also that the nunchakus reduced the risk that officers would suffer back injuries from handling demonstrators but was unable to back up this claim with any evidence that its burly and elite Metro officers had suffered such injuries at previous demonstrations.

Rescue's attorneys were convinced that their clients were singled out by the LAPD for especially brutal treatment and that nunchakus were used to teach their clients a painful lesson rather than to serve any legitimate police purpose. The attorneys were correct. Rescue certainly was singled out: Despite subsequent demonstrations by other groups for other causes, nunchakus have been used only against Rescue in Los Angeles (and in San Diego as well). In a declaration opposing a federal court ban on the nunchakus, Metro's Commander, Captain Patrick McKinley, claimed insights that help to explain why:

> Pain for the demonstrators is a catharsis for past failures to take action against abortion. Therefore, they have an unusual capacity to withstand pain. Some appear as a young child welcoming punishment for past transgressions. With this unique ability to withstand pain comes possibility of injury since a great degree of pain is required to induce compliance by arrest.[74]

Several Rescuers claim that arresting officers expressed the hope that causing them great pain with the nunchakus would convince them that martyrdom was not worth the agony. Stanley John, the lead plaintiff in Rescue's subsequent federal litigation, said:

> When I got on the bus [to the police lockup] in the front row, I said I think I broke my arm. And the officer on the bus told me: you should have thought about that before you came. I said I had considered it. I was being pleasant with him; I told him that I had considered it and had opted to come anyway. And asked him when LAPD began using "nunchakus." He said: they're new. In fact, I believe he said: they're *brand* new. At which time, I said to him: you need to practice more with them. And he said, we're practicing right now.[75]

An LAPD official who had been involved in the decision to use nunchakus told us:

> I had some qualms about it, but we couldn't think of any other way to make sure these people didn't come back. They think it cleanses their souls to be hurt. You look at some of them being carried off, and you can see that they want to be crucified. They stuck their arms straight out like Christ on the cross and made officers carry them off with their feet off the ground. So we let them do their thing and hope we hurt them enough so that we wouldn't see them again. We also wanted to send a message to the police officers who were training these demonstrators: keep doing what you're doing and we'll keep hurting these people. I think we'd do better with some more training and experience, but we got some bad reactions from people who usually support us. I don't think we'll use nunchakus again for a while.

As it turned out, this official's prediction was correct: Los Angeles's attorneys agreed to a permanent injunction against the nunchakus and they are not likely to again be used against nonviolent demonstrators. In an ironic way, however, the City Council liberals who traditionally play an important role in checking the LAPD's more extreme plans themselves encouraged the department's experimentation. Speaking of the Council's one-of-a-kind resolution urging the LAPD to put a quick end to interference with women's rights to control their bodies, a demonstrator told us:

> Telling the police to get rid of us in a hurry may have been the politically correct thing for the liberals on the Council. But it gave Gates a license to do anything he wanted to us. Why do you suppose none of the council people who are always on LAPD's back about brutality ever complained about what was done to us? Because they encouraged it, that's why. Despite all the furor over Rodney King, not one of them has ever said a word about breaking Rescuers' bones. After they sicced Metro on us, the Council would look like fools if they complained about what Metro did. Gates and his people knew that and they hurt us to teach Woo and Zarovslavsky and the rest of the Council a lesson.

Perhaps the most telling bits of evidence about the LAPD's motives in using the nunchakus are two pieces of Chief Gates's deposition testimony:

> You say [the Rescue demonstrators] are not anti-police. I think they've demonstrated to a large degree that they have been, and anti in terms of understanding what the police's responsibility is and then resisting that in every way, shape or form, crowding our courts, crowding our system, failing to identify themselves, taking up our time when we are so needed elsewhere in the City when people's, I'm sure, calls went unanswered because of this.
>
> So you say they are not anti-police, but certainly they have demonstrated in every way, shape or form their unwillingness to sit down and talk to us, their unwillingness to tell us where they were going to be.
>
> The tactics that they used in other cities of thwarting police tactics, all of those things suggest to me that they were not willing to do—to cooperate in any way and did not cooperate in any way, even though our hand was out and our hope was high that we would have had in dealing with this group of all groups.
>
> We thought we were going to have no difficulty whatsoever, that they understood the law and would comply with the law. We were shocked. I was shocked. Still am.[76]

> Believe me, this has not been pleasant for me or for this Police Department. It is extremely trying. I'm sure a lot of police officers on the line and maybe even some of the command staff of this department hold some of the same views that the demonstrators do, and that makes it doubly difficult.
>
> But no one could—no consideration was given by any of the people involved in these demonstrations, and in my judgment, it almost bordered on arrogance which, I doubt, is a Christian concept.[77]

## CONCLUSION

Gates's comments about Rescue, like his remarks about the McDonald's shooting, betray administrative reasoning that long encouraged officers to respond with contempt and violence—with vigilante-style punishment—to *arrogance* on the part of people who, in officers' eyes, should have known better. Such perceived arrogance is the link that connects Crumpton, Berry, Arango, Burgos, Bahena, Gomez, the Rescuers, Lyons, the Larez family, and King. Except for waving red flags before the police, these people had nothing in common. Indeed, even the red flags they waved varied considerably in size and shape. Crumpton, Berry, and the McDonald's robbers taunted the lethal and prideful Special Investigation Section by daring to believe that they could operate as bandits on SIS's turf. In the eyes of SIS, these were *outlaws,* beyond redemption, and for them the consequences were fatal.

The *arrogance* of the Rescuers was somewhat different. These were, as Gates testified in his deposition, people who claimed not to have been "anti-police." And, in virtually every aspect of their lives except for their participation in Rescue's annoying demonstrations, the Rescuers were people who caused the police no problems whatever. Generally fundamentalist Protestants and devout Catholics, the Rescuers were cut from the same cloth as many of the police who designed, supervised, and implemented the police actions that caused so much physical injury. Stanley John—the lead plaintiff in the Rescue case against the LAPD—for example, is a husband and father who, with his wife, operates a religious children's camp. The Rescuers hurt by the LAPD's nunchakus include telephone installers, housewives, engineers, and a cross-section of southern California that has much more in common with cops than with any demonstrators previously confronted by Metro's officers.

This was precisely the point. Although their life-styles and motivations were different from the antiwar demonstrators beaten up in Chicago in 1968, the Rescuers shared with those earlier protestors an important characteristic that helped mold the police response to them. Neither group was downtrodden outsiders or *deviants* with whom no cop could identify. The Chicago demonstrators were the children of the Establishment. They were, by and large, privileged, draft-exempt kids who, in a popular view of the time, should have known better than to challenge the police—and the Establishment that had so favored them—in the same manner as did blacks and other assorted *militants* and outsiders. In that sense, the clubbings and beatings they received were a form of education; lessons that, some might argue, have helped lead that generation of self-proclaimed radicals into a middle age of consumerism and self-absorption.

In a view popular today, the Rescuers—conservative, white, and supporters of family values, individual responsibility, law and order, and the military; often related by blood, marriage, and mindset to cops—also should know better. These are not *outsiders,* like the blacks, Hispanics, Croatians, Palestinians, gays, and AIDS activists the police have become accustomed to meeting at demonstrations. The Rescuers are people whose bloc votes helped to elect Ronald Reagan, George Bush, Dan Quayle, Pete Wilson, and Robert Dornan: They are Simi Valley and Orange County rather than Watts and East LA.

When Rescue adopted and built upon the tactics and strategies of other demonstrators—and when they reportedly were trained by sympathetic officers to foil standard crowd control techniques[78]—they were seen to have enlisted traitors to their cause and to have made adversaries of the police. Like the antiwar demonstrators of an earlier generation, they broke a trust between the police and those the police perceive as *the good people.* Hence, like their long-haired counterculture predecessors, they were seen to deserve a lesson they would not soon forget. They got it.

With some variation, this same ethos led to the Larez and King beatings and is reflected in the statements of Breier and Rizzo. The critical question raised by such reasoning, of course, is how to get rid of it. The most obvious answer is to see that it is not locked indefinitely into place by a system of lifetime appointments for police chief executives. When police chiefs have been appointed for life, they have been accountable to nobody. Milwaukee and Los Angeles recognized this when they scrapped their systems of lifetime appointments, so that no major U.S. city has a tenured chief.

But, while the capacity to hold police chiefs accountable—through fixed terms of office and/or service at the pleasure of elected officials—must exist if institutionalized police contempt and secrecy are to be avoided, it will not by itself put an end to police contempt and secrecy. Recent history offers some clues about the conditions likely to put an end to—or at least drive underground—police contempt and the veil of secrecy that lets it flourish. We turn to that next.

# PART THREE
## *Remedies*

# 8

## *Police Administrative Reform*

Police administration is not applied mechanics, but a living, breathing organism shaped by the political, social, and economic trends of time and place.

—Thomas Repetto,
The Blue Parade

Waves of reform swept over American cities at the beginning of this century. Offended by what they saw as the decadent lifestyles of recent immigrant groups and by the machine politics that allowed the vices of the ethnic newcomers to flourish, reformers in Eastern cities set about installing their own idea of good government. Typically privileged members of old-line families, these "Progressives" placed police reform at the top of their priority list.

This pattern differed in parts of the West. Most turn-of-the-century newcomers to Los Angeles, Robert M. Fogelson notes, were native Easterners and Midwesterners rather than European immigrants. Having fled the corruption of the East, the new Angelenos joined in league with the Progressives to fight for municipal virtue. Their enemies in LA's political battle, Fogelson suggests, were not the ethnic political bosses who ruled Boston, New York, and Chicago but a unique combination of public utility companies and vice operators. Between the Civil War and 1900, Fogelson writes, their efforts to control politicians' votes and appropriations by whatever means had made "the water, gas, and electric companies, the street railway lines, and the Southern Pacific Railroad . . . the most influential participants in Los Angeles politics."[1] In addition, Los Angeles reformers confronted the more typical roster of shady characters who operated brothels, gambling establishments, illegal saloons, and other dens of iniquity in which otherwise honest men sought entertainment. Then, as now, vice operators could succeed in hiding their activities from the law only by making them invisible from their clients as well. Since this would put them out of business, in Los Angeles, as in virtually every big city of the time, they co-opted police to their cause by supplementing officers' meager paychecks with healthy bribes. In Los Angeles, as in the East, brutality apparently was not much of a bother to the reformers, but eliminating police money corruption was one of their main goals.

The reformers faced heavy odds, however. In most places, attempts to straighten out the police lasted only as long as the municipal administrations the Progressives managed to elect. In the East, that usually meant only one term of office before, tired of preachy and self-righteous civic leaders who wanted to save the unwashed from themselves, the Irish and Germans voted their *landsmen* back into office.[2] Things then returned to the era's version of equilibrium between states and municipalities: State legislatures dominated by rural conservatives enacted laws against the vices; those laws were ignored by the cops, whose loyalties lay with the local ward leaders and vice operators who had gotten them hired in the first place. In this environment, the historian Mark Haller has written, police scarcely were influenced by legal norms or any sort of professionalism. Even as late as 1900, police in a city as large as Chicago were given no training. Instead, after a brief speech from a high-ranking officer, they were issued a uniform, a hickory stick, a whistle, and a call box key, and sent to walk the streets with a veteran cop.[3]

Progressivism also began its death throes after one term in Los Angeles, but for different reasons. There, soon after Progressives won the mayoralty, the sudden emergence of a powerful socialist movement forced them into an alliance with the old political machine they had just ousted. In 1911, two years into a Progressive administration, a socialist candidate, Jeb Harriman, shocked the reformers and the city's establishment by winning a plurality in a three-way mayoral election. Panicked, the reformers teamed up with their old adversaries to prevent the anarchy they anticipated would follow a Harriman victory in the runoff election that was to follow. The alliance of convenience beat Harriman in the runoff, but, by compromising with the old machine, the reformers had done irreparable damage to their own agenda for change. Business as usual quickly returned and would last, with some interruptions, for four more decades.

## AUGUST VOLLMER

While the Progressives were coming and going in many cities, good things were happening in Berkeley, California. There, August Vollmer, a man of more modest roots than most of the reformers, was working hard and with great success to professionalize the police department he had been appointed to head in 1905.[4] Vollmer, reacting against the era's loose, casual, and usually corrupt policing, became the most influential police reformer of his time. He developed the Berkeley Police Department into an internationally acclaimed model of innovation and rectitude. He recruited college students and was responsible for the introduction into policing of such technical advances as signal boxes, bicycle patrol, the crime laboratory, and patrol car radios. He stressed crime prevention over apprehension. He considered policing to be a profession rather than a mere job and opposed the formation of unions. He established the first American program in criminology at the University of California's Berkeley campus. He was appalled by the 1919 Boston police strike. Although he recognized that working conditions in most police departments were poor, he considered police affiliation with a labor union, an organization designed primarily to improve conditions of employment, to be absurd.[5]

When Los Angeles wanted to reform its police department in 1923, it hired Vollmer, who agreed to try the job for one year. In Los Angeles, Vollmer found a world very different from the one he had left behind in Berkeley. The place where he had made his mark was far smaller and was populated, by and large, by two classes of people. One consisted of generally prosperous Establishment types whose flight from the Eastern-style corruption and ethnic politics of San Francisco was hastened by that city's terrible 1906 earthquake. In search of peace, quiet, and safety, this group was joined by like-minded people who had fled from the bawdiness of neighboring Oakland, where the writer Jack London was the most famous resident. The second class comprised immigrants who came to Vollmer's Berkeley to build, staff, and study in the town's rapidly growing university, which was then the only school in the University of California system. It is hard to imagine a more idyllic setting and laboratory for police innovation than Vollmer's Berkeley.

Los Angeles was a shock for Vollmer. There he found entrenched graft and corruption, a shortage of water, a rising crime rate, and a population that would quickly exceed 800,000. The Volstead Act—Prohibition—was the law, but the reality was the free flow of booze, gambling, and the contamination of public officials. Vollmer tried to reform the government of

Los Angeles, but the city's graft and corruption were too entrenched for him to make a lasting difference. He saw how effectively gamblers and bootleggers ran the Mayor, who ran the city government, and how powerless he himself was to change things. Good government seemed impossible, and the barriers to civic reform Los Angeles had itself erected made a lasting impression on Vollmer.

Although Vollmer was unsuccessful in reshaping the Los Angeles police, he retained a powerful national reputation as the nation's leading police professional after he left. Consequently, when President Herbert Hoover appointed the National Commission on Law Observance and Enforcement—the Wickersham Commission—in 1929 to offer an overview of police problems, suggest reforms, and set standards, Hoover sought out Vollmer to head the commission's police section.

Given his experience in Los Angeles, Vollmer was understandably concerned about protecting police chiefs from corrupt politicians, especially from removal for no cause other than political convenience. He understood why autocratic police chiefs might be feared, but he thought the pendulum had swung too far in limiting the independence of police executives. "Their attempt to protect themselves from a powerful autocratic chief of police," he wrote, "has served to place them and the government in the hands of unscrupulous cutthroats, murderers and bootleggers."[6] Vollmer's depictions and language may seem hyperbolic and anachronistic, and perhaps they are. Nevertheless, corruption of and by police and politicians has been and continues to be a problem in many American cities.

Although Los Angeles had been little impressed or affected by Vollmer's stint as Police Chief, it followed his advice as a national expert on policing. In 1936, perhaps influenced also by J. Edgar Hoover's growing record of success as the FBI's increasingly autonomous Director, Los Angeles enacted legislation that gave the police chief civil service immunity from the politicians. The protection proved to be only nominal, however, and the LAPD's chiefs continued to come and go with the changing of municipal administrations. Not until 1950, when William Parker took command of the LAPD, more than a quarter-century after Vollmer had left it, was Vollmer's solution to the Los Angeles corruption of the Prohibition era—an autonomous police department run by a police chief immune from the political process—finally realized in that city. Thus, the immunity that accounted for the long tenure of Daryl Gates was the legacy of a reformer whose own term in office had little immediate effect on the LAPD.

## POLICE REFORM: SUCCESSES AND FAILURES

Since Vollmer's time, there have been many opportunities to learn from experience about the circumstances in which police reform efforts take hold and those where change withers and dies. Certainly—regardless of whether one ultimately agrees with the wisdom and direction of his reforms—William H. Parker's changes in the LAPD's philosophies and practices took hold and, under a series of autonomous chiefs, endured long beyond his passing in 1966. But even the best-respected police administrators have failed as reformers.

### O. W. Wilson

Vollmer's protégé, Orlando W. Wilson, is probably the leading example. Wilson served as a Berkeley police officer under Vollmer, then went on to head the police departments in Fullerton, California, and Wichita, Kansas, during the 1930s. Subsequently he served with distinction as dean of the School of Criminology in Berkeley and was the author of his era's two most widely read books on police administration.[7] In 1960 Chicago's Mayor Richard Daley tapped Wilson to head his city's police department. By every account, Wilson was given a free hand to make a model of the department, and it is certain that he made progress toward that goal while in office. But within a year of Wilson's 1967 departure, Chicago police, apparently out of control, engaged in the notorious 1968 Democratic National Convention riot. Thus Wilson, like his mentor, had a great impact on policing *generally* but was unable to institutionalize his ideals in the big-city department he led. Indeed, as Wilson's biographer acknowledges, he had no more than "transitory" impact on *any* of the three departments he served as chief. Soon after Wilson left them, all three experienced corruption scandals.[8]

Not all attempts at police reform have ended as fruitlessly as Vollmer's and Wilson's. It is worthwhile to examine some more recent experiences, which serve as lessons how to replace police abuse with democratic policing values and practices.

### Philadelphia After Rizzo

Vollmer and Wilson certainly would be appalled by the style of policing in Frank Rizzo's Philadelphia, where, as Gordon Misner noted some time ago, the police rarely were accused of professionalism.[9] Events that have transpired since the end of Philadelphia's Rizzo era—most notably the 1985 MOVE siege and bombing[10] and mid-1980s revelations of corruption and the ensuing convictions of more than thirty of Phildelphia's top police brass[11]—suggest that Misner's observation still holds. Yet these more recent scandals generally have been the result of incompetence and greed at the top level rather than the fruits of such open invitations to police thuggery as Rizzo's encouragements to bust heads. It may be argued that the progress from Rizzo's venality to the PPD's ill-advised air raid on the MOVE house was not a giant step forward for policing. Still, despite this incredible blunder and the absence of any leader of the stature of Vollmer or Wilson, the PPD has moved in the right direction since Rizzo and his appointees ran it. Morton Solomon, the man appointed in 1980 to succeed Rizzo's Police Commissioner, set the department on a course of change on which—albeit with great fits, starts, stops, and no little resistance—it has since continued.

Perhaps the main reason that the PPD has not come farther in a positive direction is the Philadelphia Police Commissioner's inability either to choose a management team that shares his philosophies or to hold top commanders accountable. The Commissioner is an untenured political appointee, but, with just two exceptions, all of his top managers are tenured into their positions by civil service regulations. Of the recently departed PPD Commissioner Willie Williams's attempts to further reform in this environment, the reporter Bill Miller observed:

> Williams came into office surrounded by commanders who may or may not have shared his views about policing. Some were holdovers from the years when Frank Rizzo was mayor, and some were determined to wait Williams out in hopes that their king would return.[12]

After what he deemed unsuccessful attempts to work with these commanders, Williams tried to get around them by making fourteen temporary appointments at the department's top levels and by transferring the people already in these positions to departmental limbos. That did not work: His department's labor union, a local chapter of the national Fraternal Order of Police, took Williams to court and, after a nasty and racially polarizing battle, succeeded in having Williams's promotions overturned. Williams responded by selectively promoting his loyalists from among candidates who had passed promotional examinations for permanent command positions. Again, however, he found himself embroiled in litigation, brought this time by eight of the candidates he had passed over for promotion. As a result, according to Miller, Williams found himself with "a new management team, but its effectiveness was limited by division and acrimony."[13] Williams was like a new baseball manager stuck with a popular old manager's starting nine and no choice in where they will play and when they will come to bat. In such conditions, and regardless of a chief executive's skills or good intentions, sweeping change in a police department's philosophy is virtually impossible.

## Reform in New York

An extremely painful experience for the New York City Police Department began twenty-five years ago, but it led to change that has taken that agency farther than the Philadelphia Police Department has progressed. In the mid-1960s, Officer Frank Serpico found himself assigned to a Bronx plainclothes unit, assigned primarily to enforce gambling laws. He found, however, that plainclothes work was a farce that had more to do with entrepreneurship than with enforcement. Plainclothesmen throughout the city took part in long-established agreements with gamblers in which, in return for a regular monthly payment, gambling operations—handling mostly illegal policy "numbers" betting—would continue unmolested. To keep headquarters happy, officers listed on gamblers' "pads" filled their work reports with staged "convenience" arrests of low-level gambling employees, whose days in court only minimally impinged on the regular flow of business.

Serpico, a five-year NYPD veteran before he went into plainclothes, refused to take part in his division's pad. Quietly, he also tried to call it to the attention of the department's brass and the city's administration. Although he reached as far as the mayor's office in his attempts and did receive cooperation from a few isolated, and heroic, officials, the pads and their participants continued. This went on for nearly five years, until Serpico finally got his story to reporter David Burnham. Burnham put police corruption on the front page of the *New York Times,* where Mayor John V. Lindsay was forced to confront it.[14] Within a month, Lindsay appointed a blue-ribbon panel—the Knapp Commission—to investigate the scandal. Lindsay also replaced the Police Commissioner with Patrick V. Murphy, whose twenty-four years in the NYPD had been interrupted by terms as police chief in Syracuse, Washington, D.C., and Detroit, as well by work with the U.S. Justice Department and the Urban Institute, a Washington think tank.

The Knapp investigation and hearings, broadcast live on public television, shook New York. Plainclothes pads, it was disclosed, existed throughout the department, and to some degree corruption was a part of life in almost all police units.[15] Evidence was introduced to show that patrol officers were bribed by builders and merchants anxious to avoid compliance with byzantine administrative codes and laws against Sunday operations and sales. Licensed bars paid off cops to stay open after legal hours, and unlicensed bars paid just to stay open. Tow truck operators kicked back money to cops who called them to accident scenes. Insurers and car owners whose cars had been stolen paid cops to avoid the paperwork and delays that would otherwise be involved in retrieving their vehicles from police storage facilities. Cops paid off other cops for days off, for good assignments, and for processing paperwork.[16]

Even before the Knapp hearings started, Murphy had begun changing his department irrevocably, and the crooked cops who told of their exploits on the city's television screens facilitated his reforms. Murphy put in place systems to hold supervisors and administrators strictly accountable for the integrity and civility of their personnel. He won approval to increase the number of supervisors authorized for the department and quickly filled those ranks with massive promotions. He rewarded cops who turned in corrupt or brutal colleagues and punished those who, although personally honest, looked the other way when they learned of misconduct. He introduced due process to the department's complex disciplinary system and changed an internal penalty system that previously had been so draconian and so ridden by red tape that supervisors had chosen to tolerate misconduct rather than file charges against miscreant officers.[17]

In an unprecedented series of high-level promotions and demotions that would be the envy of any Philadelphia Police Commissioner, Murphy used his authority to appoint and demote officers above the rank of captain to weed his department's 450-man executive corps of unresponsive dead wood and to advance promising young commanders quickly. He contracted with the RAND Corporation to study his executives' jobs and to determine what knowledge, skills, and abilities were necessary to succeed in it. He gave those results to the American Management Association and hired the association to assess each of his executives to identify their strengths and weaknesses. He assigned people according to their strengths and began training to correct their weaknesses.[18]

For the first time in the NYPD's history, Murphy instituted and enforced discretionary guidelines on use of deadly force, cutting police shootings by more than half.[19] He oversaw establishment of an "Early Warning Program" designed to identify and counsel officers whose work records gave indications of proneness to violence. He saw to it that training was revised to prepare new officers to deal realistically with the temptations of police work and instituted Ethical Awareness Workshops for veterans. He assigned his researchers and planners to work on solving the management and organizational problems identified in the workshops or to find ways to implement the solutions that participants had proposed. He gave his commanders greater authority to deploy personnel in response to community problems. With frequent reference to his own experience as a beat cop in Brooklyn, Murphy experimented with neighborhood team policing and a variety of other ways of bringing the department and the citizenry closer together.

To eliminate nepotism and favoritism in assignments, Murphy established a "career path" program that used clearly defined steps before officers became eligible for the detective's gold shield, which had been Serpico's goal when he entered Plainclothes. He abolished the Plainclothes Division. In its stead he created an Organized Crime Control Bureau (OCCB), which works under different rules, as well as a Street Crime Unit, which won national awards for its crime-fighting efficiency. By forbidding OCCB investigators and other officers to enforce laws against victimless crimes and ordinances unless complaints had first been made by offended citizens, he took away opportunities for corrupt cops to shake down gamblers, prostitutes, and pimps, as well as builders and grocers. He strengthened the Internal Affairs Division (IAD) and made its work the job of all commanders by establishing decentralized field internal affairs units and by creating an integrity officer position in every department precinct and squad. He authorized the IAD to conduct "integrity tests"—phoning in fictitious complaints against officers to determine whether supervisors discouraged or ignored complaints, for example—and made public examples of those who failed these tests. He created an Internal Affairs "field associates" program that recruited anonymous officers to report surreptitiously on any misconduct they witnessed at work. His IAD investigators and field associates identified "corruption hazards" in each of the city's seventy-five police precincts and held commanders, integrity officers and supervisors accountable for making certain that officers did not fall prey to them. In short, and although his department's major problem was money corruption rather than brutality, Murphy used his three and a half years in office to create an environment that loudly and clearly condemned abusive police conduct, those who engage in it, and—equally important—those who *tolerate* it.[20] Since then, two comparatively small scandals have arisen—one in 1985 involving a dozen officers in one of the NYPD's seventy-five precincts,[21] another in 1992 involving five officers in two precincts.[22] The most recent of these led the city's mayor, David Dinkins, to establish another investigative commission. Conversations with knowledgeable officials suggest, however, that there is little reason to anticipate that this commission will find organized corruption on anything like the scale that confronted Murphy two decades ago. Allegations of brutality occasionally have arisen, but they have been dealt with swiftly.[23] The response of one of Murphy's successors to a 1985 incident in which officers had shocked and burned a suspected drug dealer with an electronic stun gun is indicative that the policy of zero-tolerance for police abuse has endured:

After first accepting his own responsibility, Commissioner Benjamin Ward summoned 327 senior officers to police headquarters in lower Manhattan. He read them the riot act, then fired the entire chain of command involved in the incident—from a lieutenant at the offending precinct to the department's third-ranking official, the chief of patrol. "I didn't consult with the mayor or the district attorney, or anyone," says Ward, "I just acted."[24]

## Dade County

Like New York's Knapp scandal, other sudden crises have stimulated successful police reform. On December 17, 1979, the Metro–Dade, Florida, Police Department (MDPD) experienced a watershed event that was eerily similar to the recent encounter between Rodney King and Los Angeles police officers. On that date, MDPD officers signaled to the side of the road a motorcyclist who had committed a traffic violation. Instead of complying, the motorcyclist, a black thirty-three-year-old insurance sales representative named Arthur McDuffie, fled at high speed. After leading the police on a high-speed pursuit that traveled through eight miles of Miami's streets, McDuffie was apprehended.

What happened next is undisputed. In the presence, and perhaps with the assistance, of a sergeant, several MDPD officers—all white or Hispanic— beat McDuffie into a coma. To make it appear that McDuffie's injuries were the result of a spill from his motorcycle, the officers then drove a police car over McDuffie's motorcycle and his helmet. The officers' attempt at a cover-up was foiled, however, when witnesses—including other police—came forward with the truth. By the time McDuffie died four days later, the incident had become the focus and exemplar of all of South Florida's considerable ethnic and racial tensions. When the County Medical Examiner reported that his autopsy confirmed the witnesses' reports, the State's Attorney indicted five officers for manslaughter and for tampering with evidence.

Scarcely noted outside Florida, the McDuffie incident was the subject of nearly two hundred local news stories during the three months between McDuffie's death and the officers' trial. Because of this intense coverage, the State's Attorney asked for and received a change of venue to Tampa. The trial lasted six weeks and was sensational. Early on, lack of evidence led to dismissal of the case against one officer. A Miami Police Department officer who was not a defendant volunteered that he had taken part in the beating. Under grants of immunity, several other officers who had beaten McDuffie testified against their former colleagues.

As the trial wore on, however, the defense raised doubts about the credibility of witnesses and about the actual roles of the defendants: the question of who, if anybody, had actually struck the fatal blows loomed large. Finally, on May 17, 1980, a Saturday, the six-member jury—all white males—acquitted the defendants of all charges.

The parallels to the Rodney King episode did not end there: reaction to the McDuffie verdict was instantaneous. Miami's black-oriented radio stations exchanged their music format for full-time discussion of the case. How, callers demanded, could an acquittal have resulted when there was no doubt in anybody's mind that the police had beaten McDuffie to death? Within an hour after announcement of the verdict, random violence erupted around Miami. The police responded cautiously and began to hear reports that white motorists were being attacked. In fact, several were dragged from their cars and were killed and mutilated by angry mobs.

By 8:30 P.M., six hours after the verdict was announced, a peaceful protest at the county's Justice Building had drawn 4,000–5,000 people and had degenerated into disorder. By 9:00 P.M., looting and arson were widespread throughout a 20-square-mile area. By 10:00 P.M., the National Guard had been activated. The Liberty City riot, more violent and destructive than any of the American urban disorders of the 1960s, had begun.

Over the following nine days, in which an official state of emergency existed, the riot took a high toll. In addition to eighteen deaths and three hundred assaults documented as attributable to the riot, the Miami area suffered forty-nine additional unexplained deaths and homicides. The police made more than 1,400 riot-related arrests and recorded about $125 million in property damage and losses—sixteen homes and seventy-one businesses were destroyed, and 238 businesses were damaged, resulting in the loss of more than three thousand jobs.[25]

Liberty City sundered Miami, but out of its ashes has come a success story: the reform of the MDPD. In the years since Liberty City burned, the Miami area has undergone constant change and suffered great violence. The *Mariel* boat lift, which was at full strength at the time of the riot (and which has also been a major grievance among Miami blacks) has brought more than 100,000 new Cuban immigrants to the area. More than 100,000 refugees from Haiti have settled in the county since 1978. The area has long been the main port of entry for cocaine. Despite official successes in reducing the influence of the "Cocaine Cowboys," drug-related violence and corruption remain at high levels. Concurrently, because of its physical beauty, temperate climate, vibrant economy, and image as an exotic international city, the area draws prosperous vacationers, new industry, and new residents from throughout the United States and the rest of the world. Indeed, Dade County remains one of the most racially and ethnically volatile policing environments in the United States.

This volatility has been the cause of several more recent police scandals and riots—the "River Cops" drug and murder scandal of the mid-80s; the Overtown Riot; the conviction of a police officer for the fatal shooting of a motorcyclist and the death of his passenger in the subsequent crash, the reversal of his conviction, and the subsequent debate over the second trial's venue[26]—but none of those scandals has involved the MDPD, which is by far the area's largest police organization. Instead, despite continued changes, pressures, violence, and the temptations that confront its officers, the MDPD has dramatically improved relations with its constituency, enhanced its operational efficiency, and become an outstanding police agency.

Immediately after the Liberty City riot, the MDPD suffered the loss of many veteran officers who retired or resigned to accept positions in quieter police departments. In response, the department's then director, Bobbie L. Jones, undertook an ambitious affirmative action program designed to increase the representativeness of his agency's personnel without "watering down" entrance or promotion standards. By strengthening psychological screening and counseling and by improving the department's systems for monitoring and evaluating officers' performance, he and Frederick Taylor, his successor, apparently have succeeded. Jones also created Citizens' Advisory Committees to assist in formulation and implementation of important policies. Over the years, Jones and Taylor have decentralized authority so much that each of the department's police districts is, in effect, as autonomous as a separate police agency. They have done so at no cost to the accountability of cops or supervisors. Instead, the department's Internal Affairs Division has become more aggressive in initiating investigations, and the department has enhanced review procedures for use of force, auto pursuits, and other controversial police actions.

Perhaps the single most ambitious effort to reduce violence between police and citizens in Dade County was the Metro-Dade Police/Citizen Violence Reduction Project. This project, a joint endeavor with the Police Foundation (for which Fyfe was project director), was designed to enhance field police officers' ability to defuse potentially violent situations ("PVs"). The project drew heavily on the work of the psychologist Hans Toch, who had suggested that the best ways of minimizing violence between police and citizens were to harness and articulate the overlooked expertise of street cops, the people most qualified by experience—and necessity—to prescribe guidelines for averting bloodshed.[27]

In 1985, Jones assigned a task force of police officers, investigators, supervisors, and trainers to analyze reports of one hundred police–citizen confrontations that had resulted in use of force, in injuries to officers, or in citizens' complaints against officers. What decisions and actions by the officers in these situations, the task force was asked, had contributed to their unhappy endings? What alternative decisions and actions might have resulted in happier endings?

From this analysis, detailed lists of "Dos and Don'ts" for the four most frequent PVs (routine traffic stops; stops of suspicious vehicles; responses to reported crimes; and disputes) were developed and built into a training program. By mid-1989, all of the MDPD's patrol personnel had completed the training. In the year and a half that followed, MDPD officers' use of force, injuries to officers, and citizens' complaints against officers all declined between 30 and 50 percent.[28]

## WHAT ACCOUNTS FOR SUCCESSFUL POLICE REFORM?

It may yet be premature to assess the durability of the reforms put in place while Bobbie Jones headed the MDPD. The department remains under the leadership of Fred Taylor, Jones's immediate, anointed successor, so that one would not expect it to have changed much in the few years since Jones left. It also is rather early to determine whether the dip in police–citizen violence follow the MDPD's Violence Reduction Project is more than an accidental blip. Thus, even though the MDPD has come a long way since its officers killed Arthur McDuffie, the passage of time has made Patrick Murphy's efforts in New York a better and demonstrably more durable subject than the MDPD for figuring out what works and what doesn't. As the stun gun episode suggests, Murphy did not absolutely banish police misconduct from New York. Still, Murphy did succeed in effecting immediate and lasting change in the NYPD. Why did Murphy succeed where Vollmer and Wilson did not?

One thing that distinguishes Murphy from Vollmer and Wilson is that—despite his sojourns and successes in other places—Murphy was an *insider,* born and bred to the department he eventually reformed. Murphy came from a cop family, had walked foot beats in New York, had worked his way up through the ranks, had taught in and commanded New York's Police Academy, and knew the politics of the city and the bureaucracy he came home to lead. Vollmer and Wilson were imports who walked into unfamiliar territory in Los Angeles and Chicago.

Murphy's success in New York, however, is not an argument for police insularity. By the time he became New York's police commissioner, Murphy the insider had built a resumé of experiences broader than any other American police executive's. Further, earlier in his career, Murphy had demonstrated, albeit on a far lesser problem in a city much smaller than

New York, that an *outsider* could be a successful reformer. Called to Syracuse as a reform chief after a 1963 New York State investigation had found evidence of police corruption there,[29] Murphy worked within what the political scientist James Q. Wilson suggested was an "indifferent political environment" and had succeeded in seeing that "the police changed though the political system did not—the police moved within the existing zone of indifference."[30] Thus Murphy's success in New York probably had more to do with his own extraordinary personal ability, energy, and broad experience than with the fact that he came from a line of New York cops. He was the ideal reformer: a savvy insider who had been away learning about police life in other places before returning to reform the agency in which he had grown up.

Murphy also enjoyed in New York a degree of external support for police reform that simply did not exist in Vollmer's Los Angeles, O. W. Wilson's Chicago, or, according to James Q. Wilson's description, in Syracuse during Murphy's tenure as chief there. Whether or not embarrassed into action by the Serpico scandals, New York's Mayor Lindsay gave Murphy generous support and resources to make change. Not to be outdone, Lindsay's prime political rival, Governor Nelson D. Rockefeller, responded to the Knapp report by appointing and funding a special prosecutor and staff to investigate and present to the courts corruption and other misconduct in New York City's criminal justice system. The public, mobilized by the scandals, also supported reform. In the face of such a steamroller, no official or police union representative could afford to argue for the *status quo.* Murphy seized this opportunity: His genius was to put in place fundamental structural reforms and redundant checks on integrity and abuse in every part of the department.

While Murphy apparently changed the police system so that integrity would be institutionalized regardless of the persona or philosophies of whoever might succeed him,[31] Vollmer and Wilson had no support for such change in Los Angeles and Chicago. In both those places, the principal political actors and opinion makers were so heavily invested in the old ways of doing business that attempts to make lasting change were certain to be sabotaged regardless of the Police Chief's administrative and political talents. This had not been true for Vollmer in Berkeley, where a well-educated, relatively homogeneous, prosperous, and conservative population gave substantial philosophical and financial support to his professionalization efforts. Nor, to date, has it proved true in Dade County. There, in the aftermath of what everybody was forced to acknowledge was an unjustifiable police killing and attempted cover-up, no responsible official or interest group could oppose reform.

The message of Murphy's success is affirmed by the experiences of other famous American law enforcement reformers. For good or ill, Hoover and Parker also succeeded in remodeling their agencies to fit their ideals, not only because of their administrative skills but because of strong support from powerful external constituencies. As we saw earlier, Hoover built the FBI's cadres of supporters by winning over state and local law enforcement agencies, by mounting public relations programs that enlisted the public in his war on crime, and, eventually, by convincing President Roosevelt that a strong and autonomous FBI was imperative to the national well-being. Parker received strong support from reform-minded mayors, the press, an entertainment industry that came to idolize his department, and, most important, from politicians and a population anxious to shed the LAPD's former shady image for a version of police professionalism that, on the local level, had much in common with Hoover's FBI. Murphy's support came from a vigorous press, an outraged public, and from Lindsay and Rockefeller, two political rivals whose presidential aspirations dictated that they do everything possible to stamp out a widely publicized police corruption scandal. Except for promises to Wilson of noninterference by Chicago Mayor Daley—ruler of the last great American political machine—Vollmer and Wilson had no such support when they took office, and neither succeeded in building it while in office.

Murphy's reforms also were successful because he recognized and acted upon truths not readily acknowledge by many of those who work their ways through the ranks to the tops of organizations. Where it is needed, lasting reform cannot be imposed either by the personal charisma of a single chief executive or by simply replacing wrongdoers with fresh blood. Persistent problems like police abuse or corruption require fundamental systemic changes that, in a way, are indictments of the organizations in which chiefs have themselves labored so long and so successfully. As the Knapp Commission pointed out, it is far easier for police chiefs to blame misconduct on individual "rotten apples" than to admit that they have risen to the tops of organizations that systematically turn new members into wrongdoers.[32]

Evidence of the need for systemic change in New York was made clear by Frank Serpico's experience. Who was the deviant when, alone among a squad of more than twenty plainclothesmen, Serpico chose not to take part in a pad? The answer must be Serpico, who strayed from a group norm so strong that it had never before been betrayed by a single one of the thousands of officers who had been assigned to "clothes." Until Serpico, the pad was such an established and well-known part of plainclothes work in New York that the Knapp Commission was able to determine with some precision how much it was worth in each of the city's seventeen plain-clothes divisions. Inside Plainclothes, a police official told Knapp Commission investigators, "we had a system where any policeman could do anything in front of any other policeman."[33] Outside Plainclothes, the operative norm was tolerance of corruption.[34]

In the same way that a norm of corruption and tolerance existed in the NYPD, the King tape, the Larez and Rescue incidents, and the Crumpton–Berry and McDonald's shootings make it plain that norms of brutality and its tolerance have operated in the LAPD. Why else did none of more than twenty officers intervene to stop the beating of Rodney King? Why did none volunteer the truth about what had happened to King? Is it possible that all these officers were deviant "rotten apples" and that this situation would have played out differently if other officers had been present? The actions of the officers who actually beat King makes this seem unlikely. They had to be acting in confidence that, no matter which individual cops saw them beat King, none would intervene to stop them or report their actions.

In general, therefore, if police reform is to be more than window dressing, it must be supported by the powerful institutions among which police organizations exist. Sometimes—as in New York and Dade County—this support arises from public revulsion and condemnation of spectacular single events like the Knapp Commission scandals or the beating and death of Arthur McDuffie. It is to be hoped that the King case and its aftermath will produce similar effects in Los Angeles. Both the appointment of Willie Williams to head the LAPD and Los Angeles voters' recent decision to eliminate the anachronistic autonomy of the LAPD's chief are good signs that things are headed in that direction. Neither may be enough, however, unless the LAPD chiefs also are provided with authority to hire and fire some of the people closest to them. In or out of policing, it is hard to imagine that any chief executive can succeed in making reforms unless he can assure that his *cabinet* shares his views and philosophies. Williams did not enjoy this authority in Philadelphia, and in Los Angeles he continues to work with a top management team tenured into their positions by Daryl Gates, the man he succeeded.

Such fundamental change is critical, because history teaches that if reform is to last, it must change the systems and values to which officers adhere rather than just the officers themselves. For years before Frank Serpico brought his story to the *New York Times,* discoveries of corruption among plainclothes officers were routine. Always, however, they were treated as isolated events. If one officer in a division were caught with his hand in the till, the department assumed that he was a *bagman,* picking up money for *everybody*. Within days, everybody in the division would be summarily transferred—"flopped"—to undesirable patrol precincts, and replaced by new blood.

Within days after that, however, the old blood would have sold the new-comers all the information they needed to reestablish the pad, and the same play continued with a new cast. There were no incentives to do otherwise: The gamblers who fed the pad knew how many officers were assigned to each division and made sure that their payments included a share for each officer. If one officer did not take the share, he would be looked upon as an oddball and, like Serpico, never trusted. Further, not taking the share was no protection against being flopped back to uniform. Before sweeping clean a plainclothes division, the department did not ask—*indeed, it did not want to know*—who was taking and who was not. Everybody went, but nothing changed.

Because so many people, interests, expectations—and laws—mold a police system, changing it is no easy task. During Murphy's time, as now, the caseloads of New York's prosecutors and judges—as well as the state's jails and prisons—were bursting at the seams with muggers, burglars, and other offenders who *hurt people*. Consequently, the courts did not take se-riously the gambling arrests brought to them by the police, and slaps on the wrist were the order of the day.

The courts could do this with impunity, because nobody cared or ob-jected. In New York, most of the public knew nothing about the illegal gambling that lined plainclothesmen's pockets: Outside the ghetto, illegal gambling was the minor diversion of a few people who played the horses and bet on other sporting events. In the city's ghettos, however, policy bet-ting—"the number," "bolida"—was a welcome daily diversion and source of anticipation. There, numbers runners were known to everybody. They were trusted local figures who patted kids on the head and rewarded regu-lar players with liquor or turkeys at Christmas. In the ghettos, numbers were a way of life, and any attempts to enforce gambling laws were re-garded as foolhardy and intrusive.

By Murphy's analysis, therefore, gambling-related police corruption was the inevitable result of attempts to apply laws against behavior that offended nobody. Consequently, he reasoned, the best way to eliminate gambling corruption was to refrain from applying gambling laws unless someone was offended. In January 1972, with one stroke of his pen, he directed officers not to arrest for gambling violations (or to enforce Sunday closing laws or construction codes) unless some member of the public had first been offended enough to complain to the police. With that, he took away officers' power to arrest—or to refrain from arresting—at their own whim and removed the opportunity for gambling corruption. His police union grumbled a bit about the negative consequences of telling law enforcement officers not to enforce laws, but where gambling and administrative law enforcement are concerned, nobody else seemed to notice what he had done.[35]

Today, permanently changing police organizational norms that tolerate and encourage brutality require change in the public expectations to which those norms are responsive. However repulsed viewers may have been by the graphic display of brutality shown in the King tape—and by the fury of the riotous response to it—there is considerable support among the public for an aggressive, kick-ass style of policing. Murphy seized the moment of the Serpico and Knapp revelations to point out that corruption was the product of the public expectation that police should vigorously enforce laws against victimless crimes. In the same way, contemporary police administrators should regard the King episode as a chance to put to bed whatever remains of the public's view that cops who are quick with their hands or clubs somehow serve the cause of effective policing.

## EFFECTIVE INTERNAL REFORMS

The principle that insularity and parochialism should be avoided at the top of police departments may be applied with equal force to their internal structures as well. The organizational charts of all large police agencies are full of boxes designating individual units. Our experience suggests, however, that police should pay careful heed to the administrative principle that specializations should be created only when particular tasks are so sophisticated that they cannot be adequately performed by generalists.

The generalists in police departments are patrol cops. Like medical general practitioners, these officers have more—and more stressful—contact with the public than any of their colleagues. Like family doctors, they also enjoy less prestige than specialists, and their status and sense of self worth are diminished each time a new specialization is created. Further, the myriad units in highly specialized departments invariably justify their existence and try to enhance their status in the organizational pecking order by generating statistics and, in the former manner of the NYPD's undercover narcotics unit, by putting the most favorable spin on them. This objectification and quantification of police work—*how many arrests? how many field interrogations? how many tickets? how many minutes and seconds responding to calls? how many pounds and ounces of drugs seized? how many dollars was it worth? how many outstanding robbery cases did this shooting solve?*—then trickles down to the department's lowest level, its patrol cars and foot beats. When that occurs, everybody up and down the line becomes driven by the need to generate what New York cops used to call "big numbers," without regard to whether they accomplish any desirable end. When that happens, street cops, who know from every source that they have been assigned their department's dirtiest job, also learn that their supervisors are interested only in the figures on their activity reports, not in what the police may have done to put them there.[36]

Those are bad messages to give repeatedly to people who are expected to serve professionally as first responders to some of society's most pressing and sensitive crises. It tells them that the cardinal sin is not to break the rules, but *to be caught breaking* the rules. This message—do whatever you care to in a secluded parking lot, or in a family's home, or on a deserted street outside a closed restaurant, *just don't get caught by outsiders*—leads patrol officers in highly specialized departments to act on their worst instincts at any sign of disrespect from their clientele.[37] In a vernacular the police knew he would understand, Rodney King was beaten not because of any laws he may have broken. Instead, King was beaten because his actions *dissed* patrol cops who knew, if only because headquarters was not sufficiently attentive to tell them not to memorialize racist comments on their computer memories, that they were free to act out their anger—as long as they were not caught at it by outsiders. Indeed, in the LAPD's eyes, the sin of Koon, Powell, Wind, and Theodore J. Briseno was not the beating itself: At least 20 other cops on the scene, as well as others who were told about it by Holliday and by King's brother, did nothing to stop or report it. Instead, the sin of the four officers who assaulted King was that their transgression was captured on tape.

Specialization has other pitfalls as well. Every time a new box is inserted on an organizational chart, new agendas are built, and the route to achievement of the organization's overall goal becomes hazier and less direct. Former detective Mike Rothmiller recently has written, for example, of how hard he tried to earn an assignment in one of the LAPD's most selective organizational boxes—the Organized Crime Intelligence Division. Once in the division, however, he found that its members spent their time building and providing the department's brass with gossip-filled dossiers on show business celebrities, athletes, and politicians who were considered antagonistic to the police.[38]

When police departments build organizational boxes to accommodate new units whose names and roles are better suited to military commando squads then to policing American streets, the results are likely to be a swashbuckling style that sheds unnecessary blood.

It is difficult, for example, to see how the actions of the special LAPD units described in this book contributed in any way to the goals implicit in the department's motto, "To Protect and Serve." What did the CRASH Unit's trashing and beatings in the Larez home have to do with protecting and serving? How could SIS officers have thought they were protecting and serving when they watched while, just as they anticipated, Crumpton and Berry put a bank full of innocent people in real fear of their lives, or while the McDonald's bandits terrorized Robin Cox? Were Metro officers protecting and serving when they used deadly weapons to break the bones and crush the tissues of nonviolent demonstrators?

Obviously, the answer to each of these questions is no. Instead, CRASH officers abused the Larezes because they wished to demonstrate, as police officers spray painted at the scene of the notorious Dalton Avenue Raid, that the "LAPD Rules." SIS cops watched and waited to confront and shoot down Crumpton, Berry, and the McDonald's bandits because, as their commander and their chief suggested in public comments, they placed a higher priority on spectacular arrests than on public safety.[39] Metro used nunchakus on Rescue because, as the script on their videotape of the incident states, they wanted to show that they "make it happen."

Negative consequences of the balkanization of police departments into units competing to be the most *elite,* the *baddest,* or simply the most *productive* certainly are not unique to the LAPD. The drug corruption memorialized in the book and film *Prince of the City* was the work of an elite detective squad whose members had previously been glorified in *The French Connection* and who had come to see themselves as bounty hunters to whom the rules of policing simply did not apply.[40] In the mid-1980s, just before television's *Sixty Minutes* was to air a segment praising the work of an elite New York City transit police unit, the squad's members were caught demonstrating their high productivity with statistics that included arrests of innocent people they had framed.[41] In short, the more a police department is cut up into small units, each of which is under pressure to produce and to excel in some specialty, the more likely it is that competition and *esprit* will produce abuse. And, as the experiences of the LAPD's Special Investigation Section and the NYPD's Special Investigation Unit suggest, the more special and elite the unit, the farther above the law it is likely to rise, and the farther it will fall when it runs out of air.

Compartmentalization of responsibility also must be avoided in working out mechanisms for officers' accountability. All police supervisors and administrators should be accountable for their subordinates' work, integrity, and compliance with standards of humane policing. Too often, however, line police supervisors are led to conclude by pressures for productivity that their job is to get officers to work as expeditiously as possible without regard to the rules. In such circumstances, responsibility for officers' integrity or humaneness is seen to fall—*exclusively*—on specialized headquarters units bearing such titles as Internal Affairs and Quality Control. An atmosphere of antagonism between field units and headquarters then develops. Field supervisors see their role as protecting their units and their officers against headquarters' *head hunters, shoo-flies, beakies, spies,* and *hatchetmen,* while headquarters units define themselves as good guys charged with the responsibility of keeping in line an undisciplined horde of rogues and thugs.[42]

Since line supervisors are closest to their personnel and have the greatest day-to-day effects on their work, they must also be accountable for seeing that officers do their jobs in the most humane ways possible. This is not easy: Like university deans, police *street bosses* have heavy investments in the good will of their personnel, which are sure to be affected by anything that, however slightly and however appropriately, shifts supervisors' loyalties away from the immediate concerns of the work group to the more abstract purposes of the organization as a whole.

One way to accomplish this is to punish supervisors when officers who work for them go wrong, as the NYPD's Commissioner Benjamin Ward did after his department's stun gun scandal. Although this specific case may have been an example of overkill,[43] the principle it invoked is sound and in line with the view of supervisory liability for official misconduct articulated by the Supreme Court in *Monell* v. *New York City Department of Social Services.* Such a principle—holding bosses to account for seeing that their officers work in a constitutional fashion—would also be a big change for many police agencies that, like the LAPD, cling to the notion that police misconduct is exclusively a problem of "rotten apples" rather than an indication of deeper systemic problems.

# 9

# *Police Accountability I: The Courts*

You can't fight City Hall.

Anonymous

While we must acknowledge that law enforcement agencies are faced with an increasingly difficult job to perform with diminishing resources, far too many of those resources would appear to be squandered paying for the misdeeds of a few rogue officers. In Los Angeles County alone, between 1988 and 1991, over 65 million dollars has been spent paying verdicts and settlements resulting from excess use of force by LAPD and the County Sheriffs. These limited resources could clearly be put to better use by fiscally strapped county governments.

—California Judiciary Subcommittee<br>on Peace Officer Conduct,<br>December 19, 1991

How can an insular institution like the police be held accountable to a wider public? In the popular view, perhaps the most frequent check on day-to-day police operations is the criminal courts, which in theory see to it that police anticrime efforts conform to the Constitution. The right to be free from unreasonable search, the right to remain silent, the right to an attorney, and the right to reasonable bail are familiar to most informed Americans largely because of frequent charges that they serve to exclude the truth from criminal proceedings or that they allow dangerous criminals to run free.

Neither practice and theory nor reality and perception always match,

however, and the general conception of the courts' influence on police activity is exaggerated. The exclusionary rule, for example, is no bar to the
search practices of officers or police departments who engage in indiscriminate "street sweep" techniques with the goal of cleaning up the streets by
causing embarrassment and harassment without regard to whether any arrests they happen to make will survive cross-examination.

Even officers who care whether the evidence they seize will be admitted
into evidence have not been much affected by the courts. The widespread
belief that the Supreme Court's best-known decisions on search, seizure,
and interrogation somehow have *handcuffed* the police or otherwise have
made citizens less safe is not supported by any objective evidence. No rep-
utable study suggests that any Supreme Court decision has raised crime
rates or hampered police effectiveness. The line of Supreme Court decisions that began with *Brown* v. *Mississippi* and proceeded through *Miranda* to more recent interventions on police interrogation practices, as
cases in point, is not even a factor in the vast majority of arrests and prosecutions.[1] Most offenders are caught redhanded in circumstances so rich in
incriminating evidence that the police simply do not need to ask them for
anything but their names and addresses. When police *buy* narcotics on the
street and *bust* the seller, or search a crack house and seize the drugs, attempts to obtain confessions serve only to gild the lily of already invulner-
able prosecution cases.

The Supreme Court's decisions on search and seizure also have had
only the most minimal effects on police crime-fighting ability. Despite
great interest by both objective scholars and partisan advocates, no study of
the exclusionary rule—which keeps unconstitutionally seized evidence out
of criminal prosecutions—shows that exclusion of evidence results in dismissal of more than 1.5 percent of the criminal cases in any jurisdiction.[2]
The sociologist Egon Bittner engaged in perhaps only a mild overstatement
when he wrote:

> Our [criminal] courts have no control over police work, never claimed to
> have such control, and it is exceedingly unlikely that they will claim such
> powers in the future, all things being equal. Indeed, the courts have, today,
> even less control over the police than they have over attorneys in private
> practice.[3]

Popular overestimation or exaggeration of the court's effects on police
effectiveness is a matter of more than academic interest. Like the view of
*cops-as-soldiers,* the charges that due process protections foil the war on
crime not only distract us from more promising strategies of crime control
but also increase the likelihood of police violence and violation of citizens'

rights. Cops who feel that *their enemy* has been given unreasonable advantages by people who have not themselves experienced the battle may come to disrespect all the rules and to administer "street justice"—as in the case of Rodney King—to ensure that offenders are appropriately and severely punished. On occasion, consciously or otherwise, police administrators may encourage such activities with comments, like those of Harold Breier, Daryl Gates, and Frank Rizzo, that appear to approve of violent detours around due process.

## PROSECUTING THE POLICE

As the King and McDuffie verdicts suggest, use of the criminal process *against* police officers who respond with violence to such calls for action also usually proves an inadequate mechanism for holding them accountable. We should not be surprised at this, and we should not view the criminal law's ineffectiveness in such cases as something that occurs only when *police* misconduct is at issue. However egregious, and regardless of whatever other labels are attached to it, the police action captured on the Holliday videotape was first and foremost an abuse of police professional discretion. Our observations of what happens when people in other lines of work cross their occupations' lines of propriety suggest that the criminal justice system and the criminal law are ineffective controls on the discretion of *any* professionals.

We know that this analogy between the police license to use force and the discretionary authority of other occupations or professions may seem inexact, but we believe it is to the point. The main difference we can see between the excessive use of police officers' batons and surgeons' use of their scalpels in unnecessary hysterectomies and mastectomies is that unnecessary surgery usually lines doctor's pockets, while cops' brutality typically brings no profit. Thus we suspect our analogy may sound foreign, because the criminal law rarely is a consideration when seeking to hold most professionals accountable for performing responsibly. Officers who use excessive force occasionally are brought up on criminal charges, but our discussions with prosecutors disclose virtually no criminal assault cases brought against doctors who, contrary to all medical indications, have unnecessarily removed organs or otherwise mutilated their patients. By now, doctors who contemplate supplying "suicide machines" to their patients and aiding in their use; conceiving patients' children with their own sperm; or raping anaesthetized patients have gotten the message that discovery of their misconduct will land them in the criminal dock. But aside from such bizarre circumstances, prosecutors seem to maintain a hands off policy where doctors' occupational offenses are concerned.

## CRIMINAL LAW AND PROFESSIONAL ACCOUNTABILITY

We do not believe that prosecutions of doctors are a rarity because less outlandish professional misconduct that could justify criminal assault or homicide charges does not happen. In every big city, the medical malpractice bar dwarfs the police brutality bar in size, and many "med mal" lawyers are prosperous enough to suggest that a considerable amount of criminally negligent and reckless medical conduct is going on. Instead, two broad but unspoken understandings provide more plausible explanations for the dearth of prosecutions against doctors. The first is that *professionals are better situated than lay juries to deal with the sinners among their ranks.* Professionals—doctors, lawyers, accountants, civil engineers—are highly skilled specialists. Consequently, professionals, unlike lay people, cannot easily be swayed by specious defense attempts to place their colleagues' actions as close as possible to the good end of the continuum that begins with reasonable professional judgments gone wrong and that ends in outright venality. We are dead certain, for example, that a jury composed entirely of cops (from jurisdictions other than Los Angeles) would have rejected out of hand the defense argument that the officers who beat King were only following their training. Instead, in Van Maanen's terms, the King beating jury consisted only of *know-nothing* lay people who brought to court only their ignorance of police training and other professional police standards.[4]

Peer adjudication of allegations of professional misconduct can be a very effective deterrent and enforcement mechanism. Lawyers, accountants, and doctors contemplating professional wrongdoing, for example, worry far more about losing their licenses to practice than about going to jail. They understand that their peers will have greater insight than criminal court jurors into their offenses. They know also that the standards of due process and evidence in professional proceedings are far less protective of the rights of the accused than are those that prevail in criminal trials. Professional disciplinary proceedings typically are fact-finding inquiries that, unlike criminal trials, allow truth seekers to draw inferences from defendants' refusals to testify. Such inquiries also adhere to a condemnation standard less rigorous than the rule of *guilt beyond a reasonable doubt* that applies to criminal proceedings.

Even where police peer review works objectively and as designed, however, the analogy between it and the self-monitoring processes of the traditional professions is flawed. With the notable exception of Florida, whose Department of Law Enforcement may revoke or suspend a local officer's license to practice upon an external peer panel's finding of police wrongdoing, police professional review typically, and exclusively, is internal to the organization involved. Hence it is inherently laden with conflicts of interest and affords much room for speculation that bureaucratic interests override objective fact-finding.

It is true that surgeons and lawyers are subject to review by such internal panels as hospital "tissue committees" and law firms' committees that decide which associates will become partners and which will be asked to seek other employment. The principal provisions for professional review in both occupations, however, are *external* to immediate employers. They are, respectively, the forums convened by medical and bar associations to decide not only whether a practitioner shall continue to ply his profession with a particular employer but, on occasion, whether he will continue in his profession at all.

The distinction between internal organizational review and external professional review is significant, because employers of police officers (or doctors, or lawyers) may have a far greater stake in demonstrating that their employees' actions were justifiable than do professional colleagues not employed by the same organization. To what extent, for example, are the deliberations of a police internal disciplinary body (or a hospital tissue committee) influenced by the knowledge that a finding that an officer used unnecessary force (or that a doctor performed unnecessary surgery) might expose its employer—or even members themselves—to civil liability? While it may be argued that existing review in the professions is less than totally objective, it certainly does not have built into it the conflicts of interest inherent in the internal organizational review that typifies policing.[5]

When, as in some of the examples discussed in this book, a police organizational review of officers' conduct serves as an official whitewash rather than as a means of discovering and reporting the truth, police are professionally answerable to no one. The historic absence of accountability in the LAPD led many to hope that justice would be served by bringing the four officers accused of beating Rodney King before the criminal law. But the criminal law did not work in the King case, because it was asked to do something it was not designed to accomplish.

The criminal law was created to hold people to answer for offenses known by even the most unschooled among us to be wrong. Despite the complexities built into the criminal law since the time, centuries ago, when it dealt only with such common law offenses as murder, assault, rape, and theft, the criminal law remains so broad and presents so many enforcement problems that it cannot serve meaningfully as the parameters for any professional's discretion. When we try to use criminal law as a substitute for standards that should be applied *within* a profession or occupation, we almost invariably are disappointed with the results. Even when convicted, doctors whose misconduct has left patients just as dead or mutilated—*or as broke*—as the victims of the most vicious street criminals typically are treated far less harshly than more traditional offenders by the criminal law. So, too, are dishonest accountants and lawyers, drunken tanker skippers, and Wall Street wheeler-dealers whose frauds and greed have ruined thousands of lives. The criminal justice system appears to react harshly to occupational crime only in cases involving defendants who were household names before they ran into trouble. Typically, scheming television evangelists, highly placed government officials who subvert democratic processes, and police chiefs and union presidents who steal from slush funds are treated harshly in court. Those whose names enter the public lexicon only because they have found themselves in court fare much better. In neither the case of the celebrity nor that of the lesser light taken to court for professional crime, however, is it apparent that justice is well served.

## CIVIL LIABILITY FOR PROFESSIONAL WRONGDOING

The second understanding that accounts for the absence of prosecutions for the job-related crimes of doctors and other professionals is that *justice in cases of occupational crime is better served by victims' private civil actions than by public criminal prosecutions.* Most often, professionals' violations of their industries' standards of care generally become known only when their wrongdoing results in injuries or other damage to specific people. In such instances, injured individuals generally can be directly compensated for their losses only by initiating their own private lawsuits. Typically, this is what happens, and prosecutors—who represent the state, the injured party in all criminal cases—refrain from filing charges in all but the most sensational such cases. Indeed, even when the evidence in civil actions demonstrates with some certainty that professional wrongdoing also has involved criminal violations, prosecutors usually keep their distance.

Consider some of the cases discussed in this book. A civil court found that Jesse Larez's home was forcibly entered and trashed, and that he and his daughter were assaulted by officers whose actions far exceeded their authority. Rescue's litigation demonstrated that the LAPD's Metro Squad used nunchakus—devices strictly forbidden by California's criminal law—to break the bones and damage the nerves and ligaments of people who offered them only passive resistance. John Crumpton, Jane Berry, Jesus Arango, Juan Bahena, and Herbert Burgos all were shot in the back by people whose accounts have virtually no relation to the objective physical evidence of their actions. Had people other than police done what was shown by the evidence to have happened in these cases, they would have been up to their elbows in criminal charges. Yet, as far as we know, the Los Angeles District Attorney has closed the book on all these cases without filing criminal charges and has encountered no negative public reaction for doing so.

This is not something that has happened only in Los Angeles, or only during the administration of Ira Reiner, LA's District Attorney when all of this was put on the public record. Fyfe has testified in similar, less spectacular but frequently lethal, civil cases in other parts of California, as well as in Georgia, Illinois, Louisiana, Massachusetts, Michigan, Mississippi, New Jersey, North Carolina, and Pennsylvania. None has resulted in criminal charges, although the evidence and trial transcripts would lead any reasonable observer to believe that the police involved had committed crimes, including criminal homicide.

We think it useful to view the unsuccessful prosecution of the officers who beat Rodney King in the context of these two understandings. First, *professionals are better situated than lay juries to deal with the sinners among their ranks;* and second, *justice in cases of occupational crime is better served by victims' private civil actions than by public criminal prosecutions.* Further, we see no possibility that these understandings will become inoperative in the foreseeable future. The sociologist Gilbert Geis has suggested that much of society's ambivalence in dealing with occupational crime is related to the difficulty of distinguishing wrongdoing from appropriately sharp and aggressive business practice.[6] It is no less difficult for jurors in criminal trials to conclude *beyond any reasonable doubt* that the professional actions of the police were criminal rather than merely appropriate defensive measures. Prosecutors know this, and prosecutors do not like to lose. Prosecutors also are reluctant to take on the police, their usual working partners in criminal proceedings. Hence, prosecutors tend to charge police only when the alternative—doing nothing in the face of evidence as compelling *and as public* as the King tape—has a higher cost than proceeding to trial.

Thus, if we seek justice in cases of occupation-related wrongdoing, we probably are best advised to avoid relying on the criminal justice process and to look to other mechanisms of accountability.

## SUING THE POLICE

While police violence may have increased because of popular interpretations that courts and due process guarantees have made police work unrea-
sonably difficult, a series of relatively obscure Supreme Court decisions
probably has reduced police violence significantly. Only recently has the
Court recognized the authority of the Civil Rights Act of 1871,[7] in which
the Congress provided both civil and criminal remedies for people whose
Constitutional rights had been violated by "persons acting under color of
state law." For nearly a century, the criminal provisions of this *Ku Klux
Klan Act,* which had been designed to protect newly freed slaves from the
depredations of Southern officials, occasionally were invoked. Its civil
side—generally referred in legal shorthand as *Section 1983*—lay nearly
dormant, however, and suits alleging violations of Constitutional rights
rarely were filed against police officers. Indeed, the *Indiana Law Journal*
reported that only twenty-one suits were filed under *Section 1983* during
the law's first forty-nine years of existence.[8]

There were two reasons for this long period of latency. First was the
courts' general interpretation that abuses of authority by police or others
that violated state laws were, by definition, not "under color of state law."
In effect, therefore, police could be held liable only for actions that were
unconstitutional but were authorized by the laws of their states. Since officers who were defendants in such cases generally could convincingly
argue that they had acted in good-faith reliance on the laws of their states,
*Section 1983* was a "Catch-22." If police officers violated both a citizen's
Constitutional rights and the state law (against assault or unlawful imprisonment, for example), suits were doomed to fail, because officers had
acted beyond the color of state law. If police officers violated the constitution without breaking state law—like the Mississippi officers who tortured
a suspect to obtain a confession in the *Brown*[9] case—suits were doomed to
fail because officers could argue that, in good faith, they had done nothing
more than obey the law of their state.

The second reason for the rarity of *Section 1983* suits was less complex:
money. Like attorneys in more traditional personal injury suits, lawyers
who represented civil rights plaintiffs generally worked on a "contingency" basis. Under this arrangement, lawyers charge no fees but agree to
work for a percentage—usually 30 to 40 percent—of whatever judgment
or settlement is reached. As a consequence, victims of civil rights violations (who cannot typically afford to pay for attorneys out of pocket) faced
a dilemma that virtually precluded *Section 1983* actions. It was one thing
to show that a local official had violated one's civil rights but quite another

to interest a lawyer in taking a case against a poorly paid and therefore largely judgment-proof deputy sheriff: of what consequence is a seven-figure verdict when the defendant earns only a four-figure salary?

The first barrier to civil rights litigation—absence of liability in cases in which defendants had violated state laws—came down in 1961. In that year, the Supreme Court decided *Monroe* v. *Pape,*[10] a case that began when a group of police officers conducted an early morning raid on the home of a black Chicagoan they sought to question about a murder. There, much like the Los Angeles officers who raided the Larez home more than a quarter of a century later, the officers terrorized a large family. The suspect's six kids were rousted out of bed and marched into the living room, where they were made to stand naked. Unlike the officers in Larez, these Chicago cops had no warrant. Still, they ransacked the home tearing up bedclothes and strewing the floors with the contents of dresser drawers. They left with the kids' father in tow, interrogating him while he was held on "open" charges. Even though a magistrate was available, the suspect was not taken to court and was not allowed to call his family or to attempt to obtain a lawyer. Finally, after ten hours in custody, he was released without charges.

When the Supreme Court heard the case brought by the family, the justices reached a landmark decision. The Court's ruling holds, in essence, that *Section 1983's* "color of state law" provision applies when officials commit constitutional violations in the course of their duties, regardless of whether they also violate state law. In the face of evidence that local and state officials tolerated or encouraged Constitutional violations by police, the Supreme Court finally put the federal judiciary in the business of enforcing *Section 1983:* "Between 1961 and 1977," Justice Lewis Powell was to write later, "the number of cases filed in federal court under civil rights statutes increased from 296 to 13,113."[11]

## *MONELL:* THE EFFECTIVENESS OF AN UNLIKELY DETERRENT

The *Monroe* decision did not, however, assign liability to local governments for constitutional violations by their employees. This second shoe dropped in 1978 in *Monell* v. *Department of Social Services of the City of New York,*[12] a case about as far removed from police practice as one could imagine. Mrs. Monell, a pregnant employee of the agency she sued, had applied to her supervisor for maternity leave. Told that it was her department's policy to deny maternity leaves and to require new mothers to resign, Monell sued, arguing that she—and several other women who

were parties to her action—had been denied equal protection of law by a
policy that unfairly affected only females and their careers. The Supreme
Court agreed with Mrs. Monell and established a major legal principle:
Where a representative of an official agency (like Monell's supervisor) violates an individual's Constitutional rights as a result of the agency's official custom and practice (like the policy barring maternity leaves), the
agency as well as the individual employee may be held liable. In reaching
this decision, the Court defined *custom or usage* broadly enough to allow
plaintiffs to argue that it includes whatever officials routinely *do,* whether
or not legal or in line with written agency policy. "Custom or usage," the
*Monell* Court wrote, may be found in "persistent and widespread . . . practices of officials [which, a]lthough not authorized by written law, [are] so
permanent and well-settled as to [have] the force of law."[13]

In other words, *Monell* opened the "deep pockets" of government trea-
suries to civil rights plaintiffs who could demonstrate that they had been
hurt by employees whose wrongful acts were the results of such egregious
customs, practices, and policies, including poor training or supervision.

The results of *Monell,* evidence suggests, have included a boom in civil
rights litigation against the police. "From 1986 through 1990," according
to the Christopher Commission, Los Angeles "paid in excess of $20 mil-
lion in judgments, settlements, and jury verdicts in 300 suits against LAPD
officers alleging excessive use of force."[14] The commission probably un-
derstated this figure, which reflects a trend of steady growth. In 1971 for
example, Los Angeles paid settlements and judgments of about $11,000 to
people who had sued the police. In 1980, lawsuits against the LAPD cost
about $890,000 in verdicts and settlements; by 1986, about $4 million; by
1989, $6.5 million; in 1990, $11.3 million.[15] Although Detroit's record in
litigation is even worse—in 1990 alone, that city paid $20 million in judg-
ments and verdicts—other big police jurisdictions have fared somewhat
better. New York, with three times as many police officers as the LAPD,
paid slightly less in settlements and verdicts in 1990 than did Los Angeles.
Chicago, with a police department half again as big as the LAPD, paid out
less than half of the Los Angeles liability bill.[16]

Calculating the bottom-line cost of defending against allegations of unconstitutional behavior by officers, however, requires that several additional—and substantial—costs be added to the total for judgments and settlements. Most obvious is the direct expense of funding a sizable legal staff
and the defense of individual cases, which, in Los Angeles, total 200 to 300
annually. Most of these cases are dismissed or settled before trial, and
those that do make it to court usually result in no awards to plaintiffs: In
1990, fifty-eight excessive force cases against LAPD officers were tried,
with plaintiffs prevailing in only seventeen.[17]

Perhaps the two big reasons for plaintiffs' low success rate at trials are that cities are prone to settle their most hopeless cases before trial, and that most people who allege excessive police force are not very sympathetic. In contrast to claimants in more typical lawsuits, plaintiffs like Rodney King and—at the extreme—Jane Berry and the McDonald's bandits generally have provoked the police with some reprehensible act. Consequently, excessive force plaintiffs usually have a far heavier burden than, say, totally innocent plaintiffs in medical malpractice cases.[18] Whatever the reason, the financial implication of excessive-force plaintiffs' low success rate is that verdicts and settlements occur in only a small percentage of suits, and that a considerable amount of money is also expended in successful defenses against allegations of police misconduct.

Attorneys' fees are another cost of defending against civil rights liability. In 1976, between *Monroe* and *Monell,* the U.S. Congress enacted a law that permits judges to award successful plaintiffs "reasonable attorney's fees as part of the costs."[19] Thus, *Section 1983* litigation typically is no longer tied to the contingency fee system. Instead, while only winning attorneys are eligible for award of fees, disbursements are based upon accountings of attorney's time and expenses and are independent of the amount of the award to the plaintiff. This arrangement sometimes produces interesting results. A Los Angeles attorney, Stephen Yagman, was awarded $29,137 in fees in a case in which his clients won a $2.00 verdict against the Los Angeles County Sheriff's Department.[20]

Similar results have been reported elsewhere[21] and may not be as anomalous as they initially appear. Jury decisions—in the form of either verdicts for police or extremely small awards to plaintiffs—appear to turn upon jurors' assessments of plaintiffs' character rather than upon the merits of the police action. No matter how egregiously the police may act in the incidents that lead to some litigation, it is no easy thing for a juror to reward an authentic criminal with a judgment against the police who arrested him. In such "dollar verdict" cases, substantial attorneys' fees may serve as a sort of punitive message that unreasonable practices should end. Regardless of their purpose, however, attorneys' fees are an additional cost of defending against successful excessive force litigation.

Many police departments and professional police organizations have responded to the liability problem by codifying and implementing carefully crafted policies and directives. Typically, these directives and the training that accompanies them govern officers' behavior and decrease the chance of spontaneous brutality during such high-risk activities as car chases and use of force.

This trend to police policy formulation has been a significant change from earlier practice. In the past, apparently on the theory that officers could be held legally liable for failing to adhere to a standard of reasonableness only if such a standard existed in writing, police departments shied away from committing any rules to paper. Their reluctance to provide officers with meaningful guidance for the exercise of discretion in critical street situations was aggravated by *Peterson* v. *City of Long Beach*,[2] a case in which the California Supreme Court ruled that police departments' policies and directives could be used by juries as standards to measure the reasonableness of officers' conduct. Although *Peterson* directly affected only California litigation, it was viewed by police administrators across the country as justification for leaving as much as possible to officers' discretion. "Why should I issue policies on anything?" a police chief asked Fyfe at a 1980 FBI seminar. "If I give officers rules, they come back to haunt us in court."

This reaction was not what the courts had hoped to achieve in either *Monell* or *Peterson*. Since *Monell*, a series of decisions have made it plain that police administrators who fail to promulgate clear guidelines and to train officers in how to implement them run a higher risk of liability for inadequate supervision and training than do departments that leave critical decisions entirely to officers' discretion. In *Tennessee* v. *Garner*,[23] the Supreme Court held that police shootings under authority of laws and policies that allowed officers to decide whether to use deadly force to apprehend nonviolent fleeing felony suspects violated the Fourth Amendment. As a result, police departments in the more than twenty states in which such laws exist have been compelled to formulate more restrictive policies on use of deadly force or face future liability for officers' exercise of the broad—and unconstitutional—discretion allowed them by state legislators.[24]

In *Thurman* v. *City of Torrington*, a Connecticut police department was held liable for what was, in effect, a policy by omission. In the absence of a clearly stated stated regulation requiring officers to handle domestic assaults no differently from others, Torrington police did not arrest in domestic cases. Eventually, Thurman was stabbed by the estranged husband she had frequently asked police to arrest.[25]

In *City of Canton* v. *Harris*, even the Supreme Court conservatives conceded that where there is "a clear constitutional duty implicated in recurrent situations that a particular employee is certain to face, . . . failure to inform city personnel of that duty will create an extremely high risk that constitutional violations will ensue."[26] Other *Monell* cases have held police agencies liable for inadequate policy and training regarding nonlethal force, strip searches, and vehicle pursuits.[27]

Thus it is likely that *Monell*, a decision by the conservative Burger Court in a civil matter that most directly affected a social worker's employer, has had, and will continue to have, as broad an effect on police operations as any criminal case decided by the liberal Warren Court. *Mapp* affected police searches, and *Miranda* affected police interrogations, but *Monell* offers a remedy for wrongful conduct in virtually every sphere of police activity, including brutality and use of force.

## INJUNCTIVE RELIEF

Still, however hard their municipalities' pocketbooks have been hit by lawsuits, some police departments seem not to regard the cost of litigation as a signal that something is awry. Several members of the Los Angeles "brutality bar," as well as several officials of the LAPD, have told us that the LAPD views its losses in civil courts—and the brutality bar's consequent prosperity—as a reasonable price for the presumed deterrent effect of the department's most violent responses to lawbreaking. Los Angeles is so physically large, this logic runs, that providing it with a truly adequate number of police officers would likely bankrupt the city. Thus, the cheapest way to deter potential offenders is to encourage cops to be *aggressive*—or *proactive*—to tolerate and foot the bill for their excesses, and to hope that the sensational headlines and television news stories that follow will encourage criminals to take their business elsewhere.

There is more than casual evidence of such a philosophy in Los Angeles. According to the Christopher Commission's extrapolation of FBI crime data, violent crime rates in Los Angeles are more than twice as high as the national average and, among the nation's six largest cities, are exceeded only by New York's. The 1989 rates of violent crime (murder or manslaughter, robbery, assault, rape) per 100,000 population were as follows:

| | |
|---|---|
| United States | 663.2 |
| Los Angeles | 1601.1 |
| New York | 2021.2 |
| Chicago | n/a |
| Philadelphia | 608.5 |
| Houston | 801.1 |
| Detroit | 891.2[28] |

In describing LAPD's crime-fighting efforts, however, Chief Gates reported:

Los Angeles ranks at the very bottom in officer to population ratio (2.1:1000) when compared with America's six largest cities. Yet, Los Angeles is the safest of the big cities because Los Angeles police officers are the most productive. Studies by the Police Foundation and crime statistics released by the FBI reveal that Los Angeles has the lowest crime rate per capita among the six largest cities. The homicide rate in Los Angeles in 1990 (28.2 per 100,000 inhabitants) was also the lowest of the largest cities and far behind the 56.6 rate posted by Detroit. It is also interesting to note that our nation's capital had a homicide rate of 77.7 last year. This statistically proven way of analyzing crime data indicates that the people of Los Angeles are safer than the populace of other major cities.

The Department's proactive enforcement philosophy is one of the primary reasons it has been able to accomplish "more with less." This is clearly illustrated when comparing arrests per officer ratio of the nation's three largest cities. In 1990, New York, with a force of over 26,000 officers and an area of 301 square miles, had an officer to arrest ratio of 1:8. Chicago, with a force of 11,000 to police a city of 228 square miles, had a ratio of 1:22. In sharp contrast, Los Angeles police officers had an officer to arrest ratio of 1:60 while policing 467 square miles.[29]

These explanations are extremely questionable. Most scholars and police practitioners have long since concluded that police aggressiveness has little effect on homicide rates. Regardless of how proactive, patrol officers can do little to dissuade husbands from killing their wives, drug dealers from executing those who have cheated them, or gang kids from killing for no particular reason.[30] Neither, without knowing more about the nature of the offenses suspected in each of the cities described, do arrest statistics tell us much about the effectiveness of police work or whether it is responsive to each city's violent crime problem. Arrests for outstanding traffic warrants, for example, probably have only the remotest relationship to public safety from violent crime. In addition, it is not clear that the LAPD's arrest statistics are not inflated by police conduct unacceptable in other large U.S. cities. Paul Hoffman, Legal Director of the Southern California American Civil Liberties Foundation, told the U.S. House of Representatives' Subcommittee on Civil and Constitutional Rights about the LAPD's "Operation Hammer":

> Beginning in February 1988 the LAPD has mounted a massive military style show of force on the predominantly Black neighborhoods of South-Central Los Angeles under the name Operation Hammer. Tens of thousands of African-American young men were rounded up based only on their race and appearance without any cause to believe they had committed a criminal offense. What this has meant to youths in the community is the humiliation and terror of police stops, handcuffing, and arrest without any intention of filing criminal charges, as the statistics bear out.

In the course of Operation Hammer sweeps in 1990 more than 25,000 youths had been arrested, yet fewer than 1,500 of them were ever actually charged with a criminal offense.[31]

Nor does Gates's description explain how the physical size of a jurisdiction is related to the degree of aggressiveness officers should use in their work. By this yardstick, officers who patrol large rural areas should be more aggressive than cops who work small inner-city beats. Such a proposition has no support in the literature of police administration.

When, however misleading, such a highly quantified cost-benefit analysis is used to measure police effectiveness, cash liability may be an inadequate corrective for police abuses. Even if half of the LAPD's $11.3 million liability bill in 1990 could be eliminated and converted to police salaries and personnel expenses, it would pay for only about seventy officers, less than a 1 percent increase in the department's personnel complement. Halving Detroit's $20 million liability cost would support about 140 officers, a 3 percent increase in uniformed strength. Although these new personnel would be welcome, in neither Los Angeles nor Detroit would they increase police presence on the street enough to obtain a measurable deterrent effect on crime. Thus, to the extent that police violence may inhibit offenders, cold econometric analysis might suggest that paying even a very steep bill for police excesses is a good investment in crime control. In big police jurisdictions, verdicts and settlements are cheaper than paying for enough new cops to make a real difference in a department's ability to mount a street presence. The analysis does not hold for very small departments, where a single large verdict might easily exceed the entire annual budget.

The most apparent problem with this analysis, of course, is that it should offend the consciousness of civilized people. A license to attempt to deter crime by brutalizing suspects—or anyone else—should not be available to the police at any price. Even beyond this truth, however, such an analysis is flawed on purely quantitative grounds. As the Christopher Commission's data suggest, there is no evidence that either the degree of legitimate force or improper violence used by police in the course of their work has any effect on crime or public safety.[32]

Where police administrators appear indifferent to the financial costs of litigation emanating from abuse, the most appropriate way for courts to attempt to prevent future misconduct may be to issue an injunction, a court order that prohibits persons or organizations from engaging in some specific conduct or, alternatively, that commands some specific conduct. For reasons of federalism and the separation of powers among the three branches of government, however, courts historically have been reluctant to use the injunctive process to intrude on what they refer to as *administrative prerogatives*. Consequently, they have done so in police cases infrequently and, generally, only where it has clearly been shown that there is no other way of preventing recurrent, egregious, and clearly defined police misconduct.

In one leading case, an injunction was issued only after Baltimore police had forced their way into more than three hundred homes in a largely black neighborhood. They did so without warrants, sometimes in the middle of the night, and only on the basis of sparse information about an unknown suspect in the shooting of two police officers. Even though it was relatively clear that police had no plans to end their raids until the offender was in custody, the trial judge who originally heard the request for an injunction declined to issue it. He was overturned by the appellate court.[33]

More recent cases have demonstrated that the federal courts have grown increasingly chary of intervening in future police operational matters. In a case eventually called *Rizzo* v. *Goode,* a civil rights group tried, in essence, to get the courts to command Philadelphia's Mayor and police department to cease a "pervasive pattern of illegal and unconstitutional mistreatment by police officers," alleging that such a pattern affected all Philadelphians. In support of their petition, which was successful at the lower levels, the plaintiffs produced evidence of twenty incidents of excessive force. In dismissing the injunction, the Supreme Court eventually wrote that "in a city of three million inhabitants, with 7,500 policemen," this number was not "unacceptably high."[34] The Supreme Court also dismissed an injunction that had been obtained by an LAPD choke hold victim, Adolph Lyons, on grounds that he could not show "that he is realistically threatened by a repetition of his experience."[35] Most recently, an appeals court dismissed a preliminary injunction that had been granted against the Los Angeles County Sheriff's Department compelling it to:

1. Follow the Department's own stated policies and guidelines regarding the use of force and procedures for conducting searches.
2. Submit to the Court, in camera and under seal, copies of reports alleging the use of excessive force that are in the possession of the Department on the first of every month.[36]

Shortly after the Supreme Court's decision in *Lyons,* the criminal justice scholar Cyril Robinson noted that the Justices appeared to be

restraining the use of the injunction by federal courts as a means of social change. . . . [T]he Court seemed to be trying to push the genie back into the bottle by reducing the social content of the litigation to the simple one-on-one adversary model. Whether in its latest attempt in [*Lyons*] the Court has succeeded, only future cases will tell. In the meantime, plaintiffs will have to skillfully draft their complaints so as to come within the Court's demands for case and controversy.[37]

The more recent judicial reluctance to use an injunction to do no more than compel the Los Angeles Sheriff's Department to demonstrate that it was abiding by its own "stated policies and guidelines" may indicate that injunction is not a viable way of effecting police reform. Thus, it appears that *Monell* cases, brought on a one-on-one basis in the hope of winning money damages, will continue to serve as the most significant form of judicial oversight of the police.

## THE U.S. DEPARTMENT OF JUSTICE

The Ku Klux Klan Act also authorizes federal criminal prosecutions of local and state officials who violate citizens' rights. The Civil Rights Division of the U.S. Department of Justice and its investigative arm, the Federal Bureau of Investigation, apparently have been less than enthusiastic about bringing such cases. According to Linda Davis, Chief of the Criminal Section of the Civil Rights Division, about 85 percent of the eight thousand or so civil rights complaints

> ... received and reviewed by DOJ concern police misconduct allegations ... about one-third of these complaints are of sufficient substance to warrant investigations. ... The Department of Justice is very selective about the cases it pursues. Of the approximately 3,000 investigations conducted each year, it authorizes only about 50 cases for grand jury presentation and possible indictment.[38]

The Justice Department has never been the chief prosecutorial actor in police brutality cases—leaving that role to local district attorneys—but these fifty *presentments* apparently represent a sharp decrease from Justice's activities in earlier times. In 1981 the U.S. Civil Rights Commission groused about what it saw as the inadequacy of Justice's aggressiveness in dealing with police brutality: "Although Federal officials annually receive thousands of complaints alleging police misconduct, on the average *fewer than 100 cases are successfully prosecuted each year.*"[39]

Thus, as recently as 1981 Justice apparently was obtaining convictions in about one hundred police brutality cases every year. Today—when, for example, brutality verdicts against the LAPD cost about fifteen times as much as in 1980—Justice contemplates prosecution in only half that number. Despite the Justice Department's recent "initiative" on police brutality, we are told by House of Representatives staff that "it's still business as usual. After King, Justice said it would go back and investigate cases more thoroughly, but we haven't seen any results. They're still indicting in about 50 police cases a year."[40]

The reasons for this attrition in generally "sensitive" civil rights cases, the Justice Department's Davis has suggested, include the need to "establish the credibility of each witness under oath" at a grand jury proceeding.[41] Certainly, this is not a novel purpose of grand jury proceedings, but another—one calling to mind the Simi Valley jury's acquittal of the officers who beat Rodney King—is unusual:

> [I]t is much preferred to have members of the community assess the government's evidence. This provides the Justice Department with a better understanding of community attitudes that so frequently play a significant role in the ultimate resolution of such cases.[42]

Apparently to test community attitudes, Justice follows yet another unusual practice. American grand juries are secret proceedings in which prosecutors present evidence to community members who are then asked to determine whether sufficient grounds exist—probable cause—to indict, or file criminal charges against, the subjects of investigations. Grand jury members generally are selected by prosecutors, and it is rare indeed that subjects of investigations appear before them or are even invited to do so. Because grand juries decide only whether to charge rather than whether to convict, subjects of grand jury proceedings do not enjoy the rights of defendants in actual criminal trials. They are not entitled to have counsel in grand jury rooms. In order to ask for legal advice, they must excuse themselves and confer with their lawyers outside the rooms in which they appear. Although they may make statements, they are not entitled to cross-examine witnesses and are questioned only by prosecutors and, sometimes, by individual grand jurors. Because appearing at such a proceeding usually is a no-win situation for subjects of investigations, asking them to present themselves typically is a waste of time.

James Eisenstein and Herbert Jacob's description of a Baltimore grand jury proceeding in an armed robbery case captures how this process works in most American jurisdictions:

> While Brown sat in jail, his case continued its journey. One of the two assistant state's attorneys in the grand jury section of the state's attorney's office reviewed the file quickly to determine whether the available evidence could sustain the charges.
> ... The grand jury proceedings consumed only a few minutes. One of the arresting officers summarized the case for the grand jurors, who voted for an

indictment as they did in almost all cases presented to them. In legal theory, the grand jury had found probable cause that a crime had been committed and that Roy Brown had committed it. The indictment was returned October 10, two weeks after the preliminary examination and twenty-nine days after the arrest.[43]

The Justice Department's civil rights grand jury proceedings differ from the case described by Eisenstein and Jacob not only because they rarely result in indictments but also because their subjects are invited to appear before the grand juries hearing evidence against them.[44] Because of the secrecy of grand jury proceedings, there is no way to know whether suspect police officers take advantage of these invitations or, if so, how they may influence members' decisions on whether to proceed against them.

The end product of all this testing of evidence and attitudes is that Justice plays virtually no active role in holding local police accountable for abiding by the Constitution. The Justice Department employs 80,747 people, only forty-four of whom—*fewer than one per state, less that one-twentieth of 1 percent of Justice Department employees*—are civil rights prosecutors. In a document it submitted to the House Civil Rights Subcommittee, Justice could list but twenty-two "significant civil rights prosecutions of police brutality cases" throughout the fifty states and Puerto Rico during the nine years 1982–89.[45]

Even more recently, Justice prepared a "study" of the more than 15,000 complaints of official police misconduct it had received during the fiscal years 1985 through 1990 (October 1984–September 1990). The purpose of the study reportedly was to "determine to what extent, if any, a pattern of police brutality by employees of law enforcement agencies is shown from the data maintained by the Civil Rights Division."[46]

Justice's researchers used unorthodox methods and interpretations in their efforts to answer this question. They note:

> *The Justice Department did not receive a single complaint in six years for three-fourths of all agencies that report crime data to the FBI's Uniform Crime Reporting Program;* we received only one complaint for an additional 17% of the nation's law enforcement agencies. Fewer than 10% of all law enforcement entities nationwide generated two or more complaints of police abuse from 1985 through 1990. *Almost one-half of all the complaints received were against only 187 law enforcement agencies.*[47]

Justice then analyzed the relationships among numbers of civil rights complaints and the numbers of arrests, sworn officers, and service populations among the 187 departments at the top of its list. That is a logical next step. If *no* patterns of brutality existed, one would expect to find straight-line relationships in these analyses. If all things were equal—if police practice were the same across the departments studied by Justice—one would expect that the number of civil rights complaints against a department could be predicted by the number of cops it employed, the number of people they served, and the number of arrests they made. In other words, one might expect to find that the largest American police departments had found their way to the top of this list by virtue of their size alone, and that their places on it would be roughly the same as the order of their sizes.

As an example: Department A has been the subject of ten times as many civil rights complaints as Department B, but, when one looks to determine why, one finds that A also is ten times as big as B, serves a population ten times as big as B's, and makes ten times as many arrests as B. The logical conclusion is that, except for size, there is not much difference between A and B. In an illustration that is perhaps more familiar, this would be similar to finding that New York City—which is about ten times as big as Washington, D.C.—has about ten times as many reported cases of cancer as Washington. Such a finding probably would not affect one's choice of where to live, because it suggests that an individual's chance of coming down with cancer is the same in either city.

Conversely, if one found no relationships in such analyses—if Department A accumulated ten times as many complaints as B despite the fact that both agencies were the same size, served populations of similar size, and made similar numbers of arrests, one would conclude that there probably are differences in the operating styles of the cops and that a pattern of brutality was likely. This would be as startling as discovering that, despite the differences in their sizes, New York and Washington had the same number of cancer patients, and would suggest strongly that something other than city size must account for the difference.

In its analysis, Justice found that all things were not equal:

> The statistical analysis of these data does not reveal any strong relationship in explaining why one agency is more likely to have received a greater number of complaints than another agency. A regression analysis was performed among the variables described above but it did not show a sufficient nexus between the number of complaints received by an agency and the three variables [numbers of arrests, sworn officers, and size of service population].[48]

In plainer English, Justice found that department and city size and number of arrests did not predict the number of civil rights complaints. One might expect, therefore, that Justice would conclude that it had discovered a pattern in which some cities accounted for an inordinate number of complaints, and that Justice would continue to seek explanations other than department and city size and arrest activity. Justice, however, concluded: "After careful analysis, this study does not reveal any statistically significant patterns of police misconduct."[49]

In the gentlest possible terms, this is *non sequitur* of such obvious dimensions that it can only reflect conscious avoidance of the facts. Among data included—but not analyzed—in the Justice report is an appendix that describes the numbers of complaints against the top 187 police agencies for every year studied.[50] When one uses these figures to construct annual *rates* of civil rights complaints per 1,000 officers[51] (as one might with injury or mortality figures to determine how dangerous police work was in different jurisdictions), the patterns Justice was unable to find become obvious. Some examples from among Justice's 187 leading complaint recipients that include the largest American police jurisdictions, as well as others useful for illustrative purposes, are assembled here:

| Jurisdiction | Annual Rate of Complaints per 1,000 Officers, FY 1985–1990 |
|---|---|
| Albuquerque | 5.6 |
| Atlanta | 2.9 |
| Austin | 4.0 |
| Baltimore County | 1.9[52] |
| Birmingham | 3.0 |
| Boston | 2.1 |
| Broward County (FL) | 3.0 |
| Buffalo | 6.9 |
| Charlotte | 4.4 |
| Chicago | 1.4 |
| Cincinnati | 3.3 |
| Cleveland | 2.9 |
| Dallas | 5.1 |
| Denver | 3.8 |
| Detroit | 0.9 |
| East Providence | 22.2 |
| El Paso | 25.3 |
| Fort Worth | 3.3 |
| Galveston | 12.9 |
| Harris (TX) Sheriff | 7.8 |
| Honolulu | 3.0 |
| Houston | 4.2 |
| Indianapolis | 5.0 |

| Jurisdiction | Annual Rate of Complaints per 1,000 Officers, FY 1985–1990 |
|---|---|
| Jackson (MS) | 23.6 |
| Jefferson (LA) Sheriff | 32.4 |
| Jersey City | 3.3 |
| Kansas City (KS) | 20.1 |
| Kansas City (MO) | 5.4 |
| Las Vegas | 8.1 |
| Long Beach (CA) | 6.1 |
| Los Angeles | 1.9 |
| Los Angeles Sheriff | 7.4 |
| Louisville | 4.6 |
| Memphis | 8.0 |
| Metro-Dade | 2.1 |
| Miami | 7.5 |
| Milwaukee | 1.0 |
| Minneapolis | 7.0 |
| Nashville | 2.9 |
| Newark | 1.9 |
| New Orleans | 26.0 |
| New York | 0.5 |
| Norfolk | 8.0 |
| Oakland | 3.3 |
| Oklahoma City | 12.9 |
| Pawtucket | 21.0 |
| Philadelphia | 1.2 |
| Phoenix | 3.9 |
| Pittsburgh | 5.4 |
| Portland (OR) | 2.7 |
| Providence | 21.3 |
| Sacramento | 5.5 |
| St. Louis | 9.6 |
| San Antonio | 14.4 |
| San Diego | 4.1 |
| San Diego Sheriff | 13.9 |
| San Francisco | 1.6 |
| San Jose | 2.0 |
| Seattle | 1.8 |
| Washington, DC | 0.8 |

| Jurisdiction | Annual Rate of Complaints per 1,000 Officers, FY 1985–1990 |
|---|---|
| State Police Agencies | |
| California Highway Patrol | 0.5 |
| New Jersey State Police | 0.8 |
| New York State Police | 0.5 |
| Rhode Island State Police | 12.1 |
| S. Carolina Highway Patrol | 2.2 |
| Texas | 3.0 |

Certainly, these rates are affected by factors that have nothing to do with the actual incidence of street-level police violence. Some complaints are spurious. Some potential complaints to Justice are not made because citizens instead go to local authorities in confidence that they will thoroughly and objectively investigate grievances. In places where the civil rights bar is very active, attorneys advise their clients to forgo complaints to Justice and, instead, to seek redress in civil suits. Some of the agencies included on this table (most notably Metro-Dade and the Sheriffs in Los Angeles, San Diego, and Jefferson Parish) operate large jails and probably receive many inmates' complaints about jail conditions in addition to allegations from citizens on the street. According to Justice, "unique occurrences such as advertising to solicit complaints of brutality can increase the number of complaints substantially."[53] Still, the numbers on this table are truly startling and suggest strongly that a further look at these agencies might be worthwhile.

At the extremes among departments not responsible for holding jail inmates, cops in New Orleans (rate = 26.0) were *fifty-two times* more likely than New York cops (rate = 0.5) to have been subjects of civil rights complaints. The Sheriff's Department in Louisiana's Jefferson Parish drew complaints at a rate (32.4) sixteen times as high as the Metro-Dade Police Department (2.1). Despite the fact that its numbers include complaints by inmates, Metro-Dade's rate was less than one-third that of the Miami Police Department (7.5). The rate in Long Beach (6.4) was more than three times as high as that of the neighboring LAPD (1.9), and Kansas City, Kansas, had a rate four times as high (20.1) as its neighbor and namesake across the river in Missouri (5.4). Only four New England cities made the list of 187. Three of these are comparatively small Rhode Island communities—East Providence, Pawtucket, and Providence—that all had rates (22.2, 21.0, and 21.3, respectively) at least ten times as high as Boston's

(2.1). Indeed, the Pawtucket Police Department—144 officers strong—received more than twice as many complaints as any state, county, municipal, or territorial law enforcement agency in Alaska, Delaware, Idaho, Iowa, Maine, Montana, Nebraska, New Hampshire, North Dakota, Vermont, Wyoming, Guam, or the Virgin Islands.[54] Only six state police agencies are included on this list, and Rhode Island—the historic *smallest of the forty-eight*—leads the chart with a rate four to twenty-five times higher than any other.

In short, even this cursory look at the data compiled by Justice makes it appear that its researchers are incorrect when they "respectfully submit that no pattern emerges from these figures."[55]

Rates of disease, crime, injuries to police officers, auto accidents, consumer complaints, or any other phenomenon that varied as greatly among American jurisdictions as did "these figures"—*as much as 5,200 percent between the lowest and highest of the big cities,* where statistics are large enough to be meaningful—would present a pattern so strong that they would startle any researcher. That Justice does not see a pattern in "these figures" can only be because Justice does not wish to see such a pattern. Reluctantly, therefore, we agree with Judge J. Spencer Letts, who observed during the trial of the officers who shot the McDonald's bandits that, where police brutality is concerned, "the Justice Department has put its own interests ahead of the interests of justice."

# 10

# *Police Accountability II: The Public*

Perhaps the most common gripes that newsmen have about police records are failure to identify a woman as "Miss" or "Mrs.," failure to provide middle initials, and failure to record the ages of those arrested.

—Ned L. Wall, International City Managers' Association
*Municipal Police Administration,* 1961[1]

I object to the repetitious requirement for notification in writing [to citizens who have complained about police actions] at the completion of the investigation to notify and outline your reasons for the findings. I don't know of anybody in the police department who has that kind of writing ability that could clearly state why, in writing, certain conclusions have been reached.

—Chief Inspector Frank Scafidi, Philadelphia Police Department,
testimony before U.S. Civil Rights Commission, April 1979[2]

In recent years, the press—or, at least, some part of it—has become an important watchdog of police, to that extent fulfilling "the checking function" on local government for the public that, it has been argued, is an important purpose of the First Amendment.[3] But that is a relatively new phenomenon. The traditional police beat reporter almost never reported on the police as an organization. He, and it used be a he, hung out with cops, drank with them after work, and followed them on their rounds. The reporter's contacts within the police department gave him an inside track to impending arrests and fast-breaking crime stories. As Ned Wall's comment at the head of this chapter suggests, however, these relationships in-

217

hibited serious criticism by the press of how the police department was run. Police beat reporters didn't even think about the police department as a local institution.

That attitude began to change, at least on major newspapers, beginning in the 1960s and continuing to the present. David Burnham's stories in the *New York Times* led to the Knapp Commission's investigation of corruption in the New York City Police Department in the 1960s[4] and the *Los Angeles Times* coverage of the Los Angeles Police and Sheriff's Department, extraordinary before the Rodney King case, was even more remarkable in its aftermath. Yet all of these external checks on police, however necessary and important, can be very much after the fact.

Effective press reportage on police practices and policies can be powerfully consequential in suggesting changes that need to be made in American policing. But American daily journalism cannot analyze the effectiveness and liabilities of proposed changes on a daily basis, nor is the press authorized to run or discipline the police from the inside. The question remains, who should and how?

The most widely touted suggestions for institutional changes in policing are civilian review of police and community-oriented police. Each is traceable to the troubles between police and minority communities in the 1960s, disharmonies which, as in several cases we have discussed, we all too often see repeated in the present.

## THE TRANQUIL PERIOD

The 1960s were a truly remarkable period, especially in light of the preceding decades. Those earlier years—say between 1920 and 1960—were tumultuous in their own way, encompassing the Great Depression, World War II, and the postwar boom of the 1950s. Nevertheless, so far as crime was concerned, the period during and after World War II seemed to be a time of unparalleled public safety. Social disorder was minimal. Police and crime were not the burning political issues they came to be in the 1960s and 1970s. Even in New York City—the symbol of modern urban danger—ordinary people walked the streets at night, rode the subways, and parked their cars with minimal fear of theft or mugging.

Within the police world, the main problems were corruption and interference in police affairs by shady politicians. Professional police were those who strove for higher educational standards, technological improvement, administrative regularity, rule enforcement to combat corruption, and strong central authority. Police reformers like O. W. Wilson, August Vollmer, and William Parker of Los Angeles were less concerned with community relations than with a managerial professionalism designed to combat the graft and corrupt politics of old-line police departments. The Los Angeles Police Department, with its "legalistic" policing style, served as a model for police across the nation.

Most police departments ran on the highly discretionary and erratic "watchman" style described by James Q. Wilson.[5] In those departments, police were primarily concerned with order maintenance rather than law enforcement. Many laws were "underenforced." Cops looked away from gambling, prostitution, and illegal parking, partly because such offenses were considered minor, and partly because some cops were on the take. Police ignored the offenses of community notables and reported the delinquencies of kids to parents rather than to the courts. So long as blacks remained in "their place," in the part of town assigned to them, they were mostly ignored.

Then, during the 1960s, everything changed for the nation, the cities, and the police. "It all began about 1963," James Q. Wilson observed. "That was the year, to overdramatize a bit, that a decade began to fall apart."[6] The impact of that decade on the standing of police in American cities can scarcely be overstated. A variety of investigative commissions reported deep hostility between police and residents of ghetto communities across the nation, from Los Angeles to Detroit to Newark. These antagonistic associations were cited as "a primary cause" of the race riots that sundered American cities. But the police were, of course, not the only cause. Animosity directed toward police was symbolic of deeper, more intractable problems: the historical role of African-Americans, including first slavery, and later segregation. The inadequacies of the criminal justice system, teeming lower courts, assembly line justice, sentencing disparity, and antiquated jails and prisons were often displaced into hostility against the police.

Nevertheless, certain police practices were singled out as being especially provocative. Chief among them was "aggressive preventive patrol," a tactic that —like the LAPD's "Operation Hammer"—encouraged police to move into high crime areas without prior notice and stop, search, and sometimes demean anyone who seemed suspect. Crime in those same areas was often disregarded. Activities that would not be tolerated in white areas—street violence, addiction, prostitution—would often be ignored by "watchmen" cops.

The Civil Disorder Commission also found, as another prominent contributor to hostility, the "almost total lack of effective channels for redress of complaints against police conduct." The commission heard that many police departments countenanced rudeness and insensitivity to minority communities, ignoring even complaints that prejudiced and brutal officers were being assigned to ghetto areas. Internal affairs investigations were of little or no help. They seemed designed to protect police from complaints rather than conduct searching and impartial inquiries.

In 1967 the President's Commission on Law Enforcement and Administration of Justice concluded that such conflicts do more than generate tensions. They encourage actions against the police, which result in a spiral of animosity, embittering police and triggering combative responses. Citizens in turn retaliate against the police, who, because they lack public support, become less effective.[7]

These sorts of criticism could not be ignored. The years during and following the urban riots of the 1960s wrought the most important changes in thinking, tactics, and resources ever seen in the history of the American police, shifts centered mainly on resolving police conflicts with minority communities. Everyone who thought about the issue of police–community conflict sought methods to reduce it.

## CIVILIAN REVIEW

One important idea was to introduce a disinterested umpire to oversee and resolve such conflicts by affording citizens a civilian complaint mechanism. Such a model had already been touted by administrative law scholars based on the Scandinavian "ombudsman," an impartial general inspector who evaluated complaints against services provided by various government officials. In light of the antagonisms between police and minority communities and also because of the apparent solidarity of police as a subculture, the "civilian review board"—a variant of the ombudsman concept—was expected to provide an antidote for police–community tensions by reducing inner-city mistrust of police investigations. Civilian review was considered a key to breaching the wall of protective silence police could count on from other cops.

Civilian review boards were initiated in several cities in the United States in the 1960s, but the most famous was unquestionably the New York City board. When John V. Lindsay, a liberal Republican, was elected Mayor in 1966, the then police commissioner, Vincent Broderick, openly opposed the idea of civilian review of police misconduct. In his stead, Lindsay appointed Howard R. Leary, who had been Police Chief in Philadelphia and had worked comfortably with a review board consisting solely of civilians. (The Philadelphia board was dismantled when Frank Rizzo became Mayor.) The New York Board was established by Mayor Lindsay on July 7, 1966, when the Mayor appointed a seven-member board headed by Algernon D. Black, a leader of the Ethical Culture Society and a board member of the American Civil Liberties Union. Three members were high-ranking police officials, and the four civilians were recommended by an eleven-member panel chaired by a former Republican Attorney General, Herbert Brownell, Jr. All three police representatives had law degrees, and one had been a special agent of the FBI for twenty-five years. Minority group members included two blacks, one of them a Deputy Commissioner of Police. One member was a Puerto Rican. By putting three police representatives on the New York board, Lindsay and his advisers had hoped to deflect rank-and-file police opposition.

The strategy did not work. The prospect of review by a civilian board headed by a leading ACLU liberal, who was joined by minority group members, frightened and even outraged working cops.[8] They were convinced that a review by such a board would be stacked against them by civilians who neither comprehended nor appreciated what street policing was all about (and who, they suspected, were viscerally anticop). The Patrolmen's Benevolent Association (PBA: the rank-and-file union) quickly organized to place a referendum on the November ballot to abolish the board.

The PBA rallied its considerable resources to conduct one of the hardest-fought and bitterest political campaigns in the history of New York City. Family and friends were rallied to the cause. Police actually campaigned hard while on duty, and some of their patrol cars and wagons bore anti-review board signs. Supporters of the board claimed that at the height of the campaign, cops flagrantly ticketed cars showing pro-board bumper stickers, while those showing anti-board stickers remained virtually ticketproof.

The PBA, as well as private sources, heavily financed the campaign, which featured billboards, posters, and advertisements throughout the city. One poster showed damaged stores and a rubble-strewn street and read: "This is the aftermath of a riot in a city that *had* a civilian review board." Another poster contained a statement by J. Edgar Hoover that civilian review boards "virtually paralyzed" the police. The most widely posted, most effective, and most alarming placard showed a young girl fearfully leaving a subway exit onto a darkened street. Its text: "The Civilian Review Board must be stopped! Her life, your life, may depend on it."

Supposedly liberal New York voters turned conservative, supported the police, and overwhelmingly rejected the board by a landslide margin of 1,307,738 to 768,485. The review board was sustained in only one borough, Manhattan, with a population composed largely of liberal whites and nonwhites. Voters in Brooklyn and Queens supported the PBA by more than two to one, and in Richmond (Staten Island) the voters turned thumbs down by a margin of more than five to one.[9] A New York conservative, it was said after the vote, was a liberal who had been mugged.

Similar battles against civilian review were waged across the nation. Articles and speeches by prominent police spokesmen often invoked an anticommunist theme in challenging the board. A National Fraternal Order of Police publication offered a typical denunciation:

> No matter what names are used by the sponsors of the so-called "Police Review Boards" they exude the obnoxious odor of communism. This scheme is a page right out of the Communist handbook which says in part, "... police are the enemies of communism, if we are to succeed we must do anything to weaken their work, to incapacitate them or make them a subject of ridicule."

Such campaigns, coupled with a successful "law and order" campaign in the 1968 election by Richard Nixon, which was at least partly inspired by New York City's rejection of civilian review, seriously undercut the movement toward civilian oversight of police. Civilian review became a dead issue nationally for a number of years.

Gradually, however, as blacks, Latinos, and women became more populous in American cities—that is, as other cities began to look more like the inner-city Manhattan population that supported the New York City Board than the whiter working class and suburban Queens and Staten Island populations that opposed it—local government officials were elected who were more responsive to civilian review. In such a shifting urban political context, civilian oversight became more acceptable, even demanded, by the city electorate of the 1980s and 1990s. By 1990, of America's fifty largest cities, thirty had adopted some form of civilian review of citizen's complaints.[10] Of the thirty civilian review mechanisms, twenty-three were established by local ordinance rather than by executive order, either by the city council or, as in San Francisco, by referendum. By the 1990s, then, such a broad base of political support suggested that some form of civilian review was increasingly expected by urban voters throughout the country.[11] Even in politically conservative San Diego, a Republican stronghold, the voters amended the County Charter to provide for the establishment in 1992 of a Citizen's Law Enforcement Review Board to oversee the Sheriff's Department. This board was unique in that it was the first to monitor complaints against a sheriff's department.

Despite the apparent greater acceptance of civilian review among the public, the whole subject provokes an ugly reaction among some police, and apparently stands for them as a visceral symbol of the shifting balance of urban political power. Twenty years after the great review board battle in New York City, Mayor Ed Koch created within the NYPD a twelve-member review board composed of six police officials and six civilians. In essence, Koch's board differed from the one Lindsay had attempted to establish only in that it had an equal number of police and civilians, rather than a civilian majority; it went into operation quietly and without police opposition. During the summer of 1992, however, Koch's successor, David Dinkins, New York's first black mayor, proposed granting the board full independence from the police department and staffing it exclusively with thirteen civilian mayoral appointees. The reactions included a demonstration by 10,000 off-duty police officers, many of whom engaged in rowdy and threatening behavior, blocking the Brooklyn Bridge, roughing up reporters and cameramen, and demeaning the mayor and passers-by in the ugliest racist terms. Ironically, the early public reactions tallied in the unscientific man-in-the-street polls of radio and television news shows suggest that the vile police conduct at this demonstration has convinced even the formerly most staunch supporters of the police that Dinkins is correct in his argument that the police should not be permitted to review their own conduct.[12]

## The Forms of Civilian Oversight

Assuming that civilian oversight is becoming increasingly acceptable, a question often asked is: What form should it take? So much variation prevails across the United States that it is difficult to say precisely what organizational and power limits the concept of civilian review implies. All civilian oversight agencies have similar reasons for existence—mistrust of internal police investigation of complaints—but with different structures, procedures, and political histories. Scholars who have studied civilian review have identified at least three models depending on (a) who does the initial investigation and fact-finding, cops or civilian investigators; (b) who reviews the report—it could be a hearing officer, or a board, or a police official; (c) the right of the complainant to appeal; and (d) who imposes discipline on the offending officer.

Wayne Kerstetter, for example, identifies *civilian review,* where an agency outside the police department accepts complaints, investigates and judges them, and then recommends discipline to the chief. This is the Berkeley, California, model, where dual investigations are conducted by internal affairs and internal investigators. Another, used in Chicago, Kerstetter calls the *civilian input* prototype. Here, civilians who are part of the police department undertake the investigation of excessive force complaints, while police investigate other complaints. Discipline, as in Berkeley, is imposed by the chief. Kerstetter favors the *civilian monitor* approach, based on the Scandinavian ombudsman concept, where an outside agency is available to investigate and mediate complaints from those who think that police investigation and outcome were unfair or inadequate.[13] Other cities have different spins on these models. New York City, for example, has a system where a civilian, appointed as a Deputy Police Commissioner, oversees a board composed of police and civilians. The investigations are undertaken by police and by civilian investigators, who report to the Deputy Commissioner, an attorney who told Skolnick that she considers herself a civilian. At the same time, she is on the payroll of the NYPD as a Deputy Police Commissioner. She may, in fact, have the worst of both worlds of identity. To the public, to civilians, since she holds the Deputy Police Commissioner title, she is seen as a cop. To the rank-and-file cops, since she has never been a street patrol officer, she is seen as a civilian. In the "Introduction" to the 1990 Annual Report of the Civilian Complaint Investigative Bureau, Commissioner Sandra Marsh recognized that some members of the public mistrust investigations of police by other police and promised to "continue to expand our investigative staff to the level of 50% civilian."

Whatever the system, when citizens ask for review of police conduct by civilians, they do so because they don't trust the police to investigate themselves. The demand for civilian review thus implies a failure of police administration that, contrary to what one of us wrote a few years ago, probably cannot be put right simply by employing more responsive administrators.[14] If civilians were satisfied with police investigation of complaints, there would be no reason for civilian oversight. Once civilians have become dissatisfied with police investigations, anything less than civilian review is unlikely to change their perception that, instead of objectively reviewing complaints, the police are taking care of their own. Like the institution of the jury, which arose not because judges were incompetent to hear and evaluate evidence and reach verdicts, but because judges were mistrusted, so too with civilian review of police misconduct. Cops are not trusted to investigate and reach decisions about the alleged misconduct of other cops, even when they are perfectly capable of doing so, and even when they make the right decision. Mistrust of authorities has less to do with their *competence* than with their values, inclinations, and prior commitments, and with how these are perceived by those outside their organizations.

## Arguments Pro and Con

Civilian oversight advocates make that argument and increasingly are making it stick. They argue that police officials cannot possibly be impartial when reviewing their own subordinates. Police officials, it is said, are characteristically drawn from the rank and file and cannot fairly investigate their own. Students of police have often noted a coherence to the culture of police into which higher officials were socialized (see Chapter 5).

Furthermore, police officer misconduct reflects badly on the police department and its training and oversight functions. Higher police officials depend upon rank-and-file officers for the department's performance. So, it is alleged, police executives must show solidarity when a police officer's conduct is being challenged. But even when police investigations are fair and impartial, the process is so essentially flawed by these conflicts of interest, it is said, that the outcome is not credible. That every profession resists investigation and dispute-resolution by independent auditors is scarcely a reason, say civilian review advocates, for dismissing outside oversight. Doctors and lawyers also investigate themselves, but when they do, they aren't trusted by complainants either.

Advocates of civilian oversight understand that it involves the participation and authority of nonprofessionals and their agents. They like that feature. Members of civilian review boards are often selected because they represent a racial or ethnic group or gender. As with the selection of jurors, civilian oversight of police thus is grounded in a democratic theory of *representation* and *participation*. But, as with jurors, attempts to build representation into public decision-making are no guarantee that participants will decide cases on the merits rather than in blind solidarity with other members of their group.

Despite this potential flaw, citizen representation, particularly diversity of representation, is said to accomplish two outcomes. First, citizens can help shape police policies. One illustration: The use of police dogs, however effective, may be offensive as a method of crowd control or of apprehending suspects. CBS News, for example, showed a videotape on December 10, 1991, of an LAPD-trained police dog gnawing on the leg of a "suspect" who was screaming with pain—but was never charged with a crime. The videotape had been recorded by the LAPD itself as part of a recruitment video. CBS News had obtained a copy of the video after it had learned that during the previous three years nine hundred suspects, nearly one a day, had been bitten by an LA police dog. About half the suspects who had been apprehended by police dogs had been bitten by them. The videotape also shows a police report with the notation "lunchtime" after the description of the arrest. An LA officer who trains the dog is seen telling an interviewer that the bite is the dog's "reward" for capturing the suspect. A city attorney backs the policy of using dogs.

On the same videotape, however, former Newark Police Chief and Police Foundation President Hubert Williams is clearly astonished by what he sees. "This is incredible and unbelievable," he says. "I've never heard of this before." Obviously, the use of dogs to apprehend and then bite suspects is a policy that, if changed, would reduce complaints and lawsuits against the police. Dogs can be helpful in policing—for example, in searching out suspected burglars in warehouses—but police should employ dogs to apprehend suspects the way porcupines are said to copulate: very carefully.

Second, when citizens participate in the adjudicatory process, they are, it is said, able to incorporate the citizen perspective on the event in question. But cops are as likely to say they mistrust the civilian perspective. They view civilian review boards as kangaroo courts filled with ethnic biases, hidden agendas, and lay people who neither understand nor appreciate the nuances and pressures of policing. Police argue that a dispute between a citizen and a police officer that results in a complaint against the officer needs to be fairly judged, but civilians who represent the communities being policed do not and cannot be unbiased. That's because they cannot fulfill their representational responsibilities and still remain impartial.

Police acknowledge that codes of silence prevail in police departments but say that civilian review only reinforces those tendencies by erecting a wall of silence around civilian investigators. By contrast, they argue, while cops may not appreciate internal affairs investigators they don't question their legitimacy. The code of silence, they maintain, is not as powerful when police are investigating the misconduct of other police.

But, of course, civilians see the other side of that coin, namely, that cops trust other cops because they are unduly sympathetic to police and are likely to cover up police misconduct.

Police rebut that argument. However competent civilian *investigations* of police misconduct might be, civilian hearing officers, because they are selected on a principle of representation, lack the specialized *competence* to understand and evaluate the performance of the officer whose conduct is being investigated.

Furthermore, police opponents of civilian review argue that investigators who are responsible to civilian boards are themselves influenced by a bureaucratic imperative to find against the officer. Unless the civilian investigation can produce results different from what might be found by an internal agency or investigation, the outside investigator's work will not be appreciated.

Moreover, even if civilians are acknowledged sometimes to be helpful in shaping policy, that competence does not necessarily carry over to their capacity to function as adjudicators where police are in the role of the accused. This tension between *policy*, i.e., the legislative function of civilians, and their capacity to *adjudicate* disputes does much, cops say, to undermine the credibility of civilian review.

### Is Civilian Review a Good Idea?

John Keker, a noted San Francisco attorney who prosecuted Oliver North and was appointed to head the Police Commission during the tenure (1987–91) of the liberal Mayor Art Agnos, offers four basic reasons for opposing civilian review: (1) he is unconvinced that civilian investigators do a better job than police; (2) civilian review, he says, inevitably generates police antagonism; (3) police misconduct is the responsibility of the chief of police, and that is the only person, he argues, who can affect it; and (4) however convinced citizens are that civilian investigation and review is effective, it is not. On the contrary, Keker maintains that its purported success is "illusory and ephemeral."[15] Clearly, civilian review is neither simple nor inevitably a magical success for those who are experienced with it, regardless of how it is organized and carried out. Unfortunately, no comprehensive evaluation of civilian review has been completed. Although anticrime and antidrug efforts have been generously funded by the National Institute of Justice and other foundations interested in crime control and criminal justice, comparable funding has not been made available for studying civilian review. Nevertheless, a strong case can be made for civilian review based primarily on the notion that police cannot be impartial when investigating other police, and even when they are, they are unlikely to be credible.

Democratic institutions, such as the jury or civilian review, are instituted not because they are more efficient or able, but because they are trusted. Assuming, for that reason, civilian review to be valuable, the first question is: Which model should be adopted? A fully functioning civilian review agency needs to investigate complaints, conduct hearings, subpoena witnesses, and report its findings to the police chief and to the public. In this, the most comprehensive model, the review agency serves as an alternative to internal affairs, reporting to the police chief, who is empowered to discipline police, a task and prerogative that has to be left in the authority of the police chief. The alternative of parallel investigation by a civilian investigator and internal affairs seems needless and costly. If they agree, why have bothered? If they disagree, which should be believed?

Second, inadequate financing will devastate any system, and budgets for civilian review mechanisms rarely have kept pace with workloads. When a city introduces a civilian review agency, the number of complaints about improper police conduct is sure to rise. After all, one purpose of civilian review is to assist and encourage excessive force victims to bring their complaints forward. Just as rape complaints will mount when police establish a sexual assault unit, so should excessive force complaints climb with the establishment of a civilian review agency. An aggrieved citizen is more likely to bring his or her complaint to a civilian agency, located away from police headquarters, than to a blue-uniformed officer behind a desk at police headquarters. Thus, civilian agencies are likely to generate a higher workload than the internal affairs division of the same department and may require higher funding.

Perhaps a larger percentage of the complaints will be unjustifiable, even bizarre, precisely because a civilian review agency seems more accessible to a wider public. But a civilian agency will also generate legitimate complaints from apprehensive complainants who might otherwise have been reluctant to complain to a police officer in the department's internal affairs unit.

Third, civilian review agencies need to be staffed by competent, well-trained investigators who have the authority and the financial backing to carry out their investigations. This doesn't mean that civilian review will necessarily be more expensive than internal affairs. On the contrary, even civil service investigators are likely to be cheaper than sworn police officers. Police unions will resist civilian review for this reason alone. Civilian review does contemplate substituting civilian investigators for police, reducing the need for police investigators. Of course, the police unions will resist. No union appreciates a reduction in membership.

Fourth, it simply is not possible to have fair and effective civilian review when the hearing officers or panels are biased or less than competent. This raises a difficult issue: To what extent should hearing officers resemble jurors—in which case representativeness of the population becomes an important goal—or judges, in which case competence is a prime consideration? In this setting, diversity has to defer to expertise.

In a trial, there is both judge and jury. The jury doesn't decide without judicial guidance as to the admission of evidence, the relevancy of argument, and the scope of cross-examination. Cops won't ever like civilian review, but they—and the public—are likely to find it more acceptable when investigations and hearings are conducted not by "representative" persons but by hardnosed, experienced investigators and fair and qualified hearing officers.

Fifth, cops will resist the potential discipline of civilian review by ignoring requests for records, by being late for appointments for interviews, by withholding documents, in sum, by doing whatever can be done to disrupt the system. If a civilian review agency is to work effectively, without unreasonable delay, the oversight system must be afforded access to police witnesses and documents through legal mandate or subpoena power. Much depends on the chief and the mayor or city manager. If the latter support civilian review and enforce the demands of the agency, civilian review can be effective. If not, then civilian review will be undercut by passive police resistance.

Finally, to be successful, civilian review needs a degree of openness. This doesn't mean that the personnel files of accused officers should be opened to the public. Nor does it mean that truly personal information such as their home address, telephone number, marital history, credit rating, and so forth, should be made public. But an accuser and the accused are both entitled to know the outcome of the hearing and the reasons for the result.

For the falsely accused officer, such public disclosure should help restore public confidence in the process and in the integrity of the individual officer. Like the public trial, public disclosure serves as a general and specific deterrent. The guilty officer is less likely to do the same thing again, and fellow officers will understand that the disapproved conduct is not tolerated.

No matter how effective civilian review, most of the time cops will be exonerated, and probably should be. Most complaints against police are not sustainable. The civilian review system in San Francisco nailed cops only 8 percent of the time in 1990, which means that accusers were upheld only one time out of twelve.

## Unrealistic Expectations

Many of those who argue for the establishment of civilian complaint review boards have extremely unrealistic expectations of what they can accomplish. Only rarely will such boards settle whatever police–community problems may exist. The main reason that civilian complaint review boards are not likely to do so is that, regardless of the intensity of investigation, most citizens' allegations cannot be definitively resolved one way or the other. In most cases three bits of information are available to those who must review citizens' complaints against police. The first is the citizen's allegation that he or she was "done wrong" by an officer. The second is the officer's denial of the charge. The third is the investigator's conclusion that little or no objective evidence exists to support or refute the citizen's charge. Mr. Smith, for example, displays a bump on his head and claims that Officer Jones hit him unnecessarily, and then arrested him to cover up his misdeed. Officer Jones says he used only that degree of force necessary to restrain Smith, who had taken a swing at the officer when told he was going to receive a speeding ticket. The bump on Smith's head, Jones says, occurred when he fell during their struggle. Smith's wife gives a version of the event that parallels that of her husband; Jones's partner corroborates the Jones version. How can any objective body accept either of those stories without calling the other party a liar?

Consequently, unless the former review mechanism has habitually engaged in blatant whitewashes, it is unlikely that the establishment of external review proceedings will significantly change the pattern of dispositions of citizen complaint investigations: most are destined to be found unsubstantiated, which is certain to come as a disappointment to people who anticipate that the board will "crack down" on brutal or discourteous police. Most complaints do not involve brutality. Most do not issue from a complainant like Rodney King, whose bones have been broken. Nor is there usually a videotape to back up the complaint.

In the absence of that kind of evidence, is civilian review nevertheless justified? Is a better long-term solution to the suspicion that police are not adequately policing themselves to replace the chief with someone more willing to perform all the chief's duties, including the "dirty work" of investigating and properly disposing of citizens complaints? Possibly. On balance, however, we support civilian review primarily because of its *credibility*. In the absence of civilian review, will the exoneration of an officer accused of excessive force be believable? In the long run, only an independent investigative body can allay public suspicions of the police and render a convincing exoneration of police who have been accused of misconduct.

Like the institution of the jury, civilian review cannot be justified on purely rational grounds of administrative efficiency. Nor can civilian review substitute for informed and sensitive police administration and training to influence police activities. When investigating their own, police can do the job, and perhaps more efficiently than civilians. But when they exonerate their own, they are not trusted. The police need, indeed deserve, credibility. Instead of opposing civilian review, police would be better advised to insist that it be as fair as possible. Moreover, although there is no substitute for a first-rate, progressive police administrator, there is also no inconsistency between civilian review and accomplished police administration. The best police chiefs, even if not enthusiastic about civilian review, will not be antagonistic to it; they will support it so long as civilian review demonstrates that it can be impartial and effective.

## Complaints as Management Information

No matter who ultimately reviews them, civilians' complaints against officers should be treated as a valuable source of management information. Indeed, because officers typically work out of the sight of their supervisors, complaints are one of the few forms of feedback on officers' work—both individually and generally—available to police administrators. Hence, complaints should be encouraged and should be taken by any medium. It takes a considerable amount of courage to walk into a strange police station to complain about officers who work there, so police should be required to accept complaints even if those who wish to lodge them choose to communicate by phone or letter, even anonymously. Like those who inform on criminals, those who inform on outlaw police officers sometimes have good reasons for wishing to conceal their identities. Their wishes should be respected.

Similarly, no member of any police agency should have the authority to quash or "informally handle" complaints because, for example, he or she believes that the complainant has spelled out no clear misconduct. One reason that some police chief executives have authorized such discretion, we are convinced, is that they are more concerned with creating an impressive "bottom line" than with finding police misconduct. To many observers, the bottom line of the civilian complaint process is the percentage of complaints found unsubstantiated; the smaller this percentage, the better the job investigators and reviewers are thought to be doing.

Our own studies of police complaint procedures show clearly that this bottom line is more often an illusion than a solid conclusion. In fact, the percentage of complaints found unsubstantiated by different police departments usually has more to do with the procedures for *receipt* of complaints than with investigative intensity or objectivity. Departments that authorize field supervisors or other complaint recipients to screen out "unworthy" allegations have very low percentages of unsubstantiated complaints because only the most convincing, well-documented, undeniable, and outrageous charges are treated formally. These departments may look good on paper, but they leave the door open to the sort of stonewalling and manipulation experienced by Rodney King's brother and cameraman George Holliday when they tried to complain about the King incident. Conversely, departments that *properly* insist that field supervisors accept all complaints regardless of their apparent lack of merit reduce the risk of such short-circuiting. In doing so, however, they mandate acceptance of obviously frivolous or unprovable complaints. As a result, a relatively high percentage of complaints against their officers are found unsubstantiated. Thus, the percentage of unsubstantiated complaints against a department's officers means little without information about policies for acceptance of complaints.

Courteous receipt and proper processing of complaints should be *absolutely* required of any police official or officer who learns that a civilian wishes to complain about officers. In the absence of such a requirement—and even occasional "sting"-style testing to see that it is honored—abuses inevitably follow. When the question of whether to accept a complaint is left to the discretion of supervisors and officers, they come under enormous pressure to get rid of would-be complainants without formally recording their grievances. This pressure, especially strong when officers or supervisors work on a day-to-day basis with the cops about whom civilians wish to complain, was evident in the aftermath of the King incident. As we discussed in Chapter 1, George Holliday, who videotaped the King beating, called the LAPD Foothill Station to bring it to official attention but was turned away; so was King's brother, Paul, who was told "he should try to find the video, and that the video could be of help."[16] In some agencies, conduct such as this is a firing offense, as it should be.

The police objection to a policy of requiring supervisors or other police representatives to honor all complaints is that the majority of civilian complaints either are without merit or cannot be sustained. Certainly both statements are true: The majority of complaints come down to unresolvable swearing contests between civilians and cops. Even if they cannot be individually sustained, however, civilians' complaints may document apparent patterns of conduct that should signal administrators that further investigation of officers' behavior may be warranted. Consider, for example, what a reasonable police commander might make of this Christopher Commission finding:

> Of approximately 1,800 officers against whom an allegation of excessive force or improper tactics was made from 1986 through 1990, over 1,400 officers had only one or two allegations. But 183 officers had four or more allegations, 44 had six or more, 16 had eight or more, and one had 16 allegations. The top 10% of officers ranked by number of excessive force or improper tactics allegations accounted for 27.5% of all such allegations.[17]

Although the numbers may differ somewhat, findings of this type are common to most large police agencies. In almost every large department, a small number of police officers account for a disproportionate amount of the work of internal affairs and civilian complaint investigators. While it would violate fundamental tenets of due process to punish officers who accumulate large numbers of complaints that cannot be proven, it would be derelict to write off each chit in such an officer's personnel file as though it had no relation to all the rest. Good administrators pay careful heed to such apparent patterns, attempt to determine whether they are a form of smoke that indicates fire, and, if so, do something about them. Often such officers simply are tactless and need nothing more than some counseling or retraining. In other cases, more extreme measures—transfers to nonstreet assignments or psychological treatment—may be indicated and should be provided. In the absence of such intervention, some such officers come to regard their records of unsustained complaints as an indication that they have outsmarted the system and as a license to abuse. During their relatively short careers, for example, the Metro-Dade officers who beat Arthur McDuffie to death had accumulated well over a hundred unsustained complaints from civilians.

In addition, civilian complaints serve as a check on obnoxious police policies as well as upon offensive officers. In the course of reviewing LAPD civilian complaints in connection with a civil rights suit alleging wrongful application of a police choke hold,[18] for example, Fyfe found that more than a quarter—more than a hundred annually—made virtually the same type of complaint. Almost invariably, the summaries provided to LAPD's Board of Police Commissioners said, in effect:

> Complainant alleges Officer _____ choked him unconscious for no reason during a traffic stop. Officer states complainant became unruly and officer applied departmentally approved carotid control hold to subdue him. Exonerated.

The LAPD did not treat these complaints as a hint that there was some justification to citizens' view that it was unreasonable to be "choked out" by officers in circumstances that presented no danger to police or anybody else. Instead, the department wrote these complaints off and left its choke hold policy in place until Adolph Lyons's case was wending its way toward the U.S. Supreme Court.

This apparent parochial view leads to another suggestion concerning investigations of complaints and use of force. In many police departments, these tasks are the exclusive and closely guarded work of small special units rather than a part of the general supervisory function. In such circumstances, those who work closest to officers—their field supervisors and commanders—tend to wash their hands of any responsibility at all for seeing to it that officers behave appropriately. At the same time, those who are charged with internal investigations assume far more importance than is appropriate. This has been the case in the LAPD, for example, where the Robbery–Homicide Division has for many years maintained a small "Officer Involved Shooting" Team (OIS) that has had a monopoly on information related to shootings and that, because of its presumed expertise, apparently has been subject to little critical review by anybody in the department. Everybody in the official chain of the LAPD, for example, accepted the OIS accounts of the Crumpton–Berry and McDonald's shootings, although neither bears much relationship to the objective physical evidence.

A better system would open up the process of investigating and adjudicating complaints about use of force so that it involved supervisors and commanders. Equally important, it would hold supervisors and commanders accountable for assessing their officers' conduct by requiring that they conduct and assign investigations into use of force complaints, complete with detailed "findings and recommendations" about whether officers' behavior was appropriate, and how such incidents fitted into the context of officers' career histories. Where this does not occur—where supervisors can "leave IAD (or OIS) to figure out what happened"—those closest to the line are given opportunities to plead ignorance about their officers' most sensitive and controversial activities. Where this does occur—and where supervisors are made to know that the objectivity and completeness of their investigations may shape their careers—local supervisors and commanders have a great stake in keeping their officers out of trouble, in carefully monitoring those who accumulate inordinate numbers of citizens' complaints, and in reporting objectively when officers do get into trouble.

This is not to suggest that such investigations should be exclusively assigned to field supervisors and commanders. When this occurs, their agendas and the pressures to which they are subject are likely to take precedence over their objectivity. Instead, it is a suggestion that investigations of sensitive police actions—shootings, complaints against officers' use of force, injuries to prisoners—should involve as many people as possible in both headquarters and the field. The redundancies and checks built into such a system are the best way to ensure integrity, objectivity, and fairness.

The NYPD's "Firearms Discharge Review" process is illustrative. Any time a New York cop discharges his or her weapon, the patrol captain on duty in the area is assigned to conduct an immediate investigation and to apprise headquarters of its progress. Within twenty-four hours, this captain must also report in writing his or her preliminary findings and recommendations as to whether the shooting was in accord with department policy and training. At the same time, the commander of the precinct in which the shooting occurred must begin and conduct an independent and more thorough investigation, also including findings and recommendations, to be completed within seventy-two hours. These reports are reviewed by the commander of the borough involved and, separately, by the office of the Chief of Department, whose staff is careful to demand that all missing information or apparent inconsistencies be resolved by the precinct commander.

After these investigations have been completed, the commander of the borough in which the shooting occurred convenes a "firearms discharge review board" comprising several of his staff and an officer of the same rank as the shooter. Independently, these officials review the file that has been assembled and comment upon it in writing before the board convenes. When the board meets, it reaches a collective adjudication of the shooting and forwards a report (sometimes with dissents) to the Chief of the Department.

The Chief's staff assembles all the investigative and review information along with the personnel file of the officer involved and forwards the whole to each member of the department's Firearms Discharge Review Board, which includes the department's chief firearms and tactics trainer and about eight of the department's top officials. Independently, each member of this panel assesses the officer's actions, as well as the competence and objectivity of the investigators and board beneath them. Finally, the board comes together as a whole and the entire matter—including investigative integrity—is adjudicated.[19]

If this seems to be an extremely complex procedure, it is. Yet shootings are infrequent—and volatile—enough to warrant it, and the results seem worth the effort. So many people are independently involved in the system that cover-ups are virtually impossible. So many upwardly mobile officials know that lack of objectivity or thoroughness has effectively ended promising careers that few investigations leave any obvious question unresolved. Appeals by officers from the process are extremely rare. In fact, a veteran New York City Assistant Corporation Counsel told us, the reviews have proved "virtually unassailable" in court proceedings. Indeed, in nearly fifteen years of defending the NYPD against civil litigation, this attorney knew of only one case in which the city had lost a *Monell* case for inadequately supervising officers' use of firearms.[20] It involved an off-duty officer who shot his wife and himself.[21]

Most important, in the two decades since this system was put in place by Patrick V. Murphy, the rate at which New York cops killed people has been among the very lowest among big American cities.[22] They have also enjoyed one of the lowest mortality rates among police in any U.S. city.[23]

## CONCLUSIONS

Lest all of this sound too negative, we should also point out that a system of accountability is part of an organization's reward system. In addition to punishing supervisors whose cops go wrong, proper mechanisms for accountability require that supervisors and commanders be rewarded when their officers do well and—most important—that outstanding street cops also be nurtured and rewarded for their work.

In police agencies such as Philadelphia's, where stringent civil service rules and a militant union have limited the chief's ability to reward the stars on his staff, the opportunities for cultivating excellence and reducing police violence in this way have been virtually nonexistent. In other agencies, even in one as large as Washington, D.C.'s, the absence of even a rudimentary personnel evaluation system denies cops at all levels *any* formal answer to the question "How am I doing?"

Cops need to know how well they are doing and to be rewarded for doing well. When they are not told how they are doing, they get the idea that nobody cares, that nobody is watching. When this happens, they become understandably cynical and sometimes even brutal. Before cops can be told whether they are doing well, however, we need to define *good police work* clearly. We have not yet done so. In our next chapter, we offer some suggestions about the process of defining good police work for making sure that we get more of it, and for assuring that those who do it receive credit for a tough job done well.

# 11

## Renewing the Police

The problems of policing are not simply problems of finding "efficient" and "effective" means; they are problems of ends, of competing social values, interests and priorities, the resolution of which raise fundamental moral and political issues to be decided by an informed citizenry, not only scientific or technical issues to be decided by experts and technocrats.

—Ruben G. Rumbaut and Egon Bittner,
"Changing Conceptions of the Police Role"

A good cop is somewhere between a hot dog and a burnout case.

—Oakland Police captain, 1991

The police role is highly complex, even more than those of traditional professionals. The classic professions—medicine, law, and the ministry—offer services to those who seek out advice and assistance, who are sick, aggrieved, or troubled. Although the technical aspects of their work may require great sophistication, these professionals fill roles that are straightforward and clear: They are expected to cure or to advise their clients.

It is far more difficult to find unambiguous terms that adequately define the role of the police. James Q. Wilson once contrasted the police officer with the doctor or lawyer in two important respects: First, the police are not expected to cure or advise, but to restrain; second, while health and counsel are welcomed, restraint is not.[1] But the analogy is only partly valid, because it suggests that the only clients of the police are those in need of restraint. Police also are sought out by victims or potential victims of crime to bring to justice those who have injured them or to protect them from those who might cause them harm. Modern police, especially those who

237

are community-oriented or problem-oriented, recognize that the law-abiding citizen, the victim or potential victim, is as much their client as the person whose conduct needs to be restrained. The client may be a target of domestic assault, a small business owner who has been robbed, or a householder who has been burglarized. Just as sick people call doctors for help or ministration, crime victims call cops for advice and assistance. Other citizens, however, the assaulters, the robbers, the burglars, the drug dealers, try to hide their activities from the police. They do not call the cops, Neither do lesser offenders, such as disorderly people and traffic violators. Understanding the involuntary nature of the relationship between *perpetrators* and police is critical to any discussion involving the excessive use of force. With respect to the perpetrators of crime or even of disorder, police may be required to use force or to threaten to use force.

Those whose freedom the police are threatening may well resist, and in such circumstances the police are professionally obliged to employ force. When we say that the police are only doing their *duty,* we mean that, as an aspect of their job and of their authority, police are sometimes morally obliged to employ force. There would be no need for police to use such force, of course, if those whom they sought to arrest or place in custody did not resist or threaten to resist. But then, in such a hypothetically ideal world, there would be no need for cops. At the same time, police are obliged to use only legitimated force, that is, force authorized by statute and court decisions. In this sense, the entire citizenry of a democratic society is the client of the cop.

## POLICING, SOCIAL CHANGE, DIVERSITY, AND DISPARITY

In places where virtually everybody voluntarily acts in ways that do not require police attention, police violence rarely is a concern. In such places, people refrain from crime or disorder for reasons that have nothing to do with the police. They do so because they share a sense of community, a common understanding of the precise location of the boundary between acceptable and unacceptable behavior.

In such communities, police brutality is low on the list of social concerns, if it is there at all. As Wilson and others have suggested, one important police task is to maintain order. Where community is so strong and cohesive that order would exist independently of the police, the local constabulary generally finds that its main frictions with the community involve adolescents who, not yet fully domesticated, sow their wild oats with weekend adventures in bars and on the highways. Aside from the occasional moments of excitement provided by confrontations with these young miscreants, police work in such places is a relatively unchallenging endeavor.

The big challenges in policing are in places where the existing order is not clearly defined, is undergoing great flux, or favors some groups at the apparent expense of others. It is no accident that places and times marked by great—and at least somewhat disorderly—social change have also been characterized by vigilantism, lynching, and police overreaction. The list of such brutalities is extensive: the vigilantes of the nineteenth-century American West; the rioters of Civil War–era New York, as well as the police who stood by and watched them; the lynchings of the post–Civil War South; the police shootings and beatings of union activists in mining country after the turn of the century; the Depression-era brutality against Michigan auto workers and Dust Bowl migrants to the Far West; the police depredations against civil rights demonstrators during the early 1960s; the sometimes violent police suppression of urban riots and antiwar demonstrations during the late 1960s; the beating death of Arthur McDuffie; the Rodney King incident; and a series of Los Angeles police excesses, all of which occurred in American cities where the old order was rapidly changing.

Where wide disparities in culture, social class, geography, and affluence separate people at the top from those at the bottom, the disadvantaged are virturally certain to view the police as oppressive representatives of the group that is keeping them down. Thus—especially when race is a ready marker for differences of advantage—it is extremely difficult for police who work in inner-city slums to overcome the distrust and resentment of the very people who most need good police service. Where police departments make no effort to overcome those barriers or, worse, where they fail even to acknowledge that they exist, and cling instead to some simplistic version of "*color-blind* professionalism," latent resentments become open antagonism. It is hypocritical for police who work in cities where social class and race make so much difference in everybody's life to claim that they can perform their work uninfluenced by such considerations.

The fact is that urban police departments are bound by conditions beyond their control to an uneasy relationship with the people at the bottom of our society. The police may reduce some of the chafing between ghetto dwellers and themselves, but they cannot eliminate it. It is a reality of our social structure, and nobody should be surprised when it occasionally comes into public view in the form of allegations of police misconduct. Even where specific accusations are baseless and where police generally do the very best they can to bridge the chasm between the ghetto and themselves, people socialized to see the police as an occupying army are quick to accuse.

Thus, the public must understand that the police are not necessarily to blame for the *existence* of the uneasy relationship between the police and the residents of the ghetto. No matter how well the police do their job in the ghetto, many people there will view them with animosity. A generation ago, James Baldwin saw and wrote about the problem with extraordinary clarity and bitterness:

> The only way to police a ghetto is to be oppressive. None of the Police Commissioner's men, even with the best will in the world, have any way of understanding the lives led by the people they swagger about in two and threes controlling. Their very presence is an insult, and it would be, even if they spent their entire day feeding gumdrops to children. . . . He moves through Harlem, therefore, like an occupying soldier in a bitterly hostile country; which is precisely what, and where he is, and is the reason he walks in twos and threes.[2]

Further, whether this tension is manifested merely in a day-to-day routine of remoteness and hard stares directed at passing patrol cars or in spectacular but false allegations—and regardless of how tempting it is to react otherwise—police officers or officials should not be offended by it. They must be trained to know that it is nothing personal. Instead, it is simply *there,* a characteristic of the landscape of this society, larger and no more likely to disappear than the disaffections built into the relationships between tax auditors and small businessmen, internal investigators and street cops in rulebound police departments, legislative oversight committees and executive agencies.

This is not to say that police should be absolved of any responsibility for trying to reduce this antipathy. All organizations are responsible for selecting the people best suited for the work to be performed, for preparing them thoroughly for the ugliest parts of their work, and for structuring their work so that its ugliness is minimized. This responsibility is not met where police departments that serve and intervene in the lives of diverse populations remain by composition—or by *mindset*—overwhelmingly white, male, lower-middle-class institutions. No institution licensed to coerce and restrain every member of a large and pluralistic population can afford to be dominated by the philosophies and world view of any single group. When and where police brutality has been a significant issue in recent years, it generally has involved departments—like those in Philadelphia, Milwaukee, and Los Angeles—led by strong, charismatic officials who have adhered to and espoused a style of policing informed, influenced, and reinforced by the kind of blue-collar macho one hears in cops' bars late at night.

Our observation should not be read as an affront to blue-collar white males. Every identifiable social group holds some values and views that are out of step with—or even in conflict with—those held by the majority of the people served by the police. When, in the closed society created by the peculiar working hours and duties of policing, those views are constantly reinforced during idle-hour conversations and after-hours socializing, they come to form a sort of *groupthink;* a common set of lenses through which all members of the department view and interpret the world around them. Consequently, domination of policing by *any* single group—black inner-city males; white female college graduates; born-again Christians; liberal white Ivy Leaguers—would be unacceptable, because it inexorably would lead officers to seek to impose their group's definitions of propriety and order on everybody. Where such attempts are complicated by differences between the police and the policed as obvious as race, the result is that existing frictions are greatly exacerbated and that new ones are created. At the extreme, consider what American policing would be like if the current norm—officers commuting from homes in white suburbs to police stations in inner-city areas—were reversed. What would be the state of suburban police–community relations if the great majority of officers who policed those areas—as well as almost all those who had risen high enough to make official policy—were black men who commuted to work from their homes in the inner-city? The answer, unfortunately, is that suburbanites' view of the police might soon reflect the sentiments of the half-joking comments we have heard Washington, D.C. dwellers make concerning the work of "meter maids" who, in the capital city, are predominantly black women:

> It's the most efficient government operation in town. They stand and wait for the meters to expire on nice cars because every ticket is their way of getting even with whitey for 300 years of oppression.

The point is that, for reasons of both substance and symbolism, representativeness is critical in policing. Policing should reflect and be informed by the values and views of all the people served, and all the people should at least occasionally see others who look like them in police uniforms.

## THE NEED TO DEFINE GOOD POLICING

Although James Q. Wilson has argued persuasively that policing is a craft rather than a profession,[3] he also has made an observation that is especially relevant to policing: it is probable that the best judges of the quality of professional services are members of the profession rather than their clientele.[4] Measuring the quality of service provided by any profession or craft, however, requires as a starting point a definition of its role and a set of standards for fulfilling it. As the sociologist Peter K. Manning point outs, almost all vocations, whether crafts or professions, have done this. However imperfect their execution, doctors have defined the social *mandate* of the medical profession and its various subspecialties in terms that are understandable to lay people. With some guidance from their clientele and from the decisions of juries in malpractice cases, doctors have also developed standards for measuring how well their mandate is addressed. Similarly, the confusion that might otherwise reign at large construction sites is eased because each craft has carefully staked out its own turf and distinguished it from the work performed by everybody else on the scene.

The police, however—especially those on the line, rather than at the top bureaucratic levels—have had little input into the definition of their social mandate. Instead, Manning suggests, the police have followed the cues of politicians and others on an *ad hoc* basis and have strayed far from the ideals that originally led to the establishment of modern police departments. Manning notes the results:

> The police were initially designed, based upon principles enunciated by Sir Robert Peel, to prevent crime without resort to repressive legal sanctioning and to avoid military intervention in domestic disturbances; to manage public order nonviolently, with the application of violence viewed as an ultimate means of coercing compliance; to minimize and indeed reduce, if at all possible, the schism between police and public; and to demonstrate efficiency by the absence of crime and disorder, not visible evidence of police action in dealing with them. It might be said, subject to empirical validation, that the American police *rarely seek to prevent crime,* characteristically utilize *excessive violence,* mobilize systematic organizational effort to *increase the schism* between police and public, and seize hungrily upon evidence of police action or intervention as a verification of their effectiveness.[5]

However hyperbolic Manning's comments might seem, there is evidence in these pages that his observations can be applied to at least some American police in some times and places. Certainly they do not apply to all, or even most, police, but Manning does hint at an important point: *Both the public and the police suffer from the absence of a clear, unambiguous, and universally agreed-upon statement of the police mandate in our society.*

The consequences that flow from the lack of such a statement are great. As we suggested in Chapter 6, some police departments have come to think of *law enforcement* as their primary business, of perpetrators as their only clients. One result is that these departments may measure their effectiveness in terms of how often officers make arrests or issue tickets, without regard to whether these activities actually solve any problems. In a case as extreme as LAPD's Special Investigation Section, they may even come to give a higher priority to the *big arrest* than to preventing crime or protecting innocent citizens.

Such departments may also encourage officers to regard as a distraction any activity that does not involve enforcing laws. When this occurs, patrol officers—who spend relatively little of their time in actual law enforcement activities—become cynical and dissatisfied, because so much of their daily routine involves something other than what they have been led to believe is *real police work.* For them, *cops and robbers* is the only real police work. When, as is usually the case, they are required to perform less thrilling tasks, their disappointment shows, and they are likely to alienate and offend members of the public with whom they come into contact.

The most important consequence of failure to agree upon a statement of the police mission is that we do not have any way to tell when it is being done well. True, the police have developed standards for the performance of specific police tasks—how to stop traffic violators, suspicious people, and domestic violence, and when to use deadly force, for example. But beyond these *how-to's* and some promising but isolated studies discussed later in this chapter, there is little. The result is that it is difficult to distinguish good departments from those that are not; good officers from those who are not; good police work from that which is not. Instead, only the outliers at the negative end of the scale—officers whose records indicate violence-proneness; departments or units with histories of corruption—are readily apparent, while excellent performers are indistinguishable from the mediocre.

## Accreditation

The process of accrediting police agencies has been a promising step in the direction of defining good policing. Accreditation began with a U.S. Department of Justice grant to the four largest American police and law enforcement professional associations (International Association of Chiefs of Police; National Organization of Black Law Enforcement Executives; National Sheriffs' Association; Police Executive Research Forum). The grant eventually led to the creation of an independent Commission on Accreditation for Law Enforcement Agencies (CALEA) in 1982, and to the subsequent adoption of more than nine hundred standards in about fifty police policy and operational areas. To date, approximately two hundred police, sheriffs', and investigative agencies have applied for and received accreditation. Several hundred others are somewhere in the 3–5-year process of preparing for evaluation by CALEA's teams of peer assessors. There is a definite need for such a process, and we support it wholeheartedly.[6] The primary effect of accreditation, however, has been to professionalize administration rather than to prescribe either an overarching goal to which all police activity should be directed or a philosophy to guide the direct delivery of police services. The desire to avoid even the appearance of attempting to usurp local government prerogatives has led CALEA to refrain from specifying the substance of policies required of applicant agencies. Instead, with the single exception of its deadly force standards,[7] CALEA requires only that applicants promulgate policies and do not specify what these required policies must say. To be accredited, reviewers must find only that an agency has considered and issued such directives and procedures as the following:

1.1.1. A written directive requires the formulation, annual updating, and distribution to all personnel of written goals and objectives for the agency and for each organizational component within the agency. . . .

1.2.1. A written directive governs the use of discretion by all officers. . . .

1.3.7. A written directive governs the use of non-lethal weapons by agency personnel. . . .

1.3.14. The agency has a procedure for reviewing incidents in which there is application of force through the use of a weapon by agency personnel. . . .

1.3.15. The procedures required in standard 1.3.14 include a report of findings to the agency's chief executive officer.[8]

Thus, the effects of accreditation on police officers' interaction with citizens are limited to those directives and procedures which trickle down through the organization to the street level. Since excellence in any organization depends heavily on capable and informed leadership, these effects can be substantial. It seems unlikely, however, that accreditation, as currently understood, will ever be the means for developing a grand definition of the police mandate. Without such a mandate, it will remain difficult for even accredited police departments to specify the personal qualities that predict good police work. This, in turn, makes it difficult to identify the people most likely to make good police officers or to train them in ways that increase the chances that they will succeed in their work.

In short, accreditation is directed at the tops of police organizations, rather than at the line. In addition, the primary focus of CALEA's assessors and commissioners is on documents, facilities, and general policies and practices rather than upon the actual quality of work or the reasonableness of specific police actions. Hence, and fittingly, CALEA is closely akin to the professional bodies that accredit hospitals, universities, and law schools. It is not, however, comparable to the professional committees that develop specific standards for work in operating rooms, scientific research, or courthouses, or review peers' specific actions and work product, and that help to define good work within their professions. In policing, this task is performed almost exclusively by people at the tops of the same organizations as the people under scrutiny. These reviewers are neither unbiased nor peers, hence their work cannot be considered to be in the same category as that of professional associations' standards and peer review committees.

## A Starting Point

Clearly, there is need for a definition of the police job, but developing one is a tough challenge made more difficult by generations of misunderstanding—by both public and police—of what police do and how well they can do it. We suggest, however, that a good way to begin developing such a definition would be to take seriously some of the words that appear on the front page of almost every police department's manual: *The primary job of the police is to protect life.*

It would be simplistic to suggest that, without further explication, this statement of purpose could serve as a useful guide for the work of cops on the street. Still, it does state the overarching goal of police work that has either been missing or treated as a meaningless platitude by police agencies caught up in the quest to produce quantitative evidence that they have actually been doing something. In addition, it provides both the acid test of every police action—*Was the police action the best way to protect life?*— and the foundation for development of policies and training designed to help officers make decisions in critical situations.[9]

Skolnick once testified in a case where two highway patrolmen stopped a Mercedes-Benz going 65 miles an hour on a relatively deserted superhighway at 2 A.M. The driver, a tall black man, had passed the patrol car, which was traveling at 55 mph, the exact, but rarely observed, speed limit. The officers ordered the driver out of the car and asked to see his license. The driver opened his wallet and showed instead an emergency room physician ID card. He told the traffic cops that he was on his way to an emergency where someone was dying of bullet wounds.

The highway patrolmen nevertheless insisted that he show his license. The driver said, "This is nonsense. I'm a surgeon and a man is dying." He then turned to return to the driver's seat. One of the cops grabbed him, choked him, and dragged him to the side of the road, half-conscious and in

shock. He recovered about fifteen minutes later, subsequently suffered
from neck pains and headaches, sued, and won.

Skolnick testified that protection of life was the primary responsibility
of the police. The police in this case, Skolnick said, should have allowed
the doctor to drive to the emergency room (which happened to be only a
couple of miles distant) and assisted in getting him there.

He later learned that the shooting victim did not die, because another
surgeon, white, was also stopped by police for speeding and then was es-
corted to the emergency room by the police. The black doctor had, of
course, committed the offense of contempt of cop. He was black and affluent, and he had challenged the authority of the police, who took the opportunity to teach him a lesson in citizen obedience to police commands.

*Police Successes*

When police have started their attempts to develop policy with the principle that good policing in any situation consists of the actions that best meet
the primary police responsibility to protect life, the results have been remarkably successful. Deadly force policies that, in both philosophy and
substance, emphasize the sanctity of life over the need to apprehend suspects have reduced killings by police—and the backlash that often follows—without negative effects on the safety of citizens or the safety and
effectiveness of officers.[10] Vehicle pursuit policies developed with the
same priority of imperatives have had similar effects. When endangering
lives in order to catch fleeing drivers—who usually turn out to be nothing
more than reckless kids—is proscribed, officers lose little, if any, law enforcement effectiveness; but they do leave fewer dead and mangled bodies
in their wake.[11]

Perhaps the most dramatically successful police program directed at the
goal of protecting life was the development during the early 1970s of pro-
tocols for police hostage negotiations. Until that time, hostage-taking was
a relatively rare event in the United States, and police typically responded
to it in an *ad hoc* manner that seemed to place greatest emphasis on hasty
suppression of challenges to official authority rather than on extracting
hostages safely. Indeed, prior to the 1970s police in many places were
taught that, in planning how to deal with hostage situations, the lives of
hostages were to be considered "already lost." This view—that hostages'
survival was a result of serendipity rather than a goal of police operations—meant that the few hostage situations that did occur usually resulted
in bloodshed. Then serious police efforts to develop a policy that would
give first priority to preventing violence at hostage situations were precip-

itated by two events. The first was the 1971 Attica Prison uprising. According to the commission that investigated that event:

> Forty-three citizens of New York State died at Attica Correctional Facility between September 9 and 13, 1971. Thirty-nine of the number were killed and more than 80 others were wounded by gunfire during the 15 minutes it took the State Police to retake the prison on September 13. With the exception of Indian massacres in the late 19th century, the State Police Assault which ended the four-day prison uprising was the bloodiest one-day encounter between Americans since the Civil War.[12]

The second incident was a 1972 New York City hostage situation stemming from a bank robbery attempt. Less bloody than Attica, this incident ended when an FBI agent fatally shot one of the hostage-takers. The incident drew attention for several other reasons as well. It had lasted many hours and was broadcast live on television. Then, when it was disclosed that the dead man's partner had masterminded the crime in order to finance his male lover's sex change operation, Hollywood also became interested and dramatized the story in the film, *Dog Day Afternoon*.

The first police Hostage Negotiating Team in New York City developed a typology of four broad categories of hostage-taker, each motivated by different factors and therefore requiring different handling by police. *Criminals*—routine offenders caught at the scene of their crimes—typically were interested in escaping unharmed or with as little punishment as possible and could usually be persuaded to surrender before making things worse. More challenging were spontaneous *unorganized groups,* such as the Attica rioters, who typically wanted amelioration of some conditions beyond the control of police. In such cases, police negotiators generally were instructed to buy time while the agencies involved attempted to strike bargains with the hostage-takers. Still other techniques were specified for the two most dangerous and unpredictable types of hostage-takers, *mentally disturbed persons* and *terrorists*.[13]

Equipped with a clear goal—protecting life—the police task forces that created what are by now standard hostage negotiation strategies were enormously successful. In 1983—ten years after the creation of the NYPD's Hostage Negotiating Teams—a police officer was killed at a hostage situation. But by then, in New York City alone, the teams had resolved more than three hundred contained hostage situations without a single fatality to any hostage, police officer, or hostage-taker. It was not until 1988, after about a hundred more hostage situations, that a hostage-taker killed his hostage while negotiators were on the scene. Similar records have been recorded throughout the United States, and application of hostage tech-

niques and expertise to other police problems, such as confrontations with
mentally disturbed people, has proved equally successful.[14]

The development of hostage negotiation strategies is not the only experience that suggests the value of working around, rather than through, the
hierarchical command structure long enough to allow groups of experienced and smart street cops to diagnose challenging field problems and to
develop means of addressing them. The Metro-Dade Police–Citizen Violence Project also used this approach, which had its roots in the work conducted in Oakland by the psychologist Hans Toch and his colleagues,
J. Douglas Grant and Raymond Galvin.

In 1969, Toch, Grant, and Galvin assembled a group of officers that
included both cops with histories of violence and others identified as
"good" by their supervisors. While the officers in the subsequent Metro-
Dade project were asked to delineate specific techniques and strategies that
might help officers to defuse recurrent types of potentially violent incidents, the Oakland officers were given a much broader charge. They were
allowed to set their own starting point by defining the problem of police–
citizen violence, identifying its causes, developing a methodology for addressing it, and putting their methodology into operation.

The nonpunitive approach devised by these officers started with the creation of a "Violence Prevention Unit." That panel's work usually began
with a review of the file of an officer whose record indicated frequent "violent involvements": contacts with citizens that culminated in violence apparently precipitated by the officer. The panel would then conduct a preliminary investigation, consisting of interviews with the officer's
supervisors and co-workers, as well as a review of any other information it
could find relating to the officer. A "study group" of some panel members
would then review all these materials, develop hypotheses to explain the
subject officer's involvement in violence, and propose questions to be
posed at a meeting between the officer and the panel.

The panel's meeting with the officer would comprise three stages:

a.   Key incidents are chronologically explored, including not only ac-
     tions taken by all persons involved in the incident, but also their
     perceptions, assumptions, feelings, and motives.
b.   The summation of these data in the form of common denominators
     and patterns is undertaken primarily by the subject, with participa-
     tion by the panelists. An effort is made to test the plausibility and
     relevance of the hypothesized patterns by extrapolating them into
     other involvements.
c.   The discussion of the pattern occurs last, and includes tracing its

contribution to violence. This stage features the exploration of alternative approaches that might be conducive to more constructive solutions.[15]

Before the project began, officers who subsequently became its subjects—presumably the department's most violence-prone personnel—engaged in conflicts with citizens nearly four times as often as the rest of their colleagues (0.37 conflicts per month for participants versus 0.10 for all others). Following participation in the panel sessions, the violence-prone officers' involvement in such incidents decreased by more than half (to 0.16 per month), while nonparticipating officers' involvement remained relatively constant (0.08 incidents per month).[16] Thus, there certainly remained a measurable difference between the violence-prone and everybody else, but this one project apparently cut it in half. These are impressive results for a first-time project developed in most material ways by cops rather than by mental health professionals.

Toch and Grant were also surprised by officers' willingness to acknowledge the police contribution to violence between police and citizens. The officers who worked on the Oakland project, Toch and Grant wrote later, were willing to "accept the import of self-critical data," so that their "uninhibited exploration of intervention options yielded a departure from familiar responses,"[17] namely blaming citizens and absolving officers for everything that had gone awry.

We are not as surprised as Toch and Grant by the candor of the Violence Prevention Unit officers. Instead, in our experience, officers' historic unwillingness to comment critically upon their colleagues' work is rooted in the fact that they almost invariably are asked to do so only in interrogation rooms and in other proceedings designed to find and punish culprits. As a veteran officer told us after a disorder had erupted in a Hispanic section of Washington, D.C.:

The most glamorous part of cops' business is finding bad guys, but it affects everything the department does. It becomes a fixation—and the police department starts to think that somebody is at fault for everything that goes wrong. They don't understand that things can get screwed up even though nobody did anything wrong. So, when something gets screwed up, the officials call all the officers together and ask them, one at a time, to tell everything they know. But the cops know that the officials are just looking for somebody to blame, and the cops all play dumb. If the department was really interested in constructive criticism and in correcting problems, they'd learn a lot from officers. But they don't ask for that reason; they only ask so that can stick it to some poor cop. So they don't learn anything.[18]

This insight goes to the heart of the success of the Oakland and Dade projects. In both cases, street officers—at the bottom of their departments' hierarchy and until then rarely asked their opinions about anything—were sought out and asked to share what they knew for reasons that had nothing to do with internal investigations or disciplinary actions. In effect, the project harnessed officers' skills and experience in intervening in citizens' problems and applied them to the problems of the people closest to them: their police peers. The officers responded admirably, and in ways that should encourage other researchers and administrators to use the same technique in defining and resolving other police problems.

## COMMUNITY-ORIENTED POLICING

Two emerging philosophies—*community-oriented policing* and *problem-oriented policing*—have recently attempted to systematize the concept of broadening input into police policy that was pioneered by Toch and his colleagues. Under the label "community-oriented policing" such notions as police–community reciprocity, decentralization of command, reorientation of patrol, and generalized rather than specialized policing are commending themselves to police executives around the globe.[19] At first thought this is quite surprising. Why should police executives in places with such different cultures, different economies, and different traditions as Oslo, Tokyo, London, New York, and Santa Ana be advocating similar reforms? After all, London is perhaps the world's most diverse and cosmopolitan metropolis, not unlike New York, while Santa Ana has a population about the size of a London borough, located 33 miles southeast of Los Angeles, and Oslo is the relatively small capital (750,000) of a homogeneously populated Scandinavian welfare state.

The answer seems to be that with respect to crime—and perhaps even more to fear of crime arising from public disorder (what sociologist Albert Reiss, Jr., has called "soft crime")[20] there has developed an almost international language, a virtually reflexive set of public reactions. One part of the response is to impose heavier and mandated sentences on convicted criminals, to fill the jails and prisons to capacity and overcapacity. However mistrusted police might be, another part is to look to the police to prevent crime and public disorder.

Which leads to a larger question: Is it possible for police to prevent crime from occurring in the first place? There is some evidence that police can prevent specific offenses, but no one really knows how much police can contribute to crime prevention in the aggregate, especially since police researchers and managers have learned how unsuccessful traditional crime-fighting strategies by police were during the 1970s and 1980s. That is mainly why the new hope is in "community-oriented policing," a strategy that directs police resources away from traditional responses and attempts to foster a partnership between the "community" and the organization and direction of policing. Community-oriented policing has become widespread, prevalent, and fashionable not because it has been proved to work, but because the alternatives to it have been proved to fail. The most glaring recent failure has been the aggressive style of the Los Angeles Police Department, of which the Rodney King beating is just one symptom.

Police executives have come to recognize other failures of strategy as well. One is throw money and technology at the crime problem. But police managers, informed by criminal justice researchers, have learned that hiring more police does not necessarily result in less crime or increase the proportion of crimes solved. The same can be said for enlarging police budgets or licensing police to be *aggressive* in their prevention efforts. The most that can be warranted is that, if cops were to disappear entirely, there would be more crime. But once a certain threshold of police department size has been reached—long ago met in most major cities—neither more police nor more money helps much. Variations in crime, clearance rates, and public disorder are related to such stubbornly intractable factors as income, levels of employment, education, and population heterogeneity. Throwing money at law enforcement offers no solution to these larger persistent social factors that are so highly correlated with crime. Besides, in the declining budget climate of the 1990s, there isn't much money to throw at either police or social problems. Hence, the search for a new approach to policing.

Police managers also have learned that random motorized patrolling neither reduces crime nor improves the chances of catching suspects. It used to be thought that saturating an area with patrol cars would prevent crime. It does seem to—but only temporarily—largely by displacing crime to other areas. Yet even when police inundate an area, they rarely see a crime in progress. That happens sometimes, but mostly in the movies, as when Dirty Harry has his lunch disturbed by an armed robbery. Regular patrols by officers on foot have not been demonstrated to reduce crime either, but they do raise public confidence in the safety of the streets. The incident-driven patrol car, visible to citizens mainly when it is en route to calls for service, does not appear to offer similar reassurance.[21]

Nor does slicing response time to crime incidents—a hallmark of police management in the 1970s—raise the likelihood of arresting the criminal or satisfying the crime victim. One major study showed an initially surprising but commonsensical finding—the chances of making an arrest on the spot drops below 10 percent if even one minute elapses from the time the crime is committed.[2] But even if cops could move with the speed of comic book heroes, in a flash, it would not matter. Crime victims delay an average of four to five and one-half minutes before picking up a telephone to report the crime. After such a delay, how fast the police respond is irrelevant. And there cannot even be a response time when a woman is too afraid or embarrassed to report a beating or a rape because of the treatment she expects from police.

Researchers have learned that police who ride in patrol cars, especially two-person cars, become rather self-contained and remote, neither reassuring citizens enough to reduce their fear of crime nor engendering trust. In fact, except perhaps in the most congested areas, where it is very difficult for solo patrol officers to drive and observe the sidewalks at the same time, there is really no objective need for the two-person car. Studies have shown that police are no more likely to be injured in one-person patrol cars. And two-person patrol cars are no more effective in catching criminals or reducing crime.[23] Oddly enough, this lesson has been learned in some American cities, even in places like Oakland, California, with its machine-gun-toting drug dealers and record homicide rates. But in Europe, even in peaceful Scandinavia, police regard the companionship of the two-person car as an indispensable component of the job. We suspect that it is for these same reasons of companionship—rather than for considerations of safety or effectiveness—that police officers in some American cities fight tooth-and-nail to retain two-person cars.

These research findings are nothing short of devastating to earlier assumptions of managerial professionalism and incident-driven (911-driven) policing, which—to the horror of specialists in time management rather than policing—puts the development of police in the hands of an amorphous and faceless public. To the thoughtful police administrator, the findings suggest that traditional patrol strategies are neither reducing crime nor reassuring potential crime victims, some of whom fear the police as much as they do the criminals. Thinking police professionals have had to develop some new ideas. Community-oriented policing is the leading one.

Community-oriented policing is not a detailed, coherent program whose elements can be checked off by a novice chief assuming the job. Above all, it is a philosophy of policing, a new professionalism, which cannot succeed without a chief's energetic and abiding commitment to democratic, rather than technocratic, values. It is almost a new vision of the role of police in a democratic society. A Norwegian government report expresses the essence of this philosophy when it says that "the police are able to carry out their tasks satisfactorily only through constructive cooperation with the public."[24] Under this philosophy, the chief is responsible for generating a new normative climate—not easy to accomplish—which will assume that ordinary citizens have a contribution to make to the policing enterprise, that they are partners in the production of social order.

The distinction between traditional professionalism and democratic professionalism was made nicely by a Santa Ana, California, businessman who was asked about what had changed with the introduction of community-oriented policing to the Santa Ana Police Department. The businessman said that when the city hired community-oriented administrator, Raymond Davis, to be Chief of Police, they were looking for a police executive who was "up to date," who combined management expertise and technological sophistication with an ability to relate to the broader community. The same businessman continued, "We wanted someone who was willing to work together with the residential and business communities. The old guard didn't want to hear from the community. They told us they were professionals and that they didn't want to have anything to do with us."[25] This is probably the main difference between "new" and "old" professionals. Old professionals were insular. They were not necessarily corrupt or inefficient or technologically unsophisticated. They were adequately trained in the law of arrest, the penal code, interrogation tactics, and the fine points of when and how to apply a truncheon, and they had memorized their departments' rulebooks to prepare for promotional examinations. As trained technicians, they saw little advantage in seeking input or direction from the lay community. Like traditional firefighters, who are skilled in putting fires out rather than educating citizens to prevent fires, they were interested in solving, not preventing, crime. Unlike the tough and streetwise Davis, they also kept their distance from the street cop, regarding their own attainment of rank as the best evidence that they had a lock on whatever it took to run their departments.

Community policing involves not only sympathetic listening but the creation of opportunities to listen. This is a big step for most police forces, because what lay persons have to say may not be entirely flattering. Nevertheless, where community policing has been introduced, the police—like the officers in Toch's Oakland Project—have learned that they must be prepared to listen, even if what they hear is unpleasant. Actually, when Neighborhood Watch and similar community programs are established, there rarely is serious unpleasantness, since the police and the citizens who participate generally are interested in fostering dialogue rather than hostility.

But who are these citizens? Of what "community" are they representative? As Wesley Skogan has cautioned, "advocates of Community Policing need to spell out clearly just how the police can come to know what a neighborhood wants in the way of order."[26] The idea of community implies a commonality of interests, traditions, identities, values, and expectations. As we have suggested, these criteria may not be met in demographically complex and differentiated areas. Skogan reports that "in the outcomes of the Community Policing projects in Houston—there was a clear tendency for whites and homeowners (a surrogate measure of class) to enjoy the benefits of the programs, and for blacks and renters to be unaffected by them."[27] Community members who feel most comfortable with police— and with whom the police feel most comfortable—are the ones who enjoy stability of residence, jobs, businesses, and professions.

Whatever the limitations about assumptions of community, one compelling fact stands out in its favor in the policing context. Whenever surveys of ordinary people—of all races and political inclinations—are conducted, it turns out that most people (not most criminals, who go unpolled) prefer a police presence. Instead of despising the sight of police, people who work, ride public transportation, and send their children to school feel safer in the presence of police. Foot cops, who are the most approachable of police, are the most popular of all.[28]

In 1990 New York City, under Commissioner Lee P. Brown, envisioned a major expansion of community-oriented policing. Announced by Mayor David Dinkins, the "plan . . . maps out a strategy for weaving the fabric of community policing into our neighborhoods."[29] The plan called for hiring new officers to raise the patrol strength of the NYPD, many of whom would be assigned to the Community Officer Patrol Program. Here, foot patrol officers would be given flexibility to develop contacts with residents and community groups in order to solve problems that result in crime, rather than merely responding to calls for service.

This implementation of community-oriented policing points to two of its other tightly wound features. One is decentralization of command; the other is problem-oriented policing. Although police operations may be geographically decentralized into local precincts or station houses, local tactics, assignments, priorities, shifts, and so forth are usually centrally established. By contrast, community policing assumes that policing problems and priorities vary from neighborhood to neighborhood. To accomplish this flexibility, local commanders must be given greater freedom and authority to respond to local conditions. Santa Ana, for example, was divided into four areas, where teams of police and associated community service officers would be assigned for substantial time periods, two or more years. The first step in community-policing reform in Adelaide, Australia, was a redrawing of subdivisional boundaries to make them coincide with smaller, more organic communities. In New York City entire precincts are being organized around community-oriented policing. Indeed, in response to suggestions by the Christopher Commission, LAPD's Daryl Gates announced shortly before the 1992 riot that a community-based policing experiment would soon begin in six of the city's eighteen police districts. The extent to which this LAPD program would involve decentralization and grassroots decision-making, however, was put in doubt by Chief Gate's decision to place it under his own close personal supervision.[30]

## PARA-POLICE

Civilianizing the police force—hiring civilians to do the jobs cops formerly did so as to free patrol officers to work the streets—is a general trend in policing. Years ago, fully qualified officers, known as *sworn* police, since they had qualified to take the oath of office, undertook virtually every job in the department, from detective to dispatcher. Yet by 1973 the National Advisory Commission on Criminal Justice Standards and Goals, surveying forty-one metropolitan police departments, found an average of 16 percent civilians to 84 percent sworn. Today, urban police departments rarely, if ever, employ sworn police to serve as dispatchers and may employ as many as 40 percent civilians, although the average is about two sworn officers to every civilian.[31]

Civilianization of policing is thus quite acceptable. The controversial issue is how deeply into the policing function to civilianize, an issue that splits police chiefs who say they are otherwise supporters of community-oriented policing and that sometimes raises the anxiety and the bitter opposition of police unions.

Santa Ana, California, a department in which community-oriented policing was pioneered by Chief Raymond Davis in the 1970s and 1980s, introduced a highly developed para-policing program—a concept modeled on the paramedic or paralegal—as an intrinsic aspect of community-oriented policing.[32] In this vision, para-police were trained semiprofessionals who performed important, but more routine, preliminary or peripheral police tasks, usually connected with service to citizens. The para-cops, who were usually female, were not responsible for investigating criminal activities or for apprehending and arresting those suspected of crime. The central feature of the police role, the capacity to use force, was thus not assigned to the para-police, who wore uniforms but carried neither batons nor guns. (The SAPD had originally considered outfitting para-police in blue blazers to distinguish them from sworn police officers but found, after a brief experiment with blazers, that the blue uniform signaled the only sort of authority citizens were willing to accept.)

The SAPD believed that nine para-police could be hired at the cost of five sworn officers and could offer equally good *service*. In fact, many of the para-police turned out to be better qualified because they could enrich *communication* with the sizable Spanish-speaking population of Santa Ana. Investigation of major crimes involves a lot of talking—to the victim as well as to neighbors, relatives, and friends. If you can't speak the language of the neighborhood, you can't investigate the crime. How can police investigate a homicide of a Salvadoran or Vietnamese victim if no cops can speak the language of the victim?

As might be expected, para-police in Santa Ana participated in such commonplace community-oriented policing tasks as organizing and monitoring neighborhood watch groups and presenting crime prevention seminars, usually alongside sworn officers so as the signal the SAPD's commitment to community policing. But they also marked abandoned vehicles and had them towed; took reports of crimes, burglaries, and rapes that had occurred earlier; and recontacted crime victims. This was not to so much to solve the crime—often beyond anyone's ability—but to support crime victims emotionally, a responsibility to which the SAPD assigned a high priority. Para-police also, as it happened, turned out to be unusually effective traffic investigators. Patrol cops generally disdain traffic accident investigations, especially the paperwork accompanying "fender benders." But for the para-police, their knowledge of the necessary paperwork for traffic accident investigations evidenced *their* professional expertise. As a result, para-police took accident investigations and reports seriously and tended to be more empathetic with, and helpful to, those involved. The Chief shrewdly realized that, for the average working stiff, the seemingly minor fender bender might be the most important and traumatic event of the month. Eventually, para-police were even successfully assigned to patrol cars, alone, equipped only with a radio. When they saw signs of trouble suggesting that force or arrest was needed, they would call one or more sworn cops.

Para-police present the policing world with a dilemma: Since they are fundamentally a cost-cutting measure, their pay needs to be much lower—about half—than that of sworn officers. But the better they perform, and as they are also assigned to midnight and weekend shifts, the more they threaten the pay scales and job security of sworn police. Police unions are accordingly wary of the whole idea of para-police. Cops are not *independent* and highly paid professionals, like doctors and lawyers, and so they see para-police not as heighteners of their status and professionalism but as potential union-busters. Top police managers, on the other hand, are more interested, since para-cops save costs and perform some tasks even better than sworn cops. One way some police departments have moved to resolve the dilemma is to pay para-police salaries approaching those of sworn police, but to exclude them from the generous pension and similar benefits that sworn cops enjoy.

## PROBLEM-ORIENTED POLICING

"Problem-oriented policing," advocated by Herman Goldstein, a University of Wisconsin law professor,[33] is frequently identified with community-oriented policing, and for good reason. Both strategies stand in opposition to incident-driven policing. Traditionally, patrol police are deployed to respond to emergency calls for service. The dominant objectives of police patrol are to arrive quickly, stabilize the situation, and return to service—which means being available to answer another call. Inevitably, the response of most police officers is hasty and superficial. They may be critically important to minimize damage, but they have little time for or interest in responding to the underlying situation. Incident-driven patrol officers are usually well aware of their own limitations.

Consequently, according to Goldstein, incident-driven policing wastes time and impact. Police are neither solving problems nor preventing crime. By concentrating on incidents, the police lose control of their own resources and their own effectiveness. Most of their human resources are tied down by a commitment that diverts them from addressing the underlying crime and disorder problems of modern communities.

The solution, according to Goldstein, is for the police to become problem-oriented rather than incident-oriented. As in community-oriented policing, the emphasis is on police *pro*activity rather *re*activity. Police are advised to diagnose longer-term solutions to recurrent crime and disorder problems and to mobilize community and municipal resources to implement them. Like community-oriented policing, problem-oriented policing envisions an altered, and a more analytical and humanistic, police role. Police must be able to perceive underlying problems, evaluate the feasibility and costliness of alternatives, work with others to design and implement solutions, vigorously advocate the adoption of necessary programs, monitor the results of cooperative efforts, and redirect them if necessary. The objective of policing doesn't change. It is still the enhancement of public safety and order. What changes is the way resources are allocated to meet the goal, so that police can now make a difference.

Problem-oriented policing has been tried in several police departments. In one of the earliest examples offered by Goldstein, police in Madison, Wisconsin, were constantly summoned to the downtown shopping mall to deal with people who were behaving bizarrely and disruptively. Press reports put the number involved at one thousand and portrayed the mall as a haven for vagrants and street people. Not surprisingly, the public began to avoid the mall, and business suffered. When the police studied the problem over a period of time, they discovered that only thirteen individuals were responsible; that all had been under psychological supervision; and that they behaved strangely only when they failed to take their medication. The police began to work with mental health authorities, who developed a tighter supervision system for those people. The problem in the mall soon vanished, business returned, and the police were free to turn to other matters.[34]

As in community-oriented policing, problem-oriented policing should, above all, advocate a change in the philosophy of policing. The organization must be more flexible and willing to adapt to changing needs. The police officer, in turn, is required to be more of a generalist, more humanistic, more in tune with the underlying needs, problems, and resources of the areas being policed. Such an orientation is far less likely to generate police violence than traditional patrol policing, with which the familiar culture of policing—discussed in Chapter 5—is associated.

Two hurdles of community and problem-oriented policing can be especially difficult. One is clarifying the definition of disorder and of fitting responses to it. The other is the distance between management cop philosophy and street cop behavior discussed earlier.

Disorder, as the political scientist Wesley Skogan has observed, encompasses various kinds of social and physical disarray.[35] It incorporates everything from junk and trash in vacant lots to boarded-up homes, broken windows, stripped and abandoned cars, graffiti, and animal waste in streets. It can also include such criminal activities as public drinking, drug selling, gambling, and prostitution, along with such ambiguous legal categories as "loitering," "disturbing the peace," and "panhandling." The sort of physical disarray and behavioral impropriety conveyed by the term "disorder," combined with a mandate to police to rid the community of it, can be interpreted as an invitation to police to "crack down," to become "badge-heavy," to "kick ass and take names." Indeed, one of the most vexing problems in controlling police violence is that it is so strongly supported in the most disorderly neighborhoods. If, in conveying an understanding that policing involves a range of problems and not just crime; that problems require analysis and differentiated responses; and that police are limited in their capacity to address these problems and need to involve the community, it would be paradoxical if police were to resort to the kind of aggressive patrolling that community-oriented and problem-oriented policing were supposed to eliminate, and that are often a prelude to violence.

These orientations toward policing are just that, orientations rather than orders, perspectives rather than prescriptions. They offer ways of looking at the world of policing, opportunities to step back and to reconstitute. As Herman Goldstein observes regarding problem-oriented policing:

> I have seen elaborate but totally unrealistic schedules for "full implementation" that seem more appropriate to a military exercise than to implementing a complex, necessarily long-term plan for organizational change requiring a radical change in the way in which employees view their job and carry it out.[36]

It takes a considerable amount of thinking to effect meaningful police reform efforts. Too often, "reform" consists of hiring a new and progressive chief without any provision for ensuring that an administration's lofty ideals are understood and implemented at the street level. Hardboiled street cops are led by their work to value order and stability. Hence, they often react to innovations in policing by deriding them as pointless and unworkable intrusions into the true and eternal work of the cop—the role they were recruited into and learned when they joined the department. Their representatives, the heads of police unions, often throw roadblocks in the path of reform as well. Unions will surely oppose civilian review, and they are inclined to be suspicious of accountability to anyone other than a known superior. If community-oriented and problem-oriented policing demand organizational flexibility, chiefs may find that changes—as, for example, in shifts and assignments—will be resisted in increasingly popular "meet and confer" bargaining sessions with police unions.

There are two ways to deal with line police officers' resistance to change. One way is to force change on officers from the top; to press down on cops and *compel* them to go along with change. Once this process is started, however, it cannot be stopped. Like a hand moved off the lid of a jack-in-the-box, any relaxation in pressure is sure to activate a counterreaction that will, to mix metaphors, swing the pendulum of change back far beyond the point where it had been when reform efforts started. Reform by intimidation from the top produces great tensions and lasts in police agencies only as long as the administrations of the intimidating chiefs who initiate it. Worse, it is our experience that street cops take every opportunity and use considerable ingenuity to undermine reform-by-intimidation even while such chiefs are in office.

More lasting and tension-free changes result from *enlisting* officers in reform efforts. The highest-ranking police officials in Oakland, Dade County, and New York were absolutely committed to reform, but the actual shapes of the reforms—the hostage negotiating procedures; the Violence Prevention Unit; the violence reduction training—were developed far down the organizational chain by good street cops who had been asked to diagnose a problem and then empowered to fit to it their definitions of *good policing.* The officers in all of these projects embraced their tasks so vigorously, we are convinced, because the process in which they participated—*peer establishment of standards and development of means of assessing the extent to which they have been attained*—more closely approximated professionalism than anything they had previously experienced in their police careers.

In this sense, introducing meaningful reforms that *last* is a far greater challenge to those at the top of police departments than to those at the bottom. If a police department is to be truly *professionalized,* authority and responsibility must be decentralized. The brass must surrender some of their prerogatives and must empower those further down the line to define the challenges of their work and to develop means of addressing them. Regardless of their high-toned rhetoric and claimed commitment to police professionalism, community-oriented policing, and the like, many top police officials are unwilling to do this. As a consequence, the reality of community-oriented policing seen through the windshields of police patrol cars sometimes is very different from that described in the glowing terms of police departments' brochures and brag-sheets or by distant police chiefs who are unwilling to delegate any authority to the street cops and supervisors closest to communities and their problems. When that happens, the polarization of what Elizabeth Reuss-Ianni called the two cultures of policing—management cops and street cops[37]—grows. An officer in a police department undergoing a highly publicized "conversion" to a community-oriented policing model told us:

> This is the usual horseshit. The chief tells everybody that we're community-oriented, but we still don't know what that means. The chief goes out and makes speeches about it, but when we ask the sergeant what we should say to people if they ask us about this, he tells us to keep in mind the department's rule that we're not allowed to criticize any department policy or official. I guess it would be critical to tell people we have no idea what the difference between community-oriented policing and what we used to do is, so we just smile and nod.[38]

The officer's point is well taken. We have seen many fads in policing over the years, and police chiefs are no less likely than any other officials to wrap themselves in trendy jargon at the same time that they keep their distance from real change.

## A POLICE CADET CORPS

Many otherwise progressive police officials are adamantly opposed to one proposed change in the *status quo.* The New York attorney Adam Walinsky has proposed a national "Police Cadet Corps" (PCC) modeled closely along the lines of current military Reserve Officer Training Corps programs.[39] Under Walinsky's plan—which has considerable bipartisan support in Congress—students would enroll as police cadets early in their college careers. In return for substantial funding for tuition and other educational costs—up to $40,000 over an undergraduate career—cadets would incur two obligations. First, they would undergo police training during their college years; second, they would commit to serve as police officers within their states for at least four years after completing college.

During summer breaks from classes, students would attend training programs at which they would learn fundamental skills of policing. While the summer camps would be federal facilities, Walinsky is careful to avoid any suggestion that the PCC would *federalize* the police or otherwise interfere with state and local police policy-making. Some of the things police should know, Walinsky suggests, are universal and can be taught by the federal government with no effect but to supplement the local police academy training cadets would subsequently receive when they entered police departments. It is very hard to argue with the logic of this part of Walinsky's proposal. Even in the best U.S. police departments, no officer is overtrained, and, aside from local laws and lore, most of the knowledge that makes it possible to do the police job is generalizable around the country. Regardless of location, a car stop is a car stop, a robbery call is a robbery call.

It is also hard to argue against a program that would make college possible for many students who could not otherwise afford it, would ease the financial burden of college for many others, and would probably increase significantly the educational levels of entering police recruits. What, then, are the objections to the PCC?

The first objection we have heard is that the requirement of only a minimum four-year hitch in a state or local police agency would impose upon local governments an enormous burden. Like the military, it is argued, badly strapped local police agencies will be stuck with the cost of training dilettantes who would go on to bigger and better things after remaining in service for only the minimum stay.

We do not view this objection as valid. First, like ROTC graduates, PCC officers would be free to remain in policing after having completed their minimum enlistments. There are many reasons to believe that a considerable number would do so and that, with some organizational reforms to be discussed, short-term turnover would not be as great as it is in the military. Despite the odd duty hours many officers work, a police career is far more compatible with a stable family life than is the military. In most areas of the country, police work pays well enough to support a decent standard of living. In some places, officers who have stepped up a few ranks do quite well. Big-city police captains' annual pay—typically three steps above the entry level police officer rank—often approaches six figures.

In the military, a promotion or transfer can be disrupting, can mean a move halfway around the world; in policing, such a move typically does no more than add some time to the trip between home and police station. Punching one's career ticket in the military requires long absences from home; most police officers, regardless of where they work or how long their workday, get home every day.

Our most important reason for believing that many PCC officers would choose to remain in police careers, however, arises from the nature of the police work itself. Despite the many flaws of the American policing industry, the cop's job has been severely undervalued. Intrinsically—when done with some competence—policing is a challenging and demanding line of work. On the whole, except during economic hard times, policing currently has not been an attractive career choice for well-educated people. This is so largely because the police rarely have sought out educated people and have never afforded educated people status commensurate with that offered by other employers that recruit college graduates: the FBI, the Secret Service, and the military officer corps, for example. Instead, policing has been defined as *uneducated people's work* by those who set hiring standards. In too many cases, public respect for the whole policing enterprise has been correspondingly absent.

PCC would change this. It would give college graduates a reason to consider a career that many today regard as beneath them. Over time, the entry into police ranks of substantial numbers of PCC officers would redefine policing as respectable and appropriate work for people who have taken the time and effort to pursue education beyond high school. This would significantly enhance the socioeconomic representativeness of the police. As much as the police may have become more integrated by race and gender over the last few decades—and have changed as a result—policing remains, by and large, a working-class occupation.

We believe that some degree of *gentrification* of the police would be highly desirable, not out of any elitist sentiments, but simply because it would bring the police closer to the ideal of reflecting the entire society and its values. We hold this view while aware of the objection that integration of this type might polarize the police into two camps—the people in it now, and a new privileged class. There are ways, however, that this possibility can be minimized. Most important is the need to enhance educational opportunities for those currently in police service.

During the late 1960s and through the early 1980s, the federal Law Enforcement Education Program subsidized thousands of in-service police officers' attempts to pursue higher education. Beginning in that period, policing made unprecedented advances. As we have pointed out, a body of scientific research on police matters has grown and has debunked much of the prior conventional wisdom—including the fiction that allowing the police free rein in the use of force had any positive effects on public safety. It is difficult for us not to attribute much of the progress that has been made in policing to the broadening effects upon police of university training. This has now dwindled, however: The "college cops" who helped to bring policing so far—people who attended college between their shifts in patrol cars—are nearing retirement age and are not being replaced by a similar new cadre because funding has disappeared.

That is a great loss. The results of quantitative studies of the effects of education upon police performance are unclear—largely, we suspect, because researchers have not clearly defined their dependent variable, *good policing*. Still, as Ramsey Clark noted more than twenty years ago, support for police higher education is justified simply by the need for representation. How, Clark wondered, can a generally well-educated population legitimize the authority and intervention into their lives of officials they regard as undereducated and subprofessional?[40] To this very good question we would add another: What resentments build up in police officers as a result of day-to-day contacts with well-educated people who, not so subtly, seem to look down on the police? Our experience is that such resentments are considerable. Cops in upper-class and professional neighborhoods frequently use pejorative terms to describe a constituency that, in the view of officers, generally regards them as uncouth servants.[41]

A combination of education for in-service officers and PCC would ease this particular friction and would also encourage precisely the types of organizational changes likely to reduce violence and friction between police and citizens. Those who have studied police personnel report one finding with remarkable consistency: The worst stressors on officers have less to do with the nature of the work than with the stifling effects of police departments' highly bureaucratized and centralized structures.[42] If PCC were to become a reality, police departments that retained such a structure and the attendant philosophy, that treated bright, educated young men and women—who would have far more career options than most current cops—as unthinking cogs in a big machine, would not be able to keep them. Consequently, to avoid the costs of the short-term *dilettante* problem they anticipate, such departments would have to treat street cops with the respect and deference they deserve. That would necessarily entail a move to something more closely approximating a professional organizational model than the current—*stifling*—military model. The community-oriented and problem-oriented policing models we have discussed are the best means of doing so.

Neither of us is naïve enough to think that all PCC officers would stay in police careers. Just as some young people use ROTC strictly for the "selfish" motive of getting an education, some students would enter policing with no intention of making a career of policing. We see this as an advantage of the program.

Currently, police officers are tied together—for good and for ill—by the knowledge that almost every one of them expects to spend his or her twenty-, thirty-, or forty-year career in the same rulebound agencies where, as we suggested earlier, everybody has something on everybody else. Many older officers, who are without real marketable skills or career options, are *burnout* cases who mark their time in policing uninspired by any aspect of their work but the generous pensions that lie some years down the road. Police solidarity is admirable, but this is a state of affairs that approaches incest. Certainly it violates Peel's notion of a democratic police of the people that—unlike the military example he sought to avoid—did not define themselves as a separate class. In fact, the American police at present are a far more insular and separate class than the American military. Whatever increased police turnover eventuated from the entry and exit of short-term PCC officers would breathe some fresh air into police departments and would reduce the police insularity we believe has much to do with violence directed against citizens.

There is another important reason not to dread shorter-term PCC police careers. One rarely considered consequence of the current insularity of the police is that cops have virtually no constituency among top American policy-makers or, for that matter, among the public at large. As a result, the voice of the police rarely is heard by the people who make laws and formulate public opinion. Police input into policy and law has been easily neutralized by others with contrary views and interests—until recently, the National Rifle Association, for example. Indeed, where police have succeeded in catching politicians' ears, they usually have done so as members of organized labor in search of better working conditions rather than to affect public debate of any substantive police matter.

We believe that life would be easier for the police if some dilettantes did, in fact, come and go from their ranks. We believe this because the level of public debate concerning crime and justice would increase dramatically if young college-educated people entered policing for a time, learned what life in a patrol car or in a narcotics squad was about, and moved on to such bigger things as the law, politics, or the media, or simply became part of a better-informed citizenry.

Regardless of political persuasion, no knowledgeable street cop either of us has ever known honestly believes, for example, that national politicians' arguments about the death penalty, building more prison cells, or jailing drug kingpins are anything more than meaningless election year rhetoric. If police experience were anywhere near as common among the public—and among politicians—as military experience, simplistic debates about crime would start to disappear. Politicians without police experience who engaged in such arguments would offend far more voters than the small number of cops who now smirk at their remarks. Self-respecting politicians with police experience would simply not be able to speak with straight faces about current simplistic approaches to crime, disorder, and drugs.

This is so because, as current practice suggests, hands-on experience in a line of endeavor informs policy-makers' decisions about the endeavor, enhances their credibility and ability to communicate with those who have remained in it, and increases their interest and desire to do right by it. Right now, we can think of many politicians at the national level who oversee with wisdom, sophistication, and dedication work that they themselves have actually done. The memberships of the House and the Senate include many ex-prosecutors, ex-judges, ex-Marines, and at least one ex-astronaut; but the name of no ex-cop comes quickly to mind. In the executive branch, the Surgeon General traditionally is a medical practitioner on hiatus, the Attorney General a lawyer, the Secretary of Education an academician. But, despite the country's concerns related to the police, we can think of no ex-cop who has ever been part of any President's highest-level official inner circle. Indeed, even the last two directors of the FBI have been ex-judges, rather than ex-agents or ex-cops. At this writing, two people have held the office of "Drug Czar": an ex-professor and an ex-governor. Even though both have tried to project *tough guy* images, their credibility among the street cops and drug agents we know—as well as their ability to lead and the reasonableness of their expectations of the police and law enforcement—is severely limited. After the military's great successes in Desert Storm, a former student and veteran undercover narcotics detective told us:

When I heard General Schwarzkopf say that we had won in Kuwait because the army had gotten rid of the "military fairies" who had lost in Vietnam by trying to fight the war without leaving the Pentagon, I roared. He set a light off in my head. That's why we're losing all these wars on drugs and crime, too. They're being run by a bunch of "law enforcement fairies," who have never been out in the trenches. All they know about drug wars is what they've read.[43]

Thus, even though we believe that PCC would not produce turnover nearly as substantial as some wary police officials assert, we think it clear that whatever additional turnover does occur would be worthwhile.

## CONCLUSION

If there is an overriding theme to our suggestions for police reform, from community-oriented to problem-oriented to para-policing, and a Police Cadet Corps, it is the theme of *openness*. To the degree possible, we should routinely videotape police conduct during those occasions where propensities to excessive force are most likely to occur: high-speed chases, interrogations, protests, and riots. But the videotape is only a technical tool deriving from a larger principle of police reform, which is that anything we can do to reduce the insularity of police is a good thing. Openness about police and what they do—whether through the infusion of new strategies and new blood into policing, studies by scholars, or investigations by the press—are all useful in improving police management and practice. Eventually, such exposure should also improve the sophistication of public policy related to police issues and should furnish the police with the informed constituency they now lack. This will result in a clearer definition of what police can and cannot be expected to accomplish and will reduce officers' tendencies to use excessive force of the kind the public was exposed to in the Rodney King and more recent videotapes. Over the long run, this can only enrich the work of line cops, more clearly define *good policing*, and help to see that we get it.

# Notes

## Prologue: Whatever Happened to *Dragnet*

1. Interview with William H. Parker by Donald McDonald, one of series of interviews on the "American Character," Center for the Study of Democratic Institutions, 1962.
2. William Julius Wilson, "Imagine Life Without a Future," *Los Angeles Times,* May 6, 1992.
3. See, for example, Arthur L. Kobler, "Police Homicide in a Democracy," *Journal of Social Issues,* 31 (Winter 1975a): 163–84, which reports that criminal prosecution resulted from only three of approximately 1,500 police shootings he studied; Philip Michael, Deputy Commissioner in Charge of Trials, New York City Police Department, *Recommendations in the Matter of Charges and Specifications Against Police Officer Thomas Shea and Police Officer Walter J. Scott,* New York City Police Department Case no. 47537 and no. 47521, August 30, 1974, which concerned the dismissal of a police officer who had been acquitted in a criminal trial emanating from the fatal shooting of a young boy; City of Miami, *Report of the Mayor's Blue-Ribbon Commission on Police Brutality* (mimeo) (Miami, FL, 1984), and United States Civil Rights Commission, *Confronting Racial Isolation in Miami* (Washington, DC: U.S. Government Printing Office, 1982), both of which report on the acquittals of officers who had been charged in fatal beatings under circumstances much like those of the King case; and United States Civil Rights Commission, *Who's Guarding the Guardians?* (Washington, DC: U.S. Government Printing Office, 1981), pp. 101–8, which explains the Commission's finding (4.2) that the "criminal law is a limited vehicle for preventing or deterring police misconduct. Nonetheless, vigorous prosecution of such cases by local prosecutors is essential."

## 1. The Beating of Rodney King

1. Mike Sager, "Damn! They Gonna Lynch Us," *Gentlemen's Quarterly,* October 1991. Sager offers a vivid, detailed description of the events preceding, during, and following the beating of Rodney King.
2. Further details are contained in Warren Christopher *et al., Report of the Independent Commission on the Los Angeles Police Department,* July 9, 1991 (Christopher Report), pp. 9–12.
3. *Ibid.,* "Foreword," pp. iii–v.
4. Seth Mydans, "Decades of Rage Created Crucible of Violence," *New York Times,* May 3, 1992.
5. "CRASH" is an acronym for Community Resources Against Street Hoodlums.
6. *Larez, et al.* v. *City of Los Angeles,* Ninth Circuit Nos. 89-55541, 89-55801, p. 13603, September 27, 1991.
7. Compare this to the arrest report in the King incident: "Def't. was MT'd for abrasions and contusions on his face, arms, legs and torso areas"; also to Sergeant Koon's official description of Rodney King's injuries: "Several facial cuts due to contact with asphalt. Of a minor nature. A split inner lip. Suspect oblivious to pain." Christopher Report, p. 9.
8. *Ibid.,* p. ii.
9. *Ibid.,* p. 4.
10. Officer Singer and her partner—who also is her husband—began the King pursuit when they saw King commit traffic violations. According to the Christopher Report, both she and her husband (who apparently did not confirm her interpretation of the beating) received written reprimands from the California Highway Patrol for "failing to report the excessive use of force in sufficient detail." Ibid., p. 13.
11. Mike Rothmiller and Ivan G. Goldman, *L.A. Secret Police: Inside the LAPD Spy Network* (New York: Pocket Books, 1992), p. 33.
12. The quotes from Reiner, Ripston, and Mack are from the *Los Angeles Times,* May 11, 1991.
13. Paul M. Walters, "A Formidable Task, Well Done," *Los Angeles Times,* March 11, 1991.
14. *New York Times,* March 8, 1991.
15. Egon Bittner, *The Functions of the Police in Modern Society* (Rockville, MD: National Institute of Mental Health, 1970), p. 46.
16. Christopher Report, pp. 98–99.
17. Gates expounded on the "LAPD mentality" in Daryl F. Gates, *Chief: My Life in the LAPD* (New York: Bantam Books, 1992), pp. 174–77.
18. Christopher Report, p. 14.
19. *Los Angeles Times,* March 8, 1991.
20. *Ibid.*
21. See, e.g., Michael Kramer, "Gates: The Buck Doesn't Stop Here," *Newsweek,* April 1, 1991, p. 25; Frederick Dannen, "Gates's Hell," *Vanity Fair,*

August 1991, pp. 102–8, 168–73; "Dubious Achievement Awards of 1981!," *Esquire,* January 1982; and "Dubious Achievement Awards of 1991!," *Esquire,* January 1992.

22. Gregory J. Boyle, "Defenseless, the Poor Are Also Voiceless," *Los Angeles Times,* March 11, 1991.

23. Christopher Report, p. xii.

24. ACLU-sponsored panel on "The Constitution and the Police," Los Angeles, June 1, 1991.

25. Carol Watson, "Complaints Meet a Wall of Silence," *Los Angeles Times,* March 10, 1991.

26. Gail Diane Cox, "Who Ya Gonna Call? Copbusters!" *Los Angeles Magazine,* April 1991.

27. Stephen Yagman, interview with James J. Fyfe, September 26, 1991.

28. Robert M. Fogelson, *Big City Police* (Cambridge: Harvard University Press, 1977), p. 247.

29. *Report of the National Advisory Commission on Civil Disorders* (New York: Bantam Books, 1968), p. 302.

30. Gerald Uelman, "Varieties of Public Policy: A Study of Police Policy Regarding the Use of Deadly Force in Los Angeles County," *Loyola of Los Angeles Law Review,* 6 (1973):1–55.

31. See James J. Fyfe, "The Split-Second Syndrome and Other Determinants of Police Violence," pp. 207–24 in Anne T. Campbell and John J. Gibbs, eds., *Violent Transactions* (Oxford: Basil Blackwell, 1986).

32. See, e.g., Dannen, "Gates's Hell," p. 168.

33. These dismissals are detailed in the court papers that are filed in *Delaney* v. *Houston,* Civil Action H-89-4228, United States District Court, Southern District of Texas, Houston Division; and *Gillum* v. *Houston,* Civil Action H-89-4228, United States District Court, Southern District of Texas, Houston Division.

34. Leslie Berger, "LAPD Disciplinary System to Undergo Major Restructuring," *Los Angeles Times,* June 4, 1992.

35. *Ibid.*

36. See Martin L. Schiesl, "Behind the Badge: The Police and Social Discontent in Los Angeles Since 1950," pp. 153–94 in Norman M. Klein and Martin L. Schiesl, eds., *20th Century Los Angeles* (Claremont, CA: Regina Books, 1990).

37. James Fyfe attended the trial and heard the remark.

## 2. Vigilante Justice

1. Mike Sager, "Damn! They Gonna Lynch Us," *Gentlemen's Quarterly,* October 1991.

2. Gunnar Myrdal, *An American Dilemma: The Negro Problem and Modern Democracy* (New York: Harper & Brothers, 1941). Much of the descrip-

tion of the role of Southern courts and police in this chapter is based on Myrdal.

3. Some of the history of private violence in this section draws upon Chapter Six of *The Politics of Protest: A Task Force Report Submitted to the National Commission on the Causes and Prevention of Violence,* Director, Jerome H. Skolnick (New York: Ballantine Books, 1969).

4. Jacobus ten Broek, Edward N. Barnhart, and Floyd W. Matson, *Prejudice, War and the Constitution* (Berkeley: University of California Press, 1954), pp. 13–14.

5. *Ibid.,* p. 16.

6. Christopher Report (see note 2 in Chapter 1), pp. 74–75.

7. Williston H. Lofton, "Northern Labor and the Negro During the Civil War," in Allen D. Grimshaw, ed., *Racial Violence in the United States* (Chicago: Aldine, 1969), pp. 41–42.

8. *Ibid.*

9. Allen W. Trelease, *White Terror: The Ku Klux Klan Conspiracy and Southern Reconstruction* (New York: Harper & Row, 1971), p. xxi.

10. C. Vann Woodward, *The Strange Career of Jim Crow* (New York: Galaxy, Oxford University Press, 1966), p. 23.

11. *Ibid.*

12. David M. Chalmers, *Hooded Americanism* (Chicago: Quadrangle, 1968), p. 20.

13. Quoted in *Ibid.,* pp. 20–21.

14. *United States Civil Rights Commission Report* (Washington D.C.: U.S. Government Printing Office, 1961), pp. 266–68.

15. Quoted in Chalmers, *Hooded Americanism,* p. 27.

16. Richard K. Tucker, *The Dragon and The Cross: The Rise and Fall of the Ku Klux Klan in Middle America* (Hamden, CT: Archon Books, 1991).

17. Chalmers, *Hooded Americanism,* p. 3.

18. Quoted in Woodward, *Strange Career of Jim Crow,* p. 8.

19. Leon P. Litwack, "America Is Reaping Two Centuries of Law Treating Blacks Lawlessly," *Los Angeles Times,* May 5, 1992.

20. See John Dollard, *Caste and Class in a Southern Town* (New Haven: Yale University Press, 1937).

21. Nicholas Lemann, *The Promised Land: The Great Black Migration and How It Changed America* (New York: Knopf, 1991), pp. 34–35.

22. Charles David Phillips, "Exploring Relations Among Forms of Social Control: The Lynching and Execution of Blacks in North Carolina, 1889–1918," *Law and Society Review,* 21 (1987):361, 362.

23. E. M. Beck, James L. Massey, and Stewart E. Tolnay, "The Gallows, the Mob, and the Vote: Lethal Sanctioning of Blacks in North Carolina and Georgia, 1882 to 1930," *Law and Society Review,* 23 (1989):317, 329.

24. St. Clair Drake and Horace Cayton, *Black Metropolis* (New York: Harcourt, Brace, 1945), p. 129.

25. *Loving* v. *Commonwealth of Virginia*, 388 U.S. 1 (1967).

26. "Legal and Social Impediments to Intermarriage," in Fowler V. Harper and Jerome H. Skolnick, *Problems of the Family: A Law Casebook* (Indianapolis: Bobbs-Merrill, 1962).

27. Myrdal, *American Dilemma*, p. 563.

28. Allison Davis, Burleigh B. Gardner, and Mary Gardner, *Deep South: A Social Anthropological Study of Caste and Class* (Chicago: University of Chicago Press, 1941), p. 503.

29. *Davis* v. *Mason County*, 927 F.2d, 1473, 1478–79 (1991).

30. Jonathan Rubinstein, *City Police* (New York: Farrar, Straus & Giroux, 1973), p. 267.

31. See Gerard Murphy, *With Special Care* (Washington, DC: Police Executive Research Forum, 1985).

32. This point is discussed in detail in James J. Fyfe, "The Split-Second Syndrome and Other Determinants of Police Violence," in Anne T. Campbell and John J. Gibbs, eds., *Situations of Aggression* (Oxford: Basil Blackwell, 1986).

33. Christopher Report, pp. 26–27.

34. Using some poetic license, the manufacturer of the Taser coined its name as an acronym for Tom Swift's Electronic Rifle.

35. This apparently was not done by LAPD in the King matter. Even before the department knew that King had been beaten as he was, Koon had reported shooting him twice with the Taser. Despite the presence of several officers to help subdue the apparently unarmed King, LAPD apparently had no objection to this use of the Taser as described in Koon's report.

36. "Sorting out the Causes and Consequences of a Disaster," *New York Times*," May 19, 1985; Jerome H. Skolnick, "Murphy's Law and Order in Philadelphia," *Los Angeles Times*, May 21, 1985.

37. *Tennessee* v. *Garner*, 471 U.S. 1 (1985).

38. Mario Merola with Mary Ann Giordano, *Big-City D.A.* (New York: Random House, 1988).

39. See, e.g., Federal Bureau of Investigation, *Uniform Crime Reports Supplement: Law Enforcement Officers Killed and Assaulted—1987, 1988* (Washington, DC: FBI).

40. Fyfe reviewed these cases in preparation for testimony as an expert on police practices in the *Larez* case and in *Heller* v. *Bushey*, 475 U.S. 796 (1986), an earlier case in which a suspected drunk driver (whose blood alcohol content subsequently was found to be one-tenth the level required for a showing of drunkenness) alleged that he had been unjustifiably choked by an LAPD officer.

41. *Los Angeles* v. *Lyons*, 461 U.S. 95, 103 S.Ct. 1660, 75 L.Ed.2d 675 (1983). See also, James J. Fyfe, "The Los Angeles Chokehold Controversy," *Criminal Law Bulletin*, 19 (January–February 1983):61.

## 3. The Third Degree

1. William Morris and Mary Morris, *The Morris Dictionary of Word and Phrase Origins* (New York: Harper, 1988).
2. Richard Sylvester, "A History of the 'Sweat Box' and the 'Third Degree'," in *The Blue and the Brass: American Policing 1890–1910*, (Gaithersburg, MD.: IACP Press, 1976), pp. 71–72.
3. Quotes are from Ernest Jerome Hopkins, *Our Lawless Police: A Study of the Unlawful Enforcement of the Law* (New York: Viking, 1931; reprint, De Capo, 1972), pp. 191–92.
4. Emanual H. Lavine, *The Third Degree: A Detailed and Appalling Exposé of Police Brutality* (New York, NY: Vanguard Press, 1930).
5. *Ibid.*
6. Gene E. Carte and Elaine H. Carte, *Police Reform in the United States: The Era of August Vollmer, 1905–1932* (Berkeley: University of California Press, 1975), p. 66.
7. *Report on Lawlessness in Law-Enforcement*, National Commission on Law Observance and Enforcement, George W. Wickersham, Chairman (Washington, DC: U.S. Government Printing Office, 1931).
8. Hopkins, *Our Lawless Police*, p. 180.
9. David J. Rothman, *Conscience and Convenience: The Asylum and Its Alternatives in Progressive America* (Boston: Little, Brown, 1980), p. 49.
10. *People* v. *Mummiani*, 258 N.Y. 304 (1932).
11. *Brown* v. *Mississippi*, 207 U.S. 278 (1936).
12. See Edwin R. Keedy, "The Third Degree and Legal Interrogation of Suspects," *University of Pennsylvania Law Review* (1937):761.
13. *Ibid.*, at 284.
14. Yale Kamisar, "What Is an 'Involuntary' Confession? Some Comments on Inbau and Reid's Criminal Interrogation and Confessions," *Rutgers Law Review*, 17 (1963):728.
15. Yale Kamisar, "Equal Justice in the Gatehouses and Mansions of American Criminal Procedure," *Police Interrogation and Confessions: Essays in Law and Policy* (Ann Arbor: University of Michigan Press, 1980).
16. 372 U.S. 335 (1963).
17. *Crooker* v. *California*, 367 U.S. 433 (1958).
18. *Los Angeles Bar Bulletin*, 40 (1965):603, cited in *Miranda*, n.3.
19. 338 U.S. 49 (1949).
20. 430 U.S. 387 (1977).
21. *Kirby* v. *Illinois*, 406 U.S. 682 (1972).
22. See Richard A. Leo, "From Coercion to Deception: The Changing Nature of Police Interrogation in America," *Crime, Law and Social Change: An International Journal*, 18 (September, 1992):35–59.
23. *Florida* v. *Cayward*, 550 So.2d 971 (1989).
24. Richard Ofshe, "The Internalized Coerced Confession," lecture,

Guggenheim Crime Seminar, Center for the Study of Law and Society, Berkeley, California, April 13, 1992.

25. See Jerome H. Skolnick, "Deception by Police," *Criminal Justice Ethics,* Summer-Fall 1982, pp. 40–54; Jerome H. Skolnick and Richard Leo, "The Ethics of Deceptive Interrogation, *Criminal Justice Ethics,* Winter/Spring 1992, pp. 3–12.

26. C. Ronald Huff *et al.,* "Guilty Until Proven Innocent: Wrongful Conviction and Public Policy," *Crime and Delinquency,* 32 (1986):518–544.

27. Hugo Adam Bedau and Michael L. Radelet, "Miscarriages of Justice in Potentially Capital Cases," *Stanford Law Review,* 40 (1987):21–179.

28. *New York* v. *Quarles,* 467 U.S. 649 (1984).

29. Wayne R. LaFave and Jerold H. Israel, *Criminal Procedure,* 2d ed. (St. Paul: West, 1992), p. 298.

30. 475 U.S. 412 (1986).

31. 111 S.Ct. 1246 (1991).

## 4. Public Order Policing

1. Allen Silver, "The Demand for Order in Civil Society: A Review of Some Themes in the History of Urban Crime, Police, and Riot," in David Bordua, ed., *The Police: Six Sociological Essays* (New York: John Wiley, 1967), pp. 1–24.

2. John J. Tobias, *Crime and Industrial Society in the 19th Century* (New York: Schocken Books, 1967), p. 37.

3. See, for the history of the police, Jerome H. Skolnick, "Changing Conceptions of the Police," in *The Great Ideas Today* (Chicago: Encyclopaedia Britannica, 1972).

4. Asa Briggs, *The Making of Modern England, 1784–1867* (New York: Harper Torchbooks, 1959), p. 207.

5. Samuel Bamford, *Passages in the Life of a Radical,* quoted in Briggs, *Making of Modern England.*

6. Elie Halevey, *The Liberal Awakening, 1815–1830* (New York: Barnes & Noble, 1961), p. 19.

7. Charles Reith, *The Police Idea: Its History and Evolution in England in the Eighteenth Century and After* (London: Oxford University Press, 1938), pp. 203–4.

8. Captain W. L. Melville Lee, *A History of the Police in England in the Eighteenth Century and After* (London: Methuen, 1905), pp. 204–5.

9. Douglas Hay, "Property, Authority and The Criminal Law," in Douglas Hay *et al, Albion's Fatal Tree: Crime and Society in Eighteenth Century England* (London: Harmondsworth, 1975), p. 25.

10. Reith, *Police Idea,* p. 236.

11. E. P. Thompson, *The Making of the English Working Class* (New York: Vintage Books, 1966), p. 82.

12. Quoted in Charles Reith, *A New Study of Police History* (London: Oliver & Boyd, 1956), p. 140.

13. Stanley H. Palmer, *Police and Protest in England and Ireland: 1780–1850* (Cambridge: Cambridge University Press, 1988), p. 313.

14. Lee, *History,* p. 327.

15. Roger Lane, *Policing the City: Boston, 1822–1855* (Cambridge: Harvard University Press, 1967).

16. Michael Hindus, "A City of Mobocrats and Tyrants: Mob Violence in Boston, 1747–1868," *Issues in Criminology,* Summer 1971.

17. James Richardson, *The New York Police: Colonial Times to 1901* (New York: Oxford University Press, 1970), pp. 4–5.

18. James M. McPherson, *Battle Cry of Freedom: The Civil War Era.* (New York: Oxford University Press, 1988, p. 609.

19. Charles Loring Brace, *The Dangerous Classes of New York and Twenty Years' Work Among Them* (New York: Wynkoop & Hallenbeck, 1872), p. 26.

20. Richardson, *New York Police,* p. 277.

21. Civil Disorder Report (see note 28, Chapter 1), p. 218.

22. *Ibid.*

23. Ray Marshall, *The Negro and Organized Labor* (New York: Wiley, 1965), pp. 21–23.

24. Anthony Platt, ed., *The Politics of Riot Commissions, 1917–1970: A Collection of Official Reports and Critical Essays* (New York: Collier Books, 1971), p. 213.

25. *Ibid.,* p. 199.

26. *Ibid.,* p. 253.

27. Civil Disorder Report.

28. *Ibid.,* pp. 143–44.

29. John McCone, *Violence in the City: An End or a Beginning?* A Report by the Governor's Commission on the Los Angeles Riots, December 2, 1965, p. 1 (McCone Commission Report).

30. Robert M. Fogelson, *Violence as Protest: A Study of Riots and Ghettos* (Garden City: Doubleday, 1971), pp. 27–51.

31. McCone Commission Report, p. 27.

32. Civil Disorder Report, p. 85.

33. Jerome H. Skolnick and David Bayley, *The New Blue Line: Police Innovation in Six American Cities* (New York: Free Press, 1986), p. 50.

34. See Jerome H. Skolnick's ethnographic description of "Eastville" in *Justice Without Trial: Law Enforcement in Democratic Society* (New York: Wiley, 1975). Eastville is Newark, New Jersey.

35. "The Negro in Harlem," unpublished report prepared by the Mayor's Commission on Conditions in Harlem, New York, 1935.

36. Civil Disorder Report, p. 206.

37. Daniel Walker, *Rights in Conflict: The Violent Confrontation of Demonstra-*

*tors and Police in the Parks and Streets of Chicago During the Week of the Democratic National Convention of 1968,* a report to the National Commission on the Causes and Prevention of Violence (New York: Bantam Books, 1968), p. xv.

38. *Ibid.,* p. 5.
39. This officer, Frank Giuccari, was crippled on May 1, 1968. Despite extensive daily coverage of events at Columbia, the *New York Times* mentioned his injury only in a rear-pages story four weeks later. See "Leary Censures Critics of Police," *New York Times,* May 27, 1968, p. 37.
40. "Columbia and the New Left," *The Public Interest,* Fall 1968, p. 81.
41. Southern California ACLU, *Day of Protest, Night of Violence* (Los Angeles: Sawyer Press, 1967). Accounts of the 1960s riots rely on Jerome H. Skolnick, *The Politics of Protest* (New York: Simon and Schuster, 1969).
42. *New York Times,* October 28, 1968.
43. Robert Reiner, *The Politics of the Police* (Sussex, U.K.: Wheatshaft Books, 1986), p. 54.
44. Tony Jefferson, *The Case Against Paramilitary Policing* (Philadelphia: Milton Keynes, 1990), p. 1.
45. *Ibid.,* pp. 129–44.
46. Rodney Stark, *Police Riots: Collective Violence and Law Enforcement* (Belmont, CA: Wadsworth, 1972), p. 55.
47. Quotes are from internal report of Chief Johnston to the Commissioner, August 23, 1988.
48. *Los Angeles Times,* May 6, 1992.
49. *Ibid.,* May 8, 1992.
50. *Ibid.*
51. *Ibid.,* May 9, 1992.
52. *Ibid.,* May 7, 1992.

## 5. The Culture of the Police

1. Dennis Hevesi, "After Prison, Ex-Officer's Advice on Police Violence: 'Don't Do It!'" *New York Times,* July 12, 1991, p. A6.
2. George Will, *New York Review of Books,* June 10, 1991.
3. Joseph Wambaugh, *The Choirboys* (New York: Dell, 1975), p. 63.
4. Robert Daley, *Prince of the City: The True Story of a Cop Who Knew Too Much* (Boston: Houghton-Mifflin, 1978).
5. Whitman Knapp *et al., Report of the New York City Commission to Investigate Allegations of Police Corruption and the City's Anti-Corruption Procedures* (New York: George Braziller, 1973), p. 67.
6. James F. Ahern, *Police in Trouble* (New York: Hawthorne Books, 1972).
7. Emile Durkheim, *Moral Education: A Study in the Theory and Application of the Sociology of Education* (New York: Free Press, 1961), p. 80.

8. Jerome H. Skolnick, *Justice Without Trial: Law Enforcement in Democratic Society* (New York: Wiley, 1966, 1975).

9. Robert Reiner, *The Politics of the Police* (Sussex, U.K.: Wheatsheaf Books, 1986), p. 99.

10. Mark Baker, *Cops: Their Lives in Their Own Words* (New York: Fawcett, 1985), p. 211.

11. See David H. Bayley and Harold Mendelsohn, *Minorities and the Police* (New York: MacMillan, 1968); Virginia B. Ermer, "Recruitment of Female Police Officers in New York City," *Journal of Criminal Justice,* 6 (Fall 1978):233–46; President's Commission on Law Enforcement and Administration of Justice, *Field Surveys, III; Studies in Crime and Law Enforcement in Major Metropolitan Areas* (Washington, DC: U.S. Government Printing Office, 1967), 2:18.

12. See, for example, Bill Miller, "Police Say Pay Too Low," *Philadelphia Inquirer,* May 13, 1990, p. B-1; Frederick M. Muir, "Council OKs LAPD Pay Hike of 17% Over 4 Years," *Los Angeles Times,* March 30, 1989, Part 2, p. 4.

13. James J. Fyfe and Patrick V. Murphy, "D.C. Police: Trim the Fat (cont'd.)," *Washington Post,* December 24, 1990, p. A-15.

14. John Van Maanen, "Observations on the Making of Policemen," pp. 292–308 in Peter K. Manning and John Van Maanen, eds., *Policing: A View from the Street* (Santa Monica, CA: Goodyear Publishing, 1978).

15. Reiner, *Politics of Police,* p. 88.

16. Colin MacInnes, *Mr. Love and Justice* (London: New English Library, 1962), p. 74.

17. See, for example, H. J. Caudill, "Manslaughter in a Coal Mine," *The Nation,* 224 (April 23, 1977): 492–97, and C. Gersuny, *Work Hazards and Industrial Conflict* (Hanover, NH: University Press of New England, 1981).

18. Egon Bittner, *The Functions of the Police in Modern Society* (Cambridge, MA: Oelgeschlager, Gunn & Hain, 1970), p. 40.

19. Connie Fletcher, *What Cops Know: Cops Talk About What They Do, How They Do It, and What It Does to Them* (New York: Villard, 1991), p. 47.

20. Jonathan Rubinstein, *City Police* (New York: Farrar, Straus & Giroux, 1973), p. 271.

21. William Ker Muir, Jr., *Police: Streetcorner Politicians* (Chicago: University of Chicago Press, 1977), pp. 101–26.

22. William Ker Muir, Jr., "Power Attracts Violence," *Annals of the American Academy of Political and Social Science,* 452 (November 1980):48.

23. Baker, *Cops,* pp. 6–7.

24. 392 U.S. 1, 88 S.Ct. 1868, 20 L.Ed.2d. 889 (1968).

25. John Van Maanen, "The Asshole," pp. 221–37 in Manning and Van Maanen, *Policing.*

26. On the day that his case was argued before the Supreme Court, Lawson lec-

tured at Fyfe's class at American University, and subsequently he lectured at Skolnick's law seminars at U.C. Berkeley, explaining his motives, his life history, and his feelings about the law.

27. 554 So 2d 1153, 1154–55 (1989).

28. Paul Chevigny, *Police Power: Police Abuses in New York City* (New York: Vintage, 1969).

29. *Ibid.,* p. 136.

30. Van Maanen, "Asshole."

31. Albert J. Reiss, Jr., "Police Brutality: Answers to Key Questions," *Trans-Action,* July–August, 1968, p. 12.

32. Rodney Stark, *Police Riots* (Belmont, CA: Wadsworth, 1972), p. 138.

33. Centers for Disease Control, "Homicide Among Young Black Males: United States, 1978–1987," *Morbidity and Mortality Weekly Report,* vol. 39 (December 7, 1990); Jewell Taylor Gibbs, *Young, Black and Male in America: An Endangered Species* (Dover, MA: Auburn House, 1988), pp. 260–65.

34. Michael B. Katz, *The Undeserving Poor: From the War on Poverty to the War on Welfare* (New York: Pantheon, 1989), p. 8.

35. See William Julius Wilson, *The Truly Disadvantaged: The Inner City, the Underclass, and Public Policy* (Chicago: University of Chicago Press, 1987).

36. L. J. D. Wacquant and William J. Wilson, "The Cost of Racial and Class Exclusion in the Inner City," *Annals of the American Academy of Political and Social Science,* 1989, p. 501.

37. Robert Kuttner, "Notes From Underground: Clashing Theories About the 'Underclass'," *Dissent,* Spring 1991, p. 12.

38. Jennifer Hochschild, "The Politics of the Estranged Poor," *Ethics* 101 (April 1991):569, from *Washington Post,* January 1, 1989.

39. Martin Sanchez Jankowski, *Islands in the Street: Gangs and Urban American Society* (Berkeley: University of California Press, 1991).

40. Terry Williams, *The Cocaine Kids: The Inside Story of a Teenage Drug Ring* (New York: Addison-Wesley, 1989).

41. Christopher Report, p. 95.

42. *Ibid.,* p. 98.

43. Joe Domanick, "Why No One Can Control the LAPD," *LA Weekly,* February 16–22, 1990, p. 16.

44. The facts of the Serpico shooting are summarized from Peter Maas, *Serpico* (New York: Viking Press, 1973), and from the NYPD investigation of the incident. See James J. Fyfe, "Shots Fired: An Analysis of New York City Police Firearms Discharges," doctoral dissertation, State University of New York at Albany, 1978, pp. 337–39.

45. Fyfe, "Shots Fired."

46. Patrick V. Murphy and Thomas Plate, *Commissioner: A View from the Top of American Law Enforcement* (New York: Simon & Schuster, 1977), p. 254.

47. Albert J. Reiss, Jr., interview with James J. Fyfe, June 6, 1992.

48. Daley, *Prince of the City,* pp. 26–27.

## 6. Cops as Soldiers

1. Attorney General Richard Thornburgh, keynote address to the Attorney General's Summit on "Law Enforcement Responses to Violent Crime: Public Safety in the Nineties," March 4, 1991.
2. *New York Times,* April 25, 1991.
3. Patrick V. Murphy and Thomas Plate, *Commissioner: A View from the Top of American Law Enforcement* (New York: Simon & Schuster, 1977), p. 270.
4. John E. Angell, "Toward an Alternative to the Classic Police Organizational Arrangements: A Democratic Model," *Criminology,* 9 (1971):185–206.
5. During the early moments of the riots that followed the Rodney King verdict, Chief Gates was at a rally opposing the referendum that soon thereafter made the LAPD's chief more accountable to civilian authority. Thus, ironically, at the very moment that it most needed it, this most military of all large American police departments was without central leadership.
6. James H. Auten, "The Paramilitary Model of Police and Police Professionalism," *Police Studies,* 4 (Summer 1981):67–78.
7. Joseph Goldstein, "Police Discretion Not to Invoke the Criminal Process: Low Visibility Decisions in the Administration of Justice," *Yale Law Journal,* 69 (March 1960):543–94.
8. It is no accident that boards of education have experienced great difficulties while trying to function in hierarchical military fashion. Like police officers, schoolteachers are government line workers who exercise broad discretion that is not easily accommodated at the bottom of pyramidal organizational charts. Hard and fast rules do little to further effective teaching.
9. James Q. Wilson, *Varieties of Police Behavior* (Cambridge, MA: Harvard University Press, 1968), p. 181.
10. It would be hard to imagine a more rule-bound police department than the New York Police Department prior to the great reforms it experienced as a result of the corruption scandals of the early 1970s. Before that time, apparently to prevent officers from developing personal relationships while on duty, NYPD rules prohibited officers from engaging in "unnecessary conversation" with citizens. This rule presumably precluded virtually any officer-initiated contact with anybody who was not a suspect or traffic violator, but it was routinely violated and conflicted with the department's expectation that officers would become familiar with the people on their beats. Officers also were prohibited from issuing parking tickets without first checking by telephone or police radio to determine whether the cars involved had been reported stolen. This provision was generally assumed to be the department's response to a citizen's complaint that, instead of recovering his or her car, some ticket-happy officer had tagged it where it had been parked illegally by the thief. Except for a brief "job action" that paralyzed the department's radio communications and the Lost Property Unit's telephone lines, kept officers throughout the city tied up on phones, and effectively suspended parking en-

forcement, this provision also was routinely violated. Other rules prohibited officers from using patrol cars to transport sick or injured people to hospitals or to push disabled autos off traffic-snarled highways or bridges; required patrol car partners to wear hats at all times and to eat at different times (while they also were expected to respond together to any calls that occurred during either officer's meal period); and to leave their cars hourly in order to check in with their stations via telephone. It is fair to say that all of these rules were violated regularly and that some literally were never obeyed.

11. Peter K. Manning, *Police Work: The Social Organization of Policing* (Cambridge, MA: MIT Press, 1977), p. 165.

12. Elizabeth Reuss-Ianni quotes an anonymous memo familiar to most members of the NYPD:

> The police commissioner issued the following directive to the chief of [department]: "Tomorrow evening at approximately 2000 hours, Halley's Comet will be visible in this area, an event which occurs only once every 75 years. Have the men assemble in front of the station house in uniform and I will explain this rare phenomenon to them. In case of rain we will not be able to see anything, so assemble the men in the sitting room and I will show them films of it."
>
> The chief of operations directed the area commander: "By order of the Police Commissioner: Tomorrow at 2000 hours Halley's Comet will appear above the station house. If it rains, fall the men out in uniform and then march to the sitting room where the rare phenomenon will take place, something which occurs only once every 75 years."
>
> The area commander ordered the precinct commanding officer: "By order of the Police Commissioner in uniform at 2000 hours tomorrow evening the phenomenal Halley's Comet will appear in the sitting room. In case of rain in front of the station house, the Police Commissioner will give another order, something which occurs only once every 75 years."
>
> The precinct commanding officer issued the following order to the administrative lieutenant: "Tomorrow at 2000 hours, the Police Commissioner will appear in front of the station house with Halley's Comet, something which happens every 75 years. If it rains, the Police Commissioner will order the Comet into the sitting room."
>
> The administrative lieutenant made the following announcement at roll call: "When it rains tomorrow at 2000 hours, the phenomenal 75 year old Chief Halley, accompanied by the Police Commissioner will drive his Comet through the station house in uniform."
>
> An hour later one of the cops asked the sergeant for clarification of the lieutenant's announcement at roll call and the sergeant said: "Chief Halley, the new Area Commander, is going to test a new [patrol car] here tomorrow, if it doesn't rain."
>
> A short time later, a [civilian police administrative aide] asked the cop if he knew what was going to happen tomorrow. The cop said: "Forget it, you civilians can't get anything straight anyway."

Elizabeth Reuss-Ianni, *Two Cultures of Policing: Street Cops and Management Cops* (New Brunswick, NJ: Transaction Books, 1983).

13. David Simon, *Homicide* (Boston: Houghton Mifflin, 1988), p. 498.

14. Some collective police misconduct has resulted from officers' adherence to improper orders from above rather than from loss of supervisory control over officers who have acted out violently. Among well-known incidents of officially authorized brutality, we would include the early 1960s beatings of civil rights marchers in Selma, Birmingham, and other Southern cities; the Chicago police response to demonstrators and provocateurs at the 1968 Democratic National Convention (which also included gross supervisory failure); the 1971 New York State Police assault on Attica prison; and the Los Angeles Police Department's employment of nunchakus to arrest nonviolent anti-abortion demonstrators in 1990.

15. Larry Tifft, "Control Systems, Social Bases of Power and Power Exercises in Police Organizations," *Journal of Police Science and Administration,* 3 (1975):155–82.

16. Reuss-Ianni, *Two Cultures of Policing*, p. 64.

17. Jonathan Rubinstein, *City Police* (New York: Farrar, Straus & Giroux, 1973), p. 43.

18. See Reuss-Ianni, *Two Cultures of Policing*.

19. Herman Goldstein, "Improving Policing: A Problem-Oriented Approach," *Crime and Delinquency,* 25 (1979):236–38.

20. The largest single purchase included in these figures was an $800 buy from a small ring that included a New York City police detective. According to the commission:

> Following this exceptional purchase, the next largest buy cost $85. Thereafter, with very few exceptions, the usual operation was clearly limited to purchasing a bag or two from street addicts, with rarely more than $30 spent on any one purchase of heroin.

New York State Commission of Investigation, *Narcotics Law Enforcement in New York City* (New York, 1972), pp. 114–16. These figures do not include the activities of NYPD's elite Special Investigation Unit, many of whose members subsequently were implicated in the "French Connection/Prince of the City" corruption scandals. See Robert F. Daley, *Prince of the City* (Boston: Houghton-Mifflin, 1978).

21. As noted in Chapter 5, for example, Fyfe reported of NYPD narcotics enforcement during the first four months of 1971:

- A detective attempting to make a buy was robbed after being beaten unconscious with a "blunt object."
- A detective staked out on a narcotics "drop" shot and killed a man who attacked him with a gun.
- A detective was attacked and beaten by three males from whom he made a $12 heroin buy.
- An undercover patrolman [Frank Serpico] was shot and wounded attempting to make a heroin sale arrest.

- A detective shot and wounded the drug sale suspect who had shot and wounded Ptl. Serpico several hours earlier.
- A patrolman making a heroin sale arrest was shot at twice by the suspect; during a struggle, the suspect's gun accidentally discharged, wounding the suspect in the leg.
- A patrolman shot and wounded one of three suspected narcotics dealers after they had attacked him with a length of two-by-four.
- A patrolman in a narcotics investigation shot and wounded a male (armed with a starter pistol) who had attempted to rob him.
- A detective was shot and wounded while attempting to execute a "No-Knock" arrest warrant.

James J. Fyfe, "Shots Fired: An Analysis of New York City Police Firearms Discharge," PhD. dissertation, State University of New York at Albany (Ann Arbor, MI: University Microfilms, 1978), pp. 337–38.

22. New York State Commission, *Narcotics Enforcement,* p. 115. Neither has the obvious alternative to this particular numbers game proved effective. Despite the impressive and ever increasing amounts of drugs taken out of the market by law enforcement officers' seizures, recent data suggest that drug use among addicts and other heavy users—who consume far larger market shares than "casual users"—is increasing. See Jerome H. Skolnick, "A Critical Look at the National Drug Control Strategy," *Yale Law and Policy Review,* 8, (1990):75–116.

23. Manning, *Police Work,* p. 99.

24. Rubinstein, *City Police,* p. 44.

25. Bayley and Garofalo report that "police would seem to be reliable observers of qualitative differences in the street performance of other officers. They discriminate fairly accurately among colleagues on the basis of what they do." Some of the differences reported by Bayley and Garofalo presumably would be visible in statistical reports (e.g., ESOs "handled more jobs per shift") but others (e.g., "willingness to take charge," "versatility in tactical behaviors," reluctance "to wash their hands of matters by simply leaving or saying there was nothing the police could do") would not be readily apparent to those not observing the officers at first hand. See David H. Bayley and James Garofalo "The Management of Violence by Police Patrol Officers," *Criminology,* 27 (February 1989):1–25.

26. See Wilbur R. Miller, *Cops and Bobbies: Police Authority in London and New York City, 1830–1870* (Chicago: University of Chicago Press, 1977).

27. See, e.g., Tony Jefferson, *The Case Against Paramilitary Policing* (Buckingham, U.K.: Open University Press, 1990).

28. See, for example, Robert M. Fogelson, *Big-City Police* (Cambridge, MA: Harvard University Press, 1977), pp. 13–39, for accounts of nineteenth-century politicians' use of police to subvert elections; Richard Hofstadter and Michael Wallace, eds., *American Violence: A Documentary History* (New York: Vintage Books, 1971), for accounts of antiradical violence by police in

New York's Tompkins Square Park in 1874; antilabor violence at the Ford Motor Company plant in Dearborn, Michigan, in 1937; and police violence at the 1968 Chicago Democratic National Convention.

29. Citizens' Police Committee, *Chicago Police Problems* (Montclair NJ: Patterson Smith, 1969, reprint of 1931 original), p. 8.

30. Amid a host of minor embarrassments, two major scandals affected the Bureau. In 1921, a Senate hearing detailed the Bureau's participation in the notorious "Palmer Raids" of 1920. During these wholesale roundups, thousands of alleged radicals and subversives were summarily taken into custody with many (including U.S. natives) deported to Russia on grounds that they were dangerous aliens. In 1923 it came to light that the Bureau had attempted to silence its most famous critic, Senator Burton K. Wheeler of Montana, by spying on him from bushes outside his home, by ransacking his Senate office in a fruitless fishing expedition for damaging documents, and by trying to entrap him into compromising positions. See, generally, Richard G. Powers's excellent biography, *Secrecy and Power: The Life of J. Edgar Hoover* (New York: Free Press, 1986).

31. See, e.g., Dorothy Guyot, *Policing as Though People Matter* (Philadelphia: Temple University Press, 1991), pp. 119–33.

32. John M. Hagedorn, *People and Folks: Gangs, Crime and the Underclass in a Rustbelt City* (Chicago: Lakeview Press, 1988).

33. Richard B. Freeman and Harry J. Holzer, ed., *The Black Youth Unemployment Crisis* (Chicago: University of Chicago Press, 1986), p. 8.

34. Joseph B. Treaster, "Echoes of Prohibition: 20 Years of War on Drugs and No Victory Yet," *New York Times,* June 14, 1992.

## 7. Beyond Accountability

1. *Milwaukee Journal,* August 29, 1991, quoted in Milwaukee Mayor's Citizen Commission on Police–Community Relations, "Report to Mayor John O. Norquist and the Board of Police and Fire Commissioners," October 15, 1991, p. 9.

2. Leonard Fuld, *Police Administration: A Critical Study of Police Organizations in the United States and Abroad* (Montclair, NJ: Patterson Smith, 1971, reprinted from 1909 ed.), p. 40.

3. Milwaukee Mayor's Commission, p. 9.

4. See "LA Breaks with Precedent," *Law Enforcement News,* April 30, 1992, pp. 1, 7.

5. John Van Maanen, "The Asshole," pp. 221–38 in Peter K. Manning and John Van Maanen, eds., *Policing: A View from the Street* (Santa Monica, CA: Goodyear Publishing, 1978), p. 223.

6. See Richard R. Bennett and Theodore Greenstein, "The Police Personality: A Test of the Predispositional Model," *Journal of Police Science and Administration,* 3 (1975):439–45; Herman Goldstein, *Policing a Free Society* (Cam-

bridge, MA: Ballinger, 1978), pp. 258–81; Jerome Skolnick, *Justice Without Trial* (New York: John Wiley, 1966); and John Van Maanen, "Observations on the Making of Policemen," *Human Organization,* 32 (1973):407–18.

7. In 1981 the LAPD settled discrimination suits brought by private parties and by the U.S. Department of Justice. During the nine years that followed, the representation of females among LAPD officers increased from 2.6 to 12.6 percent. During this same period, minority officers increased from 18.6 to 37.1 percent of the department. Christopher Report (Chapter 1, note 2 above), p. 71.

8. *Ibid.,* p. 84.

9. George T. Felkenes, *The Impact of Fanchon Blake v. City of Los Angeles,* Report funded by the John Randolph Haynes and Dora Haynes Foundation (Claremont, CA: Claremont Graduate School, 1990).

10. George T. Felkenes, "Affirmative Action in the Los Angeles Police Department," *Criminal Justice Research Bulletin,* 6., no. 4 (Huntsville, TX: Sam Houston State University, 1991):8.

11. Albert J. Reiss, Jr., *The Police and the Public* (New Haven: Yale University Press, 1971).

12. Ralph Cipriano and Tom Infield, "It Was a Long and Colorful Career," *Philadelphia Inquirer,* July 17, 1991, pp. 1A, 14A.

13. Louis M. Thrasher, Charles D. Tiefer, Martha Fleetwood, and Stan Lechner, "Report of Investigation of Misconduct of Philadelphia Police Force and Recommendation," U.S. Department of Justice, Civil Rights Division, internal memorandum to Assistant Attorney General Drew S. Days, III, April 30, 1979, p. 5.

14. Interestingly, the LAPD's shootings also are investigated by homicide detectives rather than by Internal Affairs personnel.

15. Thrasher *et al.,* "Report," p. 9.

16. U.S. Civil Rights Commission, *Hearings in Philadelphia,* April 16–17, 1979 (Washington, DC: Government Printing Office, 1979), pp. 215–18.

17. This trend was interrupted by a slight dip in the number of shootings while the PPD was under injunctive order to reduce unnecessary use of force in connection with a federal civil rights case, *Rizzo v. Goode,* 423 U.S. 362 (1976). When the injunction was quashed, the upward trend of shootings continued as before.

18. Thrasher *et al.,* "Report," pp. 42–47.

19. 18 Pa. Cons. Stat. Ann., sec. 508 (1973).

20. James J. Fyfe, "Philadelphia Police Shootings, 1975–78: A System Model Analysis," Report for the Civil Rights Division, U.S. Department of Justice, March 1980.

21. James J. Fyfe, "Police Use of Deadly Force: Research and Reform," *Justice Quarterly,* 5 (1988):161–206, esp. 181–184.

22. Rizzo, running as a Republican, narrowly lost the 1988 mayoral election and was in the midst of the 1992 campaign when he died of a sudden heart attack in his campaign office.

23. Gerald Uelman, "Varieties of Public Policy: A Study of Police Policy Regarding the Use of Deadly Force in Los Angeles County," *Loyola of Los Angeles Law Review,* 6 (1973):1–65.

24. Wickersham Commission, *Report on Police* (Washington, DC: U.S. Government Printing Office, 1931), pp. 50–51.

25. August Vollmer, letter dated June 3, 1933, to Mr. Guy E. Marion, cited in Gene E. Carte and Elaine H. Carte, *Police Reform in the United States: The Era of August Vollmer, 1905–1932* (Berkeley: University of California Press, 1975), p. 61.

26. The Milwaukee Mayor's Citizen Commission on Police–Community Relations was convened after it was found that police responding to the scene of a 2 A.M. dispute call had left a bleeding, naked, fourteen-year-old boy with Jeffrey Dahmer, who claimed that he and the boy had been involved in a homosexual lover's quarrel. Shortly after the police left, according to Dahmer's subsequent confession, the boy became one of the seventeen young men Dahmer had murdered. See the Commission's "Report" (note 1 above).

27. The 1950 figures are reported in United States Bureau of the Census, *Census of Population: 1950,* Volume II, *Characteristics of the Population,* Part 5, "California" (Washington, DC: United States General Printing Office, 1952), pp. 5–51, Table 10. The 1990 figures are reported in the Christopher Report, p. viii.

28. Milwaukee Mayor's Commission Report, p. 4.

29. Parker was appointed Chief in 1950 and died in office in 1966; Gates held the post from March 1978 until July 1992.

30. Frank S. Donner, *Protectors of Privilege* (Berkeley: University of California Press, 1990), p. 289.

31. Candidates for LAPD chief are numerically rated on five competitive standards. In order to be eligible for selection, outside candidates must achieve the top score in each of the five, and may still be passed over. See. e.g., Daryl F. Gates, *Chief: My Life in the LAPD* (New York: Bantam Books, 1992), pp. 175–77.

32. Wickersham Commission, *Report,* pp. 20–21, 43.

33. See, generally, the Christopher and Milwaukee Mayor's Commission reports.

34. See, for example, John L. Mitchell, "$11.3 Million Paid in 1990 to Resolve Police Abuse Cases," *Los Angeles Times,* March 29, 1991, p. A-3; Frederick M. Muir, "Council Votes to Pay $7 Million in Officer Misconduct Cases: Included Is $5.5 Million to a Man Paralyzed After a Shooting and $1.5 Million to the Family of a Man Who Died After Being Subdued with a Chokehold," *Los Angeles Times,* November 7, 1991, p. B-3. According to Muir, these awards raised the total cost of settling verdicts and settlements against the LAPD during 1991 to more than $13 million. These figures do not include the staff costs of defending these cases. Nor do they include the cost of paying plaintiffs' attorneys' fees, which, in federal civil rights litigation,

must generally be borne by losing defendants. These fees sometimes are far greater than the damages awarded to plaintiffs.

35. *Bell* v. *City of Milwaukee,* 746 F.2d 1205 (7th Cir. 1984).
36. *Ibid.,* pp. 465–66.
37. Personal communication with James J. Fyfe, March 27, 1991.
38. Wisconsin State Committee of the U.S. Commission on Civil Rights, *Police Isolation and Community Needs* (Washington, DC: U.S. Government Printing Office, 1972), pp. 114–15.
39. David Freed, "Citizens Terrorized as Police Look On," *Los Angeles Times,* September 25, 1988, pp. 1, 3–5.
40. *Ibid.,* p. 1.
41. *Gomez* v. *Gates,* U.S. District Court, Central District of California, No. 90-0856-RB (Sx).
42. *Ibid.*
43. Lieutenant Charles Higbie, Los Angeles Police Department, Robbery-Homicide Division, "Report to Daryl F. Gates on the Shooting of John Henry Crumpton and Jane Elizabeth Berry," December 2, 1982, p. 7 (Higbie Report).
44. *Berry* v. *Gates,* Civ. No. 89-7381, U.S.D.C., Central District of California, Defendants' Answers to Interrogatories, p. 36.
45. *Ibid.* These papers give no specific indication that Berry was wearing a mask at this robbery or, if so, how witnesses were able to identify her as a Caucasian.
46. *Ibid.,* Answers to Interrogatories, p. 29.
47. Higbie Report, p. 5.
48. Higbie Report, p. 7.
49. Higbie Report, p. 3.
50. Fyfe testified as an expert in police practices in *Berry* v. *Gates.* At the time she was shot, Berry was pregnant with Crumpton's child, who was born unmarked several months after the shooting. A suit filed on behalf of this young man alleged that he was deprived of familial relations because SIS had unconstitutionally shot his father. This suit was summarily dismissed on grounds that, under *Roe* v. *Wade,* "a fetus is not a person . . . on whose behalf an action can be brought." In November 1991, however, the U.S. Court of Appeals reversed this judgment and ordered young Crumpton's case to trial. The court wrote:

> The question of whether a fetus is a "person" entitled to sue . . . is not dispositive in this case, and defendants' citation to *Roe* v. *Wade* and other cases is inapposite; each of those cases involved the rights of a fetus *qua* fetus. Further, this case does not involve a physical injury to a fetus but rather a substantive due process liberty interest in having familial relations with a parent. Because a child has relationships only after birth, it follows that the child's right to those relationships exists only after birth. Recognizing the temporal distinction between a wrongful act and the injury it causes is consistent with common law tort principles. Crumpton's injury and cause of action did not arise until his birth; accordingly, he is entitled to proceed as a proper party in his federal civil rights suit.

*Crumpton* v. *Gates,* U.S.C.A. Ninth Circuit, No. 90-55117. D.C. No. CV 89-5378-SVW, 15003-15014, at 15004.

51. Irwin L. Gordon, M.D., "Autopsy of John H. Crumpton," Los Angeles County Medical Examiner, # 82-11701, September 30, 1982.

52. Higbie Report, pp. 47–48.

53. Higbie Report, p. 48.

54. Higbie Report, p. 60.

55. Contrast this case with the Larez matter. The LAPD obtained a warrant to search the Larez home solely on the word of a jailed murder suspect that Jesse Larez, Jr., had stashed the murder weapon in his home. Aside from this uncorroborated statement, the police possessed no evidence to link Jesse Larez, Jr., or any other member of the Larez family to the murder or any other crime. In the Crumpton–Berry case, police attempted to obtain no search or arrest warrant even though both were convicted bank robbers who had been recently released from federal prisons; both were wanted for parole violations; and there was substantial reasonable evidence to believe that they had gone back into their old business. By notifying federal authorities of Crumpton's and Berry's whereabouts, police could have seen to it that the pair was returned to prison for parole violations at virtually any time during their surveillance. But they did not. Interestingly, despite the success of his family's suit against the LAPD and its failure to link him to any crime, Jesse Larez, Jr., was jailed for unspecified parole violations after the search and remains in prison at this writing.

56. Higbie Report, p. 41.

57. *Berry* v. *Gates,* Defendants' Answers to Interrogatories, pp. 47–48.

58. Fyfe testified as an expert witness in the civil litigation that emanated from this incident, *Gomez* v. *Gates,* Civ. No. 90-0856-RB (Sx), U.S.D.C., Central District of California. This history is summarized from Lieutenant William D. Hall, Los Angeles Police Department, Robbery-Homicide Division, "Preliminary Press Information Report on the Shootings of Jesus Arango, Herbert Burgos, Juan Bahena, and Alfredo Olivas," February 12, 1990; *idem,* "Report to Chief Daryl F. Gates on the Shootings of Jesus Arango, Herbert Burgos, Juan Bahena, and Alfredo Olivas," April 30, 1990; and various other papers and testimony in the case.

59. According to Olivas, Aramus Arango was an intermittent member of the robbery team.

60. *Gomez* v. *Gates.*

61. 392 U.S. 1 (1968).

62. *Ibid.,* at 30.

63. David Parrish, "Gates, Commissioner Say Police Acted Properly in Sunland Shootings," *Los Angeles Daily News,* February 14, 1990.

64. Charisse Jones, "Woo Testifies at Trial of Anti-Abortion Activists," *Los Angeles Times,* August 29, 1989, Part 2, p. 1.

65. *Ibid.*

66. *John* v. *Los Angeles,* United States District Court, Central District of Califor-

nia, No. 89 4766 AWT, Plaintiff's Memorandum of Points and Authorities in Support of Motion for Summary Judgment or Summary Adjudication of Issues, January 22, 1991, p. 7. Fyfe testified as an expert in police practices on behalf of plaintiff in this case.

67. *Ibid.*
68. Alternate spellings include "nunchukas" and "nunchuks."
69. *Forrester* v. *San Diego,* U.S.D.C., Southern District of California, Case #89-1051-E(M). This case was dismissed after a trial by a jury whose members were shown a videotape in which officers' use of nunchakus is demonstrably gentler and more careful than was the case in Los Angeles.
70. In all, thirty Operation Rescue demonstrators filed medical claims against the police, three of them alleging that officers had broken their limbs and caused damage to nerves.
71. California Penal Code Section 12020.
72. Los Angeles Police Department, Orcutt Police Nunchaku Arrest Control Tactics Course, April 26, 1989, p. 3.
73. Fyfe testified in both the *John* case and in a civil rights matter emanating from the San Diego nunchaku deployment. In both cases, it appeared that the departments had independently decided to deploy nunchakus against Rescue and that they had not talked to each other or otherwise consulted before using nunchakus against Rescue.
74. Captain Patrick E. McKinley, Declaration in Opposition to Plaintiffs's *Ex Parte* Application for a Temporary Restraining Order and Preliminary and Permanent Injunction, filed August 10, 1989, in *John* v. *Los Angeles,* United States District Court, Central District of California, No. CV 8-4766 AWT.
75. Attorney Mark Lassiter's interview with Stanley John, August 1, 1989, p. 16.
76. Daryl Gates, November 21, 1990 deposition in *John* v. *Los Angeles,* pp. 40–41.
77. *Ibid.,* p. 42.
78. LAPD officials argued in the *John* case that extraordinary means such as nunchakus were justifiable in dealing with Rescue demonstrators because officers who shared their pro-life views had trained Rescuers to use techniques that would make it difficult for police to end their sit-in demonstrations. Despite police testimony about Rescuers' sophistication in nontraditional techniques the police called "greasing," "skootching," and forming "human wormballs," videotapes show the demonstrators merely sitting on the ground when police deployed their nunchakus.

## 8. Police Administrative Reform

1. Robert M. Fogelson, *The Fragmented Metropolis* (Cambridge, MA: Harvard University Press, 1967), p. 206.
2. See, for example, Walton Bean, *Boss Ruef's San Francisco* (Berkeley and Los Angeles: University of California Press, 1952); Robert M. Fogelson, *Big-*

*City Police* (Cambridge, MA: Harvard University Press, 1977); Joseph R. Gusfield, *Symbolic Crusade* (Urbana; University of Illinois Press, 1966); Oscar Handlin, *Boston's Immigrants* (Cambridge, MA: Harvard University Press, 1941).

3. Mark H. Haller, "Historical Roots of Police Behavior," *Law and Society Review,* 10 (1976):303–23.

4. With a one-year break during 1923–24 as the LAPD's chief, Vollmer served as Berkeley's police chief until 1932.

5. Gene E. Carte and Elaine H. Carte, *Police Reform in the United States: The Era of August Vollmer, 1905–1925* (Berkeley: University of California Press, 1975), pp. 4–41.

6. National Commission on Law Observance and Enforcement, *Report on Police,* 14 (Montclair, NJ: Patterson Smith, 1968, reprint of 1931 original).

7. O. W. Wilson, *Municipal Police Administration* (Chicago: International City Managers' Association, 1938), was published in six editions (1938; 1943; 1950; 1954; 1961; 1969; 1971); *Police Administration* (New York: McGraw-Hill, 1950), has been published in four editions (1950; 1963; 1972; 1977).

8. William J. Bopp, *O. W.: O. W. Wilson and the Search for a Police Profession* (Port Washington, NY: Kennikat Press, 1977), pp. 3–4.

9. National Commission on the Causes and Prevention of Violence, *Transcript of Proceedings,* October 24, 1968 (Washington, DC: GPO, 1968), pp. 1898–1902.

10. In 1978 Philadelphia police attempted to serve an eviction notice on MOVE, a bizarre cult whose members had been harassing their neighborhood. The episode ended only after an armed seige that lasted nearly two months and that included the death of a police officer. On May 13, 1985, Philadelphia police again attempted to evict MOVE, this time from a wooden row house. The cult's members refused to leave and allegedly threatened the police with guns. The police surrounded the house and attempted to force MOVE out of it with high-pressure water hoses. After several hours of spraying and 750,000 tons of water proved unable to do the job, police conducted an air raid. Using a helicopter, they dropped an incendiary device composed of TOVEX, a mining explosive, on the roof of the house. The blaze that followed killed seven MOVE members and four of their children and leveled a city block, destroying sixty homes and leaving 240 people homeless. See, "MOVE House is Bombed: Blaze Involves 60 Homes," *Philadelphia Inquirer,* May 14, 1985, p. A-1. On May 19 Chief Gates told a national audience on CBS's *Face the Nation* that approving the bombing had made Philadelphia's Mayor Wilson Goode a "hero" who "should run for national office" because he had shown "some of the finest leadership I've ever seen from a politician." See Lee May, "L.A.'s Chief Gates Praises Philadelphia Police, Mayor: Goode Releases MOVE's Written Threat," *Los Angeles Times,* May 20, 1985, part 1, p. 4.

11. Tim Weiner, William K. Marinow, and George Anastasia, "Deputy Police Commissioner Resigns in Probe," *Philadelphia Inquirer*, April 11, 1984, p. A-1.

12. Bill Miller, "Will the Force Be with Him?" *Philadelphia Enquirer Magazine*, November 3, 1991, pp. 20–23, 32–34.

13. *Ibid.*, p. 34.

14. David Burnham, "Graft Paid to Police Here Said to Run into Millions," *New York Times*, April 25, 1970, p. A-1.

15. See Whitman Knapp, Joseph Monserrat, John E. Sprizzo, Franklin A. Thomas, and Cyrus R. Vance, *Report of the New York City Commission to Investigate Allegations of Police Corruption and the City's Anti-Corruption Procedures* (New York: Bar Press, 1972) (hereafter, Knapp Report); Peter Maas, *Serpico* (New York: Viking Press, 1973); Edward F. Droge, Jr., *The Patrolman: A Cop's Story* (New York: Signet Books, 1973); and Leonard Schecter and William Phillips, *On the Pad* (New York: Berkeley Medallion Books, 1973). Phillips, the Knapp Commission's star witness, was a corrupt officer who became an undercover operative after he was trapped extorting money from Xaviera Hollander, a prostitute and brothel-keeper. Hollander used the Knapp Commission notoriety to propel herself into a career as "The Happy Hooker," a writer and sexual adviser for men's magazines.

16. Prior to the Knapp scandals, New York City patrol officers had considerable leeway in deciding whether and how vigorously to enforce building and construction codes and "sabbath" laws. The former prohibited contractors from blocking sidewalks, crossing sidewalks with trucks, or causing dust to fly. The sabbath laws, a holdover from the seventeenth century, generally banned Sunday sale or manufacture of nonemergency services and nonperishable goods only. Thus, for example, grocers could sell fresh milk and vegetables on Sunday, but sales of condensed milk or frozen vegetables violated the law; pharmacies could sell aspirin, but not perfume; antique shops and clothiers could sell nothing. In the interests of religious harmony, the sabbath laws provided an exception for Jews and others for whom Sunday was not the sabbath. Businesses that employed only members of one family and regularly closed on another religious sabbath could operate normally on Sundays. Both sets of laws made compromise with the police virtually inevitable for anybody involved in construction or who wished to conduct business on Sunday.

17. Until Murphy organized a system of "command discipline" for minor administrative violations that could be administered by local supervisors, virtually all disciplinary actions led to the police equivalent of court-martial proceedings. They were held with counsel before a robed "Deputy Commissioner for Trials" in a courtlike headquarters "trial room." Regardless of their results, the record of such proceedings became a permanent part of officers' records and frequently were used as the preliminary screening device for choosing among applicants for special assignments or for detective designations. Thus, merely being charged with such a minor offense as smoking on duty or a

five-minute absence from post could nullify years of outstanding work and put a career-long red flag on an officer's personnel folder. In such a severe environment, minor offenses generally were overlooked, and "little ones"— complaints for a few minutes off post or failure to wear a uniform cap in a patrol car—were generally understood to have been substitute charges lodged by merciful supervisors who had caught officers in far more serious misconduct.

18. A number of the young commanders who advanced quickly under Murphy's administration subsequently became successful chief executives in other departments. Among them are Cornelius Behan (Baltimore County, Maryland), Anthony Bouza (Minneapolis), James Carvino (Racine, Wisconsin; U.S. Capitol Police; Boise, Idaho), Charles Connelly (Yonkers), Patrick Fitzsimons (Seattle), Frederick Heineman (Raleigh, North Carolina), and Joseph McNamara (Kansas City and San Jose).

19. See James J. Fyfe, "Administrative Interventions on Police Shooting Discretion: An Empirical Examination," *Journal of Criminal Justice,* (Winter 1979):309–24.

20. See Patrick V. Murphy and Tom Plate, *Commissioner: A View from the Top of American Law Enforcement* (New York: Simon & Schuster, 1977).

21. Mike AcAlary, *Buddy Boys: When Good Cops Turn Bad* (New York: G. P. Putnam's Sons, 1987).

22. Craig Wolff, "New York Police to Re-evaluate Methods Used to Stop Corruption," *New York Times,* May 9, 1992, p. 1.

23. See the late Bronx District Attorney's account of a controversial police shooting in Mario Merola and Mary Ann Giordano, *Big-City D.A.* (New York: Random House, 1988).

24. Michael Kramer, "Gates: The Buck Doesn't Stop Here," *Newsweek,* April 1, 1991, p. 25.

25. See H. Jerome Miron and Robert Wasserman, *Prevention and Control of Urban Disorders: Issues for the 1980s* (Washington, DC: University Research Corporation, 1980).

26. See, e.g., William Booth, "Miami Community's Progress Suggests Riots' Scars Heal from Within," *Washington Post,* June 5, 1992, p. A-3.

27. See Hans Toch, "Mobilizing Police Expertise," *Annals of the American Academy of Political and Social Science,* 452 (November 1980):53–62.

28. Metro-Dade Police Department, *Reports on Use of Force, Officer Injuries, and Citizen Complaints, 1988–1990.*

29. New York State Temporary Commission of Investigation, *Summary of Activities during 1962* (New York, 1963), cited in James Q. Wilson, *Varieties of Police Behavior* (Cambridge, MA: Harvard University Press, 1968), p. 105. According to Wilson, gambling-related police corruption (not unlike that subsequently disclosed in New York City's Knapp investigations) was a longstanding problem in Syracuse:

> A 1947 grand jury report had censured the Syracuse police department for "its complete lack of police work with respect to gambling." During the period

1947–1962, state police and U.S. Internal Revenue agents made a total of twenty-seven gambling raids in the city, arresting 47 persons. After—but rarely before—each raid, the Syracuse police would also make some arrests. [p. 105].

According to Murphy, police corruption in Syracuse was significant, but paled in comparison to what he subsequently found in New York (personal communications with Fyfe, 1979–91).

30. Wilson, *Varieties of Police Behavior,* p. 234.

31. One test of the durability of Murphy's reforms will have been answered by the turn of the century. If the NYPD makes it through the 1990s without a major corruption investigation and scandal, it will mark the first odd-numbered decade since the 1870s when it has done so. In 1894, the New York State Senate convened the Lexow Committee to investigate corruption; in 1911, the City itself convened the Curran Committee to investigate corruption and inefficiency; in 1932, the state's Seabury Committee repeated the process; in 1950, the Brooklyn District Attorney investigated a gambling operator's allegations that he had been carrying all the borough's plain-clothesmen on his pad; and in 1971, the Knapp Commission was convened. All these investigators found the corruption they looked for. See Knapp Report, pp. 61–64.

32. *Ibid.,* pp. 6–7.

33. *Ibid.,* p. 217.

34. Indeed, the Serpico story's big surprise for Fyfe and most of his NYPD colleagues was not that pads existed in Plainclothes, but that Serpico could claim not to have known of their existence for the five years prior to his own assignment to Plainclothes. It was understood among young officers that one did not accept an offer to enter Plainclothes duty unless one wanted to participate in a pad. The Knapp Commission observed:

> The pad was a way of life in plainclothes. According to Patrolman Phillips, the pad was openly and endlessly discussed whenever plainclothesmen got together. The Commission found no reason to doubt Phillips' opinion, echoing that held by other knowledgeable police officers and informants: "In every division in every area of plainclothes in the City, the same condition exists. There is a pad in every plainclothes precinct and division in the City of New York" [*ibid.,* pp. 75–76].

35. *Ibid.,* p. 90.

36. See Jonathan Rubinstein's discussion of Philadelphia police officers' distinction between "activity" that was statistically reported and other, no less legitimate, police tasks of *City Police* (New York: Farrar, Straus & Giroux, 1973), pp. 44–54.

37. See Arthur Neiderhoffer, *Behind the Shield: The Police in Urban Society* (New York: Doubleday, 1967), in which the author found cynicism to be greater among police patrol officers than among investigators or administrators.

38. Mike Rothmiller and Ivan G. Goldman, *L. A. Secret Police: Inside the LAPD Spy Networks* (New York: Pocket Books, 1992).

39. As we noted in Chapter 6, Chief Gates has commented that the SIS may have "accomplished something" by killing the McDonald's bandits rather than running the risk that they might be released on bail. David Parrish, "Gates, Commissioner Say Police Acted Properly in Sunland Shootings," *Los Angeles Daily News,* February 14, 1990. In addition, the reporter David Freed wrote that

> . . . SIS detectives have often ignored opportunities to arrest targeted criminals after watching them commit lesser crimes, such as car theft, attempted burglary or attempted robbery. In some cases, the detectives have overlooked existing arrest warrants.
>
> Instead, they have waited for dozens of criminals to commit actual armed robberies and burglaries—felonies that carry longer sentences and are more easily prosecuted because the detectives can testify as witnesses. [David Freed, "Citizens Terrorized as Police Look On," *Los Angeles Times,* September 25, 1988, p. 1].

40. Robert Daley, *Prince of the City: The True Story of a Cop Who Knew Too Much* (Boston: Houghton, Mifflin, 1978).

41. See Constance L. Hays, "Damage Awards in False Arrests," *New York Times,* April 10, 1991, p. B-3; Todd S. Purdum, "Transit Police Undermined by a Lack of Accountability," *New York Times,* December 5, 1987, section 1, p. 29; and Todd S. Purdum, "Transit Scandal: Do Arrest Incentives Motivate the Police or Invite Abuse?" *New York Times,* December 16, 1987, p. B-3.

42. See, Elizabeth Reuss-Ianni, *Two Cultures of Policing: Street Cops and Management Cops* (New Brunswick, NJ: Transaction Books, 1983).

43. Following this episode, Ward's discipline went as high as the forced retirement of his department's Chief of Patrol, the highly respected three-star commander of the 17,000 officers who worked in NYPD's seventy-five patrol precincts. While it is hardly conceivable that this Chief knew about or would have tolerated torture by stun gun, Ward apparently reasoned that the abuse involved was so egregious that it warranted making the most severe examples of the whole chain of command.

## 9. Police Accountability I: The Courts

1. *Brown* v. *Mississippi* 297 U.S. 278 (1936): *Miranda* v. *Arizona* 384 U.S. 436 (1966).

2. See Thomas Davies, "A Hard Look at What We Know (and Still Need to Learn) about the 'Costs' of the Exclusionary Rule: The NIJ Study and Other Studies of 'Lost' Arrests," *American Bar Foundation Research Journal,* 1983, pp. 611–90.

3. Egon Bittner, *The Functions of the Police in Modern Society* (Rockville, MD: National Institute of Mental Health, 1970), p. 25.

4. John Van Maanen, "The Asshole," in Peter K. Manning and John Van Maanen, eds., *Policing: A View from the Street* (Santa Monica, CA: Goodyear Publishing, 1978), pp. 221–38.

5. These issues are discussed in more detail in James J. Fyfe, "Reviewing Citizens' Complaints Against Police," in James J. Fyfe, ed., *Police Management Today: Issues and Case Studies* (Washington, DC: International City Management Association, 1985), pp. 76–87.

6. Gilbert Geis, *White-Collar Criminal: The Offender in Business and the Professions* (New York: Atherton Press, 1968).

7. 42 U.S.C. Section 1983.

8. Note "The Civil Rights Act: Emergence of an Adequate Civil Remedy?" *Indiana Law Journal,* 26 (1951):361.

9. *Brown* v. *Mississippi.*

10. *Monroe* v. *Pape,* 365 U.S. 167 (1961).

11. *Maine* v. *Thiboutot,* 448 U.S. 1 (1980), 27 fn. 16, Justice Powell dissenting. Justice Powell had not been yet been appointed to the Supreme Court when Monroe was decided.

12. *Monell* v. *Department of Social Services of the City of New York* et al., 436 U.S. 658 (1978).

13. *Monell,* at 691.

14. Christopher Report, p. 56.

15. John L. Mitchell, "$11.3 Million Paid in LAPD Abuse Cases," *Los Angeles Times,* March 29, 1991, p. A-1.

16. *Ibid.*

17. Gail Diane Cox, "Who Ya Gonna Call? Copbusters!" *Los Angeles Magazine* May 1991, p. 76.

18. See Rolando Del Carmen, *Civil Liabilities in American Policing* (Englewood Cliffs, NJ: Brady, 1991), pp. 3–5; James J. Fyfe, "Enforcement Workshop: The Expert Witness in Suits Against Police (Part 1)," *Criminal Law Bulletin,* 21, (May–June 1985): 244, and (Part 2), *Criminal Law Bulletin,* 21 (November–December 1985): 515.

19. 42 U.S.C. 1988 (1976).

20. Cox, "Copbusters!," p. 77.

21. Del Carmen, *Civil Liabilities,* pp. 67–68.

22. *Peterson* v. *City of Long Beach,* 24 Cal. 3rd 238, 595 P. 2d 447 (1979).

23. *Tennessee* v. *Garner* 471 U.S. 1 (1985).

24. See James J. Fyfe and Jeffery T. Walker, "Garner Plus Five Years: An Examination of Supreme Court Intervention into Police Discretion and Legislative Prerogatives," 14 *American Journal of Criminal Justice* (Spring 1990) 167–88.

25. *Thurman* v. *Torrington,* 595 F. Supp. 1521 (D.Conn. 1984).

26. *City of Canton* v. *Harris,* 489 U.S. 378, 396 (1989) (O'Connor, J., dissenting).
27. Karen M. Blum, "Local Government Liability Under Section 1983," in Massachusetts Bar Association, *Recent Developments in Police Misconduct Litigation* (mimeo, September 1991), presents an excellent summary of recent civil rights decisions involving police.
28. Christopher Report, Table 2–3.
29. Daryl F. Gates, "A Training Analysis of the Los Angeles Police Department," October 21, 1991, p. 14.
30. Wesley G. Skogan and George E. Antunes, "Information, Apprehension, and Deterrence: Exploring the Limits of Police Productivity," *Journal of Criminal Justice,* 7 (Fall 1979):217–42.
31. Paul L. Hoffman, testimony before the Subcommittee on Civil and Constitutional Rights, U.S. House of Representatives Committee on the Judiciary, March 20, 1991.
32. See James J. Fyfe, "Administrative Interventions on Police Shooting Discretion: An Empirical Examination," *Journal of Criminal Justice,* 7 (Winter 1979):309–24. This study reports that imposition of a restrictive policy on officers' use of deadly force and consequent decreases in police shooting had no measurable effect on rates of crime or the safety of police officers. See also Kenneth R. Matulia, *A Balance of Forces,* 2d ed. (Gaithersburg, MD: International Association of Chiefs of Police, 1985), which suggests that rates of police deadly force vary across America's largest cities with little relationship to crime rates, and Gerald Uelman, "Varieties of Public Policy: A Study of Police Policy Regarding the Use of Deadly Force in Los Angeles County," *Loyola of Los Angeles Law Review,* 6 (1973):1–55, finding that rates of deadly force in Los Angeles area police departments had more to do with police chiefs' philosophies than with rates of crime or violence.
33. *Lankford* v. *Gelston,* 364 F.2d 197 (4th Cir. 1966).
34. *Rizzo* v. *Goode,* 423 U.S. 362 (1976).
35. *City of Los Angeles* v. *Lyons,* 461 U.S. 95, 98 (1983).
36. *Thomas* v. *County of Los Angeles,* No 91-56047 (9th Cir. 1991).
37. Cyril D. Robinson, *Legal Rights, Duties and Liabilities of Criminal Justice Personnel* (Springfield, IL: Charles C. Thomas, 1984), p. 281.
38. John Epke and Linda Davis, "Civil Rights Cases and Police Misconduct," *FBI Law Enforcement Bulletin,* 60 (August 1991):15.
39. U.S. Civil Rights Commission, *Who Is Guarding the Guardians?* (Washington, DC: Government Printing Office, 1981), p. 108. Emphasis added.
40. Personal communication with James J. Fyfe, January 9, 1992.
41. Epke and Davis, "Civil Rights Cases," p. 15.
42. *Ibid.*
43. James Eisenstein and Herbert Jacob, *Felony Justice* (Boston: Little, Brown, 1977), p. 70.

44. *Ibid.*, p. 15.
45. These figures are taken from mimeographed documents made available by the Justice Department to the U.S. House of Representatives Committee on the Judiciary, Subcommittee on Civil and Constitutional Rights, at hearings on March 20, 1991, in Washington, DC.
46. U.S. Department of Justice, Civil Rights Division, Criminal Section, "Police Brutality Study FY 1985–FY 1990," April 1991, unpublished report, p. 1.
47. *Ibid.*, p. 2. Emphasis added.
48. *Ibid.*, p. 3.
49. *Ibid.*, p. 4.
50. *Ibid.*, Appendix A-4.
51. *Ibid.*, Appendix A-6, includes the number of officers in each agency studied.
52. The number of Baltimore County Police Department officers included in the Justice Department study (48) is inaccurate. The figure used in this calculation (1,579) was obtained from Peter Strawbridge and Deirdre Strawbridge, *A Networking Guide to Recruitment, Selection, and Probationary Training of Police Officers in Major Police Departments of the United States of America* (New York: John Jay College, 1990), p. 11.
53. Civil Rights Division, "Police Brutality Study," p. 37.
54. Pawtucket was the subject of twenty complaints in six years. The states listed were excluded from the Justice Department analysis "because no single agency in these states or territories had ten or more complaints during the [same] six-year time span." *Ibid.*, p. 20.
55. *Ibid.*, p. 37.

## 10. Accountability II: The Public

1. Ned L. Wall, "Police Public Relations Program," pp. 472–506 in International City Managers' Association, *Municipal Police Administration,* 5th ed. (Chicago, 1961), p. 495.
2. Frank A. Scafidi, Chief Inspector, Internal Affairs Division, Philadelphia Police Department, "Hearings Before the U.S. Commission on Civil Rights, Philadelphia, April 16–17, 1979," p. 169.
3. Vincent Blasi, "The Checking Value in First Amendment Theory," *American Bar Foundation Research Journal,* 3 (1977): 521–649.
4. See David Burnham, "How Police Corruption is Built into the System— And a Few Ideas for What to Do About It," in Lawrence W. Sherman, ed., *Police Corruption: A Sociological Perspective* (Garden City, NY: Anchor, 1974).
5. James Q. Wilson, *Varieties of Police Behavior* (Cambridge, MA: Harvard University Press, 1968).
6. James Q. Wilson, *Thinking About Crime,* 2d ed. (New York: Basic Books, 1983), p. 5.

7. President's Commission on Law Enforcement and Administration of Justice, *Task Force Report: The Police* (Washington, DC: GPO, 1967).

8. Including Fyfe, who was a Brooklyn patrolman and subject of a pending citizen's complaint at the time the board was established. Eventually the board dismissed the complaint as unsubstantiated.

9. See Algernon D. Black, *The People and the Police* (New York: McGraw-Hill, 1968), appendix 5.

10. Data on civilian review rely upon a research report by Samuel Walker and Vic W. Bumphus, "A National Survey of Civilian Review of the Police," Department of Criminal Justice, University of Nebraska, Omaha, 1991.

11. *Ibid.*

12. See *New York Times,* September 17–20, 1992.

13. Wayne A. Kerstetter, "Who Disciplines the Police? Who Should?" in William A. Geller, ed., *Police Leadership in America: Crisis and Opportunity* (New York: Praeger and American Bar Foundation, 1985), pp. 149–83.

14. James J. Fyfe, "Reviewing Citizens' Complaints Against Police," in James J. Fyfe, ed., *Police Management Today: Issues and Case Studies* (Washington, DC: International City Management Association, 1985), pp. 76–87.

15. John Keker, interview with Jerome H. Skolnick, December 9, 1991.

16. Christopher Report, pp. 10–11.

17. *Ibid.,* p. 36.

18. *Heller* v. *Bushey,* 259 F.2d 1371 (9th Cir. 1985).

19. Craig D. Uchida, Lawrence W. Sherman, and James J. Fyfe, *Police Shootings and the Prosecutor in Los Angeles County: An Evaluation of Operation Rollout* (Washington, DC: Police Foundation, 1981).

20. Interview with James J. Fyfe, August 17, 1991.

21. *Bonsignore* v. *City of New York,* 683 F.2d 635 (2d Cir. 1982).

22. See, e.g., James J. Fyfe, "Police Use of Deadly Force: Research and Reform," *Justice Quarterly,* 5 (1988):165–205, and Lawrence W. Sherman and Ellen G. Cohn, with Patrick R. Gartin, Edwin E. Hamilton and Dennis P. Rogan, *Citizens Killed by Big-City Police 1974–1984* (Washington, DC: Crime Control Institute, 1986).

23. See the Federal Bureau of Investigation's annual *Uniform Crime Reports Supplement: Law Enforcement Officers Killed and Assaulted* (Washington, DC: FBI).

## 11. Renewing the Police

1. James Q. Wilson, "Police and Their Problems: A Theory," *Public Policy,* yearbook of the Harvard University School of Public Administration (Cambridge, MA, 1963), pp. 200–201.

2. James Baldwin, *Nobody Knows My Name* (New York: Dell, 1962), pp. 66–67.

3. James Q. Wilson, *Varieties of Police Behavior,* (Cambridge, MA: Harvard University Press, 1968), p. 283.
4. Wilson, "Police and Their Problems."
5. Peter K. Manning, *Police Work: The Social Organization of Policing* (Cambridge, MA: MIT Press, 1977), pp. 98–99. Emphasis is original.
6. Indeed, Fyfe is a Commissioner of the Commission on Accreditation for Law Enforcement Agencies.
7. The relevant standards read:

> 1.3.2. A written directive states that an officer may use deadly force only when the officer reasonably believes that the action is in defense of human life, including the officer's own life, or in defense of any person in immediate danger of serious physical injury.
> 1.3.3. A written directive specifies that use of deadly force against a "fleeing felon" must meet the conditions required by standard 1.3.2.

Commission on Accreditation for Law Enforcement Agencies, Inc., *Standards for Law Enforcement Agencies* (Fairfax, VA, 1983), pp. 1.2
8. *Ibid.*, pp. 1.1–1.4.
9. See James J. Fyfe and Mark Blumberg, "A Response to Griswold: A More Valid Test of the Justifiability of Police Actions," *American Journal of Police,* 9 (Fall 1985):110–32.
10. See James J. Fyfe, "Police Use of Deadly Force: Research and Reform," *Justice Quarterly,* 5 (1988):165–205.
11. See Geoffrey P. Alpert and Lorie A. Fridell, *Police Vehicles and Firearms: Instruments of Deadly Force* (Prospect Heights, IL: 1992), pp. 99–114.
12. New York State Special Commission on Attica, *Attica* (New York: Bantam Books, 1972), p. xi.
13. Harey Schlossberg and Lucy Freeman, *Psychologist with a Gun* (New York: Coward, McCann & Geohagan, 1974).
14. Robert Louden, former commander of the NYPD Hostage Negotiation Unit, personal communication with James J. Fyfe, June 12, 1992. See also Frank Bolz and Edward Hershey, *Hostage Cop* (New York: Rawson, Wade, 1979).
15. Hans Toch and J. Douglas Grant, *Police as Problem Solvers* (New York: Plenum Press, 1991), p. 214. See also Hans Toch, J. Douglas Grant, and Raymond T. Galvin, *Agents of Change: A Study in Police Reform* (New York: John Wiley & Sons, 1975), and Hans Toch, "Mobilizing Police Expertise," *Annals of the American Academy of Political and Social Science,* 452 (November 1980):53–62.
16. Toch and Grant, *Police as Problem Solvers,* p. 243. As operationalized in Oakland, "conflicts" included incidents in which subjects had resisted arrest, committed battery or assault upon officers, or assaulted officers with deadly weapons (p. 232).
17. *Ibid.*, p. 246.
18. Interview with James J. Fyfe, August 21, 1991.

19. For overviews of community policing, see Skolnick and David Bayley, *The New Blue Line: Police Innovation in Six American Cities* (New York: Free Press, 1986); Jerome H. Skolnick and David Bayley, *Community Policing: Issues and Practices Around the World* (Washington, DC: National Institute of Justice, 1988); and Wesley Skogan, *Disorder and Decline: Crime and the Spiral of Decay in American Neighborhoods* (New York: Free Press, 1990).

20. Albert J. Reiss, Jr., *Policing a City's Central District: The Oakland Story* (Washington, DC: National Institute of Justice, 1985).

21. See George L. Kelling, Tony Pate, Duane Dieckman, and Charles E. Brown, *The Kansas City Preventive Patrol Experiment: Summary Report* (Washington, DC: Police Foundation, 1974); Police Foundation, *The Newark Foot Patrol Experiment* (Washington, DC, 1981); and William G. Spelman and Dale K. Brown, *Calling the Police: A Replication of the Kansas City Response Time Analysis* (Washington, DC: Police Executive Research Forum, 1981).

22. See, e.g., Spelman and Brown, *Calling the Police.*

23. See, e.g., Edward H. Kaplan, "Evaluating the Effectiveness of One Officer Versus Two Officer Patrol Units," *Journal of Criminal Justice,* 7 (Winter 1979):325–55.

24. Norwegian Official Reports, *The Role of the Police in the Society,* NOU 35 (Oslo: Universitetforlaget, 1981).

25. Skolnick and Bayley, *The New Blue Line,* pp. 20–21.

26. Skogan, *Disorder and Decline,* p. 167.

27. *Ibid.*

28. See, e.g., Police Foundation, *Newark Foot Patrol Experiment.*

29. *Criminal Justice Newsletter,* vol. 21, October 15, 1990.

30. Ted Rohrlich, "Gates' Community-Based Policing Plan OKd," *Los Angeles Times,* January 22, 1992.

31. Peter Strawbridge and Deirdre Strawbridge, *A Networking Guide to Recruitment, Selection and Probationary Training of Police Officers in Major Police Department of the United States* (New York: John Jay College, 1990).

32. See Skolnick and Bayley, *The New Blue Line,* pp. 13–50.

33. See Herman Goldstein, "Improving Policing: A Problem-Oriented Approach," *Crime and Delinquency,* 25 (1979):236–58. *Problem-Oriented Policing* (New York: McGraw-Hill, 1990).

34. Goldstein, "Improving Policing."

35. Skogan, *Disorder and Decline,* esp. pp. 3–9.

36. Goldstein, *Problem-Oriented Policing,* p. 178.

37. Elizabeth Reuss-Ianni, *Two Cultures of Policing: Street Cops and Management Cops* (New Brunswick, NJ: Transaction Books, 1983).

38. Personal communication with James J. Fyfe, July 26, 1991.

39. Perhaps the most concise recent description of the Police Cadet Corps proposal is John Carlisle, "Crime, Cops and Civil Peace: The Case for Police

Corps," *Essays on Our Times,* no. 13 (Washington, DC: Free Congress Research and Education Foundation, November 1991).

40. Ramsey Clark, *Crime in America: Observations on Its Nature, Causes, Prevention, and Control* (New York: Simon & Schuster, 1970).
41. See, e.g., Reuss-Ianni, *Two Cultures of Policing,* p. 40.
42. See, e.g., Arthur Neiderhoffer, *Behind the Shield* (Garden City, NY: Doubleday, 1967).
43. Interview with James J. Fyfe, April 17, 1991.

# Index

Printed in the United States
101330LV00003B/1-87/A